RELIGIOUS DANCES

RELIGIOUS DANCES

in the Christian Church and in Popular Medicine

E. LOUIS BACKMAN

Professor of Pharmacology at
The Royal University of Upsala

TRANSLATED BY
E. CLASSEN

London

GEORGE ALLEN & UNWIN LTD

RUSKIN HOUSE, MUSEUM STREET

FIRST PUBLISHED IN GREAT BRITAIN
IN 1952

*The original Swedish edition
was published by
P. A. Norstedt och Söner
Stockholm*

PRINTED IN GREAT BRITAIN
in 11 *point Garamond type
by Simson Shand Ltd., London and Hertford*

PREFACE

IN the following pages an account is presented of the appearance and significance of religious dances in the Christian Church and Christian society. The account comprises the period from the origins of our creed until the present day, insofar as it has been possible to give an objective description based on existing literature. Nevertheless religious history has not been the sole purpose. More particularly an effort has been made to discover an explanation of the role which religious dances have played in the history of medicine and in the popular treatment of disease.

In this respect what is of special interest is the hitherto unsolved riddle of the medieval dance epidemic. This latter has always evoked both wonder and alarm. But in order to understand the many peculiar features of these epidemics we require not only a medical analysis of their vast, varied symptoms but also a clarification of the real meaning of the dances and their historico-religious foundations. Here, as so frequently elsewhere, religion and the art of healing come together, just like two mighty branches of the same tree trunk.

In past centuries of the history of the Christian Church, just as even today in Catholic and Greek Orthodox Christianity, the legends of the saints are an object of reverent adoration, of gratitude and edification. The problem of their proven historical reality in certain details has only an academic interest; their religious meaning has no relation to such an enquiry. With what incredibly strong and widespread force have the relics of the saints and martyrs exerted their influence on Christianity, on popular religions and on medical conceptions! It is scarcely possible to exaggerate it. Even today it must be insisted that the question of their historical reality can only be regarded as of highly technical significance; the conclusive thing is the acceptance by the Churches and by Christians of the genuineness of the relics.

In the following pages very detailed accounts are given of the methods of demon-exorcism in the Christian Church. It need scarcely be said that many exorcisms were to such an extent assuredly successful, that in a condition of suggestive receptivity the various, frequently dramatic and vivid rites have compelled the various symptoms of such condition to disappear or to be modified. So also organically conditioned suffering often reveals nervous disturbances, sometimes appearing to the sufferer as most marked, and the removal of which by suggestion must give the impression of a cure. Not infrequently it has been possible to introduce another element, which made it possible for exorcism to have the appearance of a therapeutic effect, namely, the removal of the patient from the source of infection to a more healthy neighbourhood. But there is one circumstance which must not be forgotten. Many diseases, not least the exceedingly serious and dangerous ones, which are here removed from the shadows of history, show rapid and spontaneous improvement. But we shall not proceed further in these pages into these theoretically possible explanations of the statements of chroniclers concerning the restoration of the sick. The most important thing is what actually occurred.

It has been my endeavour, as regards the varied symbolism and the numerous ritualistic prescriptions, to discover the historically determined significance, the earliest explanation and motivation. But there is no certainty that simple human beings who for various reasons found themselves compelled to execute ritual acts, really understood their original meaning and significance. It is indeed more probable that they did not know at all, or only vaguely surmized, why an act should be performed in any particular manner. The ritual was inherited, the symbolism was prescribed by a tradition handed down from their ancestors. The ritual must be performed in such and such a way in order to be powerful and effective. This has always been the case with ritualistic symbolism and it is the same today. 'The interpretation changes, but the rite remains.'

I owe a great debt of gratitude to the librarians of the Royal University Library of Upsala, who with never-failing readiness have facilitated my work in the highest degree, and with the greatest kindness have procured for me access to certain literature not available within the country.

For obtaining photostatic or other copies I must thank the curators of the Hamburg Municipal Library and of the Zürich State Archives. Valuable material has been furnished by the Mayor of Zabern.

I would also wish to place on record my gratitude to the Director of the State Archives in Aachen, Professor Huyskens, for the interest he has shown in my work and for the account of the pilgrimage of the Hungarian King Ludwig I to Aachen in 1374, which he so kindly furnished to me.

For the accomplished copying and translation of *The Chronicle of the Early Roman Kings and Generals*, I thank Mr. H. Sallander, Ammanuensis at Upsala University Library; for valuable assistance in a problem of interpretation Professor J. Svennung; and for his kind translation of medieval French texts, Mr H. Lindelöf.

I am greatly indebted and grateful to the Trustees of the Regnell Foundation of the Medical Faculty in Upsala for their considerable support, which has made it possible for this work to be enriched with abundant illustrative material, and to be translated into English.

Upsala

Summer 1945 *and* 1948

CONTENTS

ILLUSTRATIONS

1

Introductory

THE early Greek writer Lucian, who lived in the second century A.D., relates in his work *On Dances* that one cannot find a single mystery induction not associated with a dance, and is of the opinion that Orpheus had already prescribed that anybody introduced to the wisdom of the mysteries should be received with dancing. It is unnecessary, adds Lucian, specially to emphasize that the old mysteries were never performed without a dance. But since far from all human beings are among the initiated, it is not possible to speak more intimately on the subject. But who does not know that it is customary to say of those who have revealed the mysteries that 'they have danced them out'?

Lucian's opinion of the inescapable role of dancing in the sphere of the mysteries in ancient times might today be expanded very considerably. There is probably not a single advanced religion in which the dance has not been, or still is, a more or less essential part of the divine service or of the drama of the mysteries. This is true not only of the ancient, pre-Christian religions; it is also true, in a very high degree, of Christianity itself. It must, indeed, be regarded as something obvious and necessary that historic customs and habits should have set their stamp upon all the spiritual movements which simultaneously appear and develop. The Jewish cult grew up in countries in which the Jews were surrounded by peoples which from ancient times regarded the dance as an essential element of their cult. The same is true of Egypt, Babylonia, Persia, Greece and Italy. It would therefore be foolish to suppose that the Jews could have dissociated themselves from such influences in their own cultural usages. But it is by no means sure that the Jewish religious service received the sacral dance as a kind of external, infectious body. Various circumstances, a common conception of nature, and so on, may, quite apart from the customs of surrounding peoples, have permitted the growth of the dance ceremonies within the cult. But certainly this occurred more easily and more rapidly because of the uniform customs in the neighbouring regions. A similar argument can be advanced in respect of Christianity and its reverence for the dance as a Church institution, although it is clear, and recognized by the Church, that the Jewish dance ceremonial determined in a high degree the development of Church dances. But in all probability the highly-developed dance customs of the pagan mysteries cannot have been without influence on the development of the Church dances of

Christianity. The terminology used by the patriarch Clement of Alexandria and Ambrose regarding the religious meaning of the Church dances, which we shall encounter later on, is the pure language of the mysteries and employs clearly and openly the terminology of the mysteries.

The Christian Church, however, was subject much later to another source of infection in the matter of religious dances, namely the pagan religions farther North. Especially the Slavonic and Germanic races possessed a highly-developed dance ritual in connection with their religious customs, both in divine service and in the rites associated with the dead. Synods and Councils, Archbishops and other Church dignitaries, as well as laymen, maintain time after time that the dance customs within the Church which occur in so many districts have penetrated from paganism and were survivals of those pagan customs. But this is by no means the whole truth; it is only a part, even if an important part. Dances within the Christian Church have other and far deeper and more independent roots, though it is certainly true that many new and strong ones developed with the advance of Christianity and the raising of its Cross in primitive pagan lands.

Early writers have preserved various accounts of the religious significance of the dance in the countries of antiquity. At this point we need only make some less important observations. Egypt displays a highly-developed dance ceremonial in its many-hued religious usages. The cults in most temples were more or less associated with dances executed either by special dancers or by the priesthood itself. Thus (according to Voss) the priests danced in definite, specially designed movements round the temple altar. According to Lucian, Plato relates that the dances of the Egyptian priests round the temple altars and the dance formations which they executed were intended to represent the movements of the planets, the constellations and the fixed stars in the heavens. Lucian in his work associates himself entirely with this symbolism. He says there that the march cadence revealed by the stars, the conjunction of the planets with the fixed stars, the harmony and the euphony of the movements of the heavenly bodies are the models in which the art of dancing has its origin. Generally speaking the dance appears to have entered as an important ritual element into most acts of a state-religious order. Engell points out how the King of Egypt, who was also the High Priest of the cult of the gods, was obliged at the initiation to perform a special dance. The dance appears as something important and essential also in the cult of the dead. In the procession in honour of the dead and at the interment a representation of the dead person, sculptured or painted, was carried or had been erected at the entrance to the tomb. When offerings were made, the ceremony was accompanied by a ritual dance to the accompaniment of a choir, usually with slow, solemn movements. Figure 1 shows a relief from the Old Kingdom. The dance appears to represent a stamping of feet, whilst other figures, presumably singers, beat out the rhythm with their hands [Erman]. In Babylon also the occurrence of the temple dance is abundantly confirmed. Thus, for example, in the text of the Assurbanipal it is related that at a cult festival the actors danced a ring-dance, to musical accompaniment, round the idol, just like Anteranna, says Jeremiah. But Anteranna is the same as the signs of the Zodiac in the skies, and just as they appear to face outwards into space, so also does the ring of dancers. This means, so far as the original symbolism of the dance is concerned, a connexion with the Egyptian ideas mentioned

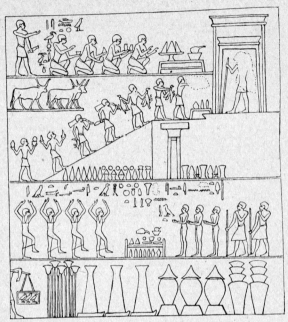

FIG. 1. Egyptian burial dance, 2500 B.C. [Weege].

above—although historically the development probably proceeded from Babylon to Egypt. The Babylonians thought that the twelve constellations, the twelve 'houses' in the Zodiac as it were, danced a ring-dance to the harmony of the heavenly spheres.

All the mystery festivals which were celebrated in the Mediterranean lands, in antiquity and during the early post-Christian era must without exception have been combined with dancing. For example, a part of the Sabazios cult was a mad, whirling, round dance on the hill tops; in the Kybele-Attis cult it was a dance executed 'with winged dancing steps' [Casel]. The Eleusis Mysteries in their later stages, which undoubtedly presented a conception of death and resurrection, and a picture too of the life of the blessed, were combined with a ring-dance which appears to have begun when the spirit emerged from its symbolic underworld journey and reached the splendid fields of the blessed [Casel, Czerwinski, Quasten]. Figure 2, from Casa Item in Pompeii, pictures a mystery induction ritual dance [Weege], apparently a slow, solemn dance, principally of twists and turns of the body. Bonnet mentions that in the Roman cult the dances consisted of backward and forward movements in cadence round the free-standing altar. In other cases the ring-dance took place around the tripod on which the oracle was introduced or the sacrifice made. The processional dances were executed with cadenced steps. Eitrem points out the common custom of performing the cult dance three times round the altar: the symbol of perfection. This circling of the altar signified partly a purification and partly a defence. A magic and protective ring was thereby formed around the altar and all who stood before it.

FIG. 2. Initiation Dance of the Dionysian Cult [Eitrem].

In Greece and Italy, as in Egypt, dances of various kinds were customary on the burial of the dead. The purpose of these dances appears to have been to gladden the dead, but still more to exorcise and expel the evil demons which wait for them [Franz]. In Greece and Italy the dead were comforted by boys and girls bearing wreaths and cypress branches, who executed solemn funeral dances with choral song. Immediately after the dancers came the priests. Cahusac reproduces a description from Plato's book on law

(Book 12) in which he describes the burial of an Athenian king: the bier was preceded by a host of youths and girls, who carried wreaths and branches; they danced slowly and solemnly to musical accompaniment. After them came priests from various temples, clothed in their different robes. Franz reminds us of the antique Roman burial tablets, which reveal that dances were performed in the presence of the bier. Similar customs existed in Greece and Asia Minor. In this connection one should also bear in mind the funeral contests which took place in Greece from the earliest time; here, as also to some extent in Egypt, these contests in the presence of the god of the dead, were meant to illustrate the struggle in and after death with the enemy and the demons, and demonstrate also a victory over evil and death. Brede Kristensen holds that the dead were supposed to wage war on the arch-fiend in the kingdom of the dead and to win a victory for life. The contests at the graveside represent and manifest this idea. Similar was the Trojan contest, which was carried on by armed, mounted men, executing complicated manoeuvres in larger and smaller circles, to and fro, but all in a pattern which reproduced the labyrinth of Crete—the symbol of the underworld. That was a dance, not so much, however, in honour of the dead as seeking their aid and succour in the battle with the powers of the underworld.

When Christianity appeared it was in a world in which a dance cult had existed as something obvious, right and necessary for the proper celebration of, or resistance to, powers which are not of the visible world. But something similar is true in respect of the power attributed to the dance in bringing healing to disease—a corollary, one might say, to its power to expel demons. The dance assists the living in their relations with the gods, but it also assists against the demons which cause disease. *The dance has its significance for life, death and disease.*

As early as the fifth century B.C. there existed in Greece the so-called orpheotelestae, a kind of itinerant healers, who offered to dance around the sick, not infrequently in the form of a ring-dance. They pretended that thus they could cure all diseases, even mental disease [Baas].

Only a few instances of similar dance customs in more modern times will be given here. In Bulgaria a dance for the healing of the sick has been discovered among the Kalin tribes: a ring-dance is performed, slowly at first, around the sick person, to a musical accompaniment which determines the pace at which the ring dancers approach or recede from the patient [Lübeck]. The inhabitants of Naples perform a very similar dance around a severely afflicted person [Andrews], while in the little village of Pratteln, near Bâle, as late as the middle of the eighteenth century, ring-dances were performed at cross-roads as soon as any pestilential disease broke out [Bloch]. Something similar is told of the people of Wertheim, who, during the plague of 1349, believed that they had found a cure by executing a ring-dance round a pine tree [Böhme]. During the Middle Ages, according to a fourteenth-century manuscript, there existed a dance with flaming torches around a new-born child; it was supposed to protect the child against evil spirits, especially against maladies which were thought to be induced by demoniac possession [Bloch].

And how they danced in the fields before and after the sowing in order to ensure a better and safer harvest! How they leapt into the air in order to force the seed to grow! Bloch relates that on the eve of the first of May the boys in the Wendish regions went forth with old brooms, which they set alight, dancing round the field with them in order to expel evil spirits and so secure a better yield. Similarly, during fasts there were a number of dances which promoted growth. The need for this high leaping is explained in the following lines from Oversulzbach in Alsace:

> If in the dance you leap not high,
> Then, when the hemp comes, you will sigh.

As early as the middle of the tenth century, probably much earlier, dances were performed on Midsummer Eve. At this period there is an episcopal condemnation of the practice which makes clear that the dancers visited wells and streams. Here also, when a fire was kindled, there was dancing and singing, and special garlands and bouquets of flowers were cast into the flames, through which the dancers leapt, believing that they would thereby secure a year's good health and a good harvest or immunity from sickness. Fire and smoke were considered especially efficacious in driving out demons [Huet, Durandus]. Against this practice also the Church repeatedly issued proscriptions and threats.

But it was not only on Midsummer Eve that people sought by bathing and washing, dancing and singing, to be healed of sickness or to find protection against it. On other nights also, notably at Holy Trinity, it was felt that such cures should be attempted. It may be said with certainty that mineral springs especially have always been the centres of the superstitious cult [Michel]. It is true of Sweden, too; where, as elsewhere in Europe, springs and streams were decorated with flowers and garlands. Many of the Midsummer Eve springs or the Holy Trinity springs have remained in use to the present day. Probably most of the real springs and baths in Sweden were originally credited with magic powers; such is the case with Medevi Sätra, Porla [Sjöberg], Sånga [Nordlander], St Olof in Albo district [Reimer], the Holy Trinity springs at Enköping [Wallensteen], Söderbärke [anonymous, 1908], Elgön and Näsby [Flentzberg], at Svinegarn [Hiärne], Askilstorp in Småland [Aldén], Nordbeck at Gagnef [Gagnér], and many more. In a recently published survey von Stapelmohr gives an account of even further medicinal springs in the North of Sweden and of their association with various saints. People gathered at the spring from far and near in order to do reverence at evening and during the night, adorning it with leaves and flowers, cleansing it and tidying it up, whilst the sick and their relatives carried water from the spring or washed their garments in it, marching round it and making small offerings [Backman]. Hylten Cavallius has discovered in

6

Småland a little sacrificial song, from the Catholic Church, which was sung during the ring-dance:

Three times I bound
My little offering around.

Then they played and danced and sang beside, and especially around, the spring. Even in our own times, these north-running streams are visited on Thursday evenings for washing garments and for cleansing diseases in the 'living water' of ancient Christianity. Some of the medieval dance epidemics we shall find most intimately bound up with springs and running water.

According to Hecker, Nicolaus Perotti (1430–80) relates how Tarantism appeared in Italy, in Apulia, for the first time. The cause was said to be the sting of a poisonous spider, the so-called tarantula, which at that time had appeared in considerable numbers. Many who had been stung relapsed into a state of maniacal confusion, and at the sound of music they were so moved that they had to dance for joy. They danced until they were completely exhausted but many relapsed into melancholy and lost consciousness. Amidst laughter and tears death itself might have ensued. Towards the end of the fifteenth century this Tarantism was widespread throughout Italy; the victims danced and believed that only in that way could the poison of the tarantula be dispersed throughout the body and expelled through the skin. Tarantism gradually developed more and more clearly into a psychic infection; it assumed enormous proportions and the remedy, which was to dance the 'Tarantella', became a great popular festival. Towards the end of the sixteenth century the Tarantella acquired a definite musical form, though the climax of this dancing mania was not reached until the seventeenth century. In Figure 3 we see a Tarantella, composed in Rome in 1654 [Czerwinski]: it consists of two phases, one fast and the other slow, and it is the latter which was designated *Antidotum Tarantulae*, i.e., antidote to tarantula poison.

It is well known that even among the pagan Germans dances with a religious colouring were in common practice. Böhme mentions how on special days people congregated for ceremonial dances to the accompaniment of songs and hand-clapping, especially in association with the cult. These dances were performed not only at worship, but also at pagan burial places, perhaps for the dead, but certainly as a protection against the malicious spirits, the demons.

Associated with the important role of the dance in these pagan Germanic cults may also be mentioned all the legends of underworld dances, of elfs and goblins, giants and trolls. It can scarcely be denied that the earlier church declarations concerning the intrusion of pagan dances into the cult of the Christian faith are correct, even though it must not be forgotten that these pagan customs encountered similar customs preserved by those of the Christian faith from earlier times and which found support in several of the writings of the holy men of the Church. This is especially true of the pagan custom of dancing in churchyards. The same may be said of the ancient Slavs, who in the Middle Ages dominated not only existing Slavonic countries, but also large parts of North-East Germany. The Slavonic dances were particularly wild. The dancers leapt into the air, stamped, distorted their bodies and grimaced [Anton]. The Polish dances were peculiarly like the Slavonic. In Moldar and Wallachia the dances were mostly ring-dances or straight dances.

FIG. 3. *Antidotum Tarantulae*—antidote to the Tarantula. The slow soothing phrase. Music written in Rome 1654 [Czerwinski].

The most important seat of the Slavonic cult was Arkona in the Island of Rügen, where the sun-god Svantevit was worshipped. It was here that, in 879, monks from Corvey erected a St Vitus Chapel, possibly in order, by reason of the similarity of names, to promote conversion. Similarly, the capital of Bohemia was situated in a place where there had once been a

8

Svantevit temple and where, in the early days of Christianity, Prague Cathedral was founded and dedicated to St Vitus [Böhme]. The Svantevit festival was celebrated in the middle of June, and June 15th was chosen as the St Vitus festival. At this Slavonic festival of the sun ritual dances were conspicuous. But the Slavs also danced at the graves of the dead. Their dance was in honour of the underworld. But the type of dance was neither sorrowful nor solemn; it was wild and abandoned, masks were worn and profane gestures made [Cosmas's *Chronicle*]. Welden considers that these pagan Slavonic dances still survive in folk customs. This is especially true of the hopping dances of early summer, which were described above as securing a better harvest by magical means. Even some of the folk dances are supposed to retain relics of the original: for example, the May dance, with its vigorous stamping and leaping.

In the Christian era the newly converted were permitted to retain some of their ancient pagan dance customs, though a Christian meaning and significance were to some extent attached to them. But their continuation led to repeated Church prohibitions, especially those of the Council of Würzburg in 1298, which, as we shall find, so strictly forbade dancing in churches.

We have seen how numerous dances are very closely associated with the cure of disease and the driving out of demons. And yet they need not have any demonstrable connexion with religious dances. They may perhaps at one time have grown out of them, but they may also be quite independent phenomena, in which the people adapted for their own special needs the magical powers which the dance had been held to possess under various conditions. We have no occasion, however, to pursue this problem in the present work. We shall limit our enquiry to religious dances as they appear in the Christian Church and in popular medicine.

II

Religious Dances among the Jews

THE Jewish cult dances have been of very special importance in the development of dances within the growing Christian Church; indeed, they are considered as having forced Christians to benefit from and to respect the cult dance. Nor may one suppose that it was only the patriarchs who put forward this motivation, for we shall find in what follows that reference to these

Jewish dances occurs again and again among Christians even to our own day.

Oesterley thinks that he can distinguish several different kinds of dance among the Old Testament Jews. A circular or ring-dance seems to be indicated in II Moses 32, 1–6, describing the dance around the Golden Calf. In this case it was a symbol of the God of Israel, who led the Jews out of captivity. When the Golden Calf was ready, Aaron proclaimed the morrow as a high festival of the Lord, to be celebrated with sacrifice and 'games' (probably dances). It is of less interest in this connexion that the Golden Calf clearly has its prototype in the Egyptian Apis bull. More important is it that the ring-dance, as a sacred dance, must have been so extremely common that when the Children of Israel wished to choose a form of dance before their Golden Calf, they chose the one which was nearest to hand.

Something similar in the choice of dance form—a ring-dance or a straight dance—seems to occur in Psalms 118, 27:

> 'God is the Lord which hath shewed us light: bind the
> sacrifice with cords, even unto the horns of the altar.'

But Oesterley prefers to translate this passage: 'Unite in holy dance, with cord, up to the horn of the altar.' If this is correct it seems to me not impossible to connect this meaning with Ignatius' Letter to the Ephesians, 9: 'Ye are stones in the Temple of the Father, ready for the building of God's house, raised on high by the lever of Jesus Christ', i.e., the Cross, while the Holy Ghost served as the cord [Hennecke]. If an inner connexion is possible, then the rope in the above-mentioned ceremony probably signifies such inner correspondence as well as a connexion with the divinity.

Another type of religious dance is the *processional* dance. In II Samuel, 6, 14, and in I Chronicles, 15, 28, we are told how David took the Ark to David's City. On the way he stops the procession from time to time in order to prepare sacrifices. At the same time he dances with all his strength before the Lord and his Ark, clad in the Levitic cope of white linen and a linen ephod, to a musical accompaniment of bassoons, trumpets, cymbals, psalters and harps. Saul's daughter observes how David hops and dances before the Lord. The Hebrew word for 'dance', according to Oesterley, means in this context to 'whirl around' or 'rotate'. Therefore the dance was primarily a *rotation dance*.

Other dances existed also, especially cult dances, and more pronounced hopping dances. To these belong, in all probability, the dance referred to in II Moses, 15, 20. When the Egyptians were drowned in the Red Sea, Aaron's sister Miriam took a kettle-drum in her hand and all the women followed her, also with kettle-drums and song and dance. According to the account in I Samuel, 18, 6, Saul, on his return from David's victory, was met by the women to the accompaniment of dance, music and song. In the Psalms 87: 1–7, it is said that Zion, the city of the Lord, stands upon the Holy Mount; it is God's city, but when the Lord counts his peoples, then he will count those who are born here and they shall say, amid song and dance, 'All my springs are in Thee'. More important is Psalm 149: 1–3, which shows the use of the dance in the divine service:

> 'Sing unto the Lord a new song and his praise in the congregation
> of the saints.
> Let Israel rejoice in Him that made him: let the children of Zion be
> joyful in their King.
> Let them praise his name in the dance: let them sing praises unto
> him with the timbrel and harp.'

We shall find in Christian quarters that a saying of the prophet Ezekiel is cited with much emphasis as a defence of, and even an unconditional call to, Church dances. The reference is to Ezekiel 6, 11: 'Smite with thine hand and stamp with thy foot.' This type of dance, with stamping and hopping, is perhaps the commonest, and we shall encounter it both in the earliest Christian Church as well as much later. Since we find in the earliest days of Christianity such definite reference to the words of Ezekiel to justify the dance, we may perhaps assume that the Jewish temple dance frequently took this form of clapping and stamping, and that the Jews saw in Ezekiel's words a motive for it.

Among the Jews of the Talmud period (500 B.C. onwards) the dance was a part of the burial rites. It was a stamping dance, which the Sephardic Jews of Spain and Portugal retained. They marched in procession round the dead, thereby showing that originally a circle or ring-dance was the prototype. The mourners moved seven times round the bier, and seven short prayers were sung or recited, each prayer ending with the words: 'May he wander in the land of the living; may his soul repose in the peace of everlasting life.'

There was a Jewish sect, the so-called Therapeutae of the first century B.C., who subsequently were quickly converted, more or less, to the Christian faith, and who were fairly exhaustively described by Filon. Some of the Patriarchs, such as Eusebius of Caesarea, and Hieronymus (according to Wetter), regarded the Therapeutae as a Christian sect. The Catholic Father Héliot relates in his history of the religious orders of monks that in the earliest days of Christianity a number of groups of men and women belonging to the Christian faith withdrew, like the Therapeutae, into the wilderness in order to avoid persecution, assembling on Sundays and holy days in the groves of the oases to dance ring-dances and sing psalms and hymns. This he finds confirmed by the sayings of the Patriarch Tertullian. Thus the Therapeutae were certainly a model for certain Christian followers. They possessed a highly-developed cult dance, which is described by Filon. After a sacred meal there followed a night watch (*vigilium*), in which the participants grouped themselves into two facing choral groups, one of men and one of women. Each group had a leader. During the alternate singing of songs, the singers sometimes remained stationary, sometimes they moved forward, sometimes backward, sometimes to right and sometimes to left, as circumstances required. Then they united in a single chorus. According to Filon this service is in imitation of the manner in which Moses allowed the Children of Israel to celebrate their deliverance on the shores of the Red Sea. Wetter, it is true, doubts the correctness of Filon's motivation, but if one considers the role of Miriam's triumphal dance as a motive in the early Christian religious dances there is in my opinion no reasonable cause to doubt the correctness of Filon's motivation.

In the period around 833 (according to *The Jewish Encyclopaedia*) there was composed in Jewish circles an exposition and interpretation of certain books of Moses. This exposition is entitled *Pirke de Rabbi Eli'Ezer*. In Chapter XII we are told how the angels danced even in the earthly Paradise and how they rejoiced with music and dance at the marriage of Adam and Eve [Brömel]. Reference is made to Ezekiel 28, 13, where Eden is described as God's Garden, which by a bold interpretation is as much as to say that there must have been music and dancing.

Nevertheless, it would appear that the ritual dance was found much later, at least in certain Jewish circles. Thus it is related among the Chassidim, an East Jewish sect appearing in the eighteenth century, of a holy man, a Zaddick, that 'his step was light as that of a four-year-old child. And all who beheld his holy dance—there was not one among them who would not have wished to return home (to the Heavenly home?) for in the hearts of all who beheld his dance there were both tears and joy' [Buber].

III

Dancing in the Earliest Christian Church

IN order to complete our knowledge of the dance in the earliest Christian Church we are obliged to turn to the writings of the Patriarchs. Even the earliest works on the history of dancing in the seventeenth and eighteenth centuries, as well as one or two more modern writers, have attempted to interpret the subject on this evidence. But the historians have been consistently content with presenting more or less detached fragments from the sayings of the Patriarchs, so that they have lost in clarity or have even contradicted the real truth. In addition, quotations have almost invariably been given in Latin, without the necessary and desirable translation. In the following pages we shall allow the Patriarchs to express themselves in our own language, and as fully as may be thought necessary for a proper evaluation of their opinions. Here and there certain opinions may be underlined if they appear to deserve importance in the interpretation of the original significance of the religious dance. Attention will also be given to the place of the dance in certain Christian-Gnostic movements, in so far as these not infrequently indicate thoughts and conceptions which were originally by no means foreign to contemporary Christendom.

At an unusually early stage, possibly even as early as the establishment of the Christian community, the dance was described as one of the heavenly joys and as a part of the adoration of the divinity by the angels and by the saved. We shall find that this conception persisted during the whole of the Middle Ages and into modern times and our own day. Existing literature likes to emphasize that within the Church the dance was conditioned by the sacral dance, which prevailed to such an enormous extent in the ancient world. Writers and numerous Church authorities have repeatedly insisted that heathen dances during worship, or magic cults, have crept into Christian practice. The dances of the Christian Church must essentially have had the same origin.

We will now mention some of the technical terms of the dance which were in use. The commonest are *chorea* and *saltatio*. Their reference to dancing is unmistakable. *Chorea* signifies a round dance, usually with song. In this book we shall usually refer to it as a ring-dance or round dance, although it is clear to me that sometimes it must signify other types of dance, possibly a straight dance, possibly something else. *Saltatio* is a dance with more or less violent jumping, and will be rendered hereafter as a 'hop dance'. But, on certain assumptions, 'chorus' is also a technical term for a dance. Choradini's lexicon defines the term as a sort of dance to the accompaniment of song, i.e., a choral dance. It is evident that 'chorus' in combination with such verbs as *ducere*, *agitare*, *agere*, *exercere*, etc. (to lead, act, exercise), must necessarily mean 'dance'. But in other cases it seems to me that 'chorus' probably only referred to the choral song, especially when it was associated with *canere* (to sing) or similar words. Similarly it is conceivable that these church choruses and hymns were perhaps never executed without the accompaniment of dance-like bodily movements. But we do not know if this applies to all cases. *Tripudium* is more difficult to translate. Du Cange gives only 'jubilation'. According to this Jesuit Father this is the medieval meaning of the Latin word. But it is quite certain that this opinion is incorrect. It is well known that the earliest meaning was 'three-step dance' and a kind of hop dance. It has been thought that *tripudium* at a comparatively early stage lost its original meaning and came to mean 'jubilation'. The verb *tripudiare* would then have meant 'to jubilate'. However, the fact is that the Catholic Church, through its various authorities, as also the civic authorities during the Middle Ages and in more recent times, preserves the meaning 'dance' for the word *tripudium*. We shall find numerous ecclesiastical prohibitions against dancing in churches and churchyards, where dancing is described as *tripudium*. The same applies to medical authorities and chronicles in the Middle Ages. But it is true that

13

during these centuries the word sometimes had the meaning of 'jubilation'. In this connexion it sometimes happens that to use the interpretation 'dance' is not altogether appropriate. For this reason it is the context of the word, as well as the other pre-suppositions, which must determine which is the correct translation. Finally, there appears the word *ludus* which is translated by 'game' or 'play', but which in all probability must refer to a game in connection with dancing. Henceforward, this word will be referred to as a 'game'.

The Patriarchs refer expressly on the one hand to the Jewish sacral dances and on the other hand to certain words of the evangel as a motive for the dance inside the church. David's dance before the Ark, especially, is referred to again and again; the same may be said of Miriam's dance after the Jewish people, with God's help, had passed unscathed through the Red Sea. Reference is also made in Ezekiel 6, 11, to God's command:

Thus saith the Lord God: smite with thine hand, stamp with thy foot.

This is regarded as God's own command that in association with praise and worship there shall also be reverent adoration in the form of a dance. But the New Testament was invoked equally clearly. Reference is made to the remarkable words of Matthew 11, 17, and Luke 7, 32:

And saying, we have piped unto you, and ye have not danced.

This, it is said, is a command which the Lord Jesus Christ himself gave, and dancing must therefore strengthen the adoration and worship of Christ. Finally, reference is made to St Paul, who is said to have danced in spirit when he strove to become a warrior of Christ. It is not clear what is here suggested, but it may refer to II Corinthians, 12, 2, in which St Paul describes how he was elevated to the third Heaven, to Paradise. Perhaps it implies that when St Paul found himself in the Heavenly Paradise he must have also participated in the celestial mysteries, to which especially belonged the round-dances of the saints and angels.

These biblical words led to a ritual Church dance as early as the third century—perhaps earlier—which was adopted by the Christian-Gnostic sects, as also—somewhat later—by the more official Church. Before we admit the evidence of the Fathers of the Church we will direct our attention to the dance within the Christian-Gnostic circles. This may be the more appropriate since we find in an ecclesiastical writer of the eleventh century thoughts and ideas concerning the dance which clearly accord with those of the Gnostics.

1. *The Christian Gnostic Dance*

Certain of the Acts of the Apostles, for example the Acts of St John, would appear to have originated in the third century. They are a part of Christian Gnosticism and were especially revered by the Manichaeans, the Priscillians and others. Here appears a cult dance, a mystery, which is performed on the evening before the Martyrdom of Jesus [Henneke]. Before Jesus was seized by the Jews he collected his Disciples and spoke to them (John 3, 94). He exhorted them to join him in a hymn of praise to the Father. He ordered them to form a ring and, whilst the Disciples held each other by the hand, he himself remained standing in the middle. He ordered them to answer 'Amen' whilst he sang a hymn. Meanwhile, the ring of Disciples moved around him. The hymn was a song of praise, filled with mystical allusions. We may quote an extract:

> Praise to thee, Logos! Praise to thee, Grace, Amen.
> I will be saved and I shall save. Amen.
> I will be delivered and I shall deliver. Amen.
> Grace dances in the round-dance.
> I will play upon the flute, let all dance. Amen.
> I will complain, let all complain. Amen.
>
> The unique eight (the ogdoade) sing praises with us. Amen.
> The twelve on high dance their ring-dance. Amen.
> It is the duty of all to dance on high. Amen.
> Who dances not, knows not what will happen. Amen.

But if you take part in my straight dance behold yourself in Me, the Speaker, and when you behold what I do then do not disclose my mysteries. When you dance, think what I do; that it is your suffering, the suffering of mankind, which I wish to suffer. I dance, but you must think of the whole and when you have thought then say 'Praise be to the Father'.

According to Augustine, both the 'Priscillians' and the 'Manichaeans' sang a similar hymn in the fourth century when celebrating their mysteries. They state that they derived this hymn from the *Memoria Apostolorum*, which constituted an actual Lord's Teaching. This is the hymn:

> I will free and I would be freed.
> I will heal and I would be healed.
> I will bring forth and I would be brought forth.
> I will sing; let all dance together.
> I will clap my hands; let all stamp.
> I will adorn and I would be adorned.

The connexion between the two hymns is obvious. Both are based upon the already mentioned gospels of Matthew and Luke. But the 'Lord's Teaching' also introduces the above-quoted words of Ezekiel. Here already we find an account of how the dance was conducted: straight dance in the form of a ring-dance, hand in hand, with chant and responses, stamping of feet with occasional interruptions for hand-clapping—probably on the occasion of the Amen responses.

The hymn of the Acts of St John describes the whole dance of creation. The Eight sing together with the dancers and for that reason may be assumed to dance also; the Twelve dance and indeed all dance on high. The Eight are primarily the seven planets with the fixed stars as the eighth—but the meaning is also somewhat wider in the Gnostic system. The Twelve are primarily the twelve houses or signs of the zodiac. Just like the Babylonians, the

Christian Gnostics believed the immense circle of the zodiac to be dancing in a ring. The words of the hymn must signify above all that the created world is dancing before its Creator: the sun, the moon and the five planets then known, as well as the heavenly constellations and the fixed stars, all dancing in praise of the Lord.

This is a very old idea. According to Plato the Egyptian temple dances were intended among other things to represent the regular harmony of the cosmos and reflect the dance of the planets and stars around the altar of the sun [Bonnet]. Lucian writes in his work on the dance that the model for the earliest dance was the choir of planets and fixed stars, their harmony and mutual dependence; he adds that the dance was performed round the altar in order to indicate the movements of the stars and especially of the zodiac round the sun. Similar performances are also supposed to have taken place among the Greeks [Bonnet].

I would interpret this remarkable hymn dance of the Acts of St John as follows: it is a mystery and the dance is intended to symbolize restored harmony in the sinful world of creation, perhaps also to promote the restoration which the approaching crucifixion of Jesus will effect. The former seems certain; for the latter there would appear to be only some probability. Only the dancer understands what is happening and what is symbolized by the dance. But the dancer must see himself in Jesus and at the same time consider that Jesus wishes to share the sufferings of mankind. The suffering of Jesus, his death, his descent into the kingdom of the dead, and his resurrection, are the symbols of the fate of individual man. But only the dancer understands, only he who takes part in this mystery can understand and share the knowledge of the significance of the mystery; resurrection and liberation from the power of death. Death is the punishment of sin; the restoration of harmony therefore requires that the power of death be broken. This, therefore, is the mystery and the substance of the dance: by salvation through Christ harmony is restored to the world of creation, and liberation from the kingdom of death is made possible, consequently also the possibility of real life in paradise.

In the Acts of St Thomas (third century) the Apostle Thomas sings a song in praise of the heavenly queen Sophia (Wisdom) whose bridegroom is Christ. In this hymn also there are references to the cosmos: the seven planets and the twelve heavenly houses (the signs of the Zodiac). From these Acts 1: 6-8 we quote [Hennecke]:

> The maiden (Sophia) is the daughter of light.
> The proud glance of Kings rests upon her.
> Ravishing is her beauty . . .
> She is surrounded by the seven bridal attendants
> Chosen by herself.
> Her handmaidens are also seven,
> Dancing a ring-dance before her,
> Twelve is the number of her servants,
> And they are her subjects.

During the same century, the third, a writing on the martyrdom of the Apostle Andrew appears to have been composed in gnostic circles [Bonnet; *Acta Apost.*]. Andrew hangs on his X-shaped cross and the following prayer is offered: 'Release my body in order that my soul, dancing with the angels, may praise 'Thee'. Thus, according to early Christian Gnostic thought, it was not only all created creatures who danced before the Lord but also the angels in heaven. Salvation includes, among other things, the privilege of dancing with the angels to the accompaniment of songs of praise.

Plotinus was born in 204 or 205 at Lykopolis in Egypt, and died in the year 270 in Campania. He represents a religious philosophy which is strongly influenced by Platonism and Gnosticism, and he became the founder of so-called neo-Platonism. His religious philosophy consequently played an unheard of role not only in early Christianity but also in Arabic Mohammedism and thereby in medieval mystic-gnostic sects of French and German Christianity. The speculations of Plotinus influenced to no inconsiderable extent such Fathers of the Church as Gregory of Nice. In his *Æneads* Plotinus writes of good and evil and of the soul which should know itself: 'uncorporeal beings are not restrained by their bodies; when the differences between them have been removed then they are all present to each other. The man who no longer possesses such bodily differences therewith becomes present to others. Just as the choir always moves in a circle around the leader and sings best when it turns towards him so also we must always surround him and when we regard him we can behold our end and our peace, our voice is in harmonious accord with him and we dance around him in a dance inspired by truth. In this dance we can find the source of life, the source of intelligence, the principle of existence, the cause of goodness and the origin of the soul.'

The image which Plotinus implies is in the main borrowed from the ring-dance of the antique chorus, which moved in a circle, singing and dancing round its leader or round the altar. To Plotinus this image represents a state of perfect harmony, in which created things obediently perform an ordered and harmonious choral dance. And he seems to mean by this that the source of all creation, both matter and spirit, is to be found in the original world of purity and harmony. But this picture from the *Æneads* is in fact still more remarkable in that a real connexion between Plotinus's symbolic picture and the one which we have noticed in the Acts of St John is inescapable. In both cases there is a ring-dance round a leader, the participants are exhorted to observe him in order thereby to obtain knowledge of deliverance from suffering and disharmony. The fundamental thoughts and imagery are so similar that one must assume some connexion. Whence did Plotinus obtain the idea that even in a world of perfection the ring-dance was characteristic of a restored harmony and perfection? There is no support for this idea in the Jewish religion; on the other hand there certainly is in some of the mystic religions of antiquity, where there is reference to a dance in the fields of the blessed. We know of the marked dependence of Plotinus on Plato, who in this respect also speaks a language of mystery. So we come back, via Plato, to the mysteries. The ring-dance in the heavenly world of the blessed can be followed in Plato's observations in *Phaedrus* on human souls and their previous existence: 'there they could behold resplendent beauty when, in a blessed ring-dance, they became aware of a blessed image and received an introduction to blessedness, which they celebrated unconscious of the evil which awaited them'. It means, therefore, that the soul in its previous existence in heaven was introduced while dancing to the supernatural mysteries and thus contemplated the world of ideas [Koch]. From Plato, and, through him, from certain of the Greek mysteries—perhaps in the first place from the Orphean and the Eleusinian—the conception of the heavenly ring-dance is derived. The expressions which we shall find in Clement of Alexandria, which indicate that the dance of the angels and of the blessed in Paradise are a mystery, must also be considered as derived from Plato. It is in this way that ancient mystery conceptions penetrated into the symbolism of Christianity.

2. The Fathers of the Church and the Religious Dance

We have now considered the role of the religious dance in Christian-Gnostic and neo-Platonic thought in the third century. At the same time it is possible to confirm the existence of an even earlier Christian literature in which the heavenly dance is included. About the years A.D. 130–150, possibly considerably earlier, there appeared Hermas's 'Shepherd', which was sometimes referred to and was loved by those of the Christian faith. Here are found, among other things, a number of similes of a marked secret and symbolic nature and in the ninth simile [Hennecke] Hermas visits God's mountain. There he beholds twelve virgins, clothed in white linen. They receive him most affectionately. Some perform a straight dance, others differently, whilst all sing. The shepherd explains to Hermas that these virgins are holy spirits, and that nobody can enter the Kingdom of God unless he is clothed in their vestments (innocence and purity). However, the twelve virgins are, it is said, also twelve forces, which emanate from the Son of God. But exactly what these twelve forces are, we are not told. We can hardly be mistaken, however, if we suppose that here also there is at least some significance in the reference to the twelve signs of the Zodiac, i.e., to the cosmic physics which give order to creation. What is remarkable, however, is that so early a Christian writing as 'The Shepherd' has a conception of the heavenly dance and that even this dance appears by the number twelve to stand in causal relation with astronomical and cosmic conceptions. As early as the first third of the second century the idea certainly prevailed that the dance was a part of celestial bliss.

We shall now consider the accounts of the Fathers of the Church and the earliest and most important religious writers on the religious dance. It is not possible for practical reasons to classify the material in respect of the conceptions of the dance in Heaven, in the churches or cemeteries. That would involve too many repetitions.

One of the passages relating to the performance of a Church dance is attributed to Justin the Martyr [Gerbertus]. Justin was a wandering philosopher of the Platonic school, born about A.D. 100 in Sichem. He suffered martyrdom in Rome in A.D. 165. In his *Quaestiones* we find the following passage: 'It is not for the little ones to sing alone, but rather together with musical instruments and dancing and rattles, just in the same way as one enjoys songs and similar music in church.' One has the impression that children's choruses were introduced towards the middle of the second century and that they took a part in divine service which was later taken over by the boys' choirs. These children then appear to have sung and danced whilst at the same time playing musical instruments. They remind us of the boys' choir, the music and dancing in the medieval divine service, as we shall find in a later chapter. One cannot avoid also comparing these children's choirs, as described by the martyr Justin, with the choir boys who danced and sang before the altar in Seville, dressed as angels. For this reason it is not improbable that the children's choirs of Justin should have been thought to represent the heavenly hosts of angels who, rejoicing and dancing, were present at divine service. We shall encounter this idea later. Moreover, it may be mentioned that the boys' choirs were by no means unknown to the pagan cults; according to St Chrysostom there also existed a kind of children's choir [Quasten]. Nevertheless the so-called *Quaestiones* of Justin originate first from the fifth century.

Clement of Alexandria was born in the year A.D. 150 and died in the year 216. He was active as a teacher of theology in Alexandria. From his 'Address to the Heathens' I quote: 'I will show you the Word and the mysteries of the Word and describe them for you as an image of your own fate. This is the mountain beloved of God. On it rejoice God's daughters, the most beautiful lambs, which reveal the reverent festivals of the Word to the accompaniment of constantly repeated choral dancing. By righteousness man may take part in them. The song is a holy hymn to the King of all created things. Oh, in truth holy mysteries! Oh, what pure light! Whilst torches are borne before me I perceive the heavens and God. I am led into the service of God. I become sanctified. These are the orgies of my mysteries. Thou also, if thou wishest, mayest let thyself be led. Then shalt thou dance in a ring, together with the angels, around Him who is without beginning or end, the only true God, and God's Word is part of our song.'

Let me first emphasize that the closing words must not be regarded as referring only to that which awaits in the future a person inducted into the Christian mysteries. These remarkable final words should also, perhaps mainly, be interpreted quite literally. If you are inducted into the Christian mysteries, then you must perform a ring-dance round the altar, with the sacrament, not only with the other novitiates but also with the angels! For they are present and participate in the mystery. These final words must be regarded as having a double meaning: one for the present and one for the future. Only then is there any meaning in Clement's statement that 'these are

FIG. 4. The dance of the angels and of the blessed in the Fields of Paradise, from Angelo da Fiesole's 'Last Judgment', painted in 1425, in the Acadamia delle Belle Arte in Florence. The Angels and the Blessed alternate with each other in a straight dance which tends to be a ring-dance [Wingenroth].

the orgies of my mystery'. The induction was made to the accompaniment of torches and dancing.

In the Babylonian conception of the world Paradise is situated on a mountain in the North. The Mountain of the Indian God is in the Himalayas, of the Persian in the North of Iran, and of the Greek on Mount Olympus in the North. The Jews designated Mount Harmoed in the extreme north as the mountain of God's congregation:

> Beautiful for situation, the joy of the whole earth, is Mount Zion, on the sides of the north, the city of the great King.

In Isaiah the leaders of the people cry out, 'For thou hast said in thine heart, I will ascend into heaven, I will exalt my throne above the stars of God, I will sit also upon the mount of the congregation in the sides of the north' [Isaiah 14, 13].

It is to this mountain in the north that Hermas's 'Shepherd' refers, and which is also seen in Clement. It is here that the mysteries of the Word are acted and with which is undoubtedly associated the solemn choral dance of God's daughters. But on the other hand this heavenly dance is both the prototype and also the final consequence of the church mysteries, for it is the latter which, for the individual, presuppose the former. We must therefore assume that the heavenly choral dance is imitated in the induction mystery of the Church, as, for example, when Clement himself, preceded by flaming torches, was introduced to the orgies of the Christian mysteries. It should be especially emphasized that Clement describes the dance of the angels as a *mystery*.

How did the idea arise that the dance in the church choir was not only an imitation of the dance of the angels but was also performed with the angels themselves? The answer is easy. Dionysius Areopagita, converted to Christianity by St Paul, and the first Bishop of Athens, is mentioned as the author of a number of writings, still preserved, on, among other things, the two hierarchies of Heaven and the Church. These writings were in fact composed during the sixth century. He declares that God has ordained that the hierarchy of the Church shall be constituted in accordance with the hierarchy of Heaven. 'Our knowledge is as yet limited to phenomena observed in the world of the senses, to visible cults, and we make use of them as a factual guide by which we imitate the world of the angels.' In the earliest Christian Church it was supposed that at divine service and the offering at Mass the heavenly angels were present in the choir and participated in the mystery and its performance. Thus Burdach points out how St Chrysostom, in his sermon 'On Regret', writes: 'Oh miracle! The table of the mystery is laid and as an offering to you God's lamb shall be slaughtered; the priest is busy for you: see how the Holy Fire sparkles from the untainted Word: the cherubim and the seraphim hasten hither, those with six wings, which veil their faces.' It is just these conceptions of the presence of the angels at Holy Communion which appear, according to Burdach, for the first time in Origen and later also in St Ambrose. St Chrysostom is the one who assures us that the angels have really been seen hovering around the altar, participating in the divine service. In the Byzantine St Chrysostom Mass the holy angels are called upon to take part. In the third part of the great Mass the singers assume the role of cherubim and sing the cherubic song of praise. The congregation sings 'Holy, holy, holy, Lord God of Sabaoth'. And the angels answer 'Holy, holy, holy, Lord God of Sabaoth. Heaven and earth are filled with thy Glory.'

In the Greek Orthodox Church this hymn of the Cherubim also appears in pure dramatic form. The cherubim themselves enter; the singers, the priest and the deacon play their parts. At the same time the great procession passes into the church and among the people, as if the heavenly hosts were really taking part. During the transubstantiation at Holy Communion the Holy Ghost is called upon, and the deacon moves a staff, on the upper end of which is the head of a cherub with six wings, to and fro over the bread and wine as a proof that the Holy Ghost and all spirits present set the air in motion with their wings. Burning fire and whistling sound are, in early Christian symbolism, the same as the heavenly spirit. Wetter has emphasized that it was once thought that Christ himself, accompanied by the angels, was personally present at Holy Communion and that all the congregation, together with the angels, assembled round Him. In the *Holy Sermon of Johannes Mandakuni*, translated from the Armenian by J. M. Schmid, it is said, 'hosts of angels descend from heaven to earth and surround the altar, where the sacrament of the Lord is preserved.'

From St Clement's curious work, *Stromata*, we may cite the following, 'Therefore we raise our heads and our hands to heaven (during prayer) and move our feet just at the end of the prayer—*pedes excitamus*. By the zest and delight of the spirit we achieve that being which can only be understood by reason; we seek by words of prayer to raise our body above the earth and uplift the winged soul by its desire for better things. In this way we reach blessedness and deliverance from the chains of the flesh which our soul despises. For we well know that he who is a gnostic gladly leaves this world behind, just as the Jews left Egypt, and thereby make it clear that in the future we shall be near to God.'

St Clement's statement that the Christians at the end of prayers 'moved the feet' is a very peculiar one. There are some who translate these little-noticed words by 'rise up on tip-toe', which seems incorrect, because we shall encounter the words 'move the feet' as a technical term for *dancing*.

Gregory the Wonder-Worker was Bishop of Pontus in Asia Minor and lived between 213 and 270. The Roman Catholic Cardinal and Church historian, Caesar Baronius (1538–1607), pointed out that, according to Gregory of Nyssa (Or. 40 adv. Mulieres), Gregory the Wonder-Worker, after the persecution of the Christians had ceased, hastened to concede to them the right to hold special festivals for those who had fought and suffered for their faith. He is said to have permitted the Christians on the festivals of the martyrs to adopt to some extent certain pagan rites which were otherwise forbidden. This applied especially to the introduction of the dance. Brömel adds that in the earliest days of the Church the early bishops, who had not succeeded by the teaching of God's word in preventing the faithful from participating in pagan superstitions, wished to introduce the dance into religion in order to adapt the rites for the benefit of the faithful. Subsequent writers adopted this view. But it seems to be contradicted by what we have learnt from St Justin the Martyr and Clement of Alexandria. Perhaps the contradiction is only apparent; perhaps we ought to interpret the facts as meaning that it was Gregory the Wonder-Worker who introduced the dance in connexion with the memorial festivals for the martyrs, whilst it already had a place among religious rites in general.

If it really was this Gregory who sought to introduce the religious dance into the Christian cult, we should have expected some reference to the fact in his writings, but this is not so. But we do find the following: 'He who has done everything preserved and prescribed by Providence in its secret mysteries, reposes in Heaven in the bosom of the Father and in the cave in the bosom of the Mother (Christ Jesus). The ring-dance of the angels encircles him, singing his glory in Heaven and proclaiming peace on earth.' In his *Four Sermons* (10.1146) he quotes a curious legend, 'To-day (Christ's birthday) Adam is resurrected and performs a ring-dance with the angels, raised up to heaven' (Fig. 5).

FIG. 5. Section of Sandro Botticelli's (1444–1500) 'Supplication Dance of the Shepherds'. Above the stable the angels dance a ring-dance. Behind the Christ Child the ox genuflects and the ass looks out. (National Gallery.)

Eusebius was born in Caesarea and died in the year 339 as a bishop of his native city. In his church history he describes how the Christians danced to celebrate the news of the victory of Constantine the Great and its happy consequences for Christianity. He gives similar accounts in his description of the life of Constantine: 'Both in the country and in towns people wanted above all to inform God, the King of Kings, of the victory by the performance of dances and the singing of hymns.' Also: 'By dancing and singing the victory was, as it were, announced to God, the King of Kings'.

A written sermon on the festival of the martyr Polyeuctes, one of the most famous martyrs of early Christianity, has been preserved from the early years of the fourth century. It is by an unknown author, and in it we read 'Today we stand here in memory of his divine anniversary; it is granted to us to appreciate his noble deeds, and it is the duty of the faithful among Christians to proclaim them everywhere. But what can we offer to the martyr

23

that is worthy of him. By what acts of grace can we return the love which he bore for God? If you so wish, then let us in his honour perform our customary dances' [Aube].

Here for the first time we find religious dances performed at the burial place of a martyr or in the presence of his relics. In other words, it is a sort of churchyard dance which we now see in official Christianity, the dance for the dead which assumes such tremendous importance in later centuries. This dance for the dead is thus an act of grace, which represents the love of God.

Epiphanius was born in the year 315 and from 367 was Bishop of Salamis in Cyprus. He died in 403. In a sermon on Palm Sunday and the entry of Christ into Jerusalem he describes in enthusiastic words how the festival should be conducted. 'Rejoice in the highest, Daughter of Zion! Rejoice, be glad and leap boisterously thou all-embracing Church! For behold, once again the King approaches . . . once again perform the choral dances . . . leap wildly, ye Heavens; sing hymns, ye Angels; ye who dwell in Zion, dance ring-dances; ye mothers dance ring-dances; . . . let us dance the choral dance before the pure Bridegroom as befits the divine bridegroom.' But Epiphanius adds in conclusion, 'Celebrate thy festival, thou Christian Church, not in the letter, not performing the ring-dance in the physical sense, but in the spiritual, perceiving the destruction of the false Gods and the setting up of the Church.'

Wetter has quite correctly observed that this vivid imagery cannot be interpreted otherwise than as the consequence of actual religious dances inside the Church. Epiphanius's words are evidently connected with some customary conception of the heavenly dance of the Angels, indeed, of a cosmic dance of creation. Two interpretations are conceivable. Either the closing words are a later addition by another hand in an attempt to reinforce action against the Church dance, or else we must suppose they have some official meaning. First of all, perhaps, we might wish to lay emphasis on the Church of Christ—though it is unnecessary to stress that it was not the Church which was to perform the dance. It would be more reasonable to suppose that Epiphanius found the material for his enthusiastic descriptions in actual dances, ring-dances or choral dances, in the celebration of the Palm festival in the Christian churches, whilst cautiously seeking to introduce a criticism of the dancing custom, seeking to represent it as spiritual and not physical. Opposition to the Church dances would thus seem to have begun as early as the middle of the fourth century.

Basileios lived between the years 344 and 407 and was Bishop of Caesarea. He is esteemed one of the most eminent of the Fathers of the Church; he is called 'The Great' and played an extremely important part in the province of healing. In his writings there are several references to the existence of the dance in early Christianity. Thus he says of one who has died in blessedness (Letter 40): 'We remember those who now, together with the Angels, dance the dance of the Angels around God, just as in the flesh they performed a spiritual dance of life and, here on earth, a heavenly dance.' Thus life in this temporal world, where it is lived in righteousness, may be described as a spiritual heavenly dance. In another letter (ad 1:2) he writes '*Could there be anything more blessed than to imitate on earth the ring-dance of the angels* and at dawn to raise our voices in prayer and by hymns and songs glorify the rising Creator.'

This last observation is particularly important, because it suggests that the early Christians greeted the sunrise with dances and songs, and that the sun symbolized God, the Creator of all things. We may remember that as late as the eleventh century many Christians were accustomed to greet the rising sun from the steps of the St Peter's Basilica in Rome by throwing it a kiss—a custom which the Papal authority found itself compelled to discourage [Dölger]. But this observation is significant in so far as it clearly claims that dancing here on earth—by which is meant the Church dance—supposes a blessed imitation of the ring-dance of the angels.

In his sermon on drunkenness Basileios in very gloomy colours describes conditions at the celebration of divine service. Easter has just been celebrated and people have watched and fasted during the seven weeks of Lent; after that they celebrate the joyous feast of the Resurrection, unhappily to the accompaniment of drinking and dancing. 'Casting aside the yoke of service under Christ and the veil of virtue from their heads, despising God and His Angels, they (the women) shamelessly attract the attention of every man. With unkempt hair, clothed in bodices and hopping about, they dance with lustful eyes and loud laughter; as if seized by a kind of frenzy they excite the lust of the youths. They execute ring-dances in the churches of the Martyrs and at their graves, instead of in the public buildings, transforming the Holy places into the scene of their lewdness. With harlots' songs they pollute the air and sully the degraded earth with their feet in shameful postures.' How could Basileios be silent, he asks. How can he sufficiently denounce these happenings? In another passage (31.459) he adds: 'You sing harlots' songs, but you neglect the psalms and hymns which you have learnt. You move your feet and hop about madly and you dance the ring dance, which you should not do, for you should more properly bend the knees in prayer. Of all this what must I most deplore?'

What Basileios here condemns so vigorously is not by any means the Church dance as such, but the dances performed by the women with frivolous and indecent movements, and the unsuitable songs which they sing in accompaniment. Against these the Church always reacted strongly, whether they were in the church or at the graves of the martyrs, especially against men and women dancing together. We shall later encounter the prohibition of dancing by women. But there is no contradiction between this last denunciation of Basileios and his previous description of the imitation of the dance of the Angels as something blessed.

Ambrose was born in the year 340 and was Bishop of Milan. He died in the year 397. He expressed himself in great detail on the subject of the church dances. Especially he associates his ideas with Luke 7, 32: 'We have piped

25

unto you and ye have not danced.' In his work *On Repentance*, he says in reference to these biblical words: 'A simple speech, but by no means a simple mystery. And for that reason we must be careful not to be snared into a commonplace interpretation of this speech and suppose that we can abandon ourselves to the actor-like movements of indecent dances and to the romance of the stage; such things should be regarded as dissolute, even in youth. No, the dance should be conducted as did David when he danced before the Ark

Fig. 6. From Donatello's singing gallery in the cathedral of Florence. Marble sculpture from 1433–38. Unrestricted stamping and gesticulating (after Schubring).

of the Lord, for everything is right which springs from the fear of God. Let us not be ashamed of a show of reverence which will enrich the cult and deepen the adoration of Christ. For this reason the dance must in no wise be regarded as a mark of reverence for vanity and luxury, but as something which uplifts every living body instead of allowing the limbs to rest motionless upon the ground or the slow feet to become numb. St Paul danced in the spirit when he exerted himself for us, when he endeavoured to be a soldier of Christ, because he forgot the past and longed for the future. But thou, when thou comest to the font, do thou lift up thy hands. Thou art exhorted to show swifter feet in order that thou mayest thereby ascend to the everlasting life. This dance is an ally of faith and an honouring of grace' (Fig. 6).

This is a remarkable polemic. Ambrose is polemizing against somebody who has maintained that the church dance should not be permitted, because it suggests vice and luxury. But Ambrose defends the church dance whenever it is virtuous and honourable and performed in the fear of God. One need not be ashamed of such a dance. The dance is bound up with faith and is a testimony to the divine Grace. He who dances in Grace dances as David did before the Ark; he participates thereby in the mystery ordained by Christ. And this dance lifts the body above the earth and into Heaven—an idea we have already noticed in St Clement. But from certain points of view the most remarkable thing here is that the person to be baptized, at least in some places, appears to have approached the font with dancing steps. It is not altogether clear, but if it is combined with the distinctly formulated thesis of Ambrose that the dance raises the living body, and with his explanation that the person to be baptized should have swifter feet in order thereby to attain everlasting life, and the subsequent opinion that the dance is an ally of faith, then we can scarcely doubt that it indicates some existing dance in connexion with baptism.

Those baptized must not only stretch out their arms to the west as was customary, abjuring the devil, and bow to the east, whilst making a confession of faith, but they must also approach the font with quickened steps. This reminds us not only of St Clement's explanation that a Christian at the end of his prayer 'moved his feet', but also of Basileios's account of how those who took part in a harlot's dance were seen to 'move their feet'. One cannot, therefore, escape the impression that these expressions 'move the feet' and 'quicker steps' really refer to a dance. Further support for this view is to be found in the words of Ezekiel that 'stamping the feet' was also interpreted as meaning a command to dance.

In his comment on the Gospel of St Luke, Ambrose goes deeper into the purpose of the church dance (15, 1670): 'For this reason Jesus expressly says, We have sung for you and ye have not danced. Behold Moses sang when the waves of the Red Sea hardened and the waters stood still while the Jews passed through them, but when the waters returned they drowned the Egyptian horses and riders. Isaiah sang (5,1) a song in honour of the vineyard (the Lord's), thus indicating those people who, defiant in their vices, had formerly flourished with many virtues. The Jews sang (Daniel 3,24) when their feet grew damp on touching the flames, when they were surrounded on all sides by hot fire (the three men in the fiery furnace). Scripture enjoins us to sing loud to music (Psalms 47, 8). It also enjoins us to dance wisely, since God said to Ezekiel (6, 11), "clap your hands and stamp your feet". The revealed mysteries of the Resurrection have nothing to do with shameless dancing.'

This passage is a further defence of the Church dance: one must dance wisely, one must clap the hands and stamp the feet. But what is most remarkable is the explanation that a dance in manifest shamelessness has nothing in common with the revelation of the mystery of the Resurrection. Expressed positively, this means that the solemn church dance is in accord with the revealed mystery of the Resurrection.

We are now approaching with great strides the mystical content of the gnostic cult dance of the Acts of St John. At any rate we can clearly see the formal connexion between the church dance and the mystery of the Resurrection. The church dance is an imitation of the dance of the angels. The latter is the symbol of blessedness and salvation and is a part of the heavenly reward. But the right of the Christian to take part in the heavenly dance of the angels can only be acquired through the Resurrection, by victory over death and the underworld. But since the church dance is an imitation of the dance of the angels, it must clearly from some points of view really correspond with the revealed mystery of the Resurrection. Similarly, it is more

FIG. 7. The dance of the Angels. From Donatello's singing gallery in the cathedral of Florence. Marble sculpture from 1433–38. A dance with violent stamping and unrestricted gesture. [Schubring.]

than possible that much wider and deeper conceptions lie behind the words of Ambrose concerning the relationship of the dances and the mysteries of the Resurrection. We shall see later that this heavenly dance is regarded as assisting in the deliverance of those who are captives of the forces of the underworld (Fig. 7).

Ambrose follows up this question in another passage (15,1679). Referring to Ezekiel (6, 11) he gives the explanation 'Thus saith the Lord God: smite with thine hand, and stamp with thy foot, and say, Alas for all the evil abominations of the house of Israel! for they shall fall by the sword, by the famine, and by the pestilence. Clap with thine hands and stamp with thy feet. The revealed mysteries of the Resurrection do not in any way correspond to the manifest shamelessness of a dance. Certainly there is a kind of hand-clapping for good deeds and endeavours, whose sound is heard over the earth, whilst these splendid gestures give a resounding echo. It is a noble dance in which the soul dances and the body is uplifted by good works when we hang our harps upon the willows' (Psalm 137, 2).

Ambrose supports the solemn church dance; it alone is in accord with the revealed mysteries of the Resurrection, though at the same time one has the impression that he is seeking a means of spiritualizing the church dance and transforming it into a symbolic dance, a dance of good deeds, since good deeds give the right to heavenly bliss and to share in the ring-dance of the angels. One cannot avoid the impression that Ambrose seeks to yield to the prevailing opposition to church dances and to co-operate in their 'spiritualization.'

In one of his speeches (No. 42) Ambrose reverts to St Luke 7, 32: 'For that reason we have announced to you the rejoicing in Heaven, and you may lift up your hearts in rapture. For this reason the Lord bids us dance, not merely with the circling movements of the body, but with pious faith in him. For just as he who dances with his body at one time floats ecstatically, at another leaps in the air and at another by varying dances pays reverence to certain places, so also he who dances in the spirit with a burning faith is carried aloft, is uplifted to the stars, and at the same time solemnly glorifies Heaven by the dances of the thought of Paradise. And just as he who dances with his body, rushing through the rotating movements of the limbs, acquires the right to a share in the round dance—in the same way he who dances the spiritual dance, always moving in the ecstasy of faith, acquires the right to dance in the ring of all creation.'

Ambrose still strives to spiritualize the church dances. If the types he describes are taken from other church dances, then the latter must have closely resembled certain Jewish cult dances, having lively, hopping steps, combined with rotating and whirling movements. The church dance also took the form of a ring-dance. The concluding words quoted above seem to me to point to the ancient conception of the cosmic dance.

Ambrose continues his efforts to counteract the extensive performance of the real church dance. He does so cautiously and diplomatically, neither condemning nor proscribing. In fact he does not seem to know where to stand. Thus he says (16:1180): 'If anybody doubts this, let him receive the testimony of the gospels, for God's Son said "We have *sung* to you, and ye have not danced". For that reason the Jews were abandoned, because they had not danced, did not understand that they must clap their hands. Therefore those were taken up into communion who gave a spiritual hand-clapping to God. That was the reverent dance of wisdom which David danced, and for that reason we rise through the spiritual dance into the dwelling of Christ, as we heard the Lord say to his Son: "Sit on my right hand".'

The argument here is not altogether clear. But probably it should be interpreted as meaning that Ambrose refers only to the spiritual dance. David's bodily dance is certainly only symbolic, but the dance of Wisdom is spiritual, it allows the spirit to ascend to the abode of Christ.

But despite his ambiguous attitude, despite his obvious yielding to probable outside pressure and the increasing ostracism of the church dance, indirectly St Ambrose is unable to abandon it altogether. Spasmodically he ied, with obvious effort, to interpret the words of Ezekiel and the stumbling blocks of the Gospels of St Matthew and St Luke as referring to matters spiritual and not bodily. It was a vain and hopeless endeavour. St Ambrose clearly understood this; hence his courteous caution. In his earlier interpretation of Psalm 118, 27, which we have already discussed in the account of the religious dance among the Jews, he evidently relied on a translation quite different from our own, and it is clear that it agreed in principle with that proposed by Oesterley: 'Join together in a holy dance, with cord, even unto the horn of the altar.' In his interpretation of the Bible, St Ambrose now says (15:1290, 1845); 'But the bodily dance in God's honour may also be regarded as praiseworthy. For that reason David danced before the Ark of the Lord.'

St Gregory of Nazianzus, born about 329 and died in 390, was an eminent theologian and officiated for a time as Bishop of Nazianzus and later in Constantinople. In one of his 'sermons' (against the Aryans) he makes certain observations on the Christian dance. 'But we follow the custom (of celebrating Christian festivals) only in the sense that we neither wreathe the door of our home with green branches nor perform ring-dances, neither do we delight our eyes, or flatter our ears with song.'

It would be both incorrect and untrue to interpret these words literally. Music and song are an original part of divine service and nobody has denied them. Yet certain Fathers of the Church have endeavoured to restrict music and song to simple, artless, even dull, melodies. Not infrequently they thought it was better that the songs should be sung without instrumental music. Chromatics were regarded as unsuitable. St Clement (Paedagog II, 4) emphasizes that only simple, modest harmonics should be permitted, and we should as far as possible reject the effeminate and the sensuous, because they mislead, by their artificial and impure airs, into an enervated conduct of life. But serious and modest modulations prevent drunkenness and licentiousness. So one must completely reject the chromatic and frivolous harmonies which are used at indecent drinking feasts, where wreaths are worn, and also the music which loose women employ [Wagner]. The passage from St Gregory of Nazianzus quoted above must therefore not be taken literally; it must rather be directed against exaggeration. It is the boisterous, high-spirited dances which he rejects, the theatrical, dramatic scenes, the modulated, many-voiced singing, accompanied by numerous instruments. It is these which flatter the ears and seduce the eyes. The confirmation of such a sublimated interpretation seems to me to be apparent in another of his speeches, in the exhortation directed to the Emperor Julius (*Orat. v contra Julianum*): 'Set free, I wish to participate in the solemnities, having always fought the battle of the good and done my duty and preserved my faith, all according to the Epistle of St Paul. Let us sing hymns instead of striking drums, have psalms instead of frivolous music and song, and as a proof of the recognition by the soul, the sonorous clapping of the hands instead of the applause of the theatre, modesty instead of laughter, wise contemplation instead of intoxication, seriousness instead of delirium. But even if you wish to dance in devotion at this happy ceremony and festival, then dance, but not the shameless dance of the daughter of Herod, which accompanied the execution of the Baptist, but the dance of David to the true refreshment of the Ark, which I consider to be the approach to God, the swift encircling steps in the manner of the mysteries' (Fig. 8).

FIG. 8. The dance of the Angels. Marble relief from 1433–38 by Donatello, executed on the exterior balcony of the cathedral in Prato. Here were exhibited on Church festivals the precious relics of the Church. Stamping and gesticulating; on the right, possibly gyratory. [Schubring.]

This is quite clear: the Emperor Julian may dance at the festivals celebrated by the Church, and this dance is in principle, in form and in function, similar to the dance of David before the Ark, a rotating dance, a whirling encirclement. Again, we may remember that the church dance is connected with a mystery, for this dance is described as an approach to God in the manner of the mystery. By dancing one approaches God. The explanation is possibly that the dance is an imitation of the dance of the angels: if one does as the angels do one can more easily approach God. Another remarkable interpretation is apparent in the explanation that David danced for the true refreshment of the Ark. It is, therefore, a refreshment for the holy ones to be surrounded even on earth by devotees who in dancing imitate the heavenly adoration and the joys of blessedness.

In an address to St Gregory of Nyssa, St Gregory of Nazianzus describes how all the martyrs should be celebrated: 'May we flee from all the chains of the devil. It is a solemn and a dangerous struggle, a mighty battle, but its prize is wonderful. If we assemble to celebrate this festival in such a way that it shall be agreeable to Christ and at the same time honour the martyrs, then we must execute our triumphant ring-dance.' And he adds: 'Great throngs of people must perform a ring-dance for the martyrs in reverent honour of their precious blood' [Brömel].

St John Chrysostom (Golden-Mouth) lived from about 345 until 407. He was born in Antioch and officiated as Bishop of Constantinople. In a lecture on Lazarus he describes how the Christians celebrated the Whitsun festival: 'Yesterday was the festival of the Devil (a pagan festival), but you, on the contrary, celebrated the festival of the Holy Ghost as far as, with the utmost zeal of spirit, you have received all that we have proclaimed. You have passed the greater part of the day together in transports of moderation, in the performance of ring-dances in the spirit of St Paul. By this your merits have increased doubly, in the first place because you refrained from the indecent dances of the drunken, and in the second place because you danced those spiritual dances which are most pleasing and most modest . . . , and while others performed dances for the Devil, you circled instead in this place and used musical instruments of the spirit, revealing your souls as do the musical instruments on which the Holy Ghost plays when he instils his grace into your hearts.'

It is the real church dance which St Chrysostom here calls the spiritual dance, evidently in contrast to the unseemly dance. Yet the faithful have circled round in this place. This dance is, therefore, said to have been performed in the spirit of St Paul, bringing to the dancers the grace of the Holy Ghost.

At Christian wedding festivals dancing appears to have been permitted at a very early date. These dances were degraded in a scandalous fashion, but it seems to me doubtful whether the dances were really performed inside the church. St Chrysostom condemns them in the following words: 'Then unbridled sensuality reigned; those present seemed to go out of their minds, some neighed amorously like horses, others kicked like asses; everything was dissolute and confused. No sanity, no dignity. Everything was the pomp of the devil: cymbals, flutes, indecent songs . . . For it was customary to combine music and song with the dancing' (Sermon 42).

In a commentary on the Gospel of St Matthew, St Chrysostom says of Salome's dance: 'For where there is a dance, there also is the Devil. For God has not given us our feet to use in a shameful way but in order that we may walk in decency, not that we should dance like camels (for even dancing camels make an unpleasant spectacle, much more than women), but in order to dance ring-dances with the angels. For if it is shameful for the body to behave thus, the more so is it for the spirit to do so. Thus dance the demons and thus dance the servants of the demons.'

It is easy to see that St Chrysostom's condemnation is directed only at lascivious and indecent dances. He approves the dance of angels; we have been given our feet in order to dance with the angels, and certainly not only after death. The dance in the choir of the church, combined with the holy ritual, was, as we have seen, a dance with and in imitation of the invisible angels.

St Chrysostom relates (*Hom. ad Agricolas*) that the Bishops and high spiritual fathers themselves performed and conducted the sacred festival dances before the relics of the martyrs. 'Ye have seen how human nature may be imbued with supernatural forces; ye have seen these splendid wreaths won by the shedding of blood; we have here in various places danced comely ring-dances under the guidance of your leader, but on this occasion sickness happens to compel us, and others who were invited, to stay at home.'

St Augustine was born in 354 and died in 430. He was educated in Carthage and became Bishop of Hippo. In his address No. 311 he devotes a special chapter to the profane songs and the loud stamping dances which were heard from the church in which the saint Cyprian the Martyr lay buried. He points in his introduction to the oft-quoted Matthew 11, 17, and says: 'May anybody dance in this place, even though psalms be sung? Once upon a time, not many years ago, impudent dancers intruded into similar places. As many of our Elders can remember, they brought their uncleanness and their insolence even into the holy place where the body of the Martyr lies. During the whole of the night they sang here shameless songs, to the accompaniment of dancing. When the Lord commanded holy vigils for our holy brother, your Bishop (Cyprian), then this pestilence added some little lustre to the festival, but later this custom fell out of use because of stricter care and from shame from the teachings of wisdom. Here we celebrate the holiness and the festival of the martyrs—here there shall be no dancing. And in spite of the fact that there was no dancing, yet we read in the Gospel: We have *sung* for you and ye have not danced. Those who have not danced are blamed, reproached, accused, banished. Though vanished until now, this insolence begins to re-appear: listen rather to what wisdom proclaims, *Let him who strikes up, sing; let him who dances, dance.* For what is the meaning of dancing if it is not to harmonize the bodily movements with song. What sort of a song, my brethren? Let us listen to the song; let us hear the dancers. Be ye harmonious yourselves in your habits as are the dancers in the movements of their limbs. Take ye care in your inner selves that ye harmonize in virtuous deeds.' And in conclusion St Augustine adds as regards St Cyprian, whose memory was being celebrated on this particular day: 'He heard the song, he revealed himself dancing, not in the body, but in the spirit.'

However severely St Augustine condemned these wild, abandoned dances, performed to the accompaniment of indecent songs or of psalms, he concedes the impossibility of entirely setting aside the Gospel exhortations to dance or the manner in which those exhortations were at that time conceived and interpreted. He appears in general to have disapproved of dancing, but grants at the same time its propriety, as shown in the words of Revelation. And he is quite clear in his own mind that those who will not dance will be blamed and reproached. For that reason he proposes a compromise, a word of wisdom. He who would dance, may dance. But more important for St Augustine is the endeavour of the congregation to make itself unworldly, harmonious in good habits—a virtuous life—in the same way as the dancers

33

seek to achieve a common harmony. I regard it as of special importance that St Augustine declared that the holy martyr St Cyprian revealed himself to his worshippers dancing in spirit. This connects itself in a special way with the Christian conception of the heavenly dance of the angels and of the blessed, which reveals this dance as a part of the state of blessedness and as inseparable from it. The heavenly dance must, therefore, be regarded as perpetual, without interruption.

In *The Kingdom of God*, St Augustine returns to the question of the celebration of the martyrs at their graves: 'Thus we neither appoint priests, nor make offerings to our martyrs, because this is unseemly, unjustified and not permitted. But it is all the more seemly before the only God. For neither by criminal transgressions nor by shameful play can we give pleasure to the martyrs or, as the pagans do, actually make a festival of the shameful practices in honour of the false gods. The martyrs themselves, were they alive, would deprecate it.'

In another address (326.1) appears the oft-quoted passage: 'Let us rejoice because the martyrs have passed from the world of suffering to the fields of rest; but they have not achieved this by dancing, but by prayer; not by drinking, but by fasting; not by quarrels, but by forbearance.' There is no doubt that St Augustine raises very strong opposition to the religious dances in the Christian church, even though he does not venture to condemn them entirely and openly. He concedes that, in spite of all, dances may be performed.

Theodoretos was a Syrian theologian, later Bishop of Kyrrhos, near Antioch. He lived between 393–457. In his church history he describes the rejoicing among the Christians in Antioch when they heard of the death of the Emperor Julian. They arranged banquets and festivals. 'They danced not only in the churches and the chapels of the martyrs, but in the theatres, too, they proclaimed the victory of the Cross and ridiculed the prophecies of Julian.'

In another work, *On Heretics*, he described the dances of the gnostic Christians in Egypt, the so-called Meletians and Messalians: 'In Alexandria there appeared a Bishop Meletius. From him came the Meletian heretical sect in Egypt. In accordance with their doctrine they were so foolish as to wash the body every other day, to sing hymns to the accompaniment of hand-clapping and dancing, to rattle bells hung upon a peg, and so on.' As regards hand-clapping and dancing, there was nothing heretical about them; they were a typical Christian usage during those centuries. The bells which were rung may perhaps be reminiscent of the so-called 'sistrum' which the priestesses of the goddess Iris rang during their temple dances, but they especially remind us that the Christian church thought that bells expelled demons.

Of the Messalians he writes: 'But they did many other things which revealed their madness. They began suddenly to dance, and threw themselves upon the demons whilst dancing (i.e., upon the sick who were possessed), and held out their fingers as if they were arrows to shoot at the demons.'

34

This passage is of especial interest, as it shows that this dance was performed for medical reasons. Many diseases, probably most of them, were regarded as the result of demoniac possession and the New Testament lent support to this view, which prevailed at this time and for many centuries later. But we shall find that this demon-expelling, healing dance was even at that time by no means peculiar to the Messalians, but was widely adopted by Christians, in so far as their dances at the graves of the martyrs and before the relics of the martyrs must have been combined with the hope of expelling demons from the possessed and of healing all sicknesses.

Caesarius was born in the year 470 and died in 542 as Archbishop of Arles. In his address on dances before the churches of the saints, he issues a warning against 'performing dances during holy festivals and singing sensual songs, when one ought to praise God and abstain from evil. There are especially unfortunate and miserable people who do not fear or blush to execute dances and hop before the churches of the saints, and although they come to church as Christians, they return as heathens—because these dances are a relic of pagan customs.'

One glimpses the dance of the Angels behind the words of Pope Gregory the Great, head of the Catholic Church during the years 590–604. He maintains that a Church festival is only worthy when it is celebrated with a dance of the angels and that it must also be a means of promoting blessedness in God.

Isidor, who lived from 560 to 636, was Bishop of Seville. He has left a very remarkable account of the dances of the earliest Christians in Spain. He refers to certain rites at the beginning of the January fast: 'These miserable creatures, and, what is worse, some of the faithful, assumed monstrous forms and transformed themselves into wild shapes; others womanized their masculine faces and made female gestures—all romping and stamping in their dances and clapping their hands, and, what is still more shameful, both sexes danced together in the ring-dance, a host with dulled senses and intoxicated with wine.'

It would seem to be a sort of carnival that Isidorus describes. Especially does he object to men and women dancing together. It was the custom, of course, for men and women to be kept strictly apart during divine service, and in general there was a strong objection to women dancing, even alone. But in my opinion the pronouncement of Isidorus has a very special importance. It seems to me to be closely connected by origin with the *festus stultorum*, the festival of fools and asses, which appeared in the churches in the sixth century and which has survived to modern times. We shall return to the subject later.

Eligius, Bishop of Noyon, was active during the period 640–659, and he too struggled against combining the Christian dancing fever with the church service. He disapproved strongly of celebrating the vigil at the solemn festival of St Paul with music and dancing. But people replied to him [Quasten]: 'However much you, a Roman, may preach, you will never succeed in eradicating our ancient customs. Nobody can forbid us these ancient games, which give us such immense pleasure.'

Pirminius came from the borderland between Spain and France. He was an active missionary and died in the year 753. During his mission he used a curiously composed handbook, the so-called *Dicta Pirminii*, from which the following quotation is derived: 'No Christian must take pleasure in performing devilish dances, songs, hops, games and jests, either in church or at home or at cross-roads or anywhere else. Comic songs and shameless songs, lascivious or indecent words must not issue from your mouths—you should go more often to church in humbleness of spirit and with steadfast faith. And nobody shall dare to raise a quarrel, or seek to chaffer, neither shall ye allow vain words to pass your lips. Flee therefore as from the Devil's arrows from all dancing and hopping, all shameful and indecent songs and do not seek to indulge in such, either in the church or in your homes or in the market place or anywhere else, for all these things are the relics of pagan customs.'

Johan of Damascus lived between 676 and 754 and was the last Father of the Greek Church. He lived as a monk in the Sabas Monastery near Jerusalem. The life of Barlaam and Joasaph (or the copy of it) is attributed to him, even if wrongly. In it we read, on the subject of the Christian life: 'Here we must strive diligently for one thing: to share in everlasting blessedness. Those who avoid error will be as the angels. And now they dance the ring-dance together with the angels, whose life they have imitated.'

Honorius was a Christian hermit who during the first half of the twelfth century lived near Regensburg. He was an eminent scholastic and represents a Christianity which is clearly influenced by Platonic, and perhaps neo-Platonic, philosophy. He writes as follows concerning the church dance: 'The choir of musicians had its origin in the ring-dance of antiquity before the false gods, so that one might believe that they, ensnared by their delusions, both praised their gods with their voices and served them with their bodies. But in their ring-dances they thought of the rotation of the firmament; in the clasping of their hands the union of the elements; in the sounds of song the harmony of the planets; in the gestures of the body the movements of the celestial bodies; in the clapping of hands and the stamping of feet the sound of thunder; something which the faithful imitate, converting all to the true service of God. For we can read how the people passed through the Red Sea and then danced ring-dances, whilst Mary played for them on the drum; how David danced before the Ark with all his strength and sang psalms to the zither. And Solomon is reported to have introduced singers round the altar who, in their voices, trumpets, psalms, cymbals and zithers let the songs resound. From that time and until now ring-dances have been performed to the accompaniment of music, whilst the heavenly bodies are said to revolve to sweet music.'

In his work on church dances Gougaud has also referred to these passages from Honorius, but he is guilty of a curious misinterpretation. He thinks that in his description of the symbolism of the dance, Honorius has borrowed features from the profane and popular dances of his own day. This is evidently a mistake; we find that his description of the symbolism of the dance is in complete accord not only with the character of the ritual dance of antiquity but also with the church dance which the Fathers of the Church have so often and so exhaustively described. Gougaud also believes that Honorius, in agreement with the general custom of the time, has sought to introduce a subtle symbolism into the details of the dance. This too is a mistake, because this symbolism is likewise in complete accord with that of the temple dance of antiquity and with the mysticism which we saw in the dance hymn of the Acts of St John. Moreover, Gougaud would wish to derive the Christian church dance from pagan customs, a view which, essentially, is not justified.

Centuries later this symbolism of Honorius crops up again, with its origin in Plato and Plotinus, Philon, Epiphanios and Ambrose. We meet it in the sermons of the Dominican monk Raffaello delle Colombe in 1622 [Rodocanachi]. In these he seeks to motivate and spiritualize the dance. He evidently agrees with the above-quoted opinions of certain of the Church Fathers, but especially with Honorius and Lucian. The dance is, he says, a symbol of the universal order and can be compared with the dance of the stars. For prayer is a spiritual dance, which takes the Saints and God himself by the hand in accordance with the words of Philo. God leads the ring-dance of the heavenly bodies. God leads inside the ring, he dances with the praying soul and holds it by the hand as it hops, dancing. For prayer is nothing else but a dance hop in so far as it releases us from earth and strives towards heaven.

3. A Summary

From the fourth century, and probably earlier, the idea prevailed in Christian circles that the holy spirits and God's forces danced in God's Paradise (Hermas, *The Shepherd*). In the latter part of that century the heavenly dance appears as a dance of the angels, in which the righteous take part. These dances of the angels belong to the mysteries of the Word (Clement). The ring-dances of the angels and of the Blessed are a part of bliss in Paradise; they are a reverent adoration of God, and of these the church dances are an imitation (Basileios). The former is connected with the mysteries of the Resurrection (Ambrose), and we must assume the same for the latter. The blessed and the righteous who, immediately after death, enter Paradise, therefore immediately take part in the dance of the Angels. If a blessed martyr reveals himself to those who venerate him, he does so dancing (Augustine). Some day all of us will perform ring-dances with the Angels in Paradise (Chrysostom).

From about the year 150 it may be that a kind of boys' choir appeared, which played music, sang and danced during divine service (Justin). In the latter part of that century church dances appear to have become a part of the divine service (Clement). At the close of prayers hands were raised above the head to the accompaniment of a brief tramping or stamping dance (Clement), which was intended to show the desire, through prayer, to lift the body above the earth. In the fourth century the solemn church dance is said to have accorded with the revealed mysteries of the Resurrection (Ambrose). This agrees with the earlier information that the dance is a part of the Christian mysteries (Clement). It is possible that those about to be baptized approached the font dancing (Ambrose) in order to indicate resurrection from a sinful life to a righteous life after death by baptism. The church dance must be performed in the same manner as David danced before the Ark and this signifies a re-annimation of the person for whom the dance is performed. It signifies a grateful approach to God through rapid rotations in the manner of the mysteries (Gregory of Nazianzus); it is closely allied to faith and in honour of grace (Ambrose). At the end of the fourth century wedding dances appear to have been performed (Chrysostom). Watch-night services in connexion with church festivals and the festivals of the martyrs were celebrated from the fourth century by dances, which took place outside the church or chapel, but sometimes inside the church and at the graveside. At the beginning of the same century the church dance was performed in order, at the moment of triumph, to come into closer contact with God (Eusebius), and during the first part of the fifth century in order to proclaim in churches and chapels the victory and triumph of the Church (Theodoretus). From the beginning of the seventh century there begins to appear the curious parody church dance which later develops into the so-called fools' festival(Isidore). During the twelfth century there became linked with the church dance a number of ideas of the symbolic connexion between the details of the dance and the order of nature and of an original or restored harmony, thus reviving similar ideas in the ritual dances of antiquity and in the dance symbolism of Christian gnosticism (Honorius).

As early as the late fourth century there occurs a frequent perversion of the Christian church dance. Women seek increasingly to participate, with high-spirited and reprehensible dances and immoral songs, both in churches and chapels and at the graves of the martyrs. From the fourth century church dances were performed in honour of the martyrs. They were performed at their graves or inside the churches in which their relics were preserved. This dance is an act of grace towards the martyr (Gregory of Nazianzus). It is a kind of triumphal dance, signifying the victory of the martyr; they were led, possibly as a rule, by the Bishop or other high dignitaries of the Church (Chrysostom).

The dances were mostly choral dances and ring-dances, probably always to the accompaniment of hymn-singing and psalms. Occasionally the musical accompaniment may have been more elaborate. Sometimes the dance had a different character, as when there was a solo dance. Romping dances also occurred, sometimes hopping and leaping and also gyrating

(Ambrose, indirectly). Sometimes there was a real rotation dance, signifying, in the manner of the mysteries, an approach to God (Gregory of Nazianzus). All the dances appear to have been led by a rhythmic clapping of the hands, which was probably only intermittent, and by a stamping of the feet. The technique of the perverted dance, on the other hand, seems to lack interest.

IV

At the Graves of the Martyrs

AS early as the fourth century it was common for Christians to visit the graves of the martyrs in order to commemorate the sufferings and the victories of the dead, and to pay them honour and reverence, and to beg their help in various circumstances. The celebrations were held on the anniversary of the death of the martyr, which day was also regarded as his real birthday, this perhaps in accordance with the gnostic, originally Platonic, conception that the human spirit is buried in the body as is the corpse in the grave. Death is therefore the same as the re-birth of the soul to everlasting life. The eve and the night of this day were also frequently solemnized in the so-called vigils, or night watches, formally taken over from similar customs in the world of antiquity. Thus great crowds streamed from early morning until late at night to the grave of the holy Hippolytus in Rome, to the grave of the holy Felix, and so on [Lucius]. Sometimes reverence of a marytr was so widespread that many went on a pilgrimage to his grave not only on his anniversary but practically every day of the year.

According to ancient Christian conceptions the martyr had baptized himself in the out-pouring of his own blood when for Christ's sake and for the preservation of the true faith he often sacrificed his life in the greatest pain rather than fail in his duty or abandon his faith. But this blood-baptism was regarded as the equal of the baptism by fire to which the Gospels and the Epistles testify and which, according to Christian doctrine, encompassed all, evil as well as good—a baptism of trial, purification and punishment in the sea of fire which was supposed to surround the extreme limits of the heavenly Paradise [Edsman]. Only by baptism in fire can one enter the Kingdom of God. But this baptism did not take place until the last hour; until then the body lay in the grave and the soul was in the keeping of the underworld. At this last hour body and soul were again united. But salvation came in a different way to the martyr. For him the blood baptism was the same as the baptism of fire and made it possible for his soul to enter directly into Paradise [Aschelis]. According to Eusebius the martyrs were the equals of the angels, and immediately after their death the angels conducted them in triumph to Heaven. Chrysostom thinks that they were received in Heaven with great pomp and were conducted to the heavenly Throne. Together with the angels they belong to the heavenly choir. The angels and the martyrs differ only in name. For this reason the martyrs are man's intercessors and protectors [Lucius].

The only effect of all the persecutions of the early Christians was to lead them in larger numbers, in denser throngs, to the graves of the martyrs, in order to hold divine services there, not only on the anniversaries of their deaths, but also at other times. When the persecutions ceased, under Constantine, magnificent churches were erected over their graves; the stream of devotees swelled and pilgrimages flourished as never before [Marx].

Augustine mentions that the graves of the martyrs were usually situated in open country [Brömel]. At an earlier date, before there was any possibility of building the increasingly spacious memorial churches, people were content with smaller, insignificant chapels or prayer houses. On the anniversary of a martyr the chapels were adorned in different ways; there was music and singing and dancing. Further details of the procedure may be seen in Gregory of Nyssa. He was born in Caesaria, and became Bishop of Nyssa in 371, and died there in 394. In his sermon on St Theodor he says as follows: 'If one comes to a place like this, where we are now assembled, where the memory of the righteous one is celebrated and where the relics are preserved, then in the first place we are rejoiced by the splendid things we behold. See how this temple has become a sanctuary, stately and perfected both by the dignity of the building and by the beauty of the decoration. An artist has carved in wood the shapes of human beings, a sculptor has polished the stone work till it shines like silver. And a painter has with his art added flowers to the picture. In his painting he has reproduced the mighty deeds of the martyr, his struggles and his pains, and also pictures of the insane, inhuman tyrants, their ungovernable passions, the flaming furnace, the blessed perfection of the warrior and the picture of the Lord Jesus Christ. All this has been presented to us as a sort of book, containing the means of interpretation in all languages, revealing in artistic colours the struggles and the pains of the martyrs. They adorn the temple like a beautiful field of flowers.'

To understand this text it should perhaps be added that the holy Theodor had been a soldier of Pontus, who set fire to the Kybele temple in Amasea and was therefore condemned to death in a furnace.

Christianity did not originally conceive of death as in any way an evil or regrettable thing, but rather as a deliverance. Hence one should not sorrow. In an old Christian tomb inscription we find testimony to the connexion between bliss and the heavenly dance [Kaufmann]. The inscription is to be found in the Roman basilica St Agnese Fuori le Mura, from the fourth to the seventh century; here the dead man says,

No sorrowful tears, no beating of the breast,
Oh, father and mother! For I possess the Kingdom of Heaven.
Neither the hopeless underworld, nor the pale shape of death,
But a safe repose has taken me. I dance
Ring-dances with the blessed saints in the beautiful fields of the righteous.

Chrysostom exhorted Christians to music and song for the dead, but warned them against songs of lamentation. Basileios mentioned flutes, zithers and drums as suitable for the performance of ritual funeral music. Tertullian, however, thought that music disturbed the dead, who know what is happening, so that caution is necessary [Quasten]. The songs which were sung and the music which was played at the graves of the martyrs must therefore be assumed to have had the character of triumph and joy rather than of sorrow and lamentation. The dances, to which we have just referred, around the graves of the martyrs must therefore by no means be regarded as mournful dances; on the contrary they were full of joy and triumph. For that reason Gregory of Nazianzus was able to refer to them as triumphant ring-dances. Very frequently only psalms and hymns were sung, but there were also special songs of honour, composed for a particular martyr [Brömel].

At these graveside festivals there was not only music, singing and dancing, but also food. These meals have also been adopted from the world of antiquity as a general and international custom. Soon, however, the Church had to intervene with warnings and proscriptions, even against meals at the graveside, since they had degenerated into drunken orgies. Nevertheless, these meals in honour of the dead have remained in Christian practice far down into modern times.

It was, however, not only to honour and reverence the martyrs that people assembled at the graves in ever-increasing numbers, to recall their lives, their struggles, and to find consolation and strength. Let us listen to Gregory of Nyssa: 'For our instruction there remained the memory of the struggles of the martyrs, uniting the peoples, cherishing the Church, repelling and casting out devils, recalling the peaceful angels, praying to God for what is good for us. Thus he creates here a workshop for the healing arts for all diseases, a haven for those who are tossed in the storms of affliction, an overflowing and inexhaustible treasury for the poor, a resting place for the wanderer, a wonderful meeting place and real day of celebration.' These words refer principally to the holy Theodor.

Very early it was realized that the relics of the martyrs possessed supernatural powers, that they exercised an extraordinary influence in driving out sickness, dispelling magic and curing numerous sicknesses. This idea is also in full agreement with the conception of antiquity as it appears, for example, in the writings of Pliny and Democritus [Backman]. Even the dust which was collected from the vicinity of the graves, the water with which the tomb was washed and every object which had been in contact with it, possessed something of the powers of the relics and could effect miracles and cast out devils. Several of the Patriarchs testify to this, e.g., Chrysostom, Gregory of Nazianzus, Gregory of Nyssa, Augustine and others [Lucius]. These opinions were held right through the Middle Ages and into modern times.

Let us now listen to some of these Fathers of the Church. In an address on the holy Julian, Chrysostom says: 'Both men and devils look up to heaven and the stars, but the faithful look at the wounds of the martyrs, whilst the devils dare not look upon them. For if they did so they would for ever lose the sight of their eyes, but in addition they could never endure the splendour which streams out from the martyrs . . . For everybody who has been possessed and frenzied by demons and who is led to this sacred grave, in which the relics are preserved, in him you will see how the demons leap up and take flight.' In another address on the forty martyrs the same patriarch says: 'When you have thus left your home and gone forth from the city, then we all meet here at the church of the martyrs, saying farewell to all unrest, admiring their glory, forgetting our cares, enjoying peace and quiet. We mingle with the saints, praying them to be the faithful protectors of our well-being, and we offer up many prayers to them.'

Gregory of Nyssa, in the address already quoted, in honour of the holy Theodorus, ended with a litany-like prayer, in which he says: 'For we also, who have hitherto remained unscathed and healthy, we repay thus the good deeds we have known.'

Gregory of Nazianzus says in his address No. 24: 'It is now for you yourselves to add what remains, in order that you may make an offering to the martyr himself for the manifest casting out of devils, the prevention of sickness and the knowledge of things to come; all of which can be accomplished by the very ashes of Cyprian if only faith is present. This they know well who were together in the days of danger and handed down the story of the miracle to us, just as we shall hand it down to those who come after us.'

St Cyprian was Bishop of Carthage and died about 200. He fought against idolatry and suffered martyrdom by beheading. The miracles to which Gregory refers were performed by Cyprian when a pestilence raged in Northern Africa. Gregory's words are highly significant, because they prove that these festivals and dances at the tombs of the martyrs were in expectation of great blessings: the healing of sickness, the expulsion of devils, and the knowledge of things to come. We shall find later that the same prospect urged large hosts to visit churchyards and tombs century after century. That which in the earliest periods of Christianity was addressed to the dead martyrs gradually came to be addressed to the dead in general, but the purpose remained the same.

Basileios (Or. ad Mamas-Dict. Christ. Antiq.: Martyrs) points out that all should remember how the martyrs, when called upon, helped the sick, prolonged life for the sorely afflicted, and brought dead children back to life. Ambrose (ib.) discovered, as the result of a revelation in a dream, the burial place near Milan of the holy martyrs Protasius and Gervase, and had the relics preserved and borne in solemn procession through the town to the episcopal church. During the procession these relics worked numerous miracles; they restored sight to the blind and, amidst violent cramps, the devils fled from tortured bodies. Theodoretus (*ib.*) calls the martyrs healers of the body and of the soul.

In his writings, especially in *The City of God*, Augustine repeatedly returns to the power of the relics of the martyrs to heal the sick and to expel devils. Indeed, in this work he expresses the curious view that miracles are effected through the Sacrament of Christ and through the relics of His saints. He insists that the places to which the sacred relics have been taken have a special sanctity and are endowed with the power to work miracles. How enormously potent have these words been for many centuries in stimulating the Christian churches to enormous efforts to discover and acquire as many precious relics as possible!

Augustine likes to tell of the miraculous powers of the relics of the Christian arch-martyr, St Stephen. A Bishop Praejectus had taken the relics of St Stephen to Aquae Tibilitanae. A blind woman was led to the Bishop. With her she had some flowers to leave as a tribute to the martyr and they were laid beside the relics. She then took them back and, by the powers which they had acquired from proximity to the relics, they restored her sight. Another, by being near these relics, was cured of a serious abscess. A third was freed from a chronic stone; others were cured of gout, bodily sores, tremors and convulsions, and even the dead became quick.

What did Gregory of Nazianzus mean when he declared: 'Now it is for you yourselves to add what remains, so that you may offer a gift to the martyr himself'? That gifts and offerings were really made appears beyond dispute, despite contrary declarations, already quoted, from the patriarch Augustine. Possibly this did not happen to any large extent until the martyr's chapel was transformed into a burial church. In addition, one must not forget that for a long time there was not a single chapel by the grave of the martyr. If we bear in mind the already quoted sermon on the martyr Polyeuctes, we shall remember the question raised as to what one could offer the martyr that would be worthy of him and his deeds. And the answer was: our customary dances. And Gregory himself said that on the festivals of the martyrs triumphant dances must be performed. It is therefore not improbable that this is precisely the gift which the faithful must bring at last. But this gift, the dance at the grave of the martyr, shall above all also complete the work of the martyr, the casting out of devils and the healing of the sick.

V

The Dance and the Church Hymns

VARIOUS Catholic hymns and church songs contain references, more or less precise, to the heavenly dance of the angels or to the church dance. The Catholic church preserves from the early Middle Ages a particularly rich treasure of religious poesy. What has already been published is of imposing magnitude. There are songs sung by the congregation in the celebration of divine service. This applies not only to the Church festivals such as Easter, Whitsun, etc., but also to those sung at the celebrations of the anniversaries of the saints and martyrs. They have been very little used for the purposes of science. Although the examples which follow can lay no claim to being complete, yet they seem to me not without considerable importance in relation to the occurrence and significance of the religious dance in the church. We shall find evidence that conceptions of the church dance inherited from the earliest Church were actually preserved throughout the centuries. We quote from the *Dictionnaire d'Archéologie Chrétienne* fragments of these hymns, all of which show that the heavenly dance of the angels is a characteristic of bliss in Paradise. At the All Hallows festival there was sung, according to the ritual of the Bernhardine Order:

> Always you are encircled
> By the Angels' ring-dance.

At the confirmation of girls a hymn was sung in praise of the Virgin Mary in which we encounter the words:

> Thou who made merry among the lilies,
> Encircled by the ring-dance of the virgins.

On November 17 was celebrated the annual festival of the holy Gertrude. She was a high-born Abbess of Southern Brabant and died in 659. We shall meet her again in connexion with one of the sixteenth-century dancing epidemics. On the anniversary of her death a hymn was sung showing her own fate in heaven:

> The holy ring-dances of the virgins may celebrate
> The bridegroom of the virgins and the King of the Heavens.

In a hymn which was sung for one martyr or another on the anniversary of his death and which was composed at the earliest in the tenth century (*An. Hymn* 49, 372) the congregation sings:

> Dancing martyr,
> Comforting thyself with heavenly missions!
> The righteous rejoice in the Lord
> Whom he has always loved
> Always trusting in him.

The Latin expression here is *tripudiante martyr*, which could also be translated by 'jubilating martyr'. But 'dancing' seems to me more correct. For there is always the certainty that heavenly bliss consists of a never-ending dance. We have seen already that when a martyr reveals himself, he does so dancing. Still, the dance of the angels in heaven is obvious, indeed necessary. It is just participation in this dance of the angels, this heavenly mystery, as Clement called it, which must be regarded as constituting the 'heavenly missions' which bring to the martyr his well-earned consolation.

On October 1 was celebrated the feast of roses of the Virgin Mary. It appears to have been solemnized since the year 1210 (Augusti). In Spain we find the following medieval hymn, which was sung at this festival (*An. Hymn* 16, 72):

> Virgin, thou dost rise to everlasting triumph!
> Thou dost rightly share the heavenly ring-dance,
> Beautiful there, through the flower of virginity,
> Bearing the mantle of the sun of righteousness.

So the Virgin Mary was also considered to have taken part in the round dance in the community of heaven after her death and entry into heaven. The sun of righteousness, with whose mantle Mary is adorned, refers to Christ the victor and the judge. We shall return to the symbolism in our account of special sacred church dances.

In extra-liturgical devotions and in church processions held in honour of the holy Ursula a medieval hymn was sung which referred to the heavenly bliss which she had won by her martyrdom. Ursula was the daughter of a British king who had embraced the Christian faith. Together with eleven thousand virgins she went on a pilgrimage to Rome. On the return journey, on arrival in Cologne, they were all murdered by Guan, a king of the Huns. Soon afterwards the Huns were put to flight by eleven thousand angels. The relics of Ursula and her virgins were afterwards preserved in Cologne. The song to her contains the following lines (*An. Hymn* 1, 137):

> Beautiful Ursula,
> Blooming rose among flowers,
> Glistening jewel,
> Mirror of virginity,
> Beauty of the lily,
> Brightest of stars!
>
> Lead thou the host
> Of eleven thousand virgins
> In the ring-dance of the angels
> To the rejoicing of the heavens
> And to everlasting eternal life!
> Trampling vices under foot.

The old idea persists: the dance of the angels brings joy to Heaven, as a part of its bliss. We should also note the expression that the heavenly dance tramples vices underfoot. The dance is, therefore, not only a heavenly mystery and connected with restored harmony, but it is also in a magical way directed against evil and consequently against the demons of hell.

At the Easter celebrations and the festival of the Resurrection of Christ from the dead and from the underworld there was sung, during the eleventh and twelfth centuries, and later, a song which related this departure from the underworld (*An. Hymn* 37, 27):

> The proud but loathsome underworld
> Is robbed of its virtuous denizens,
> Who, happy and dancing (*tripudiantes*),
> Enter into Paradise.

This translation is in full accord with the circumstance so often noted, that on deliverance from affliction, on entry into Paradise, a man begins immediately to dance with the angels. But we shall also find that popular medieval thought insisted that the road to Paradise from death and the underworld was passed while dancing.

The most peculiar and for the present discussion the most significant medieval hymn is the following. It was first recorded during the twelfth century, though it is clear that it may have been composed considerably earlier. It was sung in connexion with the Easter festival and is therefore intimately associated with the death and resurrection of Christ. But these are also the fate of man, for whoever during his lifetime follows Christ may rest assured that for him the portals of the kingdom of the dead are not for ever closed. The hymn (*An. Hymn* 21, 37) is as follows:

> Zion, rejoice, dance the ring-dance!
> Sing for our brethren!
> Stamp the feet, clap the hands,
> No restraint in gesture!
> Thy David strikes the tambourine,
> He turns unto the dead.
> Thus is exorcised the king of the underworld
> Snared in sins renewed.

In this hymn we seem to hear the patriarch Ambrose speaking. Or the Lord's commandment to Ezekiel: Stamp the feet, clap the hands. The dance is intense and frenzied (Fig. 9). From the earliest days of the Church its dances were thus performed, and this also was how the artists of the later Middle Ages and the beginning of modern times represented the dance of the angels in heaven. David appears once again in this hymn, the great prototype of the church dance whose dance to the true reanimation of the Ark one sought to imitate. He strikes the tambourine, but, having regard to the opening of the hymn, which describes it as a dance of rapture, which Zion itself, God's heavenly city, may perform, we may assume that David also dances. But David turns towards the dead and presently the other dancers follow suit. David appears more as a leader, completing that which in his life on earth he had performed with such skill. The dancers in heaven turn towards the dead, showing that it is for them too that the dance is executed. Its purpose clearly stated: *thus is exorcized the king of the underworld*, ensnared in sins renewed. This dance, with its stamping and clapping is therefore an exorcism of death and the Devil, of demons and of evil. It thus becomes clear why in the hymn to St Ursula it is emphasized that those participating in the dance *trampled the vices under foot*.

FIG. 9. Church Dance. Marble relief from the 1430's in the singing gallery of Florence Cathedral, executed by Luca della Robbia. It is a stamping dance and is accompanied by castanets [Schubring].

The king of the underworld is ensnared in sins renewed. This symbolism recalls to mind St John's description in the Apocalypse of death and the Lord of the Kingdom of the Dead, who populates his realm by new sins (the Fall of Babylon, *Apoc.* 18). Death is the evil in our material world. Human endeavour strives with the aid of Christ to conquer death, to overcome the power of the underworld and to find a way of escape from the kingdom of darkness. The Lord of the Underworld is also the Lord of Death; and each time the scythe swings the number of his crimes increases; by the heavenly dance he is exorcized. But exorcism is synonymous with ruling and casting out, and the song says, too, that the dance of the angels *breaks the power of Death and the Underworld for the benefit of the dead*. This in turn must imply that the captives, the dead, find a way of escape or that their deliverance is at least made easier and their salvation assisted.

The dance of the angels thus facilitates escape from the Underworld and ascent to Paradise. This is perhaps the real significance of the mystery of the

47

dance of the angels of which Clement spoke. This must be the real content of the obscure words by which Ambrose indirectly explained that the solemn church dance accords with the revealed mystery of the Resurrection. The dance of the angels represents not only blessedness and salvation, but also the exorcism of the demons, and resurrection. Thus the dance of the angels tramples vice underfoot.

Dancing was common in Christian churches at the Easter festival. In the tenth century hymnary of the monastery of Moissac there is a hymn for morning mass during the celebration of the Easter festival of the Resurrection (*An. Hymn* 2, 62).

> His (Christ's) life, His speech and miracles,
> His wondrous death prove it.
> The congregation adorns the sanctity
> Come and behold the host of ring-dances!

From the latter part of the Middle Ages there comes another Church hymn that was sung during the Easter celebrations (*An. Hymn*, 1, 207):

> The salvation of the earth is at hand
> Ye mortals; clap your hands,
> Ye who are saved, sing
> Your songs of triumph!
> Sing and dance to music (*tripudiantes*),
> And with honest mind
> Before the Lord of the Heavens.

In many of these medieval hymns there is proof that Church dances were performed at the celebration of the anniversaries of the martyrs. They were doubtless the old dances of triumph, 'our customary dances', dating from the earliest days of the Church. A fifteenth-century hymn, in honour of martyrs, exhorts us (Mone, 743):

> Play, play, ye men,
> Give yourselves up with pure heart and understanding,
> And dance with great leaps (*summa tripudio*).

At church festivals for certain saints songs were perhaps often sung suggesting the performance of dances at divine service (Mone, 1213). We shall see later what an enormous role St Willibrord played in the popular church dances, in so far as the processional dance in honour of the saint is still performed annually at Echternach, and has been performed since the early Middle Ages. The relative song runs:

> In honour of Christ
> On this day
> Celebrate everywhere
> All the faithful
> With great dances (*magna tripudio*)
> And deepest reverence
> The wonderful father
> Saint Willibrordus.

In the eleventh century, on the birthday of Mary, the following hymn was sung (*An. Hymn* 53, 97):

> Now clap in applause
> Ye men and women!
> Tune up in harmony
> Beautiful communal songs,
> And dance ring-dances
> In holy Mary's honour!

For St Lambert, whom we shall later encounter as the object of numerous church dances, the choir sings this song, written during the twelfth century (Mone, 1018):

> With loud voice is given you
> The highest prize of all by all,
> When in lively heavenly ring-dance
> We rejoice in such a peer.
> The earth, made worthy by a Bishop so mighty,
> Re-echoes with applause.
> O! holy martyr Lambert,
> Receive our gifts.

The song relates that when, after suffering martyrdom, St Lambert entered into heaven, all the angels offered him the highest prize and they danced as a sign thereof. St Lambert immediately took part in the dance, and thus became a peer of the heavenly host. But the earth also echoes the applause of the martyr, for it has become 'worthy' of such a Bishop. St Lambert was, in fact, Bishop of Maastricht. It may be asked if there is not a double meaning in the word 'bishop', a kind of pun; for the Latin word is *praesul*, which originally meant 'dance leader'. We have seen in the case of St Chrysostom that at that time the bishops were leaders in the church dances, and only gradually, according to du Cange, did the word *praesul* acquire the meaning of 'bishop' and lose its original sense. Therefore, it is not impossible that in this hymn *praesul* has its old double meaning and that St Lambert was conceived not only as the former bishop on earth but also as the worthy dance-leader in heaven, by virtue of his special sanctity. The gifts of which the hymn speaks may certainly have been material but may also be conceived as being like those of which the early Church affords evidence, the dance of the angels, imitated in the church dance for the refreshment of the saint.

This brief survey of the church hymns and songs which touch more or less upon the dance of the angels and the church dance has afforded us some information of value and of special importance in determining their real meaning. It has considerably deepened our understanding of certain obscure references in Clement and Ambrose and affords a satisfactory background to the peculiar proposition that the dance of the angels is a kind of mystery. Popular religious hymn writing might possibly reveal more material for the explanation of profane thought concerning the dance as a heavenly mystery.

We shall later, in our account of the dance of the dead, encounter such songs; here we quote only a popular fourteenth-century hymn to the Virgin Mary:

> I greet thee with garlands of roses,
> Ah! help us to the heavenly dance
> And lead us to the wondrous light
> Which shines from the house of the saved!   [Yacobs.]

VI

Sacred Church Dances

1. *The Festival of Fools*

CHRISTIAN religious dances may be divided into two main groups, the sacred and the popular, of which the former includes dances performed by persons belonging to the Church, such as bishops, priests, monks, choir boys and nuns, and the latter those performed by members of the congregation without the participation of the clergy. I shall endeavour in what follows to adhere to this classification, though I am aware that there are objections. The fact is that certain 'popular' religious dances were performed in close association with purely church ceremonies, both at service within the church and in church processions, with the full approval and guidance of the Church authorities. Indeed the dancers themselves appear to have been selected and appointed by these authorities. It is doubtful, therefore, whether these dances should be regarded purely as 'popular' and whether they should be regarded at the same time as typically sacred. By sacred dances I shall in what follows mean only those religious dances in which the clergy—in the widest sense of the word—themselves took an active part.

But even in the case of popular church dances the classification is not entirely safe; nor is it true of the churchyard dances. In the latter case we know that in earlier centuries the clergy also took a part; their character was both sacred and popular, but preponderantly popular. To the popular religious dances belong also the numerous dancing epidemics of the Middle Ages and more modern times, but their medical character is in many respects revealed so clearly that they may suitably be considered as a separate exclusive group.

John Beleth, living in the twelfth century and for a time Rector of the University of Paris, relates that 'there are some churches in which it is customary for even archbishops and bishops to play with their subordinates and to indulge in ball games. This conviviality was called *Decembrica*, because among the heathens a custom had once existed by which during the month of December male and female slaves and shepherds were given a certain liberty and were permitted, on equal terms with their masters, to celebrate the festivals following the gathering in of the harvest. Although even large churches, such as that at Rheims, retain this custom, yet it would seem more proper not to play (Divin. Offic. explic. C. 120 and Ration, col. 885). Beleth also mentions that four kinds of dances (*tripudia*) were in use at the various church festivals. They were the Deacons' festival dance on St Stephen's Day, the Priests' on St John's day, the choir boys' on Innocents' Day and the sub-deacons' on the feast of the Circumcision or Epiphany. It was the last of these which came to be known as the Festival of Fools.

The sacred church dances of which Beleth speaks are thus those which we would regard as connected with festivals celebrated in ancient Rome at the end of December and the beginning of January. We shall now follow their further development.

Beleth died between 1182 and 1190, at a time when these festivals were held in Nôtre Dame in Paris. They were called the Festival of Fools or the Asses' Festival or the Festival of the Rod. Other names were also used, which pointed to the large part played in them by the clergy, as Beleth relates. The dancing festival in which the choir boys took the principal part came to be called the Children's Festival. The most important, however, was that which was originally organized by the sub-deacons and which was more generally called the Festival of Fools or of Asses. It would seem, however, that one of the other festivals bore this name and that occasionally the sub-deacons and children's festivals were held jointly. Whoever presided carried a ceremonial staff; it was originally given to the leader of the church choir, and was richly and expensively decorated. The one in Cologne Cathedral is illustrated here (Fig. 10). Hence the occasional name, the Festival of the Rod. But out of its original crude and light-hearted character much disorder and even bloodshed frequently developed during these festivals, and for this reason Pope Innocent III in 1207 issued a decree to archbishops and bishops, principally in Poland, forbidding these dancing festivals. It had little or no effect. Similarly, in Paris in 1212 the Church forbade this festival just when it was beginning to be called the Festival of the Asses [Chambers]. We shall later find that the Church zealously endeavoured to prevent them, threatening and condemning participants, but was unable to end them until a new age had begun. The decrees against the Festival of Fools appear, however, to be much older than the thirteenth century.

These festivals were celebrated at the beginning of the year, and sometimes in the latter part of December. Each category elected its own 'Bishop', or 'Archbishop', or even its 'Pope'. The sub-deacons and also the others, with the exception of the choristers, probably wore ivy wreaths on their heads, and held burning candles in their hands, whilst the authorities present wore green wreaths, fashioned with gold and purple ribbons [Schrörs].

Certain authors, such as Dreves and Walther, have sought to minimize the importance of the Festival of Fools, and to deny that it had any blasphemous character. We shall allow the Theological Faculty of the University

FIG. 10. Ceremonial Staff at Cologne. This church ceremonial staff is of wood covered with richly ornamented silver. It is 147 cm. long. It is crowned by a mountain crystal in the shape of a baluster and globe. Above this are the three Holy Kings in prayer, dating from 1350. The staff was wrought in 1178. An inscription reads, 'I am the staff of the leader of the choir and I may be borne in the hands of those who participate in the Festival of the Staff . . . In the year 1178, the Festival of the Staff was celebrated for the first time here.' [Clemen.]

of Paris to speak for itself. A circular letter, dated 1444 and addressed to the prelates and chapters in the kingdom of France (Copia, Migne: P. L. 207, col. 1169) relates specifically to the Festival of the Asses and all the 'abominable' practices which attended it.

This filthy custom, says the Theological Faculty, has been taken over from the heathens and commemorates them. History tells us how the various heathen countries, in which the true God was unknown, were deceived by the tricks of the devils, were spurred on by various passions and abandoned themselves to vain superstitions. In this Festival of Fools within the Christian Church people do not shrink from any vulgarity, any excesses, any shame, but abandon themselves to anything which their imagination prompts. Openly and unpunished they relapse into lewdness and harlotry and other criminal monstrosities. The shameful traditions of the repulsive Janus are still preserved during the month of January and in many churches they have been adopted by priests and clergy, at the instigation of the Devil and under the protection of the birthday of our Lord and of the joyous days which follow. And this accursed congregation, which is called the Festival of Fools—the words of the Faculty—is now upheld in churches and consecrated places by those who have themselves been consecrated to God, thus bringing damnation upon themselves, because they profane the sacred places by celebrating the rites of Janus.

These priests and clergy, continues the Faculty, who appear in masks at divine service, or with distorted faces, or women's clothes, or dressed as bawds or actors, perform ring-dances, sing indecent songs, eat coarse bread at the horn of the altar during mass, and play dice. They carry incense amidst the stink of worn-out shoes. Leaping and jumping they course through the church without shame. Then they are led through the town in shabby carts and carriages to witness indecent spectacles in the theatres, whilst they themselves distort their bodies in scandalous manner to the derision of the spectators, speaking the foulest and most stupid words.

The Faculty's epistle forbade all this, as also the election of bishops and archbishops and the handing over to them of the episcopal insignia, mitre and crook. Neither were they permitted to conduct divine service or to give the blessing. In addition, all sorts of dances, all eating and drinking at the altar, were forbidden during mass, as well as the wearing of masks, of women's clothes, or paint on the face.

These festivals appear to have been most widespread in France in the later Middle Ages, but they occurred too in Germany and in Spain. Innocent III, in his interdict of 1207 against the Festival of Fools, condemned also those held in Mainz and Cologne. During the thirteenth century Durandus relates how on Christmas Eve the deacons danced in the church and sang in honour of St Stephen. But the old customs still persisted and it was usually the Feast of the Circumcision which was celebrated in the most grotesque fashion. This was the real Festival of Fools.

Du Tilliot describes a Festival of Fools according to a fifteenth-century document from Sens and this account is supplemented by details given by Walther. The procession in fifteenth-century Rouen, for example, started from a monastery; it was headed by two criers and two of the clergy as leaders of the singing, and in the middle of the procession was an ass, on which Balaam rode. In Beauvais, on the other hand, a virgin and child rode on the ass. The custom evidently varied a great deal from place to place, According to du Cange the ass was covered with a golden saddle-cloth, the corners of which were held by four of the most eminent canons. On arrival at the church doors there was sung, in 1411 and for probably a couple of centuries earlier, the so-called Asses Song. This was composed perhaps by the Archbishop of Sens, Pierre de Corbeil, who died in 1222, so that it may date back to the beginning of the thirteenth century. But the ass's part in the festival is of much older date. While this song was being sung, the ass was led in a great procession through the nave of the church up to the altar. Sometimes, on the other hand, it was left standing at the church doors and then subsequently taken into the church. The following is my translation of the 'Song of the Ass':

From Eastern lands once there came
A modest Ass.
This Ass was fine and very strong,
No burden was too heavy.
　　Hail, Mr Ass, Hail!

Reuben rode to the heights of Sichem,
Rode this fine strong Ass.
Through the battling waves of Jordan
Swift it ran to Bethlehem.

Roebuck, mule or goat,
None can dance as thou,
And the camel from Madian
Would soon be conquered by thy dance.

Gold from Arabia,
Sabian incense and myrrh,
All are taken into church
By the great strength of the Ass.
Now he pants before his cart,
Drags his heavy burden,
Now with strongest teeth he bites
The tough straw in pieces fine,

Clean straw and dry chaff,
Sharp thistles he eats,
Thrashing on the box floor
From early morn till night.

Now say Amen, thou little Ass,
Thou art sated with all thy straw.
　　Amen, Amen, over again
Fly from that which was!
　　Hail, Mr Ass, Hail!

At the end of the Song of the Ass there followed a short *Introit*, of which the contents were equally grotesque,

This is the famous day, the most famous of all famous days!
This is the festive day, the most festive of all festive days!

Lateinisches Refrain-Strophenlied zum Bakelfest der jungen Kleriker (,,asini") am Tage Epiphanias oder Circumcisio (nach der St. Martial-Hs. London add. 36881, dort mit Organalstimme ähnlich wie Beisp. 55)

(*Refrain*)

Gre-gis pa-stor Ti-ty-rus,
A-si-no-rum do-mi-nus, Pa-stor est et a-si-nus E-y-a,

e-y-a, e-y-a! Vo-cat nos ad va-ri n Ti-ty-rus ci-ba-ri-a.

FIG. 11. The Asses Song at the Festival of the Rod. A medieval Asses Song at the Sub-deacons' Festival of the Rod, or Festival of Fools on Epiphany or Circumcision day [Besseler].

Besseler gives another Latin Asses Song at a Festival of the Rod, which was sung by young priests (Fig. 11), completed by a gradual from Mosburg, 1360 [An. Hymn 20, 133].

> Shepherd of the herd, Oh Satyre,
> Thou Lord of the Asses,
> Thou art Shepherd and Ass!
>
>   Eya, Eya, Eya!
>
> The Satyre calls us
> To food of many kinds!
>
> The Satyre's worthy
> Rod-feast now celebrates
> Chieftains and Asses.
>
> Let us clap the Satyre
> To the pleasing sound of song
> And to strings and drums.

It may be added that this song was sung during the celebration of the Mass at the altar. It is the celebrant who is designated as the Satyre and as the shepherd of the congregation and as representing the Ass. It is he who is called to the 'banquet' of coarse bread, blood pudding or blood sausage which, during Mass, is consumed at the corner of the altar.

At the festival in Rouen the ass was left standing at the entrance to the church, whilst the procession continued down the middle of the church. An alternating song was then executed between six Jews, six heathens and the choir, whereafter Moses and a number of Old Testament prophets appeared and prophesied the coming of the Messiah. Next there was a shout: 'Balaam comes!' and he rode in on the ass. A young man with a sword (the Angel of the Lord) stood beside the ass, and somebody, probably concealed under the ass, then spoke. Balaam spurred on the ass, which thereupon cried out, 'Why do you spur me so hard, wretch?' The angel answered 'Cease to obey the commands of King Balak.' The congregation exhorted the ass to prophesy. It cried out, 'He shall come from Jacob.' A number of priests then appeared, dressed as Samuel, David, John the Baptist, Virgil and others. A dramatic scene of the three youths in the burning oven was acted. Sibyls appeared and prophesied.

55

All this information is of importance to us because it makes clear what sort of costumes and acts preceded the expulsion of demons from the priest-performers. When all this theatrical show was finished the Mass was begun in the manner already described. It is then that the loose and indecent dances of the priests began. In the year 1544 we hear of ring-dances and other dances. People danced in the choir during divine service, and when it was over they danced throughout the whole church, often throwing off their clothes [du Tilliot].

Spanke quotes from a diary kept by an Archbishop in the thirteenth century on a visit of inspection to the church of St Yldvert in Gournay (Seine Inférieure): 'Clergy, vicars and chaplains violently and foolishly perform ring-dances in the streets and sing virelays at certain festivals, especially that of St Nicholas (Christmas).' A virelay is a swift vigorous dance to the accompaniment of a song. This brief reference shows, however, that these Festivals of Fools were celebrated not only within the church but also—as shown by the letter of the Theological Faculty in Paris—in the market place and in the streets. It is almost a carnival.

Every category of the clergy had its leader, who bore the ceremonial staff. An old direction from Sens prescribes that the leaders on the second day of Christmas shall execute a dance in the choir of the church or around it, holding staffs in their hands (*Binterim II*, 2, 80).

These accounts of the Festivals of Fools are especially rich in detail and picturesque. They afford overwhelming proof of the blasphemous character of these church dancing festivals. But the attempt of the Theological Faculty in Paris to find their origin in the Greek and Roman festivals of Janus is entirely unreasonable and mistaken. Clearly the Faculty has merely followed the statements of the eighth-century Abbot Alcwyn. Janus was one of the oldest of the Roman divinities and his sanctity in the Forum still had its significance 300 years after Christ. It is he who guards entrances and exits and his emblems are the key and the staff, the latter being the badge of office of the Roman doorkeeper. The beginning of every month was dedicated to him, especially the beginning of January. The *Kalendas Januarii* were popular feasts, but of a solemn, serious kind (Dict. Ant. Gr. et Rom). Any connexion between the solemn Janus festival and the light-headed Festival of Fools is therefore inconceivable. The ceremonial staff can have no meaning in this connexion, for there exist numerous and varied ceremonial staffs to choose from as prototypes, if indeed it be necessary. The Festival of Fools, moreover, was celebrated in December and not in January.

Many writers have urged that the Festival of Fools may have had its origin in the saturnalia of antiqity. These began [Dict. Ant. Gr. et Rom.] on December 17 and continued for seven days. They were characterized above all by great feasts, and by mutual gifts, being held at the same time as great fairs. During this festival slaves were the equals of their masters and were sometimes even served by them; they had complete freedom of speech and were permitted games of hazard. But according to the early Christian apologists, this festival had a peaceful, friendly and happy character, with a complete absence of pagan cruelty and dissoluteness. So one can say now that the Festival of Fools cannot possibly have arisen as a relic of these saturnalia. But it is clear that the date agrees in some cases better and in others worse. Certain features are identical: the cast-down shall be raised up, the mighty shall be laid low, freedom of speech is complete, dice games are allowed, banquets are laid. But in the Festival of Fools freedom of speech was blasphemous and the banquets were of the poorest, and clearly blasphemous also. The resemblances are formal, not real. In the song of praise of the Virgin Mary, which was later called the Magnificat, we find mention of the social change.

Du Cange thinks that the Festival of Fools in the Christian church had its origin in the curious profane festival games of the pagans called Cervulus or Cervula (the little deer, the little hind). It is said to have been customary at the beginning of January for men to leap about, dressed as beasts or cattle, and commit outrageous acts. All this the Christians had banished, but they had nevertheless instituted similar practices. Healing processions and general fasts were thus hastily organized in order to suppress the pagan custom. We shall see what the earliest Christian writers have to say about the disorders which led up to the Festival of Fools.

In the sixth century Caesarius writes, 'If you know anybody who performs the indecencies of the Ass or the Little Hind, then rebuke him most sharply so that he may repent having fallen into this sacrilege'. This is probably the earliest suggestion that the Ass played a part in any festivals which might be connected with the medieval Festival of the Ass and Festival of Fools. Caesarius says nothing to indicate that this indecency was derived from the heathens. In an account of the life of Bishop Eligius of the seventh century [*Vita S. Eligii, lib. 2. cap.* 15] we read, 'Nobody may take part in the shameful and ridiculous January vetulas or cervulas or jotticos'. These are various names for the same thing. Bishop Faustinus [*Serm. in Kalend. Jan.*] expresses himself thus, 'What reasonable being could believe that any man of sound mind would dream of taking part in "The Little Hind" and would disguise himself as a wild beast. Others clothe themselves in the skins of cattle; others wear the heads of wild beasts, thus assuming animal shapes so that they may no longer seem to be human beings' [du Cange].

Here we are reminded once again of the remarkable and strangely similar account in Isidor from the sixth and early seventh centuries, which in all probability refers to the same events, although Isidor does not give them any name, nor does he assert that their origin was pagan. Bishop Boniface relates in a letter to Pope Zacharias in the eighth century, that 'in certain years in Rome one could see, quite near to the Basilica of St Peter, and just at the beginning of January, people executing choral dances in the market place in pagan fashion, day and night, to the accompaniment of loud shouting and godless songs, loading the tables with food [du Cange]. The remarkable thing about this passage is that no suggestion is made that the custom is

57

taken from the pagans; it says merely that people danced in the pagan manner, that is, wildly and dissolutely, and it is very remarkable that the dances were performed so near the Basilica of St Peter that they had to be expressly forbidden. During the first half of the eighth century Pirminius admonishes the Christians [*Excerpt. de Sacr. Script.*] not to take part in these Stag festivals and adds, 'Men must not dress themselves in women's clothes nor must women dress themselves in men's clothes either at this feast or at any other games.'

Between 730 and 803 the Abbot Alcwyn lived in St Martin's monastery in Tours. To him is ascribed, possibly wrongly, an account of the January festivals. He begins with a joke which cannot be rendered in translation, 'The mad Kalendae of these pagans should be called "avoiding" rather than "following".' (*Hae Kalendae secundum dementiam gentilium potius dicendae sunt cavendae quam calendae.*) 'At one time there was in Italy a prince of the pagans of the name Janus after whom the month of January was named. Ignorant people, who knew not God, worshipped this Janus as a King and a God and represented him with two faces signifying the rise and fall. Sometimes he was called the four-headed or the Janus twins because there are four elements and four seasons of the year. But in doing so they created a monster rather than a god. To celebrate the end of the old year and the beginning of the new ignorant people worshipped him as a god and by various obscenities consecrated this day to him. Thus they transformed themselves into monsters and into the shapes of wild beasts. Others appeared with female gestures and womanized their masculine features and, not undeservedly, those who clothed themselves in women's dress lost their strength. Others debased themselves by mad tricks of prophecy, romping and hopping to the clapping of hands. Others believed they could see omens in their own hearths or elsewhere, or were able to prophesy good things for those who desired them. Others, again, claimed to receive messages from the Devil and communicated them. They had their tables laden with food throughout the night in the belief that New Year's Day would repeat itself throughout the year. And whilst the whole world was full of this misery the Church decreed that during these days a general fast should be observed.'

It is easy to see that the fifteenth-century Theological Faculty in Paris derived its historical data concerning the Festival of Fools from Alcwyn, but their reliability seems to me not very great, for there is no support for them in the literature of antiquity. It seems to me more probable that these customs arose among Christians, even though certain features may have been derived from ancient feasts.

Burchard from Worms, in his decretals, only makes a passing mention of the existence of these January festivals, but says nothing of their pagan origin.

Balsamon, the ancient Patriarch of Antioch, who lived between 1140 and 1195 in Constantinople, formulated proscriptions in accordance with the resolutions of the Council of Trullo. He asserts that it was the Greeks who by ancient custom celebrated the January festival: 'Public dances by women, in which men are clearly incited to passion.' This custom was strictly forbidden to Christians. It is not permitted, we learn, for a man to appear in woman's dress or a woman in a man's. Nor is it permitted to appear as any kind of actor. He also complains that on the day of the Three Kings (Jan. 6) it was customary to commit a thousand obscenities in the church of Constantinople.

Cedrenus (according to Du Tilliot) relates how, in Constantinople in the tenth century, dances were performed at Christmas and Epiphany with clownish processions, loud laughter and shouting—and all this in the middle of the church and before the altar. These devilish dances were combined with incantations and indecent songs. Cedrenus maintains that they were introduced by Theophylactes, Patriarch of Constantinople, in the tenth century.

The connexion between the festivals described by these authors and the so-called Festival of Fools seems to be quite obvious. It is very remarkable that these authors do not point out that these 'monstrosities' were taken over from pagan customs; it was only Alcwyn, or whoever is concealed under that name, who maintains that the Janus festivals gave rise to the Christian abandonment. But the supposition of such Janus festivals is very probably incorrect.

It is therefore better to assume that the 'Little Hind' or the 'Mule', and subsequently the Festival of the Ass and the Festival of Fools, originated in early Christian circles and without any direct pagan influence. Only a few features have been taken from pagan ceremonial. It was low-level vulgarian Christianity and crass magical conceptions which gave rise to the Festival of Fools. But this cannot be all, for the mule or the ass must have had some meaning, and one may ask oneself whether the real solution of the problem is not to be found in just the interpretation which one puts upon its role. We saw that Caesarius at the beginning of the sixth century knew that the festival was called the 'Mule'. Many, perhaps most, of the later medieval Festivals of Fools assigned a principal part to the ass. Which ass is meant? The answer is easy to find. Walter mentions that in Spain there was religious reverence for the ass, because it stood beside the Saviour's crib in Bethlehem and was the beast on which Mary and Christ rode in the flight to Egypt, and even the one on which Christ rode into Jerusalem. In the two former cases there is only very early legend to support the belief; only the last finds support in the Gospels. The ass was in any case closely associated with the life of Jesus. It is even regarded as having played an important role—be it only a mechanical one—in the work of salvation.

In Madrid at one time an ass was led in a great church procession every January 17th, adorned with a saddle-cloth, coloured ribbons, panaches of plumes, etc. The ass was conducted to a magnificent manger and around it congregated the choir, singing songs of a religious character [Walter, Batillard]. It seems for this reason that the Festival of the Ass was from the beginning regarded as a memorial festival to the ass of legend and of the Gospels. The costume of the participators—animal masks—may be regarded as indicating that all the animal world shared this reverence for the ass. The very names 'Little Hind' and 'Little Stag' may support this view. One immediately thinks of Psalm 42, 'As the hart panteth after the water brooks, so

FIG. 12. The Birth of Christ in the Stable at Bethlehem. Mary kneels before the Child, lying on a bed of straw. From behind the manger an ox and an ass peer out. The shepherds are shown the way by an angel, and angels pray to the new-born Child. Painting by Stephen Lochner, dated 1442–5 [Winkler.]

panteth my soul after Thee, O God.' Perhaps it was this favourite simile which gave rise to the original name for the Festival of the Ass, namely 'The Festival of the Hart'. If the Festival of the Ass was formerly regarded as the reverence of the animals for the ass, then it is also comprehensible that it soon assumed the character of a carnival, with burlesque, grotesque forms of parody.

There is an old legend concerning the further fate of the ass of the Gospels. In despair at the crucifixion of Christ in Jerusalem, the ass fled from the Holy Land and passed the islands of Cyprus, Rhodes, Crete, Malta and Sicily to Aquileia and Verona. This legend was still alive in the seventeenth century, as appears from a letter of 1687 by the author of *Max. Misson*. This letter describes how, after the death of the ass in the church at Verona, a reliquary was quickly prepared, representing an ass, in which the relics of the dead beast were deposited. This was set up in the church of St Mary in Organo, and was later incorporated in church processions two or three times every year. The President of the Parliament of Dijon, Ch. de Brosses, writes in 1739 that the monks of St Mary in Organo told him that the ass reliquaries had not been shown for many years, but that the reliquary was preserved in that church. Voltaire relates a similar story of the ass in Verona. But the belief that the Festival of the Ass had its origin in the celebration of the Verona ass is quite certainly incorrect [Batillard, Allg. Enc. Wiss. Künste: Eselsfest].

Meanwhile it seems to me that investigation into the origin of the Festival of the Ass should be pursued much further. One might connect these festivals intimately with the role of the ass in pious Christian narratives and legends. How extremely common it was for artists to represent the birth of Christ in a stable, with the child lying in or beside a manger, and an ox or an ass in the immediate vicinity. The animals stood on either side of the manger or they lay in front of it or looked out from behind it. When the shepherds kept watch or the Three Magi brought their gifts, the two animals looked out from the stable windows (Figs. 5 and 12). So too with the narrative of the flight of Christ, Mary and Joseph into Egypt. But neither of these representations is to be found in the Gospels or the Epistles. Here we deal entirely with legendary material, though of great antiquity.

The representation of the Christ child between the ox and the ass can be traced to the earliest days of the Christian church. In the accompanying picture (Fig. 13), an ivory plaque of the fifth century, we see the child in the manger whilst the ox and the ass look out from their respective stalls behind it; the other half of the plaque shows the Three Magi offering their gifts to the Child on Mary's knee. The earliest known pictorial representation is in a relief of 343 (Fig. 14); the child lies in a low manger, or possibly on the ground, whilst the ox and the ass stand, as if in reverence, at its side. The Christ child is surrounded by three shepherds. The presentation may well be called biblical but not evangelical. According to St Matthew, Jesus was born in a house; according to St Luke in a manger, 'for there was no room for them in the inn'. St Mark and St John say nothing of the circumstances of the birth.

But nowhere is there any mention of the presence of the animal in question. Both picture and legend are based on Isaiah I, 3. 'The ox knoweth his owner and the ass his master's crib.' This passage was taken up by the Elders, who explained that Jesus was born in a crib between an ox and an ass. Whether they meant this as a reality or solely and simply as a curious symbol is

61

uncertain. Ambrose [Luke II, 40, Migne, P.L. 15, 1568] starts from the above quotation and continues, 'So this ass, a picture from heathendom, has come to know its master's crib. And therefore the ass says "the Lord shall feed me. I shall lack nothing" ' [Ps. 23, 1].

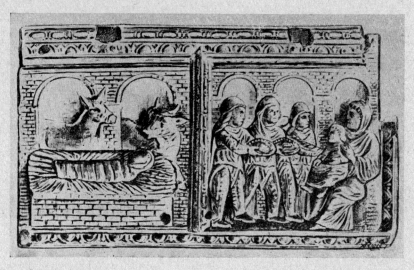

FIG. 13. Jesus in the Manger. Ivory plaque of the fifth century. The ox and the ass of legend look out from their respective stalls. To the right the Three Magi and Mary and Child [Dict. d'Arch. Chrét].

FIG. 14. The Birth of Jesus in Bethlehem. Relief of 343. The earliest pictorial representation of the legend of the ox and the ass beside the manger of Jesus. In the picture the three shepherds (of one of them only the right hand is visible) keep their watch [Dict. d'Arch. Chrét].

Gregory of Nyssa [Addr. on Christ's birth. Migne, P., Gr. 46, 1142] is more explicit: 'The stable in which the Word was born is at the same time the home of cattle, since the ox knows its owner and the ass its master's crib. By the ox we must understand the one which is obedient under the yoke of the law, and by the ass—the animal which is born to bear burdens—you must understand those who in their sin are weighed down by the worship of false gods. For this reason the Lord is born between them breaking the wall and himself leads them into a new life, lifting from the one the heavy yoke of the Law and delivering the other from the sin of worshipping false gods.'

Gregory of Nazianzus [Addr. 37, 17, Migne, P., Grec. 36, 331] carries this symbolism still further: 'Remember how Isaiah exhorts you, like the ox, to know your owner and—like the ass—the crib of your master. You may be pure and obedient to the Law and ruminate on perfect teaching and be zealous in your offerings, or you may have been hitherto impure, unworthy to eat and make offerings, a pagan . . . Together with the shepherd do thou worship God with songs of praise, sing hymns together with the angels, take your part with the archangels in the choral dances.'

So this is the meaning given by the Church Elders to the ox and the ass beside the crib in which Jesus lay. The ox symbolized the Jews and obedience to the Law, the ass symbolized heathendom and idolatry; the ox and the ass at the crib of the miraculous birth together symbolized Jesus Christ offering salvation to all peoples, drawing them together into a common faith and creed. So widespread was the legend that Christ was born between an ox and an ass that in the sixth century it was included in the account of the miracle in Bethlehem given by the apocryphal pseudo-Matthew, 'Blessed Mary entered the stable and laid her child in the crib and the ox and the ass worshipped it' [Grousset].

At least as early as 1223 the ox and the ass were introduced into the Christmas celebration of the birth of Christ. It is said that St Francis of Assissi was the first to obtain papal permission to install a stable and crib, together with the two animals. The mass was then celebrated around this pictorial reality [Clement, F.].

Similarly it must be regarded as quite certain that in Church festivals a much more important role was allotted to the ass than to the ox. Had the two animals merely symbolized pagans and Jews respectively, there would seem insufficient motivation for the difference. One would then have to admit that the 'evangelical' role of the ass was one of the reasons why it was allowed to appear in a much more distinctive manner. This must be due to the role of the ass in the flight to Egypt and the entry into Jerusalem. To some extent there may be associated with it the scorn of the pagans for the Christians, who were called *asinarii* (ass drivers), or who were stated to pray to a god with the head of an ass. But we do not know the ultimate motive for these assertions.

Bishop Eligius recounts that in the Festival of Fools people not only dressed up as various animals, but also in 'the skins of cattle'. Hence the ox was also present, not only the ass and the mule. Quite certainly there were other animals too, as shown by the name 'Little Hart'. The encyclopaedias of Diderot and d'Alembert mention that, at the festival of the sub-deacons on St Stephen's Day, the Song of the Ass or the Song of the Fools was sung, but at the priests' festival of St John they sang *'la prose du boeuf'* (the song of the ox). In that case, centuries ago, the priests' festival must have expressed the desire to Christianize all Jewish converts, whilst the festival of the sub-deacons implied the eager hope of gathering the heathens about the Christian cross. The festival of the priests, with its dances, never seriously degenerated, but that of the sub-deacons did, for the reason that this festival at a very early date, as early as the first epoch of Christianity, was combined with the worship of the ass of Gospel and legend, developing into a worship by all creation, especially animal creation, of the ass. A mass in honour of pagans and beasts became more and more grotesque; this was quite natural, and in the beginning it certainly was not deliberately blasphemous. In 1595 the last of the Festivals of Fools was held in the cathedral of Troyes [Chambers], but it continued to be celebrated outside the churches, possibly even in the churchyards, the last of these occasions being in 1614. We shall later hear of numerous proscriptions of the Festival of Fools, frequently repeated during the later Middle Ages and the early centuries of modern times, which indicate that they were held not only within the churches but also in the churchyards. This becomes more comprehensible if one reflects, on the one hand, that the processions started from outside the parish and had therefore to pass the churchyard on the way to the church, and, on the other hand, that churchyard dances were very common at that time. Certain of the ceremonies must therefore of necessity have taken place in the churchyard. But we know nothing further on the subject.

2. *Children's Festival*

The so-called Children's Festival, or the Festival of the Choristers, at which a child-bishop was elected, was celebrated mostly on Innocents' Day, December 28. As we have seen from Beleth it occurred at least as early as the twelfth century, and may be even older. Its celebration was accompanied by dancing at divine service and at the celebration of the Mass. The church at Puy has a so-called *prosolarium* of 1327 in which there are a number of directions concerning the choristers' dance at the Feast of the Circumcision, i.e., the second date on which the Children's Festival and the election of a child-bishop might be held. It states that, in the procession to the choir of the Holy Cross, the choristers must dance with great vigour (the Biblical description of David's dance before the Ark), but that at the end of the mass they must dance even more vigorously—*tripudiant fortiter* [Villetard, Gougaud].

In the year 1360 Mosburg elected a child-bishop in connexion with the choristers' dance, and at this 'episcopal' election the following song was sung:

> Let us rejoice; let us sing
> To the new bishop!
> In honour and glory
> Receive the excellent staff! [Chambers]

At Sens cathedral a 'boy archbishop' was elected in the middle of the fourteenth century, together with a '*Praeses*' for the Festival of Fools.

And it was in the fourteenth century that a German monk, who was also a schoolmaster, composed several songs and hymns which the choristers sang during the performance of their ring-dances and three-step dances at the election of the child-bishop [Spanke]. During the sixteenth century the Children's Festival flourished more than the Festival of Fools, since, as already stated, the latter had been suppressed as a church dance in the year 1547. In France, Germany, and England the choristers' festival was very popular. Probably the Germans made more fun of the child-bishop, for they called him the 'school-bishop' or the 'apple-bishop'. In English churches mitres and crooks are preserved, which were carried by the child-bishop, and in the records of the Council of Rouen of 1313 there is mention of an episcopal ring intended for the little bishop [Chambers].

At Rouen there are instructions for the Choristers' Festival [du Cange, Chambers]. After second vespers on St John's Day or on Innocents' Day, the choristers formed a procession from the Sacristy; those in the lead were dressed in gown and pall and held burning candles in their hands. After them followed the other choristers. With them was the newly elected 'bishop', and a song was sung about the innocents slaughtered by Herod. The procession proceeded through the choir to the altar of the Innocents, where it stopped and sang part songs. When the choristers had sung a hymn of joy, the 'bishop' uttered a prayer. Thereupon the choristers asked for a blessing and the 'bishop' complied in customary fashion. Then the choristers assembled in the upper choir for the celebration of the mass and sang hymns and danced. The bishop concluded the service, and after the *Magnificat* had been sung the choristers entoned: 'He hath put down the mighty from their seats and exalted them of low degree' (Luke I, 52, and *Magnificat*), whilst the ceremonial staff was handed over to the new 'bishop', who was clothed in a silken tunic and wore the mitre and carried the episcopal staff.

Schneegans, with the support of Grandidier, describes the Children's Festival in Strasburg Minster. Existing records at this church seem to prove that these four *decembrica*, as well as the Festival of Fools and the Children's Festival, were celebrated there in the year 1136. Even then they must have had a very old tradition behind them. The Children's Festival was held on the usual day, Innocents' Day, but began with a watch-night service, preceded by vespers. Immediately before vespers the choristers elected their 'bishop' and when, during the service, the *Magnificat* was sung, the choir reached the words '*deposuit potentes*' (he cast down the mighty), the new 'bishop' advanced, clad in episcopal robes, bearing the shepherd's staff, and sat on the episcopal throne. The rest of the service was conducted by the choristers; the 'bishop' uttered the usual prayers and concluded with a blessing, and the choristers officiated in the place of the priests. All this was repeated the following day. Although Schneegans and Grandidier have nothing to say on the subject, according to Beleth the priestly sacramental acts of the choristers must have included sacral dances. On the completion of vespers the choir-boys in their robes, with the 'bishop' in the midst of the procession, romped noisily through the streets of Strasburg, frequently parodying church songs. Many of the choristers were masked, though we do not know what sort of masks they wore. The procession forced its way with great noise into churches and monasteries, in which 'thousands' of pranks and malpractices were seen.

Schneegans mentions just such masquerades as distinctive of the Children's Festival in Metz in 1444. Here also the choristers were masked and the 'bishop' had his face blackened and his clothes smeared with mud.

An English statute at the end of the twelfth century says, 'It is the duty of the priest on Innocents' Day, when food has been eaten, to conduct his boys, dancing and carrying candles, to their quarters.'

According to Buchberger it was Pope Gregory IV (827–844) who in-augurated the Children's Festival and its child-bishop as a memorial to Pope Gregory I, the great sanctified Pope, who afterwards became patron of schools and students. To some extent we may consider that remnants of these festivals survive, for example, in the children, who, on Christmas Eve, preach in the church of Ara Coeli at Rome.

3. Pelota

The Dance in Auxerres Cathedral

The performance of the Dance of the Angels as characteristic of heavenly bliss was taken over from the ancient church and preserved for centuries, surviving in certain places even to our own times. We have found evidence of this in old hymns and songs afforded by the churches themselves and by members of their congregations. It is also intelligible that this heavenly Dance of the Angels and the Blessed should be accompanied by repre-sentations from the Revelations of St John. Thus in a codex (730), preserved in the university library of Graz and originating in the thirteenth century, we read the following from a number of sermons on Innocents' Day, 'In the sixth place a song of joy: this is sung by the angels and the holy virgins before God and the Lamb, dancing and stimulating each other to joy! The Apocalypse! They shall sing a new song but nobody can interpret this song' [Schönbach]. None the less the old idea has not been forgotten: that this heavenly dance had a mystic connexion with the Resurrection and its re-vealed mystery. We shall now describe in further detail the sacral church dances which symbolize the Resurrection and Blessedness. We have just quoted from the Rector of the University of Paris, John Beleth, a passage showing that in the twelfth century it was a custom in various churches that at church festivals even bishops and archbishops 'played' with their sub-ordinates and participated in ball games. Most characteristic of these 'ball games' was the so-called *pelota* in the cathedral of Auxerres.

The Bishop of Mende, the eminent theological writer, G. Durandus, who lived between 1230 and 1296, describes the remarkable *pelota* dance in his highly-esteemed handbook on divine service. He relates that in a number of places, sometimes at Easter, sometimes on Christmas Eve, either in the monasteries or in the episcopal palace, the priests played ball games with their clerks, accompanied by songs and dances. But it was especially in the cathedral of Auxerres, dedicated to St Stephen, that this ball game took place. Here the game had been played from ancient times on the afternoon of Easter Day and was first proscribed by a Parliamentary decree in 1538.

The rules of this church ball game are preserved in a decree of 1396. The Dean or his deputy received the ball from the newly inducted canons; it had to be of such a size that it could be held in both hands. With one arm round the ball the Dean seized with his other hand the hand of the nearest priest and in this way a long chain, possibly a ring, was formed. The Dean struck up the Easter hymn, *Victimi Paschali laudes*, in which all joined to the accompaniment of the organ. The long chain of men performed the three-step dance (*tripudio*) round the labyrinth inlaid upon the floor in the nave of the cathedral, at the extreme west, and the Dean threw the ball alternately to one or more of the dancers. When the singing and dancing was over, they hastened to the expected meal. There they all sat on benches, members of the Chapter, chaplains, officiating priests, as well as nobles of the town and district. They all offered small gifts, sweets, fruits, etc., as well as dishes of wild boar, venison and hares, washed down by red wine 'in moderate quantities'. During all these proceedings the text appropriate to the festival was read from the lectern or the pulpit. Then all proceeded to evensong. (Mercure de France.)

This festival was conducted in a very similar way for centuries. It was regarded with reverence and won the esteem and admiration of the most highly placed personages [Lebeuf]. From April 14, 1471, we have a record of a dispute which occurred in connexion with the pelota. The new canon, a certain Master Gerard Rotarius, had omitted to procure a large, new ball, as custom and the statutes of the cathedral prescribed. In order to avoid an open scandal the Dean and Chapter conferred with the highest magistrate of the city. Then Master Rotarius was informed of this ancient custom and of the constitution which he himself had sworn to observe when he was admitted to the priesthood. Rotarius excused himself by saying that it was not from contempt of the Church or its statutes that he had committed the offence but because he had read Beleth's above-quoted work in which such ball-play is condemned ('so it seems more praiseworthy not to play'). The reply to him was somewhat evasive and pointed out particularly that he ought to have informed the Chapter of his views in advance. But Master Rotarius submitted and acquired the ball from the previous year. The procession then moved into the nave of the church and in the presence of the Mayor and a large number of guests Master Rotarius was obliged to confess that he had been ignorant of the statutes; he now publicly declared obedience to them and in accordance with ancient custom proffered the ball to the Dean and the other church dignitaries. Thereupon, according to ancient custom, they at once proceeded with the dance and the feast.

Chambers has surmised that in the ball we may find a symbol of the sun, and that the game and dance were probably associated with the peculiar belief that if one rises early on Easter Day one will see the sun dancing. We will examine this idea further, on the assumption that the game and dance form a mystery play intimately connected with the mystery of the Resurrection.

FIG. 15. *Victimae Paschali laudes* until 1518 sung at Easter in the cathedral of Auxerres. It accompanied the pelota dance round the labyrinth inlaid in the floor at the far western end of the church [Besseler].

Easter is the supreme festival of the Church; it celebrates the death and resurrection of Christ, which are the foundation of the Christian faith. The Easter hymn, *Victimae Paschali laudes*, is of very great age and is linked to the Gospel account of the mystery of the Easter festival (Fig. 15). Its words are:

'Christians bring forth their songs of praise to the Easter offerings.
The Lamb has delivered the sheep: Christ the irreproachable has reconciled the sinners to the Father
Death and life struggle in wondrous strife, and the prince of life rules, living though dead,
Tell us, Mary, what have you seen on the way?
I have seen the grave of the living Christ, the glory of the Resurrection!
To this testify the angels, his napkin and clothes.
Christ, my hope, has risen, he goes before to Galilee.
Believe rather in the true Mary than in the deceitful Jewish host!
We know that Christ hath truly risen from the dead, but Thou Conqueror and King, have mercy upon us.'

So the song which accompanied the pelota is concerned primarily with Christ's resurrection from the dead and his victory over death and the underworld.

As regards the labyrinth round which the dance was performed, its symbolism is as follows: Labyrinths have been known from very early times in Babylon, Egypt, Greece, and Italy. But it was the Cretan labyrinth which became the model for so many labyrinths in Christian churches [Frazer], as also for stone labyrinths in the north. Legend has it that at Knossos in Crete the Minotaur dwelt at the centre of the labyrinth, and to him were offered

every year seven youths and seven maidens, until Theseus, one of the pro-
jected sacrifices, succeeded in conquering and slaying the Minotaur. At that
time, and later, dances were performed around this labyrinth which, according to Frazer, were possibly intended to facilitate and assist the course of the
sun in the firmament.

Brede Kristensen describes the Trojan game, played by armed and
mounted youths, mentioned in the *Aeneid*. This game, a part of the cult of

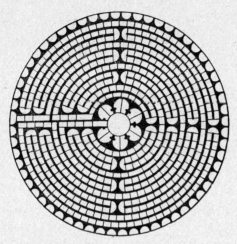

FIG. 16. The Labyrinth. In Chartres cathedral, dating from the twelfth century, and inlaid in the
floor with blue and white slabs. It is 12.2 metres in diameter [Matthew].

death and burial, was dedicated to Anchises. The pattern which the riders
made was that of the Cretan labyrinth. But the game was very ancient in
Italy and was performed in other places, but on foot. It was also well known
in Greece. On the shield of Achilles dancing men and women were represented holding each other by the hand, the line of dancers following the bends
of the labyrinth. This dance was ascribed to Theseus, instituted in memory of
his escape from the labyrinth, and was supposed to represent the way out.
Brede Kristensen emphasizes that the labyrinth, even in antiquity, symbolized the Kingdom of the Dead. In early Christian art the Minotaur was
identified with Satan, and Theseus became Christ, who descended into the
underworld, overcame Satan and emerged victorious, together with the
saved, through the gates of the Kingdom of the Dead. When the labyrinth
dance was performed by armed men this was done because departure from
the kingdom involved battle and victory.

Christianity adopted very early the symbol of the labyrinth (Figs. 16 and
17). Labyrinths of multi-coloured stones were laid in church floors, and
sometimes on the walls. The earliest known is that on the floor of the
Reparatus Basilica in Orleansville in Algeria, which dates from the fourth
century. Near the north-west entrance there is a labyrinth measuring
eight feet in diameter. In the middle of it is a square in which are repeatedly

69

inserted the words 'sancta ecclesia' (the Holy Church), probably in reference to the universal church and the third article of faith. As a rule, however, the church labyrinths seem to date from the eleventh century or later. Many were quite large. The one in Chartres cathedral measured forty feet in diameter and that in Auxerres cathedral, which was destroyed in 1690, was probably as large. They are to be found in many churches in Italy, France, England, Germany, in the Rhine province and in many monasteries; in the

FIG. 17. The Labyrinth in Amiens cathedral, dating from the thirteenth century. Inlaid in the floor of the nave, it measures about 12.6 metres in diameter [Matthews].

crypt of the St Gereon church in Cologne (eleventh century) the signs of the zodiac and the symbols of the seasons surround the inlaid labyrinth. In the labyrinth of St Michael's, in Pavia, of the eleventh century, one could see at the centre Theseus and the Minotaurs and the inscription, 'Theseus entered and slew the two-headed monster'. The labyrinth in St Savino, Piacenza, of the tenth century, bore the inscription, 'This labyrinth reveals the structure of the world'. Interesting also is a statement that in the sixteenth century a student named Didron saw, in a monastery in Athos, a labyrinth painted on the wall in red; it was said to represent 'Salomo's prison'. A monk is supposed to have found the prototype in a book and to have copied it on the wall [Launay]. Salomo was, in early Christian terminology, another name for Christ; his prison is therefore identical with the underworld into which he was obliged to descend. Still further weight must we attach, however, to two other labyrinth inscriptions. That at Piacenza reads:

> This labyrinth shows the picture of the world,
> Free to him who enters
> But very narrow to him who returns.
> But he who is ensnared by this world and is weighed down by the delights of vice,
> Will find it difficult to solve the riddle of life.

70

On a stone from a labyrinth preserved in Lyons Museum the following inscription is carved:

Look upon this mirror and behold in it thine own mortality!
Thy body shall become dust and food for the worms,
But thou thyself shalt live eternally; this life is hard to live.
Beg and pray to Christ that thy life may be lived in Christ
That by the Easter festival thou mayest be awakened and come out of the labyrinth.
By these five lines of verse I instruct thee in the secret of death.

When Palestine was lost to the unfaithful, according to Matthew, the Church permitted 'pilgrimages to Jerusalem', the pilgrims crawling on their knees along the winding passages of the church labyrinth. For this reason the labyrinths in France were often called 'The Road to Jerusalem' or simply 'Jerusalem' or 'Heaven'.

In Northern countries, too, in Sweden for example, stone settings in the form of labyrinths are preserved. They seem as a rule to mark the burial places of the iron or bronze ages [Alin]. On the other hand they were not laid in Christian times, though this is only a supposition. Alin mentions that, according to the people in Nordholland, their forefathers in their childhood went out early in the morning of Easter Day to such a labyrinth and 'go treddenborg', i.e., went through the passages of the labyrinth. This custom, in Alin's view, goes back to prehistoric sun and fertility cults, an unnecessary assumption, since the custom is in full accord with early Christian usages in respect of the labyrinth. Here too the labyrinth represents the underworld and the rite suggests death and resurrection.

We may say, if we so wish, that there were two different conceptions of the labyrinth. On the one hand it has been conceived simply and solely as representing the underworld; Minotaur-Satan sits at its centre, and the labyrinthine underworld sinks lower and lower until it reaches the bottomless depths. On the other hand, the Kingdom of the Dead was conceived as a mountain, associated with the Old Testament conceptions of the mountain far up in the North within which is the underworld and on the top of which the new Jerusalem is enthroned; one clambers higher and higher up the winding ways in order at last to reach the Heavenly City at the top. In this case we see the Sancta Ecclesia in the centre of the labyrinth, and the journey through the labyrinth represents a pilgrimage to the heavenly Jerusalem, to Heaven.

The sun has been a symbol for Christ since early Christian times. According to Dolger one was referred to Malachi, 4, 2, 'But unto you that fear my name shall the sun of righteousness arise with healing on his wings', the 'sun of righteousness' being Christ. The Latin term is 'sol justitiae', the sun of righteousness or justice, to which was early added the term 'sol resurrectionis', the sun of resurrection. We find these terms with these meanings in Origen, Cyprian, Kyrillos, Ambrose, Hippolytus, Eusebius, Jerome, etc. From the third century the expression 'Sun of Righteousness' belongs to the terminology of the Church in reference to Christ who, as victor over death and the underworld, shall judge all, both good and evil.

St Gregory, the Miracle Worker, in addressing the Virgin Mary regarding Gabriel's annunciation, says: 'There was sent out a weak light which signified the Sun of Righteousness.' He explains to Mary that through her the Sun of Righteousness has arisen for all those who sit in the darkness (Hom. III, col. 1174).

Clement of Alexandria writes in his address to the heathens [8:84 1, 2— Dölger]:

> Awake from sleep,
> Rise up from the dead,
> Christ thy Lord enlighten thee,
> Christ, the Sun of Righteousness,
> Created before the Morning Star,
> Giving life by his rays,

The Catholic Church has retained this terminology even to our day. The expression *sol* or *sol justitiae* is used in hymns and psalms and other church songs. A medieval hymn to the Virgin Mary on the Rose Festival begins [An. Hymn 16, 71]:

> Thou light of light, rising,
> Thou glory of Paradise,
> Thou sun of righteousness, flower of the gracious mother,
> Mayest thou thyself wreathe us in roses,
> Judge when thou comest to the glory of the Kingdom!

In the monastery of Moissac in the tenth century the following song was sung at matins [An. Hymn 2, 36]:

> Just now, O Christ, sun of righteousness,
> Vanish the shades of night,
> Now vanishes the blindness of the soul,
> The light of virtue returns.

In the sixteenth century and later there was sung at Easter [An. Hymn 21, 31],

> The true son of righteousness
> Has risen again today.
> What the Jews gave us passes!
> Today the King of Glory has arisen!

We shall find the Sun of Righteousness again in modern hymns.

In England (according to Chambers), Switzerland (according to Riser), Scandinavia, and especially Sweden (according to Nordlind and Hagberg), and elsewhere, it has been popularly believed from early times that if one rises on Easter morning, just at sunrise, one can see the sun dancing. It rejoices at the resurrection of the Saviour and dances for hours [Hagberg]; it is very brilliant, wheeling back and forth, and is said to curtsey three times. Or, according to Norlind, it dances, like a great cart-wheel, with joy at the resurrection of the Saviour or it turns and dances at the grave of Christ. How early these ideas were held we do not know. According to Pessler [II, 61], George Rollenhagen, at the end of the sixteenth century, relates how on Easter morning young and old ran out together into the fields to see the rising sun·dance in the East. Perhaps this is a survival of early medieval mysticism in which Christ the resurrected was conceived as dancing forth from the underworld.

Both in Babylonia and in Egypt 'West' became the symbol of the underworld. This was for two reasons. To the West of these ancient empires lay the barren deserts, which early came to symbolize the underworld and the home of the devils. Moreover, the sun sets or dies, so to speak, in the West, and during the night passes through the Kingdom of the Dead, to arise in the morning in the East. Thus the West became the symbol both of the underworld and its entrance, and from it proceeded the winding road to the interior of the mountain in the North. Early Christianity adopted this symbol. Jerome [*Amos lib*. III, c. VI, 14—Dölger] says of baptism, 'For this reason in our mysteries we refuse above all him who lives in the West, we die from him and from our sins. Therefore we turn to the East and join the Sun of Righteousness and promise to serve him'. According to Dölger, the Elders of the Church compared the descent of Jesus into the underworld with the setting sun in the West, but they compared the resurrection, on the other hand, with the rising of the sun in the East.

On this basis we may perhaps draw the following conclusions. The sacral dance and ball game in the cathedral of Auxerres and elsewhere constitute a religious mystery play ultimately connected with the Easter celebrations, i.e., with the death and resurrection of Christ. When the ball game was practised at Christmas it was associated with the birth of the Saviour and with his work. When people danced to the Easter hymn, '*Victimae Paschalis*', this was done in memory of the death of Christ, his victory over death and his resurrection. The ball represented Christ as the Sun of Righteousness or the Sun of Resurrection and was thus associated with the terminology relating to Christ the Resurrected and Christ the Judge which had been retained in the Church since the third century. The labyrinth now as always represents the underworld and the dance round the labyrinth retains its original significance as the exit from the kingdom of the dead. The dance symbolizes both the resurrection of Christ and also the firm hope that every Christian will follow Him. The ball which was thrown to the players possibly symbolizes the passage of the Saviour to the underworld and His resurrection is a necessary pre-supposition for every individual Christian.

In this way we may freely and consistently interpret the pelota of Auxerres in respect of its most important details, or preserved and in association with early Christian conceptions and symbolism. This sacral church dance is connected in the most intimate manner with what Ambrose called 'the revealed mysteries of the Resurrection'.

4. The Bergerette

Durandos relates how, as early as the thirteenth century, a sacral church dance called the bergerette was performed in Besançon. It was also found in various other places in France, and it continued until the Revolution of 1789.

On the first day of Easter the Archbishop of Besançon invited his clergy to dinner. After dinner they performed roundels and other dances, either in the cloisters or—in wet weather—in the nave of the cathedral. During the dance the following song was sung:

> Let the clear voice of the faithful resound
> And awaken Zion to joy!
> Let all join in a common rejoicing
> Purchased by limitless grace!

Gougaud has left an extract from a ritual of 1582 of the Mary Magdalene church in Besançon, which describes this bergerette. The dance was performed, as late at 1662, with the canons and chaplains holding each other by the hand, so it must therefore have been a ring-dance or a line dance. Afterwards there was a meal in the chapter house at which red wine was served.

The bergerette was thus also connected with the Easter festival of the Resurrection and the hymn to which it was danced also describes the miracle of the Resurrection, which by boundless grace delivered mankind from the power of death and the underworld, from the gates of the Kingdom of the Dead. Zion may rejoice because the powers of the underworld no longer imprison him who has been released from captivity. In rejoicing people danced; the servants of the Church clasp each other by the hand, forming a chain—the Dance of the Angels. The great artists of the time liked to represent the angels and the blessed dancing ring and line dances in just this fashion. It is the Dance of the Angels on the heights of Zion after the Resurrection which is here demonstrated and imitated—in full accordance with the ancient custom of the earliest Church.

As in the case of the pelota, so also the bergerette was followed by a banquet, and a special emphasis is clearly laid on the fact that the wine served was red. What the real significance of this banquet was we do not know. It may be thought that it was simply banal and had no other significance than a festive communal meal, but it is also possible that it was symbolic, and, as a guess, perhaps connected with the meal described in St John's Revelation, which was a part of the mysteries of divine bliss and concerning which the Apostles have something to say. The heavenly banquet after deliverance from the temporal world was an extremely important element in the symbolic decoration of the Christian catacombs outside Rome. It seems to me probable that this heavenly banquet was something even more significant than the dance among the heavenly blisses. So these festive meals may quite possibly have had symbolic reference to the heavenly feast. The wine would recall the outpoured blood of Christ—the necessary preliminary to heavenly bliss.

Other Easter dances performed in the church by the clergy are described by the Jesuit Father Menestrier in his very curious work on dancing published in 1682. He mentions there [Cahusac] that on Easter Day, in a number of churches he himself had seen canons and choristers holding hands and dancing to the singing of joyous hymns. They would appear to have danced a ring-dance to the song *O filii et filiae* [Gougaud], a hymn of resurrection which begins,

> O ye sons and daughters,
> The King of Heaven, the King of Glory
> Has risen from the dead (Chevalier)

Regarding the ceremonies of the Easter festival there is preserved, according to Villetard, in the metropolitan church in Sens, a manuscript of the sixteenth century. It describes in much detail the dance which the clergy were to perform at Easter, the so-called Easter carol. This was a ring-dance in which the dancers held hands. The dance took place in the cloisters on Easter Eve. The Archbishop assisted and all the clergy participated. They first moved round two by two, followed in the same manner by the most prominent citizens, all singing songs of the Resurrection. Thereupon the carol was executed. The dance is described as a *chorea*, i.e., a ring-dance, but with no hopping, which was allowed in other special and more individual dances. The dance is said to have been performed in the 'cloister walk' but seems to have continued into the church, round the choir, into the nave, to the singing of the part song *Salvator mundi* (Saviour of the World). The ceremony is preserved in a processional of 1772 and the dance only ceased at the Revolution. There is no doubt, it seems to me, that the Easter dance in Sens was also a bergerette. It has quite the same character and clearly also the same symbolism.

Whitsun was also celebrated by sacral church dances. The Whitsun miracle is the outpouring of the Holy Ghost, a baptism. In appearance at least the Gospels contain a threefold baptism: water, spirit and fire. Actually there are only two—water and fire. Whether the baptism of the spirit coincides with the baptism in water or just in fire, it is difficult to decide; possibly it coincides with both. Even water was thought to flame at the baptism of Christ in the Jordan [Edsman, Kmosko], because of the presence in it of the Holy Ghost. In this connexion it is significant to remember that the angels have a garment of fire, that God himself is a flaming fire, that everyone who wishes to enter Heaven must clothe himself in a robe of fire and that the pouring out of the Holy Ghost is therefore the same as the pouring out of fire. For that reason the Whitsun festival was celebrated in the Catholic Church with the casting down in the church, round the altar, of bundles of burning chips [Veit]. But the pouring out of the Spirit then becomes the same as the attainment of heavenly bliss, the entrance into paradise, and for that reason the Whitsun festival has close symbolical associations with the Easter festival of the Resurrection. The dances which the priests performed in the churches at Whitsun appear to have illustrated heavenly bliss, which everybody who receives the Holy Ghost and who follows its behests may confidently hope to attain. In the church at Angers the canons danced during the Whitsun festival [Stieren] and in Châlons-sur-Saône the canons and the choristers and others danced in the porch of the cathedral and in the neighbouring cloisters. This is described in further detail by Martene. First, on a meadow, the Dean began with the song *Veni Sancte Spiritus* to the accompaniment of the dance; others followed the Dean with their own songs, if

183.

VEni Sancte Spiritus, reple tuorum corda fidelium; & tui amoris in eis ignem accende : qui per diverfitatem linguarum cunctarum gentes in unitate fidei congregafti. Halleluja, Halleluja!

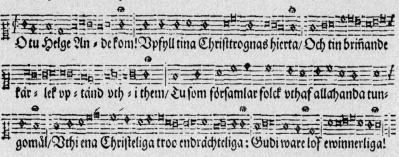

Fig. 18. *Veni Sancte Spiritus* (Come Holy Ghost). To this hymn, at the Whitsun festival, the priests danced the bergerette at Châlons-sur-Saône. [Svensk Koralhandbok 1697.]

they so wished, but in Latin. This dance is also called a bergerette. It was danced in choristers' robes. The senior dignitary went first, followed by a chorister who carried his train. Then followed all the other canons, one by one, and each followed by his own chorister, bearing his train. After this dance, which might well be called a processional dance or, more properly, a line dance, all entered the monastery, where they made three circuits of the great hall or its garden whilst the music played and the dancers sang *In hac die Dei* [Chevalier].

> On this day of God
> The Galileans can relate
> How the Jews destroyed the King.

Curiously enough, this is an Easter hymn composed at the earliest in the thirteenth century. But the fact that this Easter hymn was sung when the bergerette was danced at Whitsun seems to me to show that the dance had a symbolic connexion with the miracle of salvation and therefore also with the bliss which was won by the Resurrection.

From the fifteenth century, possibly one or two centuries earlier, dances have been performed in Seville Cathedral in connexion with divine service. At certain church festivals this dance was performed by *los seises* in the choir in front of the high altar; for example, during the week before Corpus Christi, before Annunciation Day or on the three last days of Carnival, before the fast. This dance survived until quite recently. In the third part of his work, *Mitt livs minnen*, the Marquis Claes Lagergren gives a description of this

FIG. 19. Chorister at Seville, 1844, dressed in his dancing costume [Bueno].

dance. It was on the afternoon of December 8th, 1878, that Lagergren visited the Cathedral; the 'Ave Maria' had just been sung and the blessing and sacrament administered, when *el baile de los seises*, the dance of the six, began. The performers were choristers and originally there had been six of them, later increased to ten. The high altar glittered with candles and gold, the church was filled with organ music, the Archbishop had just raised the jewelled monstrance above the heads of the kneeling worshippers and there was complete silence. Then entered the ten choristers, dressed magnificently as pages of the seventeenth century. Standing before the high altar, first they dropped on their knees, then they rose and sang a curious melodious song; then they put on hats, divided into two groups and stepped backwards and forwards, making figures and singing, sometimes accompanying themselves with castanets. 'The dance, which resembled a minuet, lasted about a quarter

FIG. 20. *Los Seises* in Seville, 1933. Choristers in their Renaissance costumes for the dance in Seville cathedral and for church processions [Capmány].

of an hour and made a very remarkable spectacle. The deep reverence of the spectators emphasized the strangeness of the performance. All knelt and I saw well up in the choir the Duke and Duchess of Montpensier with their two children, Donna Christina and the twelve-year-old Don Antonio, with their heads lowered in prayer.'

Then Lagergren describes how Archbishop Palafox of Seville (1642–1701) one day forbade the performance of the dance. Amazed at this, the inhabitants of Seville collected the necessary funds to send *los seises* to Rome, where they performed their dance before the Holy Father to the accompaniment of song and castanets. The Pope said, 'I see nothing in this children's dance which is offensive to God. Let them continue to dance before the high altar.' And they did.

Three times a year the choristers dance in the church, in December for the Virgin Mary, in June for Corpus Christi, in the presence of the most holy sacrament, and at the end of Carnival. In honour of Mary the dresses are predominantly blue, in honour of Christ red and white. The former signifies Mary as Queen of Heaven, the latter signifies Christ's innocent blood. Lagergren reproduces the music and song which he heard on his visit to Seville, and part of it is here reproduced, together with some of the music of an earlier period. Both music and song seem to have varied considerably during the centuries.

A Bull of Pope Eugene IV of 1439 authorizes the dances of *los seises*.

Yet these *seises* existed before that date, though under the name *los mozos de coro*, i.e., choristers. They were also called *ninos cantoricos*, little singers, which reminds us of the name in *Justin the Martyr*, 'the small' [Rosa, Davillier]. Originally the intention was that these choristers should sing the responses and other ceremonial songs. But very soon the dance was added to their duties. In the years 1464 and 1467 existing documents confirm that they danced before the Ark on the altar, the Arca del Sacramento, the most ancient and most valued treasure in the cathedral and that they were dressed as angels. During the whole of this century they seem to have been dressed thus when they danced during divine service. The costume was as follows: short,

FIG. 21. Choristers' Dance 1844. *Los seises* before the altar [left] in Seville cathedral. Arranged in two parallel rows [Bueno].

wide knee breeches of Moorish cut, short sleeveless mantle, a tight-fitting jacket, silvered half-length boots with gaiters, wreaths of intertwined flowers on their bare heads, and gilded wings fixed to their shoulders [Rosa]. Thus the dancing choristers really represented the angels in heaven, who had descended to the church choir in order to continue there the dance of bliss in Paradise. The very fact that the boys were dressed as angels shows in a remarkable way that the sacral dance was still interpreted exactly as in the days of Clement of Alexandria: as an imitation of the dance of the angels. During the sixteenth century the costume began to vary; sometimes they were dressed as pilgrims, sometimes as shepherds. In the year 1613 they appeared dressed as soldiers of Christ, carrying shields and spears. After that they probably definitely adopted the courtly page costume of the late Renaissance [Rosa]. This consisted of a blue or red coat, white neck-frill, white bandolier, dark hat with white plumes, white cockade with upturned brim on one side, short yellow breeches, red stockings, large rosettes on the lower edges of the breeches, black shoes with white tassles. [Cuendias and Fereal.]

The *seises* had to be between ten and fifteen years of age, says Davillier, who describes the dance as a kind of glide with movements like those of a very slow waltz and not unlike the old pavan of the sixteenth century. Palamedes describes it as a slow gliding dance in the form of a quadrille. Lagergren compares it to a minuet. The dance must therefore have varied in

Fig. 22. Choristers' Dance, 1904. *Baile de los seises* before the altar in Seville cathedral. The choristers perform a ring-dance with passes. Section of an oil painting by Gonzalo Bilbao [Rosa].

character on different occasions. Rosa describes in detail the very peculiar figures which the choristers performed. For example, the *seises* formed two parallel lines of five, probably in imitation of the Spanish *immaculata*, as becomes the Holy Virgin; one of our illustrations reproduces this figure. Or they may have grouped themselves in the shape of two S's, suggesting the *Sacro Sacramento*. In another figure they were grouped in the form of a St Andrew's cross, or in a similar grouping with two choristers moving in a narrow circle around the centre of the cross, the oblate, or perhaps the disc of the sun which was fixed to the cross and symbolized the crucified Christ. These two last figures only appear in connexion with the Corpus Christi festival. Rosa thinks, and quite rightly, that in these two figures there is a deeper mysticism and symbolism and it is difficult not to draw a parallel between them and certain Egyptian cult dances which are much older than Christianity.

FIG. 23. Choristers' Dance, 1916. *Los seises* dance before the high altar in Seville cathedral. The Archbishop is under his baldaquin. The choristers, in two rows of five, face each other. The steps of the high altar are seen to the left. They have castanets in the hands. Section of a watercolour probably English [Buschan].

The songs of the dancers varied very much with different occasions and at different periods. According to Rosa they sang the following song in 1690:

(*Standing still*) We believe in the bread of life
From Christ to our overflowing joy;
By our dance we supplicate him,
As once the Baptist supplicated.

(*Dancing*) Therefore by this dance
We strengthen our firm faith,
All to the sounds of music!

In the following two refrains 'our love' and 'our hope' are confirmed. In other words the three Catholic virtues: Faith, hope and love.

Davillier quotes other dancing songs, of which the following is one:

Hail, Virgin, purest and most beautiful,
More than the red dawn, more than the star of day!
Daughter, mother and spouse, O Mary
Thou gateway of the rising sun!

81

Fig. 24. Sacral Church-Dance Music. The opening music of a song for *los seises* in the *Baile al St. mo Sacramento* before the high altar in Seville cathedral. The song in translation runs, 'We mortals assemble at the Royal Banquet and eat the heavenly bread of the blessed' [Rosa].

From Bueno we quote a song from the dance on the festival of Corpus Christi, reminiscent of the medieval *Sol Justitiae*:

> Sun of righteousness,
> Rising in the heaven,
> On fire for thee,
> Secretly setting me afire.
> Thy face sets free within my breast
> Love unflaming towards thee.

From the songs which Lagergren copied on his visit to Seville we may quote one here (Fig. 25). The dance on this occasion was to the Virgin Mary.

> Who shall describe these warbles
> Of lovely nightingales, of biblical song,
> The notes of harmony?
> Who can describe the burning glow
> With which the angels sing aloft!
> Thou purest Mother and Virgin
> Behold the exalted!

These *los seises* dances begin immediately after the Archbishop has raised the Host at vespers. They are accompanied by a large orchestra and when they are ended the Archbishop administers the blessing from the high altar and grants absolution to all present for eighty days [Palamedes].

Los seises, however, also take part in certain church processions, more particularly at Corpus Christi. These processions start at the cathedral and are preceded by the upper clergy; the holy sacrament is borne in the procession under a magnificent baldequin. From time to time the bier on which it is carried is set down or occupies a so-called station or halting place, and the choristers begin to dance around it. This dance clearly reminds us of David's dance before the Ark. As early as 1508 the choristers danced and sang in such sacramental processions [Cuendias and Fereal].

Davillier relates that, according to St Thomas of Villanueva, who lived in the first part of the sixteenth century, similar sacral dances were performed before the sacrament in the churches of Toledo, Valencia and Yepes. Some of them continued much longer.

BAILE DE SEISES

Á LA PURÍSIMA CONCEPCIÓN

FIG. 25. Sacral Church-Dance Music. The first part of the music in four parts, in honour of the Holy Virgin on December 8, to accompany the dance of *los seises* and sung before the high altar in Seville cathedral [Lagergren].

Thus Palamedes states that as late as the eighteenth century there is reference in the records to *los seises*, the six choristers, in the cathedral of Toledo, who appear to have played the same role as the *seises* of Seville. According to Cahusac, it was Cardinal Xéménès (1436–1517) who reintroduced the sacral dance at Toledo. In actual fact this was a renewal of the common dance which flourished in the best days of the Mozarabic mass. The Mozarabic mass required the performance of a dance in the choir or the nave during the service. *The Spanish-American Encyclopaedia* holds that the Catholic Church, inspired by the dances of youths and children before the Ark, singing the songs which David sang, accompanying themselves on the harp (the dissimilarity with the Old Testament account is clear), preserved this custom in the Spanish liturgy, which since the fourteenth century was propagated by Spanish-Roman and Mozarabic peoples. In order to conciliate and convert the Mozarabic population of Toledo the Cardinal felt that he ought to preserve the ancestral ritual of Corpus Christi and the dance which had been performed earlier in the Mozarabic divine service, but had been suppressed. This was found the more appropriate since the Latin liturgy prescribed costumes for choristers to be worn at the Christmas festival, when they had to perform in representation of the dance and song of the sibyls. This was supposed to be the origin of the dance which was later performed during mass, symbolizing the prophecy of the Saviour's coming. The costume for these dances was simple: a wreath of flowers on the head, a long shirt, a narrow belt at the waist, a broad stole (symbolizing the priest's stole or yoke), and low shoes, all in white. We can doubtless recognize in this costume either the Levitic shroud in which David danced before the Ark or the white clothes in which, according to Revelation, the blessed in heaven are dressed. The music of the dance is reported to have varied and was often specially composed for the occasion. The songs were Mozarabic songs of praise or hymns with a deep religious feeling. They are reported to have been lost.

6. *Sacral Church Processions*

Numerous texts preserved from the relatively early Middle Ages permit us to confirm [Berlière] that at church festivals, for example at Whitsun, congregations assembled with crosses, banners and relics, and made the offerings in the churches. A Cardinal Legate, Guy de Palestrina, relates that in 1202, in the Bishopric of Liége, it was already customary for congregations annually to bring their offerings to certain churches for the upkeep of God's servants, as it was put. Earlier, in 1143, these offerings seem to have been regarded more as a sign of the gratitude of the baptized to the Papal power, and at the same time as a sort of tax paid to the church. Similar processions were known in England, France and Germany. In France they can be traced still farther back, for between 918 and 933 there were great processions every year at Auxerres, headed by the priests and bearing cross and banners, which made their way to St Stephen's Cathedral, already mentioned in connexion with the pelota. Many such processions are recorded in other places. One circumstance should be specially noted: the processions bore with them a gift from every household and in the procession at St Michel the members were asked to promise to return every year. We know of similar processions in Würzburg and Salzburg between 1100 and 1500.

These church processions seem always to have been dancing processions. In the seventeenth century Bodinus writes of the processions of his own day that they still have the character of the old sacred dances. Either the processions advanced with rhythmic steps or else the so-called sacral dances were performed at the so-called stations. Possibly both methods were employed. Bérenger-Féraud also emphasizes the point that the church processions had formerly taken the form of a more or less pronounced dance. Especially was this the case at the meeting of two processions, when there were ceremonial greetings; the bows, turns, advancing and retiring, all performed in front of the cross and the sacrament, the images of the saints, the relics, were all choreographic figures. Many of the processional songs have also been adopted as music for other church dances, as for example *Salve festa dies* [Spanke].

Margit Sahlin, who, in a work on medieval carols, gives a comprehensive survey of church dances, quotes from a *Dictionnaire de plain-chant* (Paris, 1860), an account of church processions: 'The word procession means a moving chorus advancing in harmony and with a sort of cadence through the various parts of the church. The processions passing through the choir and aisles, swinging the censer, do so to measured movements prescribed in the ritual . . . representing by their symbolical movements and figures holy and mystic dances.' The Abbé Villetard says the same thing and is of the opinion that the processions through the aisles were so conducted that the choristers executed figures which were nothing but liturgical dances.

The purpose of numerous church processions since the earliest days of the Church was to ward off individual or public distress, or to bring relief from pain or epidemic. They were then called prayer processions or healing processions or litanies; this last word came later to mean only the prayers [Augusti]. Such processions took place throughout the Middle Ages and even into modern times, preceded by cross and banners, the Sacrament in the monstrance, images of the Holy Virgin and saints and relics. Frequently the procession was barefoot and lighted candles were carried.

There was dancing particularly in those processions which bore relics of saints and martyrs from their original graves to some newly prepared repository, most frequently a burial chapel. Thus the relics of St Vitus were transferred in 836 to Corvey in Saxony. During the actual transfer miracles were performed: the sick were healed, contractions of fingers, arms, legs and feet were cured, and in all probability there was occasional dancing on the route. When the relics were deposited, on June 13th, large numbers of Christians congregated before and around the church, singing devout songs and dancing all night. The commonest dancing song was *Kyrie eleison* (Lord, have mercy). During that night many miracles were performed and contractions of many years standing were cured. [*Acta Sanctorum.*] When the relics of St Aegilis were transferred to the St Bonifacius basilica in 819, the translation is described thus:

> The holy relics,
> Were borne amidst happy dancing.

The translation of the relics of St Martial is described in a poem of the thirteenth century. In deepest reverence the procession surrounded the saint; the clergy sang loudly and the whole procession danced with joy while the relics were transferred to the new church. The Augsburg chronicles relate how in 1223 relics of St Vitus and St Modestus were recovered in the church of St Andrew and taken to Salzburg to the dancing (*tripudio*) of numerous people. Under Pipin the Less the relics of St Germain, Bishop of Paris, were also translated. They were carried by priests and selected clergy to the singing of hymns and the accompaniment of dances [Sahlin].

We shall now give three more detailed examples of church processional dances.

In the fourteenth century, in the small town of Moosburg, between Regensburg and Munich, the priests performed a processional dance, which drew out from the old church, the so-called Minster, in order to form up. Both the words and music are preserved and are here reproduced. The song was composed by the Dean, John, and was written down in 1360. [*An. Hymn* 20, 178.] It bears the superscription, 'When one dances (*chorea*) outside the church' (Fig. 26). The three first words of each Latin line begin with letters which combined spell 'Mospurga', i.e., the name of the town where the dance was performed and from which John came. I translate *puellae* not as 'girls' but as 'nuns', in accordance with Kelle, and by analogy *pueri* as 'monks'. The correctness of this view is vouched for much earlier by Martene [II, 560].

Geistliches Tanzlied aus dem Mosburger Graduale des Dekans Johann von Perchausen (München, U.-B. 156, geschrieben i. J. 1360)

„Cum itur extra ecclesiam ad choream"

Mos flo-ren-tis ve-nu-sta-tis Pu-e-ro-rum a-ci-e Gna-ra ca-ra sors re-du-xit
Jo-cis dig-nis at-que gra-tis Lae-ta fin-gat fa-ci-e, Er-go ter-go re tro-da-ta

Prae-su-la-tus ju-bi-lum, Pel-lens, vel-lens, ut il-lu-xit, Cap-tae men-tis nu-bi-ium.
Qua-vis jam moe-sti-ti a, Plebs Mos-bur-gae doc-tri-na-ta, Gau-de sub pe-ri-ti-a.

FIG. 26. Melody and song from 1360. Written for the church on the occasion of a dance before the saints.

This custom most delectable
Through the great hosts of monks,
And by its joyous seeming
Gives worthy form to grateful games.
This well-known, highly-esteemed act
Brings again our Bishop's blessing,
Dispersing as if in the light of dawn
The dark clouds of the depressed mind.

CHORUS:
    Therefore I free myself
    From all sorrow that comes.
    Moosburg's clever people
    Rejoice in your able leaders.

Before the eyes of the nuns
Stands in purple splendour,
Deeply and devoutly honoured,
The Bishop, guiding the cult.
Numerous hands
Join and clasp in dance,
This broad and joyous path
Gives ample space for the chain of dancers.

CHORUS:
    Those who would be lured
    Hence to vicious habits are quickly stopped
    And obey strictly and willingly
    And with joy the Church order,
    Strengthened by its wondrous shepherd.
    All these festive gestures
    Intend the gift of inward joy.

The Moosburg dance does not appear to have been solely a dancing procession. Probably it ultimately became a ring-dance or a line-dance. This seems to be indicated by the words 'chain of dancers'. It would also seem that the dance ended with the episcopal blessing. As in the earliest days of the Church, so also in Moosburg in the fourteenth century, the Bishop was the leader and guide. He supervises the cult, as the song tells us, and this would seem to imply that he led the dance also. He is therefore the *praesul* in the fullest sense of the word: both bishop and dance leader. The reference in the song to the people of Moosburg, who are described as having experience and skill, may signify that members of the congregation also participated.

A manuscript from Hildesheim, dated 1478, describes the Easter ceremonies at mass [Bartsch], and the writer adds various details in order to make the symbolism of the ceremonies intelligible to the reader. In translation the account is as follows: 'Thereafter comes the solemn procession in memory of the procession which Christ, King of Glory, solemnized when he returned from the underworld, leading out those he had delivered into the paradise of ecstasy, dancing and hopping. He introduces both music and dance in consideration of the liberation of so many souls. He sings to them a song which none should utter except to God's immortal Son after his wondrous triumph. And we all, happy and adorned with spiritual perfection, follow our highest master, who himself leads the solemn ring-dance. Then we say,

> Lord Jesus dances first of all.
> He leads the bride by the hand.
> He it is who jubilates;
> Jubilus is his name.
> Blessed he who jubilates!
> The soul grows warm in memory
> And filled with heavenly food.

At the subsequent communion we read

> O, gracious Lord Zabaoth,
> Thou art the God of all the world.
> Lead us on in Easter dance;
> There we shall find our joy.

Later in this same manuscript, endeavouring to describe the heavenly paradise, the author exclaims, 'Ah! how brilliant is that bride! See how she dances a thousand steps before the bridegroom, before the lamb, before the throne! Before the bridegroom she dances as many steps as once she sent up pious thoughts from earth.' Here we find the same spiritualization of the dance and the same equation of good deeds and pious thoughts with a spiritual dance as we have clearly seen in the words of the early fathers. But the resemblance is now coarsened and sensualized. But the most valuable part of this old manuscript is the evident parallel with Christ's departure from the underworld; we may assume that it was so formed as to resemble that described in pious legend. The manuscript is clearly of clerical origin, and among the clergy at the end of the fifteenth century the church dances were regarded manifestly as belonging to the cult. This is proved by the words, the Lord will lead us 'in the Easter Dance'.

From the latter part of the Middle Ages there is preserved in Cologne an annual 'great, holy, sacramental procession', the magnificent 'Gottestracht'. It is supposed to have been instituted by the Bishops Heribert (fourteenth

FIG. 27. The Little Fool Bernhard who, from the Middle Ages onwards, preceded the great annual Gottestracht procession in Cologne. The costume is not the original one, which was 'oriental'. He is supposed to have represented the Devil fleeing before the Sacrament and the relics which were carried in the procession.

century) and Theodor (fifteenth century) of Cologne. It was celebrated on the second Sunday after Easter, and continued until the first decade of the nineteenth century [v. Mering]. The procession was primarily in honour of the holy lance of Longinus which was driven into the side of Christ, also of one of the Crucifixion nails which was preserved in the reliquaries of the cathedral and was a part of the old German coronation treasure [Browe]. Both of these were borne in the procession, together with the monstrance.

All the clergy and the city authorities, as well as visiting ambassadors, took part in the procession. All were clothed in splendid costumes or uniforms; the choristers carried special processional crosses of silver; the baldequin over the body of Christ was borne alternately by the mayors and the choir leaders. There followed in the procession the various fraternities and guilds, all with flags and insignia. The procession passed through a number of the city streets, mainly along the old boundary wall, and finished at the Church of the Apostles and Archbishop Heribert's tomb. Here the procession halted and mass was read. Up to this point nothing in the nature of a dance had occurred; and yet such it was, for it was preceded by a dancing harlequin, the so-called Gecken-Berndtchen, the Little Fool Bernhard. At the head of this brilliant church procession he hopped and danced 'the most curious steps'. Earlier, according to Schrörs and Krier, he was dressed in a fantastic oriental costume and later in one from the Renaissance, described and reproduced by v. Mering (Fig. 27).

In his right hand he carried a wind instrument in the form of a large horn with a flag attached to it, but this may, in fact, have been a cornucopia. On the flag was painted the figure of David dancing to his lyre before the priest-borne Ark, and Mering says that Bernhard reproduced that very scene. Beneath this picture on the flag were the arms of the guild of locksmiths, which are not shown in the picture. In his left hand he carried a silver shield, on which was written, *Dieu protège les jongleurs*, and in the middle of it there were antlers and a laurel wreath, the former symbolizing the speed of the stag, the latter King David's victory over Goliath—a banal and disconnected interpretation. The underclothes, like the mantle, were both decorated with floral wreaths and fox brushes; the former were said to represent the peasant benches placed outside the city gates from which a certain jurisdiction was exercised, the latter representing cunning and flattery. To the left of the figure hangs an enormous battle sword with an inscription in German on the bandolier 'Whoever would have honour, let him follow my example'. On the head is a silver helmet with white and red feathers, the colours of the city of Cologne. The helmet is crowned by two buffalo horns, surrounded at the base with bells, and lined with fox brushes.

It seems to me evident that the costume is of comparatively late origin. Its symbolism is impossible and disconnected. Moreover, earlier accounts relate that Bernhard the Fool wore a fantastic oriental costume. The appearance of inscriptions in both French and German is difficult to understand, and there is a suspicion that they are a later addition. It seems most probable that the curious French inscription is the older, the more so as it can be connected with early medieval legends of buffoons who danced before the saints. The clumsy horn and flag also seem to me of later date, for it is scarcely possible that Bernhard the Fool represented the dancing David. On the other hand the fox brush, helmet, horns and bells, and possibly the shield and sword, without their inscriptions, are probably relics of earlier times. Horns are characteristic symbols of demons and devils; bells expel them, though we shall find in Spain that they are also assigned, in connexion with homeopathic magic, to devils; the fox is the cunning and deceitful creature, and his red brush reminds one of the devils who are generally called 'the red'. I therefore agree with Krier, who has already suggested that Bernhard the Fool represented the demons, perhaps the Devil himself, in flight from the relics and the Corpus Christi. In later times his costume changed and it is no longer possible to give a consistent interpretation of its meaning. When the great sacramental procession passed through the streets of Cologne in the Middle Ages it certainly acted in the manner characteristic of these medieval processions, i.e., dancing or moving with solemn rhythmical steps. In front of the sacrament Bernhard the Fool cut his capers as if in flight from holiness and godliness.

7. Other Sacral Church Dances

Even at Church festivals for particular saints or on other special occasions the clergy performed dances in churches and monasteries. Cahusac mentions that in the middle of the seventeenth century the priests in Limoges were seen performing a ring-dance in the choir of the Church of St Leonard. This may have been the festival of St Martial. It also seems probable that they took part in the dances which the congregation performed in honour of that saint and which we shall describe later.

When both monks and nuns were inducted into their order, or their monastery or convent, and laid aside their worldly dress, a lively dance was performed in order, it was said, to give the world a last kick [Stubenvoll]. In 1385 these dances and the wild behaviour which usually accompanied them were prohibited.

In some bishoprics a custom prevailed in which the priest, when he conducted his first mass, was obliged to perform a sacral dance to special music [Gougaud]. This custom, which we find in various countries, is confirmed by the Council Minutes of Strasburg for 1518, which show that the prohibition of music which was enforced on account of the dancing epidemic should not apply to a priest celebrating his first mass [Wencker]. In 1547 the Parliament of Paris prohibited the old custom.

Church dances in Italy are almost entirely untraceable; yet there cannot be the slightest doubt that the Italian churches were the scene of numerous sacral and popular dances. There is some evidence of this. According to Rodocanachi, religious ceremonies in Italy were, as late as the fourteenth century, introduced by dances. Casanova tells of them in one of his letters. In Cana there was a religious dance until 1486. The statutes of Ancona show that in those parts of Italy church dances were performed until 1560 and, despite the prohibition, at Loreto, in Ancona province, a great and magnificent church dance procession took place in 1609 in connexion with the canonization of Ignatius de Loyola. We shall return to this in the next chapter.

We shall now consider one of the most beautifully written legends of the

Middle Ages, *Del Tombeor Nostre Dame* (Our Beloved Lady's Dancer)'. It is written in a manuscript of about 1286 [Faerster] and treats of a jongleur, dancer and buffoon, who has wandered all over the world and in the end, tired of wandering, comes to the monastery of Claravallis (Clairvaux), into which he was admitted after giving away all he possessed. The language of the manuscript seems to show that the story is of much earlier origin, and Faerster thinks that it came from the Ile de France in the twelfth century. After admission to the monastery the jongleur noticed that it was not possible for him to participate in the prayers, songs and services of the monks, because he was so ignorant and could not read. Deeply depressed, he sought some means by which he could remedy this and at the same time serve the Holy Virgin. He found such a possibility one day when he was in the crypt of the minster of the monastery. In front of an image of the Virgin Mary on the altar in the crypt he had a sort of revelation that he might serve the Holy Virgin by dancing, and in a prayer to Mary he declared his purpose and dedicated his dancing skill to her service. He hastily undressed and threw away all his clothes and began to dance. He bowed low before the Madonna 'Most beauteous Queen and beloved Lady, do not despise my art and my service. With God's help I shall serve thee in faith and with all my strength.' Then he began to dance with small graceful steps to right and left, sometimes with longer and higher steps. During this dance he performed the Metz dance, the French hop dance, the Champagne hop dance, the Spanish, Loraine and English hop dances. To these he added the Roman hop dance. He addressed prayers to the Madonna and begged her not to scorn his efforts, but to accept them. Then he danced on his hands and spun his feet in the air, whilst tears streamed from his eyes. Now he had become Her player and dancer. When the monks held divine service and read their mass he danced to the Madonna in the crypt. Always he danced until he was exhausted, even to unconsciousness, and after clothing himself he again showed his reverence for Mary. His behaviour was discovered by a prying brother, who informed the Abbot. Both descended one day into the crypt and through a peep-hole watched what happened. There they saw how, when the jongleur had danced until he was completely exhausted and lay unconscious on the ground, the Virgin Mary descended to him in all her glory in a robe of red and gold set with brilliant jewels. She was followed by the hosts of angels and archangels and all of them, with Mary at the head, were at pains to bring him refreshment and solace. Finally Mary gave him her blessing and made the sign of the Cross over him.

This miracle the Abbot and the other spectator witnessed several times. The Abbot not only permitted the jongleur to continue his dancing, but also expressly assured him that in this way he served God and the Virgin just as well as did the other brethren by their masses, songs and prayers. But finally he danced himself to death, and in the hour of his death the Virgin Mary and the angels again descended to him and Mary took his spirit in her arms and guided him, followed by the angels, to Paradise. After his death the jongleur was designated a holy man and was buried in the church with great solemnity. His grave was regarded as the monastery's most precious relic.

Later on we shall hear of another jongleur, the holy Gontran, whose relics are also treasured and revered.

This touching story of an ignorant but God-fearing man shows what could be regarded during those centuries as natural and reasonable, as something which could have happened and perhaps sometimes did happen. The words of the Holy Father of the Church, Ambrose, come back to mind: 'Everything is proper which is done in fear of the Lord'.

8. *The Dance of the Coptic Church*

The Coptic Christian Church appeared after the Council of Calcedon in 451 as a separatist movement within Christianity, ascribing to Christ only a divine nature. It founded its liturgy on the Alexandrine rites, with the support of St Cyril, St Basileios, and St Gregory of Nazianzus. In this church the sacral dance has been preserved in all probability from the earliest times, and to this day exists in full operation in the Abyssinian section. It is certainly remarkable that the liturgy goes back to Basileios and Gregory of Nazianzus, both of whom were, as we have seen, upholders of the solemn sacral dance.

It seems, according to Rey, that there are two main occasions in the ecclesiastical year when dances are performed in the Abyssinian church: the September festival in connexion with the recovery of the Cross by the Empress Helena, and the January festival for the blessing of the water. The former, the so-called Maskal festival, is celebrated from the 21st to the 27th September, and priestly dances are performed on the first and last days; the latter, the so-called Temkat festival, is celebrated the 18th–20th January, and on these days too the priests dance. Rey describes these dances as follows: 'First there is low-pitched singing without musical accompaniment, to which soldiers and their officers beat time with their weapons. Then come the cymbals and finally the big drums. Meantime the long line of priests advances and retires and others turn first to one side and then to another, swaying their bodies to the rhythm of the music. More and more people join the dance, the tempo quickens and voices are raised to a climax. Then there is a sudden stop; all are silent and the long rows of priests are still. Then the Bible is read.'

Lüpke describes divine service in Northern Abyssinia on festival days. The church is commonly surrounded by a protected area, sometimes with graves and sometimes with rights of asylum. It is here that divine service is held on festivals, mainly to provide sufficient room.

The author describes such a service in the Zion church in Aksum. The priests sang songs and performed dance-like movements, partly in the open and partly in the church porch. Priests and deacons grouped themselves in a ring, in the centre of which were two pairs or two groups of three, each group closely followed by a deacon, who beat a drum. They then performed a sort of counter-dance, resembling a quadrille: *en avant*, *en arrière*, *traversez*, *chassez, croisez*. All the other priests sway the upper body in rhythm with the drums, whilst raising or lowering their crooks and sistra. In much the same way McCreagh describes a dance during divine service before the Emperor of Abyssinia. The intoned music seemed extremely old-fashioned, and employed quarter and half tones. Anstein notices a similar priestly dance in honour of the angels in heaven in Fidsche. Towards the end of the dance all members of the congregation joined in.

The German expedition to Aksum [Littmann] describes a church festival on January 13th, 1906, probably in honour of the expedition. The bassoons blared and the spectators thronged round the church. Below the steps of the crypt stood the priests, whilst they, together with choir boys, pages and soldiers, crowded the steps. The remainder of the churchyard was filled with visiting priests and members of the public. The choristers and deacons participating were costumed in magnificent mass robes and bore three heavy golden crowns on their heads; some priests stood beneath great sunshades of red silk—all gifts of the Emperor. When the bassoons were silent the priests began to sing, at first simply and slowly, with peculiar Abyssinian cadences. Then they sang in Old Ethiopian a song of greeting:

> Aksum is a much esteemed city;
> The great of the earth have entered it.
> The people of Jerusalem (Europe) have honoured us with a visit,
> From far Germany they have come to us.

When the priests paused the bassoons blared again. Then the song of the priests became more lively; the leader sang louder and louder; the choir joined in with vigour. Then began the dance; the couples danced to the same rhythm as the song, advancing towards each other and then retiring or changing places.

Swedish travellers describe the Abyssinian sacral dance similarly. It is mentioned by Siwertz and is further described by Virgin. The latter happened to be present at the Festival of the Cross from September 22nd to 28th. A great amphitheatrical platform had been erected on a hillside and the Imperial throne was placed at its top. The Emperor and family and the higher priesthood, foreign ambassadors and the highest dignitaries of the land sat upon the platform. At the foot of the hill was an open space, covered with flowers. At a sign from the Emperor there entered hundreds of priests and clergy in procession, dressed in splendid costumes carrying images of the saints, crosses and censers. Gold-braided and gold-embroidered red and blue parasols were borne behind the church dignitaries. Divine service began with a mass, which was followed by songs from children's choirs and a recital of the legend of Helena and the Cross. Then appeared ten priests carrying long staffs tipped with crosses; to the accompaniment of their songs and to the sound of cymbals and drums, a dance began, consisting of set figures with bowing and gentle genuflexions. It was the same dance, it was said, as David had once danced before the Ark of the Covenant. After the dance there was a children's chorus and a mass by three priests, whereupon the Abuna (the High Chief of the Abyssinian Church) arose and preached a short sermon, concluding with the blessing of the Emperor, his house and his subjects.

One circumstance should be noted: the remarkable similarity between this dance and that of the (probably) Christianized sect of the Therapeutæ described in detail by Philo Judaeus. It is not improbable that the ceremonies of the Coptic church may have direct roots in the dances of the early Christian church.

VII

Popular Church Dances

SIDE by side with the sacral church dances there existed church dances of a purely popular character, i.e., dances in which only members of the congregation took part. The distinction, however, is not particularly sharp, for the Church, at least locally, permitted these dances and the priests were present; indeed it frequently happened that these popular dances were organized as part, and even as an essential part, of the Church festivals. By no means infrequently the dancers were appointed by the Church authorities and danced at their instigation. The distinction between the popular and the church dance, therefore, is very fine, and in what follows we shall designate as 'popular' those which were performed by members of the congregation or by dancers appointed *ad hoc*, but in which the clergy did not themselves take part. The abundant material is here classified according to countries of origin. We should note, however, that because we have little knowledge of the extent to which these dances at one time flourished, or even still flourish in certain countries, the fact of their existence is not excluded. It only proves that the material preserved in various publications is scanty.

1. *Spain*

The so-called 'Jazgo Law' reveals that in Spain during the seventh century there were nocturnal festivals and night watches with offerings and dances. In this body of law, according to Capmány, the dancers are threatened with punishment. Conditions are here exactly the same as in the rest of the Christian world. But Spain is the country in which the religious dance flourished more abundantly and most vigorously. It is there that it has been best preserved into our own time and there it has remained almost completely under the control of the Church and its authorities.

Capmány has left an illuminating account of the evident purpose of the popular church dance in the divine service of the fourteenth century. In the year 1313 a number of Christian men and women kept watch in the Church of St Bartholomew in Saragossa, when a Jewish scholar Solomon, a surgeon of Ejea, began to perform a dance, 'as was proper' and took the lead over the Christians. Then this scholar was accused of deliberately blaspheming the mass at the altar, because, being a Jew, he had led the dance. Having regard to the gravity of this accusation, which was supported by the Jews themselves, it was demanded that he be condemned to death. Luckily for the Jewish dancer, sentence was left to the civil authorities, who only inflicted a fine [Arch. d. Maestro d. R. Patrimonio Barcelona No. 1688, fol. 83–96; anno 1313].

Much later, in 1777, the Government sought by Royal decree to forbid dancing at solemn festivals either before the images of the saints or in the churches or in their porches or in churchyards. This Royal command, as we shall see, was completely ignored, for dancing was much too firmly established in custom, in early Christian beliefs and in the writings of the Fathers. Moreover, in that century the old Christian custom was prevalent by which young girls danced at night watches, before the festival of the Holy Virgin, at the doors of the churches of St Mary, and then spent the night dancing and singing hymns and psalms in honour of the Virgin [Bonnet].

In the far-famed and much visited place of pilgrimage, Montserrat, the pilgrims were wont, at least from the thirteenth century, to keep their night watches in the monastery Church of St Mary, and they passed the time singing and dancing. Their songs, however, were far from devout; they were repulsive and indecent. Since it was not possible to uproot the desire to dance, the monks of Montserrat themselves composed religious dancing songs for the use of the pilgrims [Spanke]. A codex of the fourteenth century, preserved in the monastery, conveys the following information, 'since the pilgrims sometimes during a watch night service in the church of St Mary in Montserrat wish to sing and dance (*tripudiare*), as also in the market-place in the daytime, several songs of different kinds have been composed for the purpose' [Villanueva]. The pilgrimages to this monastery were in honour of the image of the Virgin Mary in the monastery church, and the songs therefore concerned Her, and took the form of ballads, virelais, etc. Songs about death also occurred [Ursprung], and may perhaps signify that some of the pilgrims also wished, with the help of the Virgin, to be cured of serious diseases.

Sánchez Cantón mentions that Basque and Galician sailors even today perform a sort of sword dance in front of the images of the Virgin and Her Saints. In an account of travels in the Basque provinces, published in 1929, Harispe mentions the existence of such popular dances in the twentieth century. Here vespers usually excite more enthusiasm than the High Mass, and

this enthusiasm is especially kindled by the singing of the Magnificat.*
Every verse of the song to the Virgin is followed by the ringing of six small
bells and beats on six tambourines, in honour of the Queen of Heaven.
During the singing some youths danced a quick-step with 'reverent' hopping
in the porch of the church.

Marienantiphon Herimanns des Lahmen in freier Sequenzform

FIG. 28. 'Hail, Queen of Mercy'. By Herrimann of Reichenau, 1013–1054. It was the closing song in
the dance procession of the Hopping Saints of Echternach [Besseler].

In certain congregations in the district of Nules, Castellón de la Plana, on
the east coast of Spain, north of the Valencia district, Christmas Eve was
celebrated by throngs around a fire which was kindled in the market place
outside the church. These throngs sang and danced. Some parishes in
Mallorca celebrate St John the Baptist on Midsummer Eve. Men and women
dance through the streets to the music of a shawm, played by a man in clothes
of grass representing St John the Baptist [Capmány].

But it was especially the festival of Corpus Christi which in Spain was
associated with religious dances, and there was not a single Corpus Christi
procession but was accompanied by dancing. This dance is said to symbolize
the triumphs which, according to sacred legend and biblical texts, were once
celebrated, though occasionally we must admit that there were other symbolical notions.

The blessed Juan de Avila, the Apostle of Andalusia (died 1569),
relates how in those processions the Holy Sacrament must be reverenced.
He adds, 'Let the priests swing their censers, may laymen dance before

---

* The Magnificat is the song of praise of Mary, which she sang on her visit to Elizabeth in the
house of Zacharias, after the Annunciation. Its name derives from the opening words. This
so-called evangelical hymn of praise reproduces Luke I, 46–55. Also at the celebration of the
Festivals of Fools and the Feast of the Innocents, the climax was reached with the singing of the
Magnificat. 'The Lord hath cast down from their Thrones,' etc.

them in innocent joy, as David danced before the Ark'. And Hernando de Talavera, the first Archbishop of Granada (died 1507), adds, 'Moorish dances may precede the Holy Sacrament in the Corpus Christi procession, as also on other solemn occasions'.

Let us just glance at some of the dances which were still performed in 1931 in the Corpus Christi processions.

FIG. 29. The Eagles of Valencia, 1855. They accompanied the Corpus Christi procession in Barcelona and entered the churches, where, during Mass, they danced before the altar. They are said to represent St John the Evangelist [Capmány].

In Barcelona the Dance of the Eagles is the favourite of all the religious dances, and there is scarcely a single religious or profane festival at which they do not appear, but this is more especially the case with the Corpus Christi procession. These eagles perform a special dance both in the procession and later inside the church at divine service. The performance takes place in the choir, and the eagles are thought to represent St John the Baptist, who from early Christian days had the eagle as his symbol. In the year 1603 we read, 'the Eagle advances to the altar and dances there'. But in 1753 the custom was suppressed by the Bishop of Barcelona. Nevertheless the eagle has survived in Barcelona, Valencia, Mallorca and in the district of Polensa in the Balearic Islands. We reproduce two pictures (Figs. 29 and 30), one of which shows two eagles—there are always two—from about 1855, the other a pair from modern times. Formerly they were completely dressed as birds and wore head masks. Nowadays they are normally somewhat banal girls carrying before them models of an eagle [Capmány].

Both in the Corpus Christi procession and at various other Church festivals there were 'Giants' (Fig. 31) and 'Dwarfs' (Fig. 32). In Barbastro [Palamedes], for example, in Palencia Cathedral [Rosa], Burgos [Capmány], and Santiago di Compostela, where they also appeared in connexion with the festival for the Patron Saint of the city, the Apostle St James [Palamedes]. They always entered the church dancing [Capmány], and did so in many other churches as late as the beginning of the twentieth century [Rosa]. The custom dates back to the seventeenth century. Thus in 1616, in Madrid, was celebrated the translation of the monastery Encarnacion by a great pro-

FIG. 30. The Eagles in the 1930's. At Polensa, Mallorca, two girls appeared, clad in a special costume and carrying an eagle's head. They danced in the Corpus Christi procession and in the church [Capmány].

cession in which men and women took part, dressed as giants [Capmány]. These giants and dwarfs wore enormous head masks of papier-maché, the former on long poles, enveloped in mantles, the latter wearing them on their heads. They are said to represent the devils who flee at the sight of the body of our Lord or of the relics, or they may represent idolatry and heresy driven out by godliness. Another interpretation is that they illustrate how everything great and small is subject to Divine Providence. This latter must be regarded as a misinterpretation. In the year 1780 there was issued a Royal edict decreeing that in future there should be no Dance of the Giants and that they might not take part in church processions. But evidently the decree was not observed.

Villanueva describes the processional dance with which the Archbishop of Tarragona was received after his enthronement. The whole of the Cathedral Chapter was sent to a place just outside the town, where the Archbishop and all the priests mounted their mules, which were hung with black saddle cloths down to their hooves. The priests were robed in long, splendid caftans and wore Spanish collars and low, round hats, from which a richly embroidered ribbon and tassels hung down upon the chest. By degrees the procession reached the San Carlo gate. Here it was joined by the civic authorities and the Archbishop received the numerous dancers and players and their respectful addresses, as well as those of more eminent personages. All then sat down, and the Archbishop took the oath at an altar which had been erected at the entrance to the monastery of St Francis. Then all the dancers danced in front of the procession. On arrival at the cathedral they

99

FIG. 31. Giants. They executed dancing movements in the Corpus Christi procession at Barcelona in 1860. Sometimes they entered the church dancing. In the background we glimpse the priestly members of the procession.

were met by members of the Chapter dressed in their copes. The dancers might, however, be supplemented by the so-called Titans, also a kind of giant. There were thirty or forty of them dressed in Turkish costumes. The Titans moved only their heads, bending them to one side or the other as if in sorrow or discontent, whilst each in turn hopped in time with the music, which consisted of a simple melody on two clarinets or oboes. The major processions of the clergy, mounted on horses or mules, have been known since at least the sixteenth century [Baronius].

In Onna there was another processional dance on the occasion of the Corpus Christi festival. The procession moved off from the church and around the Sacrament danced twelve youths, grouped in twos, on each side. When the procession started they knelt before the Sacrament and then began their dance, advancing among the devout spectators. They danced in a somewhat more rapid tempo ahead of the procession. After a while they turned and, as it were, flew back to the Sacrament and knelt down before it. Then the dance began again; it was a sort of hopping dance, a real 'tripudium'. Backward and forward they swayed and knelt before the Sacrament. It reminds us again of David's dance before the Ark [Krier].

In Alaro, a small town in the Balearic Isles, there was a church dance, of which the record is preserved in a statement of Archduke Salvator. It celebrated the Ascension of the Virgin Mary on August 15th, and was partly processional, the ceremony being repeated the following day. The per-

F𝙸𝙶. 32. The Dwarfs or the little Giants. They danced in the Corpus Christi procession at Burgos, Santiago di Compostela, Oviedo, etc. Sometimes the dancers entered the churches [Capmány].

formers were six youths who were called *les cosiers*, who might be described as a kind of chorister, in which case the dance might be classified as a sacral church dance. Three of them were clad in white, adorned with coloured ribbons and carrying flower-decorated birettas; one was dressed as the Virgin, and two as devils with horns and cloven feet. They formed up in the church immediately after vespers. The Virgin walked in front; occasionally the other five made a caper. In the market-place and at cross-roads the procession halted and the six *cosiers* executed a dance. When the procession returned and re-entered the church a dance was performed around the image of the Virgin. On the following day, which was the local Saint's day, the *cosiers* danced in front of the high altar [Vuillier]. It is clear that the Virgin represented Mary, the three youths in white the angels, and the remaining two are expressly described as devils. The meaning of this mystery play is clearly that the Virgin Mary, after the Ascension, obtained heavenly bliss and as the above-quoted hymns show, joined in the Dance of the Angels and overcame the lurking devils.

At the Corpus Christi festival in Valencia there was a processional dance, introduced by the blessed Juan di Rivera, who died in 1611 and who wished to enhance the splendour of the festival. The dances were executed by men and children, to the accompaniment of a sort of motet, which always ends with the refrain '*toro, toro*' (bull, bull), suggesting the allegorical dance. The children are represented as fighting the devil as toreadors; they are threatened and attacked by the devils and pretend from time to time to seek refuge in the accompanying Sacrament.

In the seventeenth century these dances were also performed inside the churches before the altar and monstrance. The dress of the children was

Fig. 33. Ribbon Dance. This dance is performed in a number of places in Spain at Church festivals, in front of, or inside, the churches. The dance seen above takes place in front of a church in Tenerife [Capmány].

'biblical': white costume and gold edging, a bright red sash with ribbons and rosettes round the waist, white sandals, long hair, plaited and parted in the middle in Nazarene fashion, as they called it, and wreaths of flowers on their heads. There are not usually more than four children. Although nothing is said on the point, one may assume that the men dancers were the 'bulls', i.e., the devils. It would appear to represent the struggle between the angels and the devils, between good and evil, with the help and protection of the Saviour. In the eighteenth century this dance ceased [Rosa].

The dance *las faixes* (ribbon dance) is performed in a number of places in the district of Maldá, in the province of Lerida, in the bishopric of Tarragona (Fig. 33). It is performed at the festival of Macarius on January 2nd. The number of dancers is twenty-four. They wear a ribbon secured to their wrists and they move in time with the music of two flutes and a drum. During service in the church and when the Credo has finished and prayers to the Sacrament are in progress, the doors of the church are opened and the dancers enter to the sound of music. From the right hand of the leader of the dancers a ribbon is released. The same operation is then performed by the other dancers. These ribbons are then placed on the altar as an offering to the Saint's relics. Then the dancers retire in order, each one passing under the ribbon on his left hand. There follows a procession into the open to the accompaniment of various dances and figures [Capmány].

There are also other ribbon dances generally named *los cintos*, but having other local names. Thus the Valencia dance is called 'the Pomegranate', because of the appearance of the figure which is formed when the ribbons are unfurled from the top of the pole to which they are fixed. In Catalonia the dance is called a 'gypsy dance', because it is usually performed by gypsies.

The number of dancers depends upon the number of ribbons. From a high pole are suspended multi-coloured ribbons. Each dancer seizes a ribbon in one hand and dances round the pole, winding the ribbon around him and then unwinding it. In Elche (Alicante) this dance, called 'Granada', is danced inside the church, where a high platform is erected on which the priests also have their seats (Fig. 34). There is a musical accompaniment and the dancers play castanets. During the dance the performers sing:

> Of men we may praise
> Their deeds and their prayers,
> Both of which lead on
> To heavenly Zion.

When the winding process is finished and the unwinding is about to begin this song is intoned:

> In the sweet name of Jesus
> We wind ourselves in ribbons;
> From them we shall be freed
> By Mary's holy name.   [Capmány.]

In the little town of Yacca, in the province of Huesca, the patron saint of the town, Santa Orosia, is celebrated in dances. These dances are also performed at the watch-night services before the festivals, and are repeated on the day of the Apostolic Prince, St Peter. There are six dancers and they are called 'St Orosia's dancers'. They are clad, according to Palamedes, in white sandals with black ribbons, white stockings, white knee breeches, white shirts and red stole, with gold edges which pass over the left shoulder and under the right shoulder. During the dance they rap the castanets or similar instruments, old-fashioned string instruments and flutes covered with snake skin. The dance begins in the western porch of the church. In 1895 it was performed by two boys, three youths and an older man. Rosa thinks that the church dance is scarcely older than modern times. It first came into use when the population first saw the Saint's relics when they were translated from the mountain on which she suffered martyrdom.

Rosa describes the flute as an old-fashioned shepherd's pipe, and the string instrument as a kind of psalter with six strings which are struck with a small drumstick. The dance is performed on June 25th, which is the day of the finding of the relics. When King Alphonso visited the cathedral of Yacca in September, 1903, the St Orosia dancers performed before him.

In Catalonia, especially in Castelltersol, in the province of Barcelona, during the last week of August, dances have been performed in front of the Consistory Palace since olden times. There are six couples who dance *El Ball del Ciri*, the 'Candle Dance', so called because formerly they used to hold candles in their hands. The dancers are clad in bright colours, and wear the Catalan mantle and tall black hats. The dance is solemn, and symbolizes the translation of the patron saint Victor and his companion St Ætius. They

FIG. 34. Pomegranate and Ribbon Dance. Interior of the church at Elche, Alicante, 1912. A large platform is erected, surrounded by numerous spectators. On it stand the dignitaries of the church. The pomegranate is suspended from the roof and from it spread out the ribbons which are used in the Ribbon Dance [Capmány].

were both bishops and were among the first missionaries to Spain, where they suffered martyrdom, probably in Barcelona. The six couples group themselves in the market place. The females of the first three couples each hold in their hands a *morratxa*, a curiously shaped and decorated glass bowl, filled with aromatic water and a sprig of artificial flowers. These bowls or chalices were intended to adorn the church altar beneath which the two Saints repose. The dance is performed by the women in a circular figure, surrounded by an outer circle of men. Then a hop dance is executed. The spectators are sprayed with aromatic water. Another candle dance was performed in the town of Maullen in the district of Vich at the festival of St Anthony the Hermit on January 17th. This dance originated at the end of the eighteenth century [Capmány].

The four most important parishes of the town of Leon have from early times been under an obligation to equip a number of girls for a church dance. This was performed annually in connexion with a great festival for some historic saint. The four groups of little girls are dressed in silk and brocade and adorned with ornaments of gold and silver, pearls and jewels. Each group consists of twelve girls aged from ten to twelve years, and they are conducted in procession to the church. This procession is very ceremonious and consists of the notabilities of the four parishes, with the mayors, councillors and priests. It enters the church and advances to the high altar, whilst the girls dance. When the procession enters the church, divine service is already in progress and is interrupted by the music and din of the procession.

After reverence has been made before the altar the girls again dance in the middle of the choir to the singing of a psalm. The four groups dance in turn and the girls then advance to the altar, at the side of which the Bishop sits in his robes. They kiss his ring and receive the blessing, after which they dance, two by two, down the choir steps. Evensong is similarly celebrated with dancing. The following day there is another great procession through the town, and the girls dance again [Capmány].

In the valleys of Albaida, Onteniente, Játiva and Cocentaina, and many valleys around Valencia, a special dance is performed on the eve of the great Church festivals, such as, for example, the festival of the Virgin Mary in September. We may confidently assert that these dances are reminiscent of the old vigil dances. Here *la donsaina* and *el tabalet* proceed through the streets and wherever a door is unlocked they have the right of entry. If a woman is found within she is led by the hand into the street and may not refuse to take part in the dance. During the dance the frivolous song *las foliès* is sung, a name which indicates that it consisted of foolish trifles. In spite of the gaiety of the song and dance, says Capmány, the great church festival of the following day is foreshadowed.

In Mallorca there is a dance called *cociés*, in which six or seven dancers perform. Four of them are the *cociés*, one represents *la dama* and one or two are devils (Fig. 36). It need scarcely be added that *la dama* is the same as Notre Dame, Our Lady, or the Virgin Mary. The four *cociés* are dressed in white breeches, silk belts and silk shoes. Belts are hung from the lower edges of the breeches and on their heads they wear cylindrical, gilt hats, wreathed with flowers. *La dama* appears as a shepherdess (though played by a man) dressed in a mantle and train and ruffs, all in white; on her head is a straw hat, with brilliant red ribbons and flowers on either side.

Fig. 36. A Fallen Angel. From a group appearing as devils dancing in the Corpus Christi procession at Lorca, Murcia [Capmány].

The devils are dressed in coarse cloth, draped with many-coloured ribbons. They are wrapped in dark cloaks; on their faces they wear loathsome masks with horns attached and they also wear black hairy tails. On their costumes hang bells and in their hands they carry long iron rods or tubes of agave.

The seven dancers are accompanied by musicians dressed as Mallorcan shepherds, playing guitars and beating drums. During mass in the church and the offertory *la dama* dances up the nave to the altar. The remaining dancers remain stationary at the porch. Then *la dama* dances back to them, fetches one of the *cociés* and leads him, dancing, to the high altar. This she repeats with the others, i.e., dances up and down seven times [Capmány]. It is evident that this church dance relates to the Virgin Mary; it was probably performed on the eve of Mary's ascension.

A very curious church dance has been preserved in Seville. On Innocents' Day, December 28th, the very day of the election of the Innocents' Bishop to the accompaniment of choristers' dances, or at the Festival of Fools with its blasphemous dancing orgies, there was celebrated in Seville a dancing festival which was called *Christians' Spring*. It is in reality a dance of fools. The troop consists of twelve male fools and one female. The latter must be fat and strong, wearing great ear-rings and bracelets of gilded brass. The whole quadrille is dressed in white. The dancers appear in short coats, adorned with ribbons and richly embroidered. Around their waists they wear Moorish girdles. On their costumes are fixed innumerable crosses, amulets and relics, and in their hats are diadems of glass and chains and coloured plumes. The dance is accompanied by castanets. At the mass which precedes the procession, and which is celebrated in a chapel in a vineyard, or near an olive mill, both the population and the fools take part. During the mass itself the fools dance around the inside of the porch [Capmány]. This dance is without any doubt a poor and confused relic of the earlier Festival of Fools.

2. *Portugal*

Castil-Blaze gives a description of a dancing procession in Lisbon in 1610. The occasion of the festival was the canonization in that year of the Cardinal and Archbishop of Milan, Carl Borromeus, who died in 1584. His canonization was celebrated in the same way in numerous other places. On the day of the festival a richly ornamented boat approached the port of Lisbon. In this boat, under a magnificent baldequin, stood an image of the Cardinal. All the boats in the harbour went to meet it. On disembarkation the image was received by all the church and civil dignitaries and also by members of the church congregation. In a great procession it was then conducted to the cathedral. In the procession were four enormous waggons richly decorated with symbolic representations of Milan, Portugal, Honour and the Church. Around these four waggons troops of dancers and actors performed dances which gave a symbolic representation of the life of the Saint.

3. *Italy*

There is also an account from Italy of similar popular church processions of dancers. This account is given by Castil-Blaze, after Menestrier, and thus originates in the seventeenth century. In 1609 there was celebrated in Loreto, in the province of Ancona, the canonization of the Jesuit General Ignatius de Loyola, who died in 1556. On the day before the festival, which represented the Trojan War, a play was performed in front of the church of Notre Dame de Loreto. This church is of very special interest, because it is supposed to contain the house in which the Virgin Mary dwelt when she received the Annunciation. On the market place had been erected the city and walls of Troy. Thither was conducted the famous giant horse, filled with Jesuits and surrounded by dancers, and the Trojan War was re-enacted. The following day four richly decorated vessels ran into the port, with numerous dancers and musicians on board. Each of the vessels had its own 'ambassador' conveying gifts to the canonized Loyola, as well as offerings of thanks. After disembarkation the ambassadors took their place in the four waggons and were taken in procession to the Jesuit college, followed by three hundred mounted Jesuits in Grecian costume. Four troops of dancers, representing the four quarters of the globe, and clad accordingly, danced around the waggons.

In Italian churches there were dances also at weddings, and these were excepted from the decrees against church dancing issued in Ancona in 1560, being permitted by day or night, as desired. But this exception shows that wedding dances in churches must have been so extraordinarily common and were so beloved by the people, that it was dangerous to forbid them.

4. *England*

In England various kinds of church dances have been performed from very early days. In the sixteenth century, during the reign of Queen Elizabeth, men and women danced to the music of pipes and drums both inside and outside churches, and in churchyards [Chambers]. In the seventeenth century students and servants in York were even obliged to dance in the nave of the cathedral on Shrove Tuesday [Anonymous, 1871]. In the whole of the county of Yorkshire it was also usual at Christmas to dance in country churches to the cry of 'Yole, Yole' (Christmas: Yule) [Gougaud]. In England, however, dancing in churches was on various occasions forbidden. In Wiltshire there was another ancient custom, according to which the inhabitants of Wishford and Batford met every year and danced in Salisbury Cathedral [Anonymous. 1871].

5. *France*

According to Stieren there was a dance procession in the little village of Percquencourt, in the district of Douai, as late as the beginning of the sixteenth century. It was performed in connexion with the festival of St Aegidius on September 1st. Aegidius lived as a hermit outside Arles and died by accident in 725. He was one of the fourteen relievers and was especially invoked in cases of severe spiritual need, but he was also the patron of epilepsy and cramps. In his procession a large number of clerics and musicians took part, the latter playing all sorts of instruments. To what extent laymen participated we do not know with certainty, but the procession was forbidden because of the abuses which had begun to creep in.

On April 28th, the anniversary of St Vitalis, patron of the cathedral of Evreux, who suffered martyrdom under Nero, there was a dance procession in that city. The procession was led by the clergy in their robes, and proceeded to a little wood just outside the city, where the priests gathered green twigs, which were then borne by the participating parishioners. The procession, dancing, then returned to the church, where the images of the saints were decorated with the twigs. During the next three days the lower clergy conducted the church services, whilst between services the higher clergy played skittles on the church roof. In the church itself there was public dancing and the dances were at one and the same time both sacral and popular church dances. There was a similar dance procession at Châlons-sur-Marne on Midsummer Eve [Stieren].

Until as late as the seventeenth century the parishioners danced in the choir of the church at Limoges [Martene]. The dance was for St Martial, the apostle of Limousin and Aquitania. He was one of the seven bishops who were sent from Rome to Gaul in the time of Decius, about the year 250, to preach the gospel [Buchberger]. He is invoked against the plague, epidemics and general misfortune. When highly placed persons such as Kings or Princes of France came on a pilgrimage to Limoges the reliquary containing his relics was exhibited for the reverence of the faithful. After 1526 the reliquary was exhibited every seventh year [Segange]. The festival in his honour was celebrated on June 30th and July 1 [Stadler]. At the festival the parishioners danced a kind of ring-dance in the choir, whilst the congregation sang the psalms appropriate to the service, but at the end of each verse of the psalm there was a refrain in which the congregation joined:

> Holy Martial, pray for me
> And I will dance here for thee [Bonnet].

But according to Cahusac, Menestrier—himself a Jesuit—states in his work on the dance (1682) that the priests also took part in this choir dance of the congregation.

From olden times until as late as 1913 there was a processional dance at Barjol on January 16th, the festival of the Patron of the church, St Marcel, who was Pope from 304 to 309. He was martyred because he refused to lay down the pontificate and pray to false gods. When his relics were translated to Cluny it is possible that his intestines were given to Barjol for preservation. At any rate an old legend has it so [Bérenger-Féraud]. On the eve of the festival and just at the end of divine service the priest rose from his seat, and those whom he had invited grouped themselves around him, holding hands. Then all together danced for a short time before they left the church. The following day the festival of St Marcel was celebrated with an imposing divine service. It was then that the *danso dei tripettos* (the dance of the small intestines) was performed by the congregation. During the solemn mass the sacred songs were interrupted at a given moment and the whole congregation sang:

> We shall have them, the small intestines;
> The small intestines, we shall have them.
> The small intestines of St Marcel!

Hereupon the mothers lifted up their small children and let them kick their legs as if dancing. The older children were then exhorted to dance and the parents executed rhythmic movements in accompaniment. The performance became more and more intense until finally the whole congregation sang the *'Dei tripettos'* [Gougaud, Bérenger-Féraud].

Immediately after divine service the procession set out at the slowest possible pace. It was thought that the longer the procession lasted the more fruitful the coming year would be, and the fewer would be the misfortunes befalling the participators. From time to time the hymns and psalms sung in the procession were interrupted for the singing of '*Dei tripettos*', whilst the whole procession performed a rhythmic dance. Formerly, says Bérenger-Féraud, an ox was led in the procession, which was afterwards slaughtered and eaten; the entrails especially were eaten by the children. But the actual meal was consumed only on the following day, which was the appointed festival of St Anthony the Hermit. At this festival most of the betrothals of the neighbourhood were effected.

In all the churches in Bordeaux, Palm Sunday was celebrated by a church dance. Just at the moment in the mass when the lessons had been read and the organ played the psalm, as late as the nineteenth century the mothers let the small children hop, and finally the whole congregation was hopping too [Bérenger-Féraud].

At the festival of the patron saint of the little town of Arcs, near Draguignan, it was usual to arrange a procession in such a way that at certain stations the children performed a kind of dance. This custom continued until the end of the nineteenth century [Bérenger-Féraud].

In a number of districts in Provence it was the usual custom to allow the children either on Easter or Midsummer Eve, and sometimes at Corpus Christi, or Ascension Day, to wear shoes for the first time. Wearing their shoes the children were then carried to mass in the church. When the bells rang out the mothers set the children down on the ground and held their hands while they hopped. At the same time those older children who were late in learning to walk were allowed to hop [Bérenger-Féraud].

Bérenger-Féraud describes another church dance for children in Roquebrussanne, near Brignoles. This dance began towards the end of the mass for the celebration of the patron of the church. Here too we find the children who have been late in learning to walk. With their children in their arms the mothers take their places in front of the altar of the Christ-child, and sing:

> Hop on the right foot,
> Hop on the left foot!
> My dear Jesus!
> Hop on both feet!

The words of the song are illustrated by gestures or by the hopping of the children, as the mothers hold them by the hand.

In Brittany in the seventeenth century boys and girls danced in the numerous small chapels on the anniversaries of the various saints. Cambry, who undertook a journey in these districts in 1794, relates that he then, as also ten years earlier, saw dancing in chapels and churchyards near Brest [Gougaud].

One of the most magnificent Corpus Christi processions was inaugurated in 1462 in Aix, the capital of Provence. It was the pomp-loving King René I of Anjou who was its originator [Larousse]. In what follows I give the account which Castil-Blaze took from Menestrier. The primary purpose of the procession was to illustrate how the Christian religion with its pure light had dispersed the darkness of paganism. In the vast procession were included almost all the ancient deities: Saturn and Cybele, Mars and Minerva, Neptune and Amphytrite, Pan and Syrinx, Pluto and Proserpina, and many others. They were surrounded and led by fauns and dryads, tritons and the nymphs of Diana, who danced to the music of tambourines, castanets and other instruments. Then followed splendidly decorated waggons with other Olympian gods, and between them were groups of actors and dancers, large and small. Finally came the 'armed men' and the troops. Among the dancers were some representing devils, wearing black mantles with red flames and hung with hundreds of bells. Amidst them was a tall and powerful she-devil. All together they danced around Herod, tormenting and punishing him as he repeatedly attempted to escape. Others danced around a soul protected by an angel, but the angel finally triumphed over the demons, dancing and hopping with joy. Another group represented the Jews who danced around the Golden Calf. At the end came a large group representing Christ and His disciples, led by St Christopher in giant shape, followed by a group dressed as lepers. The dancers, both great and small, were dressed in bizarre costumes and the 'armed men' performed weapon dances. The troops wound up the procession, but behind them all danced Death, armed with his scythe and having a terrifying countenance, as if chasing them all before him.

This brilliant Corpus Christi procession was repeated in Aix until the French Revolution, which swept it away with so many other things. But in the year 1805, or possibly 1806, this dance procession was revived and was executed in all its splendour in honour of Princess Pauline Borghese.

According to Sahlin, it is stated in the records of a visitation of the Bishop of Grenoble to the church of Vatillyon in 1399 that the pastor sent out by the bishop could not see the details of the church because it was so crowded with dancers at the celebration of a noble wedding. Consequently church wedding dances must have been very common in France in the later Middle Ages.

6. Belgium

During the eighteenth century the students of Huy's College, which is in the country just outside Liége, used to dance in the college chapel at the beginning of Lent [Gougaud].

A very big procession was formerly arranged in Liége in honour of the blessed Gontran. He is said to have been a jongleur—just like the sainted jongleur in the monastery of Clairvaux—who was converted to Christianity in 976 at the grave of St Lambert in Liége. Later he is said to have had a part in the building of the St Aegidius monastery there. This procession continued until the end of the eighteenth century. On the Wednesday after Midsummer Eve the deacon and canons went in procession from the St Lambert Church to the town hall, where they joined a large company of musicians. Then they went to the St Aegidius monastery, which is situated on a height outside the town. The Abbot then sent a saddled horse to meet the Deacon so that the difficult road to the monastery might be made easy for him. As soon as the Deacon was settled in the saddle the dance began. Hundreds of people danced back and forth along the whole of the road to the monastery— a dance which reminds us of the one which we shall see in Echternach. The musical instruments which were played were worthless home-made things; the music was false and painful to the ears; the dancers contorted themselves frenziedly, drawing up their legs and stamping upon the ground. They gave the impression, as the author whom we here follow says, of a hellish dance or a witches' sabbath. The dance melody may best be compared with a bear's dance or a march of camel drivers. In this manner the procession proceeded with drums and trumpets to the monastery church, and made the round of the altar which contained the relics of the blessed Gontran and St Aegidius. From the church it proceeded to the monastery garden, where the so-called *grande bourré*, or the great 'peasants dance', was danced. When the pilgrims had heard solemn mass, the procession returned to Liége. The musical instruments which had been played were hung up in the monastery church as votive gifts.

The various ritual instructions for this processional dance point certainly to an original demon-expelling significance. The loud music, the strident and bellowing instruments were the familiar means of expelling demons in pre-Christian and early Christian times. The violent movements of the dancers and their contortions all show that the original purpose of the dance procession was probably much the same as that which characterized the Echternach procession, i.e., the expulsion of demons in cases of epilepsy, possession and cramps. And it was just against these diseases, as well as madness and the pestilence, that St Aegidius was patron.

Probably from the Middle Ages, and certainly since the sixteenth century, a dance procession was held annually on Midsummer Eve in Sint-Jans-Meulenbeek, near Brussels. Nowadays Meulenbeek is within the city boundary of Brussels. The church is said to have been founded by St Gertrude in honour of God and St John the Baptist [Wauters]. A spring which was situated quite close to the church and of which the water was reputed to possess supernatural powers, and the soil of the churchyard surrounding the church, were also dedicated to St Gertrude, and thither came crowds of pilgrims on Midsummer Eve; so great, in fact, was the reputation of the spring that the number might reach sixty thousand. To the accompaniment of prayer the procession danced round the spring and the church. In the year 1399, when an infectious disease raged furiously, several miracles took place. St John the Baptist announced to a comatose child that whoever should creep three times round the church on his knees would for ever be protected against the ravages of the disease; the promise of immunity still holds, but only for one year, as we shall see when we meet this spring and church again in our account of the dance epidemics. Most people came to them for the healing of diseases of an epileptic character [Reinsberg-Düringsfeld]. As late as 1642 epileptics danced round this spring [Hdb. Deutsch. Volksk. I, 274], and the processions continued into the eighteenth century [Wauters].

On September 14th, the day of the raising of the Cross, a dance procession has been held in Tournay since olden times [Stieren]. At the beginning of the month about thirty neighbouring Flemish and French towns were invited, and at the same time a 'privilege' of Phillip IV was proclaimed, proclaiming that all who joined the procession at Tournay would receive free convoy for nine days for themselves and their belongings. This is a very old pilgrims' privilege. Enormous hosts streamed thither. The main procession was preceded by two smaller processions, one of them led by workmen with lanterns in their hands, entering the town at midnight, and the second setting out at four o'clock in the morning. The former is known from its occurrence on various occasions in the thirteenth century; the second was composed principally of citizens of Ghent, who proceeded with their own singers and musicians in order to offer a robe for the statue of the Virgin in the church. In the first place went the members of the ecclesiastical orders, followed by the cathedral chapter and members of a brotherhood carrying a precious reliquary containing relics of a number of saints. Then followed the members of various societies and associations. In later times pictures of religious scenes were also borne. At certain stations scenes from the story of Christ's passion were acted. As late as the seventeenth century people danced in the procession, though the dancing was confined to certain groups. In a regulation of 1554 it is laid down that the *fols saiges*, 'the foolish wise', may no longer participate in the dance in the St Martin church. In 1689 they were further forbidden to dance in the procession.

The dance of the citizens of Verviers bears the old name of *Creux d'Vervi*. The ceremonial was followed from the fourteenth century until 1794 [Neyen]. On the Tuesday of Whitsun week there arrived at the Amercoeur bridge in Liége a deputation from Verviers preceded by three men, one of whom bore the processional cross, on which was hung a small purse, while each of the other two bore a banner. The Mayor, the Councillors and the Pastor accompanied the procession. During the sixteenth century there were several thousands in the procession. The gates to the bridge were opened by the Mayor of Liége with special ceremonies, in the course of which the Mayor of Verviers declared that he had come to fulfil the obligations, entered into by his forefathers long ago, to the church and to St Lambert, to whom the church was dedicated. Then the procession proceeded through Liége, but on arrival at another bridge, the Pont des Arches, it stopped again, whilst the most recently married couple danced publicly. Thereupon the dancers dispersed in the town and awaited the morrow. On

Wednesday at 11 o'clock, at the end of a very solemn mass, the music announced that the people of Verviers were approaching the entrance to the church of St Lambert. They then entered and halted beneath the enormous crown suspended in the middle of the church, a crown which was dedicated to St Lambert. Then a ring was formed and they danced, or rather hopped, holding each other by the hand. During the whole of this time they held up the thumb of the left hand and occasionally lowered it whilst the whole congregation cried out, 'thumbs up! thumbs up!' After the dance they proceeded to the sacristy, where the church dignitaries were given the purse which had been brought for them, and in exchange they were given a purse of green silk containing a special incense, which on return to Verviers was to be burnt at the altar of the church of St Remacles. After their departure from the church they went in procession to the palace of the Bishop, and danced in front of it, continuing afterwards to the market place. There they were given by the town police the head of an ox, and when they arrived at the Pont des Arches the above-mentioned newly wedded couple set the head down; it was then cut to pieces and, to the accompaniment of renewed dancing, was thrown piece by piece into the river.

St Lambert is buried in this church; he was born in Maastricht and became the apostle of Toxandria; he was contemporary with, and a friend of, St Willibrord, whom we shall meet again in connexion with dance at Echternach. St Lambert was murdered in Liége in 705.

The Verviers dance has been variously interpreted. Neyen maintains that it was nothing but a solemn payment of tax due from the surrounding parishes to the church at Liége and merely expressed the satisfaction and friendly feeling of the taxpayers.

According to Hahn, Jacques de Hemricourt, born in 1333, gives an account of this Verviers dance. The dance was known at that time and it had to be performed from the city boundaries to the cathedral, where the offering was made. De Hemricourt emphasizes that every household in the neighbouring parishes was liable to send a representative and to pay one denier Tournois. A sixteenth-century text states that the dance must be performed under the giant crown and that the purse must be attached to the processional cross. But in the de Hemricourt account it is said that after the dance beneath the crown, the procession advanced to the choir and danced round the altar, whilst the tax was paid and the incense received. Thereupon all were obliged to take an oath to return the following year and dance beneath the crown. On leaving the church the cross was placed in the market place in a large barrel, together with grain seed, and it was around this that the dance continued. Detrooz mentions that in 1805 (according to Hahn) not only the pieces of ox-head were thrown into the river, but also the barrel and its contents.

Hahn quotes from a work by the Bishop of Waldecq from the beginning of the fourteenth century. In it we learn that the citizens of Verviers once upon a time received help from Liége during a terrible famine which sent the price of grain rising steeply and bringing false measures into use—an inch too little—and that the citizens of Verviers were the first to make a complaint. As a reward for this the people of Verviers were promised that they might return every year to Liége and form a dance procession. As a further reward they were freed from all taxes and had only to make a token payment at the time of the procession. It is thought that these events took place during the life of the Prince Bishop of Liége, Albert de Cuyck, between 1193 and 1200.

This explanation may be quite acceptable so far as the origin of the dance procession and the church dance is concerned, the more so since the purse attached to the processional cross only contained a token payment: a gold coin, a silver coin and a copper coin [Anonymous. 1871]. The inhabitants of Jupille, Amercoeur and St Pholien were under similar obligation to attend and dance with the citizens of Verviers beneath the great crown in the church of St Lambert.

To all this, however, there is much to be added: the dance of the newly wedded pair, the cross which is placed in a barrel with grain, the head of the ox and the barrel of grain sacrificed in the river—all during the performance of the dance—can scarcely be anything but old fertility rites, having the purpose of ensuring a richer harvest. We may assume that these parts of the ceremony are ritualistic and were added at a later date and interwoven with the original purely church ceremony. This was not quite certain, however, because the dance in the church evidently also has a magic significance. It is just of the kind which we have already seen as characteristic in promoting fertility, in making grain, hemp and flax grow tall and strong. It is noteworthy that according to legend this dance originated at the time of a raging famine. It therefore seems to me probable that all, or at least most, of the details of the ceremony are connected and originally had the purpose of preventing famine and promoting fertility. The ceremony of the purse seems to me quite banal: all pilgrims' processions have always had such purses or money-boxes containing a small offering to the church or saint to which or to whom the pilgrimage was made.

It is very remarkable that in Sweden there is a dance reminiscent in certain respects of the Verviers dance. There is a melody of an old fiddler of Dalum parish in Västergötland which went under the name of 'thumbs up'; it belongs to an action-dance which was often performed in the seventies of the last century. The dancers formed themselves into two groups facing each other in such manner that each group formed a ring, one inside the other. The members of the inner ring held up their thumbs to each other. When the melody of the dance reached its final notes there was a cry of 'thumbs up! thumbs up!', whereupon the outer ring advanced and took the place of the inner ring [N. Anderson]. It seems to me not impossible that this folk dance may be a relic of the Verviers dance transplanted to Sweden by immigrant Walloons.

The sacrifice of a beast at the Verviers dance is of great interest. We have seen such offerings at the dance in Barjol, where an ox was slaughtered and its intestines consumed. In the Corpus Christi procession in Marseilles, until the middle of the nineteenth century, according to Bérenger-Féraud, there was a fat ox in the middle of the procession; it was decorated with flowers and was ridden by a small boy dressed as John the Baptist. The ox and rider were surrounded by a group of children dressed as Hercules. Bérenger-Féraud thinks that the ox is a kind of memento of Celtic customs, according to which oxen were sacrificed on certain days to certain gods, the names of which 'are long since forgotten'.

The actual sacrifice of animals is far from unknown to the Christian religion. Reinsberg-Düringsfeld mentions that in Brabant, as late as 1850, on the festival of St Anthony the Hermit, a pig's head or a piece of bacon was offered; others offered what they could—chickens, ducks or pigeons. So also in Brabant the peasants used to offer calves at the festival of St Servatius. According to Andree, chickens were offered to St Valentine and St Vitus, the former in Marzoll, the latter in Goldegg. In the little Gothic chapel of St Vitus in Schwaz, chickens were offered in the sixteenth century; Pfleiderer mentions that in all the chapels of St Vitus the offering was usually of chickens, especially cocks, and this is supported by Doyé. The offerings of cocks to St Vitus were made by sufferers from cramp and epilepsy [Schultz]. Until the beginning of the nineteenth century one could see on St Vitus's day, June 15th, numerous pilgrims journeying to Riesengebirge from the districts round the Elbe, the Iser, etc., where offerings were made in the seven springs beneath the Schneeberg [Grohmann]. A similar custom existed at Hürthigheim in Alsace, where black cocks were offered to St Vitus on behalf of children suffering from cramp [Stoeber]. From ancient times the cock was regarded as a protection against, and an expeller of, demons.

7. Luxembourg

The hopping dance of the saints in Echternach is a tradition which has been preserved from the Middle Ages until our own day. This dance procession is held at Whitsuntide in honour of St Willibrord (Fig. 37). He was the apostle of the Frisians, became Bishop of Utrecht and founded what was soon to become the famous monastery of Echternach, where he died in 739. Very soon after his death he became the object of ever-increasing popular reverence; his relics were reputed to perform miracles, to effect cures of various diseases, especially cramps, and restored health in numerous cases [Acta Sanct.]. In his church at Echternach, beneath the altar of which his relics are preserved, there hung shortly after his death numerous votive offerings, consisting of iron chains, probably symbolizing deliverance from the fetters of the underworld, jars and all sorts of limbs made of wax [Stadler]. Numerous churches in Holland and Belgium, on the Rhine and on the Moselle, are dedicated to St Willibrord.

This procession has proceeded to Echternach annually since the four-teenth century and probably considerably earlier [Kurth]. In the *Acta*

Sanctorum we learn that certain authorities are of the opinion that it had its origin in the great dance epidemic of 1374. What is certain is that as early as the eighth century the church of St Willibrord in Echternach was the goal of great pilgrimages. The Abbot Thiofrid (1078–1110) relates how the church was full to overflowing with votive gifts, and adds 'In Whitsun week there come, not only from the neighbouring districts but also from France and Germany, according to ancient custom, . . . numerous persons with offerings and litanies and with great reverence to the dance of the saint'. The word

FIG. 37. St Willibrord. Miniature from *Vita Willibrordi* in Gotha, from the time of the Emperor Otto III, at the end of the tenth century [Künstle].

for 'dance' is *tripudium*, and early writers translated it by 'threshold', which as Martin correctly observes, is a quite ridiculous translation. *Tripudium* here certainly has its customary meaning of 'three-step dance'—for such in fact was the nature of the dance. It therefore seems to me quite certain that the dance at Echternach was performed as early as the eleventh century and earlier, and I shall show in another connexion that it even preceded the time of St Willibrord, only later being attached to his cult. A chronicler named Heinrich Brandt of Prüm, who wrote about 1628, mentions that under the Abbot Heinrich von Schönicken in Prüm (who died in 1342), a hopping dance procession took place in Prüm, which had the same character as the dance at Echternach, which latter must therefore be regarded as the earlier. Ever since that time it has been generally accepted that both the Echternach and the Prüm processions originated in times of general need and suffering [Reimers].

In the year 1512 the Emperor Maximilian summoned a Reichstag at Trier. The plague raged in the district, for which reason he undertook a pilgrimage, with a great following, to Echternach, where he attended the hopping dance procession. On this occasion a picture was painted which was preserved in the church, but which appears to have vanished afterwards

E

FIG. 38. The Dance of the Hopping Saints. St Willibrord in episcopal robes with an angel by his side. Behind are pilgrims and sufferers, praying and carrying the processional cross and standard. Behind them the dance procession has already begun, also bearing the processional cross, flags and standards. In the background is the basilica of Echternach, whither the procession is bound. Painting by A. Stevens, dated 1605, and preserved in the town church of Echternach [Meige].

FIG. 39. The dance procession of the hopping saints, 1849. The vast dance procession through the streets of Echternach, preceded by the priests and the processional cross and standard. Lithograph of 1849 [Erens].

(cf. Fig. 38). But the pilgrimage was also to the special plague saint, St Sebastian, whose skull, with one of the arrows that wounded him, is in the church at Echternach, having been given to St Willibrord by the Pope in Rome [Krier]. Much earlier, in 1131, another Emperor, Lotharius, visited Echternach to implore the protection of St Willibrord [Muller].

On the eve of Whit-Monday pilgrims from far and near assembled, not only from Luxembourg, but also from other countries, and on the following morning divine service was celebrated. Other processions then arrived from various directions, all with bands, processional cross and banners. Even today, as five hundred years ago, a specially solemn procession arrives from Prüm, preceded by two youths dressed in a curious costume and bearing enormous richly decorated candles. When the great procession has assembled immediately outside the town of Echternach it has to pass over a bridge— i.e., over the river which flows through the town—then through the main street and up the long flight of steps leading to the churchyard surrounding the parish church, dedicated to the apostles Peter and Paul, where, beneath the altar, the relics of St Willibrord are preserved. The procession is preceded by the priests and choristers, carrying the processional cross, banners, etc., as Fig. 39 shows. They are surrounded by sextons and beadles, who are dressed in ankle-length red robes. In the midst of all the flags and banners there is one bearing the image of the saint, followed by the pastor of the church. Next come the children and youths, and after them the hosts of pilgrims, amounting sometimes to several thousands. From time to time the

119

procession is interrupted by the musicians. The priests sing the St Willibrord Litany:

St Willibrord, first apostle of the Netherlands, pray for us,
St Willibrord, thou who cast down the false gods, pray for us.
St Willibrord, through whom God's voice has spoken to the heathen, pray for us.
St Willibrord, thou tireless worker in the vineyard, pray for us.
St Willibrord, thou light to the blind, pray for us.
St Willibrord, thou healer of the sick, pray for us.
St Willibrord, thou comfort and joy to the tormented, pray for us.
St Willibrord, thou benefactor of the peoples in plague, famine and war, pray for us.

311. Jubelmelodie
zur Echternacher Springprocession.

FIG. 40. Popular Church-Dance Music. Melody of Rejoicing from the Dance of the Hopping Saints at Echternach [Böhme].

During the singing of this litany the bands play the dance melody, the well-known melody which in Germany is played to the profane song 'Adam had seven sons', which is here reproduced (Fig. 40). Only the pilgrims and the children dance; the priests and choristers take no part. Most of the pilgrims are sick; often they have epilepsy, sometimes other diseases. Similarly some of the dancers are healthy. They dance for others, for the sick at home, or at the request of those who are unable to dance. The women taking part in the dance often keep their place by holding cloths, umbrellas, etc. This also is a very ancient custom in the dance. We give here a couple of pictorial illustrations, one of this custom in Echternach and the other of a seventeenth-century popular dance (Figs. 40 and 41).

In principle the dance is the same in different years, but in detail it varies somewhat. Thus there might be three steps forward and one back, or five steps forward and two back, or three or four steps to the right and three or four steps to the left, but in any case in a diagonal direction [Meige, Krier]. It is therefore a question of a dance with the original character of the old 'tripudium'. Every time the backward or forward movement is changed

FIG. 41. Popular Dance of the Seventeenth Century. Peasant festival with dancing. Painting on canvas by Matthias van Hellemont (1623–after 1679). Section showing the dancers linked together by cloths, possibly also by a hat.

the whole procession stops for a moment; the knees are raised high and then the feet stamp down—in other words it is the old stamping dance of early Christian days. Certain swinging movements of the body, together with a sort of balancing movement with the arms, were executed simultaneously. The processional dance in Echternach may for this reason be described as at one and the same time a hopping dance and a standing dance (Figs. 42–44).

After arrival at the church the procession dances in on the so-called evangelical side, i.e., the right aisle. It continues dancing up to the choir and the high altar. Many burst into tears at the sight of the tomb of the saint. They kneel at the altar, embrace it, kiss its walls and lay rose wreaths, medals, pictures and books upon it. Then they continue the hopping dance round the altar and back by the epistolary aisle, i.e., the left aisle. Then the dance proceeds out of the church into the surrounding churchyard, three times circling the large cross [Krier].

Yet sometimes the dance terminated in the middle of the nave, under the

FIG. 42. Dance Procession at Echternach. The hopping saints during the Whitsun dance procession. The priests with the banner of St Willibrord have passed; here follow the sextons in red mantles and birettas, the choristers with the processional cross, flags and standards. The youths follow. Priests and choristers do not take part in the dance, but sing the St Willibrord Litany [Meige].

great candelabrum with its seventy-two candles reminiscent of the seventy-two disciples of Christ. In that case, however, the dance circled the great cross in the churchyard before entering the church. When the dance was in the middle of the nave the crown was dipped three times over the dancers, who on each occasion knelt to the ground, stretched up their arms, clapped their hands (compare the early Christian hand clapping), praised God and cried out in a loud voice: 'Jesus, Mary!' Then the officiating priest struck up: 'Hail to thee Queen, Mother of Mercy!'* [Krier] (Fig. 28).

---

* 'Salve Regina Misericordiae' originated at the end of the eleventh century. The word *mater* was introduced before *misericordiae* in the sixteenth century (*An. Hymn* 50: 245, 1907).

> Hail, Queen of Mercy,
> Our life, our happiness, our hope, Hail!
> To thee we call, Eve's fugitive child,
> To thee we sigh 'midst complaint and weeping
> In this valley of tears.
> Ah! for this mayest thou, our intercessor,
> Turn to us thy gracious glance,
> And after this our exile let us behold
> Jesus, thy blessed offspring!
> Oh thou, full of mercy and of love!
> Oh thou adorable Mary!

FIG. 43. Dance Procession at Echternach in 1904. The dancing hop can be seen. The procession is led by a band, which plays the tune of *Adam had seven sons* [Meige].

In ordinary circumstances the flag-bearers placed themselves beneath the immense church crown after offering a trifle at the altar, as was also done by most of the pilgrims [Meige]. Neyen mentions that these offerings were commonly placed in small bags attached to the flag poles. They were a reminder of earlier obligations imposed on neighbouring parishes as payable to the Abbot of the Echternach monastery. But this assumption has no justification, for the offering was a part of the ceremonial in the very earliest pilgrims processions.

The character of the Echternach dance procession corresponds surprisingly with the old church dances as we have been able to deduce them from the writings of the Church Fathers. Here we find the stamping of feet and the clapping of hands—a real hopping dance, a *tripudium*; here it is performed inside a church in honour of the relics of a saint; here also is the churchyard dance, which is remarkable as being preserved into our own time. The dance not only 'refreshed' St Willibrord, but also the dead. The litany which the priests sang during the hopping dance seems to me also of interest because it shows that the dance was performed not only by those suffering from cramp and epilepsy, but also by those who were smitten by other infectious diseases, and by those afflicted by hunger and misery. Saint

Willibrord is invoked as a protector against the plague, as the healer of the sick, as the comforter and the bringer of joy to the tormented.

One may perhaps recall that the words of the litany referring to plague, famine and war may be technical terms derived from the Old Testament. In II Samuel, 24, the Lord gives David the choice of three punishments:

FIG. 44. Dance Procession at Echternach in 1904. The women adopt the old-fashioned method of keeping together with the help of umbrellas, sticks, handkerchiefs, etc. [Meige].

famine for seven years, exile for three months among enemies, and plague for three days. Plague, famine and war are therefore the three divine punishments.

Many writers have believed that the Echternach dance was a survival of the medieval dance epidemic, so-called, of which the most terrible and most widespread was in the Rhine Province and surrounding area in 1374. To some extent there is little to object to in this view, but the Echternach dance is in all probability much older, possibly older than St Willibrord himself. For we must remember that he sent dancers to Echternach who would not (or, perhaps better expressed, could not) stop dancing, and this may mean that even at that time there was some question of healing by the dance. It is of the greatest importance to be able to confirm that in the crypt beneath the church, in which is the tomb of St Willibrord, there is a spring of miraculous water from which many pilgrims devoutly drink in the hope of a cure or the assuagement of the suffering [Krier]. Frequently the pilgrims take the water home with them. We shall find later that underground water, springs and running water do in fact play a role in healing dances. It therefore seems not improbable that it was the existence of this underground spring which first gave rise to the dances later associated with St Willibrord. The church itself was built over the spring in the eleventh century.

The Catholic Church has a number of hymns or psalms addressed to St Willibrord. In addition to the one already quoted, we may give one other. In the fifteenth-century song we find [*An. Hymn* 37: 327: 9]:

> Radiating health's
> Wondrous strength,
> He restores to the feeble
> The strength of their limbs!
> He gives to the confused mind
> The gift of reason!

I attach a certain weight to the words in the song which say that St Willibrord restores reason to the demented mind, for this song was composed shortly after the 1374 dance epidemic, in which one of the most characteristic symptoms was acute dementia.

Browerus relates that formerly, in the seventeenth century and earlier, there were two other kinds of procession in Echternach. They took place at the same time as the hopping dance of the saints, that is, at Whitsuntide, and often on the same day. They were the 'standing dance' and the 'creeping procession'. On the Friday after Whitsun a bell was rung, which was a call to the performers to assemble. Those participating in the standing dance took their places in a row and then stood still for seven or eight minutes. Then another bell rang with the signal to advance three or four steps, when the first bell gave another signal for a new stop of seven or eight minutes, during which a community psalm was sung. The procession advanced in this manner until it reached the church. Both this and the procession of the hopping saints are said to be reminiscent of David's dance when he bore the Ark of the Covenant to Zion, for as soon as the Levites advanced six steps they stopped and let David make his offering. The second of the processions, that of the creepers, assembled round a great cross which was raised on the other side of the bridge over which the hopping procession passed. The creeping procession passed round this cross, after which every participator had to creep under a large stone, the underside of which formed a narrow arch; the procession then made its way to the church.

One or two details seem to me important. The terms 'standing' and 'creeping' were surely not chosen haphazard. We can find something similar in principle in the oldest church. Binterim recounts how, as early as the time of Gregory the Wonder-worker, the healers were divided into four classes, of which the first was the lowest. These groups were named: the weeping, the listening, the lying, and the standing [V:2:362]. At divine service the first group assembled outside the church and remained there; it was not even allowed to enter. The second group remained in the porch, the third group remained kneeling inside the church doors, that is, inside the church, while the fourth group was allowed to be with the faithful, but probably had to take back seats. The two lower groups were thus apparently excluded from the service. The third group was called the lying because it was their duty at all solemn prayers to fall on their knees or to cast themselves on the ground, and this they also had to do at the laying on of the hands. When the penitents were received among the fourth group, the standing, all external tokens of healing disappeared, as also the obligation to wear the costume of a healer. Then they remained together with the other faithful during the service. But the healers were not permitted to take part in the offering or in the night watch. It seems to me probable, therefore, that the participants in the 'standing' and the 'creeping' processions in Echternach were special penitents, and that these two groups corresponded most closely to the two highest classes in the ancient church: the 'standing' and the 'lying'.

8. *Germany*

It was the custom from very early times for a large crowd of pilgrims from Prüm to take part in the procession of the Hopping Saints at Echternach. But in the Middle Ages Prüm had its own procession, which closely resembled that of Echternach. It was held thirteen days before the Echternach procession, that is, about the time of Ascension Day. The chronicler Heinrich Brandt relates that the Prüm procession originated under the Abbot Heinrich von Schönecken, who lived between 1288 and 1342. On the appropriate day the parishioners of the various estates of the Prüm monastery assembled under cross and banner for a procession in which every participant had to dance with all his strength to imitate the dance of David before the Ark of the Lord. According to Krier this procession was organized in times of deep distress in order to escape God's scourge or, as the chronicler Servatius Otler of Prüm wrote in 1623, the dance was performed to avoid barrenness and the visitation of God. When the parishioners reached the monastery church at Prüm, they began to dance. They continued in dance procession to a little chapel at the entrance to the town and danced round it three times. Thence they moved to a similarly situated spring, round which they also danced three times. Then they entered into the town and danced with hopping steps three times round the monastery church and then inside it. When they had reached the choir they cast themselves down in front of the altar. The whole proceeding ended with a solemn mass.

The dance procession in Prüm ceased in 1777, after which the inhabitants of these districts more usually went to Echternach to take part in the procession there [Stieren]. That the Prüm procession is very old appears from a miracle which was wrought there [Hyginus]. A chronicle of the Benedictine monastery in Prüm relates, 'about this time (1342) a miracle was wrought during the dance procession (*in processione saltantium*) which is held every year in Prüm on the day after Ascension Day, and which is performed with great reverence. It originated in a time of great misfortune and was held to avoid the scourge of God. Among other things it happened that a man who had been unjustly imprisoned and put in chains asked to be taken to the church of the holy Saviour in order that he might, together with others, make his offering there. This was permitted and when he approached the altar containing the relics of the Saviour, God intervened and in front of the whole procession cast off the chains and restored him healthy and sound to his people. He left his chains behind as a proof of the miracle. They were hung in the arch of the church and are preserved there to this day.'

III

E-ſo-net in lau-di-bus cum
Chri-ſtus na-tus ho-di-e ex
Pu-e-ri con-ci-ni-te, na-
Si-on lau-da Do-mi-num Sal-

iu-cun-dis plau-ſi-bus Si-on cum fi-de-li-bus,
Ma-ri-a vir-gi-ne ſine vi-ri-li ſe-mi-ne
to re-gi pſal-li-te, vo-ce pi-a di-ci-te
ua-to-rem ho-mi-nũ, pur-ga-to-rem cri-mi-nũ

Ap-pa-ru-it quẽ ge-nu-it Ma-ri-a.

FIG. 45. *Resonet in Laudibus* (Swedish Psalm Book, No. 61). To this melody people danced in the churches at Christmas and sang 'Joseph, beloved spouse' [from *Piae Cantiones*].

It would seem, therefore, that we may trace the hop-dance procession in Prüm back to the first part of the fourteenth century, when it was fully developed. This is not without importance, since it proves that it existed long before the first plague seriously raged in Europe—the Black Death of 1349—and long before the dance epidemic of 1374.

In the town of Hof, between Leipzig and Regensburg, there was a specially solemn service on Christmas Eve. During the fifteenth and sixteenth centuries the so-called *Pomwitzel* dance was performed in the church, a dance which conveyed a symbolic rocking of the Christ child in the cradle. Amidst songs of praise for the birth of Jesus the organist passed over to an old rhythmic dance tune, to which the congregation sang:

Joseph, beloved spouse of mine
Help me to rock my child!

Hereupon boys and girls hastened up the church to the altar and began to dance around it. Even a few of the adults were allowed to participate in the dance [Böhme].

In actual fact this Christmas Eve dance certainly began as early as the later part of the fourteenth century, and from the same time dates the above-mentioned song, which was sung to the melody of one of the Christmas Eve songs of rejoicing, *Resonet in laudibus* [Wackernagel, *Piae Cantiones*]. Sometimes this was sung in such a way that the verses were interrupted by Mary's prayer and Joseph's reply from the cradle. We reproduce the *Resonet in laudibus* in Fig. 45, and the cradle song was as follows:

> Joseph my beloved spouse,
> Help me to rock my child!
> God will give you reward
> In Heaven
> For the Virgin Mary's son.
>
> Gladly, beloved spouse of mine,
> Will I help to rock thy child!
> God will give me my reward
> In Heaven
> For the Virgin Mary's son.

Johannes Boemus in 1520 relates of these Christmas Eve dances in the churches of old Franconia: 'With what rejoicing did not only the priests but also the people, celebrate in the churches the birth of Christ. This we can see from the fact that they placed on the altar a doll representing the Christ child, after which the boys and girls hopped a ring-dance round the altar, whilst the others sang, all in a way which differed little from the manner in which, according to the myth, the Corybantes once hopped around Jupiter over the cave on Mount Ida.' Later, in 1550, this testimony was confirmed by Vuicelius in his description of church song and action dances in the contemporary Catholic Church: 'On Christmas Day there is an exhibition in some places at vespers. Then are shown the blessed birth of our Redeemer, the star of Bethlehem, the angels, the shepherds, the three wise men, etc. When the *Resonet* is sung the small boys hop up and down in front of the congregation and clap their hands to show the great joy that all feel at the birth.'

In Saxony also they danced round the altar, but this Christmas dance was forbidden by the civil authorities towards the end of the eighteenth century [*Hdb. d. D. Volksk.* II: 145].

During the seventeenth century there were two types of popular dance in a number of German churches, both connected with entry into the state of matrimony, which were called *Lehenschwinken* and *Kronentanz*. These are real wedding dances and both of them were forbidden by the church authorities in Cologne in 1617. By *Lehenschwinken* is meant '*schwingen der Lehen*' in which *schwingen* is identical with '*dance*' and *Lehen* means 'lend' or 'grant'. Consequently *Lehenschwinken* is the same as *Mailehen*. This latter, which has survived into modern times, was performed in such a way that on Easter Monday or on the eve of Walpurgis Night the girls were 'auctioned' among the boys of the village and were then under an obligation for the year to come to dance with the boy to whom they had been 'loaned'. This was called a 'betrothal for a year' [Junk]. The Crown Dance has continued until our own time in Germany, Holland and Belgium; it was danced under wreaths of flowers and greenery suspended over streets and cross-roads, especially on Midsummer Eve, the festival of Peter and Paul, and on the inauguration day of the church [Böhme]. We have however already seen other crown dances in Liége and Echternach.

There were also other wedding dances in German churches. The archiepiscopal decree from Cologne in 1617 points to this: [Binterim, II: 2] 'The plays which are performed in many places after the marriage ceremony, in which the wedded couple stamp their feet, must stop completely . . . since such a custom is contrary to the dignity of God, the Church and the Sacrament. Let them (the priests) declare this to the people in their cure and let them exhort them . . .' Just the fact that, standing still, they stamped their feet brings out with renewed emphasis the already quoted words of St Clement of Alexandria: to 'move the feet' at the end of every prayer, as also the exhortation of St Ambrose to those about to be baptized to 'have quicker feet'.

9. *Russia*

The church dance certainly flourished in the earliest days of the Greek Orthodox church. We are entitled to draw this conclusion from the mention of such dances by so many of the fathers of the Greek church. But there is nothing in literature to tell us what form it took in the Middle Ages and after. There is nothing published on the subject. Curiously enough one can still today catch a glimpse of the relics of such a dance, a wedding dance, which we shall now describe. After the wedded couple have touched the consecrated wine and water with their lips, the priest takes the hand of the best man, who takes the hand of the bridegroom, who in his turn takes the hand of the bride. She then takes her bridesmaid by the hand and she in turn takes the deacon's. In this chain they move slowly past the two side altars and the holy doors, to the singing of songs. According to Gougaud, this ceremony was called a ring-dance by Simon of Thessalonica (who died in 1429), and by Goar in his commentary of 1730, a 'chorea' or 'choraula'. This is very convincing proof that this chain movement before the all-holy and the high altar was a popular sacral wedding dance.

10. *Sweden*

Hyltén-Cavallius describes a Swedish form of popular church wedding dance. It occurred in Varend at the end of the eighteenth century, perhaps also at the beginning of the nineteenth. It was the custom, we are told, in the older weddings for the bridal pair to be led to the church in a special procession with drums and fiddles. When the procession was ready to enter the church the tune of the wedding dance was played and the pages had to perform a sort of dance on the path, which an old Finved woman describes as follows: 'They hopped and swirled around, clattered with their chains, held up their hands and jumped up and down.' When the service was over and the procession re-formed and left the church and altar, all the others remained in the church, whilst the pages resumed their 'hopping and jumping inside the church'.

11. *The South American Republics*

The literature of travel has little to tell us of the religious dance among the Catholic Christians of the South American Republics. We shall find a dance of the dead in northern Brazil in the latter part of the 1920's [Funke]. The obvious naturalness of its execution seems to indicate that here too the dance was, and is, fairly widespread.

In Mexico Thompson mentions that at the Catholic religious festivals 'heathen' dances and exotic ceremonies occurred among the Christian Indians, but he gives no further details.

In a Swedish newspaper in 1927 Elliot gave an extremely detailed and vivid account of the religious dances of pilgrims before the Holy Madonna in Andacollo on the slopes of the Chilean Andes. The festival of the Madonna is celebrated there on December 26th. Many thousands of pilgrims then come to the cathedral of La Serenas not only from the surrounding districts, but also from Southern Chile, the Argentine, Bolivia, Peru, etc., which seems to me to prove that the religious church dance was far from being rare in the Catholic world of South America.

Mass is in progress in the cathedral of the Madonna when the dancers arrive in procession, preceded by fluttering banners and drummers. The different groups of dancers are dressed in bright many-coloured costumes and they dance to the music of a sort of Pan pipe. They move slowly forward, taking one hop with the right foot and one with the left in time with the music of the pipes. It is thus a hopping dance, a kind of *tripudium*, during which the bodies swing and twist. Higher and higher the dancers (*chinos*) hop in honour of the Virgin; the rhythm becomes wilder and wilder, and the pipes sound more and more loudly. The crowds of dancers are led by a greybeard with drawn sword, surrounded by drummers who sway their bodies from side to side in time with the pipers. The hops of the sidesman grow higher and higher. Some of the leading men have no musical instruments, but dance nevertheless, and bear instead small flags or silken banners, which they lower at a given sign, falling upon their knees before the Virgin. The leader speaks an address to the Virgin, asking for help and protection, or complaining of her indifference. When the mass in the church is finished the image of the Madonna is carried in procession out of the nave into the porch and is held there, raised on a silver bier, and before it the main dance is performed. From the main doors across the stone floor of the entrance to the sand of the plaza a group of pipers form a fence. When the dance has been in progress for several hours the procession, with the image of the Virgin, moves round the plaza and back to the church, followed by the dancers who, still dancing, conduct the Virgin through the main entrance and up to the altar. After this, numerous offerings are made to the church. The festivities actually began, however, on the preceding day, when the image of the Madonna was brought from the old basilica to the new cathedral, led by other groups of dancers. A larger group of them is composed of *dansantes*, dressed in white, wearing bright caps embroidered with pearls and curios. The dancers play on guitars or strike triangles. Another group of dancers is called *damas* and is veiled and regarded as the honorary guard of the Bishop. A third group is called *turbantes*, because they wear oriental turbans or old-fashioned, brilliant Spanish uniforms.

The historical connexion between these religious dances of the South American republics and those which we have already seen in Spain is evident and indisputable.

VIII

The Dance and the Dead

1. *The Dead as Demons*

AMONG the Jews of the later period and in early Germanic heathendom the dead were regarded as dangerous and hostile to the living. But at one time the dead were buried in the soil beneath the house or in its immediate neighbourhood and were still the dear companions with whom one wished to remain in contact and to have near one after death. Circumstances changed and the dead became dangerous demons against whom one sought protection by secret means. It is not easy to understand the causes of this change. Yet it is in the highest degree strange that these dead, however near they may have been to the living during their lives, were immediately regarded as demons as soon as they left the circle of the living. One might perhaps be tempted to find the principal reason in the Old Testament laws as laid down in Numbers 19:14: 'This is the law, when a man dieth in a tent: all that come into the tent, and all that is in the tent, shall be unclean seven days.' This is further amplified in the same chapter by the declaration that anybody who comes near the dead shall be unclean and, if he does not purify himself, he shall be cast out of Israel. Aurelius points out that the idea clearly is that there issues from the dead body something which makes unclean. But simultaneously the idea exists that the spirit of the dead finds it difficult to separate from its lifeless body: it would wish to return to its dwelling and grudges its heir the new possession. Although the Jews taught that the underworld was the great repository of the spirits of the dead, yet at the same time it was thought that the spirits of the dead were in some way fettered to the grave, in which they continued their existence. Aurelius describes as an offshoot of primitive ideas the Jewish view that a continued connexion between the living and the spirits of the dead can be maintained, a view which led to the conjuration of the dead. This appears from I Samuel xxviii, 7–21, in which Saul conjures up the spirit of Samuel, and still more in Isaiah viii, 19, rendered by Aurelius as 'and when they shall say unto you, Seek the spirits of the dead and the prophesying spirits, whispering and mumbling—should not a people seek counsel from God, should they turn to the dead for help for the living?'

One might be tempted to assume that these ideas of the uncleanness of the dead and their ability to communicate this uncleanness to everything which approaches them might be the powerful influence which in the late Jewry and also in Christianity transformed the dead into demons. It is indisputable, however, that Germanic heathendom, for example, had such conceptions long before Christian missionary activity reached the various countries. It is more important that we find similar thoughts in other religions, for example the Central Asiatic, long before the Christian epoch. For this reason it seems to me more probable that other circumstances and experiences have forced the conception of the dead as demons. Confronted with epidemic diseases and mass poisoning it must have been easy to think that those who died first dragged more and more of the living after them. Possibly such experiences presuppose the rise of culture and a certain density of population. Then it becomes possible to understand why primitive man in Europe—the men of the Neanderthal, Aurignac and Cro-Magnon civilizations—buried their dead in the soil below their dwellings or very near to them and provided the dead with parting gifts [G. Backman]. Much later the dead were buried farther away from dwellings and to the accompaniment of a number of magic rites intended to fend off their evil influence.

Possibly we are justified in seeing in Mark v, 2, a suggestion of the idea that the possessed, i.e., the sick, dwelt among the graves because they considered themselves possessed by the spirits of the dead [Clemen]. That dangerous and injurious forces emanate from the dead is confirmed by various passages in the Old Testament, e.g., Jos. vii, 26, where it is related how a sinner was stoned to death and a cairn thrown up over him. In II Samuel xviii, 17, an enormous cairn was erected over the dead Absolom, after which everybody fled. Duhm thinks we cannot escape the conclusion that the Jews thought that under certain circumstances these dead became dangerous and vengeful demons.

There is in Europe a very old and widespread idea that the dead are ill-natured beings who wish to injure the living. Numerous magical means have therefore been employed to prevent them from walking again. The dead desire the living [Kleinpaul] and thirst for their blood; they drag the living to them; they appear as vampires, were-wolves, and ghosts, etc. The dead kill! Every dead person, says Kleinpaul, stretches up a hand from the grave in order to drag down a living person. Such ideas are to be found not only among the Germanic peoples, but also the Slavonic and Romanic [Krauss]. One can scarcely point to any marked difference between the various peoples in this respect. Only at one point in the year do people think that the dead are better disposed to the living: at Christmas. Hyltén-Cavallius tells of a dance of the angels in Finveden which was danced on Christmas Eve to the singing of Christmas psalms. It was a kind of sacrificial dance which was performed towards the end of the eighteenth century for the so-called dead. It was believed that the angels, that is to say, in this case, the spirits of the dead, participated in the dance. From Sydösterbotten in Finland there are similar reports that on Christmas Eve a visit was expected from the dead [Tegengren]. In Germany also it was believed that at this time the spirits of the dead paid a visit [Reichhardt].

Everywhere the most varied methods have been employed to prevent the dead from walking the earth again, from returning and creating misfortune or sickness. In her work *When Death Calls*, Louise Hagberg gives us an excellent and comprehensive survey of many such customs: needles were stuck into the skin or the feet of the dead; nails were driven into their feet, firmly securing the dead to their coffins; their legs were bound together, as also their feet and big toes; the arms were bound together; the body was enmeshed in a fishing net; seed, usually of flax, was strewn behind the dead when they were taken away from their homes; there were numerous ceremonies when the dead body was stood upright in the cottage room and when it was taken away, etc. These customs are well known in the Northern countries and in Germany [Franz], in England [Clemen], etc. In Lincolnshire the custom of binding together the feet of the dead was practised as late as 1916 [Clemen].

2. The Dance for the Dead

However, all these magic rites to protect the living against the dead were insufficient. It was necessary to perform other rites for and against the dead during the time in which they were above ground after death. One was a part of the so-called death watch. Also we now encounter the dance as a means both of satisfying and fending off the dead.

The death watch had much the same character in all countries. Louise Hagberg gives numerous examples of the procedure, and both she and V. Backman give very much the same account of the conduct of the dance of death in Bjuråker. Here there is a wall from the church to the shore at Norra Dellen which is called the *leckvallen*. Until the 1840's the dance of death was performed there. The dead body had previously been conveyed there either by rowing boat across the lake, or in winter by sledge across the ice. The dance took place immediately on arrival. The mourners held each other by the hand in pairs facing each other and these pairs formed up side by side in a large circle around the coffin. Then a kind of slow ring-dance was danced to the left. A special fiddler provided the music. The dance was performed on Saturday evening, the day before the burial.

FIG. 46. Burial Dance from Norrland. Copied by Björn Halldén [Valentin and Halldén].

I have found a burial waltz from Norrland, probably from the latter half of the nineteenth century, copied by B. Halldén (Fig. 46). But according to information given to me by N. Andersson, variations occur in several Swedish counties, both as wedding marches and as funeral marches. Its earliest use seems to have been as a bridal march.

The actual death watch was ordered in this way: friends and relatives assembled round the body in its coffin. There was neither wailing nor lamentation, but the telling of stories, riddles and legends; there was song and dance.

When we pass to the eighteenth century the Swedish sources concerning the death watch and its dance become relatively abundant. We find some examples in Bergstrand's sketches of the culture of Västergötland in the eighteenth century. At an episcopal visitation to Saleby in 1705 it was ordered: 'Since it is forbidden by Royal church law to hold wakes, then this malpractice as well as the night dance in connexion therewith shall be entirely abolished. If anyone acts to the contrary, let him be brought before the local court and if he mend not his ways let him be brought before the higher court.' Similar orders were issued in connexion with visitations in 1746, 1751, 1753, 1756, 1761 and 1799, as also at a visitation to Linköping in 1687. In all probability there were similar warnings and proscriptions against dances at wakes in other Swedish counties in the seventeenth and eighteenth centuries, and it appears from these orders that at these wakes large crowds of youths assembled for dancing and games, music and drinking. It is related that in 1687 the time in the death chamber was passed in frivolous dancing and jumping—possibly the old hopping dance. At these wakes the body often lay on its bier in the middle of the room.

Accounts from Denmark agree with those given above. Grundtvig relates that during the latter part of the eighteenth century it was customary in the north-eastern part of Sönderjylland to dance around the coffin and to sing what was called the *Ligvejt*. Feilberg describes how at the end of the eighteenth century, and possibly the beginning of the nineteenth, they watched over the dead during the night before burial and how in West Jylland youths assembled and played and danced, sometimes round the coffin and sometimes in the adjoining room of the house of mourning. This was to play the *Ligved*. Mollberg quotes from Bishop Bircherod's diary: 'On December 13th (23rd) I was with my mother at Peder Pedersen Lerke's house for a death watch for his blessed wife until late at night. Our death watches seem to become more like Christmas parties, as all sorts of games and frolics are played by guests old and young.' Kinch relates: 'Before the body was buried death watches were arranged, to which a number of people came and were offered food and drink, and there was noise and merriment.'

From Norway Reichborn-Kjennerud recounts: 'There was an unpleasant custom in some homes. When a young boy or girl died they placed the coffin without any lid in the middle of the floor and made up a party around it. The guests sat around the coffin and played all sorts of games.'

In Germany the death watch was just the same. People assembled around the dead; beer, bread and brandy were offered; cards were played and stories told. There were dancing, games and noise around the dead until lately [Sartori, Reichhardt].

What is the real meaning of such jesting and merriment, music and dancing, at the death-watch? It has always been believed that music exorcized the dead, forced them into compliance at being taken to the grave and prevented them from walking the earth again. It was only later that the belief arose that music protected the dead from the demons and put the latter to flight [Quasten]. Music thus acquired a significance very similar to that of the bells. Quasten relates that in antiquity the hearse and the corpse were furnished with small bells, the sound of which drove the demons away, and that in the Christian world small bells might be laid beside the body in the coffin. Durandus, in the thirteenth century, declared with great emphasis that church bells expelled demons; bell-ringing at a burial formerly had precisely this significance of keeping the demons away. The Fathers of the Church were also not unfamiliar with the thought that music in the churchyard might reach the dead [Tertullian].

So much may be regarded as certain: music for the dead served both to drive the demons away and to protect the dead; it could also be heard by the dead. The purpose of the death watch was evidently to comfort the dead and to make them happy on their last night on earth. I interpret the dance round the dead as a continuation and development of the early Christian churchyard dance for the martyrs. The Church regulations which I shall describe in greater detail in the following chapter show quite clearly that these churchyard dances very early, probably in the fourth century, were developed into dances for the dead in general. They then continued century after century and thus reveal the strong roots of ancient custom in popular religious conceptions and their close connexion with traditional early Christian usage. It is extremely probable, however, that similar customs among the heathen peoples of Middle and Northern Europe contributed to the maintenance and intensification of the earliest Christian customs.

The dance for the martyrs was a dance of the angels and for that reason at the same time a dance of resurrection. For that reason it was comforting and consoling to the dead. It was for their refreshment. But at the same time it had the power to ward off demons, and was thus in agreement with the old Christian belief that the dance of the angels was a mystery associated with the resurrection, that is to say with the triumph over the forces of death.

The best account I have found of a death-watch dance is by Davillier from the middle of the nineteenth century in Spain. He has also reproduced the situation in the accompanying picture (Fig. 47). His account is as follows: 'In Jijona we were witnesses of a death-watch ceremony which surprised us. As we were walking along the street we heard the sound of a guitar, accompanied by the harsh tones of a mandolin and the clash of castanets. We entered a workman's dwelling and thought it was a wedding—but it was not. Instead, the last services were being rendered to the dead. At the back of the room lay a small child of five or six years, stretched out on a table and covered with a cloth. It was dressed in festive attire with a wreath of flowers on its head, which lay on a cushion. . . . Beside the child stood a jar of holy water and at the four corners of the table stood tall lighted candles in their candelabra. All this showed that a death had occurred. But everything else that happened in such curious manner was in conflict with such an assumption. A youth and a girl in the festive dress of Valencian workpeople danced a *jota* (a vivid, merry dance), accompanying themselves with the castanets, whilst musicians and guests danced a round dance, following the two leaders around the body. Simultaneously they sang and clapped their hands. We could not understand how such gaiety could be reconciled with sorrow. "He is with the angels", a member of the family explained. In actual fact the belief has long prevailed that it is natural that those who die in childhood

136

go direct to Paradise, and that "little angels in heaven" beyond purgatory, rejoice in everlasting life in the heavenly home.'

As late as the 1920's Funke found a similar dance for the dead among the Catholics of north-eastern Brazil. Here too it was the death of a child that caused a day of rejoicing. A violin was played, the old songs were sung, the whirling *samban* was danced and the little 'angel', dressed in its best, lay between lighted carnauba candles. It was thought, says Funke, that the little child, because of its innocence, had gone to heavenly joy.

Fig. 47. Dance for the Dead. In Jijona, Alicante, in 1870, a youth and a girl danced a *jota* in Valencian workers' festive dress, followed by those present in a line-dance round the body. Observed by Davillier and drawn by Gustave Doré.

These death-watch dances are clearly very old. During the Middle Ages it was not uncommon for the dead to lie on their bier in the church, whilst in the porch, or even inside the church, a meal was eaten, after which a ring-dance was danced round the body to the accompaniment of frivolous songs or conjurations. In other respects also the whole procedure was bound up with frolics and jest [Balogh]. In the eleventh century we find the confessional questions, which Burchard from Worms found himself compelled to put, referring particularly to the death-watch, its dances and conjurations, its laughter and drinking. At the beginning of the tenth century Regino of Prüm enforced similar questions upon his subordinate priests, and these too related to conjurations and dances. It is possible to glimpse similar night watches behind the reminders of the bishops in the eighteenth century concerning the general practice of singing and laughing in the presence of the dead during the night. In the next chapter I shall return to the consideration of these matters.

After burial, memorial feasts were arranged. People returned from the churchyard and arranged for a meal in the house of mourning, at which there might also be dancing. Hagberg gives us several examples of this. Dahlgren relates how there was dancing in Wärmland after the funeral of Kristofer Gustaf Geijer in 1768, 'so that it was a day of rejoicing', as one of his nearest relations said. Lloyd mentions in his account of his travels in Sweden that in the first part of the nineteenth century it was customary to arrange a feast in the house of mourning after the funeral, at which there was

FIG. 48. Churchyard Dance. Music for the girls' dance and song as they returned to the church from the grave of a friend. On this occasion the bier cloth was carried at the head of the procession. Copied in 1840 from Bailleul, Flanders [Coussemaker].

also dancing. Similar customs are recorded in other countries, such as Switzerland [Riser] and Germany in the nineteenth century [Bloch]. It was said that one danced away the dead. During the Middle Ages a party was held on the anniversary of a death and frequently there was dancing as well.

From Spain there are also accounts of dances for the dead after the funeral. Capmány says that they are preserved, to this day, in some small places in Murcia, in the so-called Dance of the Souls or the Dance of the Innocents, originating in earlier times. When a child has died among the people of Perello, near Tortosa, and has been buried in the churchyard, the mourners return direct to the market place, where a dance is held. The members of the family participate in this dance and 'often tears run down their cheeks during the dance'.

Until 1840 there was a similar funeral dance in Bailleul of which the music is given here (Fig. 48). This dance took place at the funeral of a young girl. After the body had been lowered into the ground those of her comrades who followed her to her last resting place took hold of the splendid sky-blue

138

FIG. 49. Hungarian Funeral Dance. Danced as a czardas to the Rákóczi March, it was performed during the first half of the nineteenth century on leaving the churchyard after a funeral [Balogh].

bier cloth with its white embroidered cross, and, carrying it between them, proceeded in a sort of procession out of the churchyard, dancing and singing:

> In Heaven there is a dance. Hallelujah!
> Where all the maidens dance.
> May the Lord bless us. Hallelujah! Hallelujah!
> This is for Amelia. Hallelujah!
> We dance like those young maidens.
> May the Lord bless us! Hallelujah!

The reference to the dance of the blessed in heaven and to the girls' dance as an imitation of it recalls the words of Clement of Alexandria or Basileios. Everything is preserved from the earliest conceptions of the ancient Christian church.

In more recent times, writes Balogh in 1926, it happened in Hungary that the youths of one village or another arranged after a funeral to dance a *czardas* at the gates of the churchyard to the tune of the well-known Rákóczi march (Fig. 49). He probably refers to the first part of the nineteenth century. We should be wise in this connexion to remember the belief that one should not sorrow at the departure of a human being but rather celebrate the day as one of joy and as a real birthday—of everlasting life in heavenly bliss.

Böhme mentions how in 1271 the inhabitants of Appenzell buried the Abbot Berthold of the monastery of St Gallen and danced the whole way on their return from the churchyard.

3. *The Churchyard Dance*

Very important was the role of the dance for or against the dead, performed in the churchyards, the churchyard dance proper, which has persisted for many centuries, and against which both church and lay authorities have exhorted, threatened and punished from the fourth century until 1777, when the last lay prohibition was issued. If one looks at the actual words of the prohibitions we shall find, as regards the popular churchyard dances, the following picture, though it must be remembered that there is no objective evidence outside this source. In the next chapter we shall give an account of these prohibitions and their special significance. We learn from them that the dancers were accustomed to assemble in the churchyard at night, sometimes naked, except possibly for their shirts. Sometimes they wore masks over their faces. They beat drums and kettle-drums and from time to time laughed loudly or derisively. And then they danced, especially ring-dances, hop-dances and three-step dances. They sang devil songs, that is to say conjurations, as well as indecent ditties, all of which were at the same time dancing songs. They also arranged song and action dances, ball games, arrow-shooting and stone-throwing. Drunkenness and fornication were common.

The proscriptions prove that these churchyard dances occurred in the Northern countries, in Lund among other places, in Germany, Belgium, France, England, Hungary, and also in the Slavonic countries. In Bohemia in the thirteenth century the heathen custom of dancing in churchyards at night and singing devilish songs and indulging in loud laughter continued among Christians [Czerwinski]. In the year 1555 a number of people were condemned to prison in Dresden because during the night they had assembled naked in the churchyard, or dressed only in their shirts, and, armed with swords, danced all sorts of dances [Bloch]. In a fourteenth-century document we are told that the inhabitants of Champeaux, near Avranches, executed certain dances in the churchyard and clapped their hands. At Estouy, near

Beauvais, in 1381, numerous persons danced in the churchyard [Villetard]. Lavater relates that in 1569 a number of men disguised themselves and danced in a churchyard, holding parts of a skeleton from the charnel house in their hands. People thought it was the dead who were dancing, and expected that a great plague would very soon ensue [Bächthold-Stäubli].

This churchyard dance was in my view best described by the German poet Jakob Balde, who wrote in Latin and lived between 1604 and 1668. He called his ode *Choreae Mortuales* or the ring-dance of the dead, from which the following is an extract:

> Let us dance, joined by our clasped hands.
> Now the dangerous dusk calls forth the spirits.
> Through the white-gleaming clouds
> Horned Diana casts her glittering light.
> Frail virgins with indecorous drapings
> And rust-coloured mantles!
> But the frail host is bedecked with chains of violets!
> Let us dance with changing steps,
> So that we train our feet for the dance,
> So that the earth no longer hinders;
> Light, unweighted, imponderable!
> Standing still, three times we mutter our song,
> Three times we turn towards the blessed Heaven.
> Three times we dispel, midst candles else slaked,
> The shades of night with the pale torch.
> Whoever thou beest and seest us clap our hands to the spirits:
> Thou also shalt sing death songs in these words:
> What thou art we have been!
> What we are, thou shalt be!
> Follow the departed!—till then farewell!

This is in fact at one and the same time a churchyard dance and a dance of death. When night falls the dead arise from their graves, illumined by the moon (the horned Diana), clad in their winding sheets and trailing mantles stained by the rusting iron walls and fetters of the Underworld. But at the same time they are adorned with ribbons of violets, the flower of Proserpine, Goddess of the Underworld [Dierbach]. But it is not only the dead but also the living who dance, in a protective, conjurative sense, clapping their hands, reminding us once again of the oft-quoted exhortation of Ezekiel. The acts of the conjuration are repeated three times, for the number three is the number of divine fulfilment [Eitrem]. The conjuration song is muttered whilst standing still; heaven is invoked; the shades of darkness are dispelled. This muttering is not without significance, for we have seen earlier—in the translation of Aurelius—that Isaiah viii, 19, says of the dead, 'and when they shall say unto you, Seek the spirits of the dead and the prophesying spirits, whispering and mumbling—should not a people seek counsel from God?' The dead only speak in whispers, and we must respond in the same way. In his famous *Requiem*, Verdi has made use of this idea: at the last judgment the dead begin their journey through the sea of fire to receive sanctification or punishment, singing the last prayer for salvation or deliverance from everlasting death in extreme pianissimo and as a *recitativo tuba* in one and the same tone, the old *vox mystica*. The death song quoted by Balde was, as the manner of expression shows, the song which the dead were meant to sing. This means that he who beholds this dance will one day die, and himself sing just this song with the host of spirits.

Handclapping is the clearest survival of old Christian custom, when approval was communicated to God in that way. But in the course of time it came to have significance as a protection against demons. We shall meet it again in the history of dance epidemics, where this significance is obvious. Here it is a question of homeopathic-apotropous magic; that is to say, one does just what the demons do. All the figures and masks of devils on Gothic churches were intended to force the demons to flight at the sight of their own images. The demons were often thought to imitate divine actions: just as the angels dance, so also the demons dance and clap their hands, and according to legend the water demons clap their hands and laugh loudly when anybody crosses a bridge—representing the bridge over the river of death [Bächthold-Stäubli].

The loud laughter and derision mentioned in the decrees of synods and councils are also of interest, and we have already met them in the accounts of the Festival of Fools, in which the priests also laughed and derided as they danced in the churches. Laughter, it was thought, broke the power of death since the dead could not laugh. In Sardinia, until the nineteenth century, it was the custom when the coffin was carried away for a woman to jest in such manner that the other women had to laugh. In the Middle Ages it was believed that laughter put the evil spirits to flight, but if one wanted to raise the spirits one must not laugh [Bächthold-Stäubli]. For this reason, according to the Balde account, the churchyard dancers did not laugh loudly, because it was a question of watching the dead dance and of listening to their song, at the same time preventing them, by such magic means as the invocation of the blessed Heaven and swinging the torches, from approaching and harming the living. The muttered songs of conjuration were probably intended to raise the dead and force them to dance and also to prevent them from harming the living.

The church authorities repeatedly condemned the devil songs (*carmina diabolica*) of churchyard dancers. Kelle has shown that the expression has no reference to indecent songs (*carmina turpia*), as was once thought, but was a technical Church term for popular conjurations, sung, according to Regino of Prüm, over the dead. Other sources, as Kelle shows, call them by the right name, *incantationes*; that is to say, readings, conjurations, magic formulae. They were directed against the dead as demons and sought to compel them to ward off disease, to alleviate famine, etc. Attempts were sometimes made to induce the dead to lend their aid in some matter beneficial to the district or to its population, or to reveal the future. Incomparably the greater number of these incantations were of a medical nature, most commonly to drive out disease, to free from possession, to heal injuries in both man and beast. It is also very probable that many of these conjurations, preserved in popular medicine into our own time, are relics of these old churchyard songs. Kelle adduces an example from a manuscript of the tenth century, a magic German formula against gout: 'The worm with nine small worms', the source of the evil, 'from the marrow into the bone, from the bone into the flesh, from the flesh into the skin, from the skin into this arrow'. Afterwards, says Kelle, the arrow was probably thrown away, taking the disease with it, or rather, taking the demon back to the demon. This, however, is fairly characteristic of many such magic formulas against disease, and the type can be traced back to Babylonian medicine, and from my collection of popular medical charms I will quote two of which the origin in the incantations of the churchyard dances may now seem probable. Vistrand has preserved a charm against lumbago from Småland in the 1880's:

> The redeemer stood on a mountain; there he saw the sorcerer with drawn bow.
>> What do you shoot?
>> We shoot folk and fairy.
>> We shoot in the wood where no one dwells,
>> We shoot in a lake, where no one rows,
>> And shoot into the Red Sea.

The second example I take from Rääf, who has copied an incantation from Kinda against ringworm:

> Hence shalt thou go,
> Hence shalt thou thrive,
> Like a corpse in the earth!
> In the name of the three holy ones!

As has already been mentioned, the churchyard dances included both singing and other activities. In popular medicine many charms were thus uttered simultaneously with the shooting of arrows and guns, especially against shooting pains of various kinds, probably signifying that the disease was bound to the arrow or stone and thus flung to the demons. A very valuable account is given by Bodinus of the activities of the devil, published in the seventeenth century. He says that educated and prudent men must feel a loathing for what others do, such as running to graves at midnight and there practising loathsome sorcery by enquiring of the dead concerning hidden things or seeking a cure for disease. We may now remember what Gregory of Nazianzus said of the Christian visits to the graves of the martyrs and of the songs and dances there: they were 'for the manifest suppression of demons, for the warding off of disease, for the knowledge of things to come'.

Among the Slavonic peoples there was a dance called the *kolo*, which was performed in connexion with funerals or in the churchyard, and which was danced backwards; this was thought to signify a strengthening of the power of magic against death and the dead [Kemp]. On old Bosnian memorial stones we can sometimes see a reversed ring-dance or line-dance depicted. From the same area comes an old song to a deceased bridegroom [Blümmel]:

> When the handsome pages saw this,
> They took reversed lances in their hands,
> And trod the line-dance backwards,
> And began to sing a song of sorrow,
> Praising the warrior dead.

Pieter Brueghel the Elder, in 1568, painted a remarkable picture, now preserved in the Darmstadt Museum (Fig. 50), which has been called 'The Merry Way to the Gallows'. In the foreground is a high hill on which a gallows has been erected; immediately to the right is a newly dug grave, which stands out from its surroundings. The red soil is peculiar to Flanders and from it the motive of the picture is probably derived. By the side of the grave stands a cross, evidently to emphasize that there the dead lie buried; but this cross is an impossible anachronism, for the gallows hill was certainly not sanctified ground and the Church of that time would certainly not have permitted a cross in such a place, where executed criminals lay buried. In the middle and background of the picture is a broad valley flanked by hills, on the left of which, in the middle distance, is the village where people are walking. On the path to the gallows come some of the villagers; some have already arrived and two stand in the foreground with their backs turned, looking at the others. One of them points to the gallows. Beside him two men and a woman dance a ring-dance, the medieval dance of two and one, to the music of bagpipes. Other villagers are on the way up. Far to the left a man has let down his trousers and squats. Van Mander insists that a magpie sits on the arm of the gallows, and he thinks that the picture is a sort of ironical skit on all gossips and slanderers, but *Das Bruegel-Buch* does not accept this interpretation; it points out that another magpie perches on the rock at the foot of the gallows, which has nothing to do with the gallows. Another interpretation comes from Jedlika, who argues that the villagers have not noticed that they have reached the gallows and that the two nearest spectators hasten to draw their attention to the fact. This seems to me improbable since we must assume that these are local inhabitants, and that they must know full well where they are. Jedlika further supposes that the picture may be an illustration of some proverb, for there is one which says that the way to the gallows passes through pleasant fields, and that it is here represented by a dance beside the gallows; while another proverb says that the gallows must be smeared, and this is supposed to be done by the man emptying his bowels.

I myself would prefer to interpret the picture in another way. It represents a churchyard dance, in this case on the gallows hill amidst the law-breakers

FIG. 50. 'The Merry Way to the Gallows', by Pieter Brueghel.

buried there. The cross is to impress the fact that such a law-breaker has recently been buried there. The man who points to the gallows is only telling the others that they have at last reached the goal of which they were in search. And immediately the dance begins. Possibly down in the village the plague is raging or there is famine or the threat of famine—the purpose is to propitiate the hostile demons and to force them to put right the wrong they had wrought. The man who answers the call of nature is making an offering to the Underworld of the vital force which the dead lack and always seek, and which, according to ancient and medieval lore, is to be found in all the excretions and secretions of the body. In an earlier work I have emphasized the very important role played in medicine by faeces and urine, owing to the fact that they were thought to have magic power derived from their vital origin. Faeces are by very ancient conception closely associated with the Underworld and its inhabitants. In a comprehensive work published in 1576

145

by Scribonius and entitled *The Treasury of the Poor*, there is a chapter entitled 'The Dissolution of Sorcery and the Expulsion of Demons', which reflects contemporary medical knowledge. It emphasized that human faeces have an extraordinary power of destroying sorcery, *maleficium*. For this reason I would interpret Brueghel's picture as describing a characteristic churchyard dance on a gallows hill.

We should remember that the gallows and dead malefactors had a special magic significance in popular superstition. As they did not lie in consecrated ground and never found rest, they were thought to be dangerous demons walking the earth and eagerly promoting misfortune. The gallows hill was enveloped in secrecy and fear and after dark these ghosts and evil spirits had their way. Near the gallows hill suicides were also buried and they were regarded as being, if possible, even more dangerous [Mathiessen]. It was a common view, both in the Middle Ages and late into modern times, that suicides and executed persons never found rest in the grave but wandered around as ghosts [Reichhardt].

4. *The Dance of Death*

That the dead dance is a very ancient belief. A plaster relief from a grave in Cumae, near Naples, of late antiquity (Fig. 51), shows them dancing— perhaps on the fields of the blessed, perhaps as ghosts [Weege]. The latter is more probable, since they are represented as skeletons. In this case there is no question of the dead dancing as spirits in the heavenly paradise or in the fields of the blessed, but of a dance of the dead who have been buried in graves. People thought they saw lights shining on the burial mounds, and both heard and saw dancing and games, and heard the dead sing:

> We warriors lie buried here below,
> The soil above is heavy!
> Happy he who is allowed to live
> And enjoy his young life!   [Hyltén-Cavallius.]

Perhaps we may discern in this song one of the explanations why the dead so willingly danced: they sought to recover the joys of living.

There are numerous similar accounts from other countries; usually they relate how the dead danced in the burial places. Musical history is full of *dances macabres* or *dances tristes* composed on just this theme. In France it is even stated that the dead danced the national dance, the dance they preferred in life [Sebillot]. But the dance of the dead is dangerous for the living, because the dead draw unto themselves all they can, and then life itself is at stake. In Germany it was thought that the dead not only danced between and on the graves, but also held processions and masses. Henne-Am-Rhyn found a link with Platonic and neo-Platonic thought, arguing that the dance of the dead represented the perpetual dance of the moving stars round the earth, the stars being souls, but there is no need to show the fallacy of this interpretation.

During the Middle Ages the view was quite general that the dead liked to dance in the churchyards; that they sought to draw the living into the ranks of the dancers, but whoever danced with them would die within the year [Stammler].

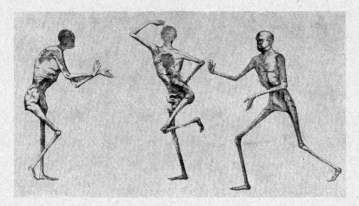

FIG. 51. The Dance of the Dead. Antique stucco from a grave in Cumae [Weege].

Kozáky mentions that a certain Amru Ben el-Haris Ben Modh-adh, in the third century A.D., wrote the following poem:

> Ye men, hasten to the palace,
> For tomorrow ye may no longer enter in!
> Spur your horses, loose the reins
> Before the man with scythe can reach you!
> We were once the men that you are now,
> You will soon become what we are now.

We have already met the two last lines in one of the death songs quoted by Balde. This death song is perhaps older than is commonly supposed; for example, we read on an ancient grave:

> What thou art, I have been,
> What I am, thou shalt become.
> I have been and am not,
> Ye are, but shall not always be.
> No one is immortal.

This old saw survives for centuries; sometimes it is engraved upon Christian tombstones, sometimes over the porches of churches, sometimes over their charnel houses. Thus we read over the charnel house of a church-yard in Berne [Köhler]:

> Here lie our bones!
> To us dance high and low.
> What you now are, once were we,
> What we now are, you shall become!

147

Freidank, who wrote in the thirteenth century, makes the dead speak thus [Massmann]:

> Thus speak they who are buried here,
> Old men and young boys:
> What you now are, once were we,
> What we now are, you shall become.

It is my opinion that in this death song, sung by the dead when they revealed themselves dancing in the churchuards, there lies a threat to the

FIG. 52. The Dance of Death. Marchant's imitation 1485 of *La Danse Macabre* on the wall of Le Cimetière des Innocents in Paris from 1424. Cardinal and king dancing [Mâle].

living: what the dead now are the living will be. It is an incantatory song; the expressed wish will compel the desired death by the magic force of the word. It is their own dangerousness, their own ill-will, their own hatred of everything living which the dead thus demonstrate. Their dance is therefore fraught with dire consequences; for the dead drag the living down to the grave during the dance.

Mâle relates that a document was once found in the archives of the church at Caudebec, and later lost, from which it appeared that in 1393 a dramatic dance was performed in the church, in which the actors represented the various ranks and professions and in which, after every turn of the dance, one of the dancers withdrew and vanished. This meant that one and all move towards death; one and all are subject to destruction. Mâle considers that this was a sort of dance of death. At a later date, 1453, we know that the Franciscans in Besançon, at the conclusion of every meeting of the provincial chapter, performed this dance in the church of St John [Gougaud]. Probably verses were sung which indicated to each and all the inevitability of death and the need to leave all behind. Such performances in verse are also known in other countries, for example in Spain. Soon, however, the representation of this dance of death began to be made in pictures. But in them it was not Death which led the living to the grave, but the dead, each one of whom dragged one of the living to destruction. Curiously enough it was the Strassburg zoologist A. Goette who was the first to realize this, and his conclusions—now self-evident—were quickly confirmed by Fehse. So it is the dead who drag the living with them in a line dance. Fehse argues, like so many other authors in the same field, that it was the texts of the earlier dances of death and the plays in the churches which gave rise to the painted pictures

Fig. 53. The Dance of Death. From a painting, dated 1424, on the wall of a churchyard in Paris. The physician and the printer are led to death by the dancing dead [Buchheit].

of the dance. The walls of the churchyard and its charnel houses, or even of the churches and monasteries, were used for painting the Dance of Death. In 1424 it was painted on the churchyard wall of the monastery of Aux Innocents in Paris (Figs. 52, 53); similar paintings followed elsewhere in France, Germany, England and Switzerland. Buchheit is of opinion that the Dance of Death in the monastery church of La Chaise Dieu in Auvergne may be somewhat earlier, from the fourteenth century. In the church of St Mary in Lübeck there was a representation, originally on wood, but later transferred to canvas, and in the church of St Mary Magdalene in Hamburg there was another similar painting. As a rule the dance was rendered as a line-dance, sometimes as a dance of pairs in procession, as, for example, in Bâle. Most frequently it is the dead who dance and hop; it is seldom that the living take any part [Mâle, Buchheit].

Very famous is the painting on the churchyard wall of the Preachers' Monastery in Bâle (Fig. 54). It was fully described by Merian in 1649, who stated that the picture was executed in the time of the Emperor Sigismund at the request of the Great Council of Bâle (1431–1448), in memory of the great mortality in the plague which raged in the year 1439. The figures in the dance are said to be portraits: the Pope is Felix V, the Emperor is said to be Sigismund and the King is Albert II. Schnurrer, in his *Chronik der Seuchen*, confirms that the plague began in 1438 and that in 1439 it was so widespread in South Germany and Switzerland, not least in Bâle, that people died in thousands.

Fehse, however, contrary to the generally accepted view, has advanced the not impossible idea that the dance of the dead may have its origin in the custom of churchyard dances. When one considers how extraordinarily widespread the custom was from the early days of Christianity until the end

FIG. 54. The Dance of Death. Painted on the churchyard wall of the Preachers' monastery in Bâle. From the end of the fifteenth century. Copper-plate by Matthäus Merian the Elder (1593–1650). Here a corpse dances with a knight [Buchheit].

of the eighteenth century, and when one considers the motives behind these protective incantation dances, then we must fully accept Fehse's surmise. It is not possible that the dramatic performances of the Dance of Death which took place in the churches in the fourteenth century were the only motive for the paintings of the Dance of Death. In that case it remains to explain, on the one hand, the origin of the former and, on the other hand, the appearance in the latter of the dead who drag the living with them. All attempts to connect the Dance of Death with the early medieval legends of a meeting of three living persons and three dead seem to me to fall to the ground in view of the fact that there is here no question of three, but of a countless host. The motives behind the churchyard dance and the dance of the dead are obviously identical. As regards the dramatic dance against death and its connexion with the motive of the churchyard dances we may feel more hesitation. This dance cannot have been anything but a dramatic illustration of the old truth that all living things pass away and that there is no inequality in death. In addition, the living dance as they approach their death. But we find this motive in religious mysticism. The motive of the Dance of Death surely is purely magical: the dead, in the shape of demons, force the living into an early grave, and so, in the verses of the Dance of Death, the living complain and ask for delay. The Dance of Death seems to be also a dance of triumph; for the dancers it seems a pleasure to force the living into death. But the churchyard dances are directed against the dead; their songs have the purpose of exorcizing them, of keeping them and their evil away. Merian's view is probably quite correct: the dance of death painted in Bâle was associated with the plague which raged there. The dance of death has its origin in the motives which centuries ago gave rise to the churchyard dances.

But in the Dance of Death is found the peculiar suggestion that the living themselves dance towards their own death. To die is to dance; death is a wedding dance; one dances in death towards the bridegroom; one is conducted by Christ, the Virgin Mary and the dancing host of angels through death to Paradise. All these ideas are a part of late medieval mysticism.

Freidank writes:

> God did well when he forbade
> That man should know when he shall die!
> For if man knew this
> The dance they then would miss.

In a manuscript of 1428, entitled *The Prophecy of the Sybil*, Christ tells the Virgin Mary, together with the dancing and singing hosts of angels, to conduct the souls of the dead to the Father in Heaven. According to Heinrich von Nördlingen (1346) Christ dances before the soul set free from the body, and according to the pronounced mystic Henrik Suso, of the fourteenth century, Christ is the dance leader of the blessed arriving in Heaven [Kozáky]. We also find in medieval mysticism the idea that the soul celebrates its marriage to Christ, who takes it by the hand and leads it in the heavenly dance [Stammler]. Indeed, the mystics of the fourteenth century let Christ lead the dance to the grave. They saw in death 'a happy transition to eternal life from this death in the world' [Stegemeier].

But the Devil, like his demons, dances. He imitates Christ and the Blessed. Suso thought that the Devil likewise led his followers in a dance [Stammler]. It was thought that the accursed danced in hell just as the blessed danced in Heaven. And at one time, when the blast of the angels' trumpets awakened the dead, it was thought that this awakening must be to a dance; the resurrected bodies must dance, one row up to Heaven, the other down to hell [Wackernagel].

It is this resurrection of the body which, in my opinion, is so often represented in the late medieval pictures depicting skeletons or half-decomposed bodies arising from their graves to tread a dance to the music of other dead. This is the real *danse macabre*. We find support for this view also in Schedel's chronicle, published in Nüremberg and illustrated with woodcuts by Wohlgemuth. The picture here reproduced (Fig. 55) depicts just such a Dance of Death. Schedel's text reads: 'We believe in all certainty that God has created man in his own image. What can happen to us with greater equanimity than to leave this unclean earthly body, and to return to Him who has not scorned to create us in his own image, so that the human spirit, filled with the spirit of God, may live in eternity, sharing divine bliss among the angels and the choir of the saints?' But the resurrection from the grave presupposes the Pauline transformation of the body; it is both the spirit and the spiritualized body which, through resurrection, dance into Paradise. Thus there still

FIG. 55. The Resurrection Dance of the Dead. Woodcut by Michael Wohlgemuth (1434–1519) in Hartmann Schedel's *Liber chronicarum germanice*, Nüremberg, 1493.

survives the old idea of a dance in Heaven. There is a German popular lay, according to Kozáky, which strongly reminds us of the song which the girls in Flanders sang at the funeral of their dead friend. It runs:

> In Heaven, in Heaven joy is great;
> There dance the dear angels, there they play;
> They sing and hop and praise God;
> They praise Mary, the Mother of God.

The Dance of Death has found its way into purely profane dances. Among Hungarians and Slavs there is a social dance which is called the Dance of Death. A dancer lies down 'dead' and the others dance round him singing songs of sorrow. One or another leaves the ring and advances to the 'dead' and changes his position in some way. Finally somebody kisses the 'dead'. Then comes the resurrection and then begins a wilder dance, with comic hopping steps, to the accompaniment of joyous songs [Böhme, Czerwinski]. This Dance of Death persisted from the fifteenth to the seventeenth century in wedding dances in various parts of Germany [Böhme]. The procedure is essentially much the same.

FIG. 56. The Dance of Death in the Corpus Christi procession at Verges, Catalonia. During the eighteenth century it conducted the Archbishop of Tarragona on certain occasions. To the left is a scythe bearer, in the middle the banner bearer, to the right the dead with a pendulum clock. In the background Death (or Time) as drummer [Capmány].

In Spain there is another *Bal de la Mort* (Fig. 56), a dance of death still performed in the 1930's, principally in Catalonia, particularly in certain districts of Ampurdán. It is part of the church processions during Holy Week. It is composed of a quadrille, executed by twelve men and three women, in black clothes on which white skeletons have been painted. The face is covered with a mask representing a skull. One of the dancers carries a scythe, another a pendulum clock, and a third a banner. The musician, with only a drum, is clad in armour, enveloped in a black mantle. They follow the Corpus Christi procession and therefore are a part of the popular church dance. The one who carries the scythe must not take part in the dance, but just swings his scythe towards the bystanders. The others dance and hop. In the eighteenth century a similar Dance of Death led the procession which received and followed the Archbishop of Tarragona when he first joined the fraternity of the Holy Blood.

To sum up, it may be said that the dead are comforted and rejoiced by the dance performed for them in the night watch, before their last journey. The demons are forced by the dance to leave the dead alone. When the body is buried there is another dance in its honour, and for its comfort, a dance which illustrates both bliss in the heavenly paradise and also the approaching bodily resurrection. Similar ideas no doubt at one time underlay the dance which was performed at the memorial party. Perhaps the intention was also to express satisfaction that the departed had reached bliss through death. But at the same time the dead become demons—this the obverse of the medal; they seek to injure the living and drag them down to a premature death. They dance in churchyards by night, and seek to draw the living into their disastrous performance. Being of the Underworld, they are above all demons of disease; they cause illness and severe suffering by possessing men. Their evil must be warded off; they must be compelled to put right what they have distorted. They can even be forced to assist or to prophesy coming events. The nightly dances and incantations and magic rites performed in churchyards and on gallows hills serve the same purpose. The dance is protective, partly because it comforts the dead by the resurrection and the bliss which it illustrates and promises, and partly by the imitative dance of the angels which by its magic has the power to fend off the forces of the Underworld and to force the latter to give up their prey. Possibly the dance had this last-named faculty because it revealed something of the mystery of the divine creation, the wonderful harmony by which the created world is ruled and constructed.

IX

The Prohibition of Religious Dances

THE struggle of the Church against religious dances in churches, chapels and churchyards began as early as the fourth century with Epiphanios and Basileios. At first the Fathers of the Church were cautious and hesitating. There can be no doubt whatever that the chief objection was to those forms of the dance which were vicious and indecent, with improper songs, and to the participation of women and the dancing together of men and women. For example, even when it seemed that St Augustine would have liked to forbid and condemn every form of church dance, he finally gave way when confronted with the often quoted biblical commands in the gospels of Matthew and Luke that whoever wishes to dance may dance. But neither is there any doubt that the opposition of the Church had already begun; the dance had led to such serious abuse that it had to be resisted. We have seen, however, that this resistance was not very successful and that not infrequently it was quite in vain. The Fathers of the Church and other theological writers were certainly correct when they pointed out that pagan influence was the cause of the energetic efforts of the newly-converted to retain the dances of their cult. These pagan dance customs contributed, without the slightest doubt, to the vigour of the dance even within the Christian Church. These pagan customs are to be found preserved by those of pure Christian faith since the earliest days of the Church. Throughout the centuries it was just the writings of the Church Fathers which were the principal object of study in monasteries and in the training and education of the priesthood. Their views on the meaning of the dance in the Church and in divine service have never been forgotten, and have always been preserved. This is also perhaps the principal reason why the priests and monks never quite concurred in the repeated prohibitions of the dance. In the following pages we shall survey the various prohibitions, from the fourth to the eighteenth century.

The Provincial Synod in Elvira, near Granada, in 300–303, ordered that women should not be permitted to hold night watches in churchyards, at which, under the cloak of prayer, they fell into sin [Hefele]. It seems safe to assume that these night watches in churches and churchyards were combined with dancing, and the proscription has a very special significance since it affords proof that the churchyard dance already existed at the very beginning of the fourth century.

Proscriptions multiplied in the sixth century. The Council of Toledo in 539 expressed the hope that the practice, contrary to religion, of dancing and singing shameless songs at the festivals of the saints and whilst waiting for church processions might, with the help of the priests, be rooted out of all Spain. The Council of Auxerres, 573–603, forbade the public to dance choir dances or nuns to sing in them [Gougaud]. Towards the end of the sixth century King Childebert II (who died in 596) issued a circular letter in which he deplored dancing, singing, drunkenness and dissoluteness during night watches at the great Church festivals.

In the seventh century the Council of Toledo (633) inveighed against the Festival of Fools with its music and dancing in the churches [Stubenvoll], and the Council of Châlons-sur-Saône, 639–654, against the shameless and indecent songs sung at female choir dances in connexion with inauguration festivals of churches and at the festivals of the martyrs, and these were all forbidden in the vicinity of the church [Gougaud]. We are reminded how, in the middle of the seventh century, Bishop Eligius of Noyon objected to the night watch dances at the festival of St Peter, and he forbade the Germans to perform dances or sing 'devilish' songs on Midsummer Eve or on any other saints' festival.

In the eighth century a number of episcopal instructions were issued to subordinates (*Commitorium*) in which dancing and singing by women in the church porch were forbidden, as well as the 'devilish' songs which the public used to sing for the dead at night time to the accompaniment of loud laughter. In the year 743 the Council of Lessinas, in Hennegau, forbade laymen to dance choir dances, and nuns to sing in churches, for it is written: 'My house shall be a house of prayer' [Böhme].

The Council of Rome in 826 complained that women, especially on holidays and the anniversaries of saints, only came to church in order to sing shameless songs and to perform choir dances, whereby they followed pagan example [Quasten]. In the middle of the ninth century Pope Leo IV ordered that women should be prevented from dancing and singing in churches and porches. Further, the public were enjoined to refrain from 'devilish' songs and loud laughter at night in the presence of the dead [Gougaud].

At the beginning of the tenth century the Patriarch John III threatened with excommunication those women who visited graves in order to beat drums and dance [Quasten]. Similarly, at the beginning of the same century Regino, Abbot of Prüm, who died in 915, intervened with the same object [Kelle]; in his work, *On Church Discipline*, he posed the confessional question, 'Have you sung devilish songs for the dead?' and forbade the public to sing them at funerals, or to dance, since it was the pagans who, at the instigation of the Devil, had invented them. The Bishops, during their visitations, were to inquire whether 'the priests have really resisted the singing of devilish songs by the people at night, for the dead'. Regino relates that in France an annual festival was instituted on the day before Ascension Day in thankfulness to the Lord for warding off a raging epidemic of rabies; at this festival women were forbidden to take part in ring-dances. In another work, *De Synodis Causis*, Regino wrote, 'Laymen who hold a death watch must do so with fear and reverence. Nobody shall on such occasions sing devilish songs or play games or dance. All these are pagan inventions of the Devil. Who cannot know that these are the work of the Devil and are not only repulsive to the Christian religion but are also contrary to human nature, all this singing, merry-making, dancing and laughing in the churchyards, all this rejection of piety and feelings of delicacy combined with hopping in the presence of friendly death, when, instead, there should be sorrow and lamentation and voices bewailing the passing of a beloved brother? But if anyone should want to sing, let him sing *Kyrie eleison* (Lord, have mercy)' [Kelle]. Regino also posed this confessional question, together with an injunction, to those who sung in the church and to the women who danced there instead of listening in silence to the Word of the Lord [Balogh].

At the beginning of the eleventh century Burchard from Worms laid it down that during confession the question should be asked, 'Have you taken part in a death watch and sung devilish songs and have you danced and hopped, as the Devil taught the pagans to do?' [Kelle]. In the same decree Burchard continued, 'Take care at death watches, for it has happened that Christian bodies have been watched in pagan fashion, when devilish songs have been sung and hopping dances have been performed, as the pagans learned them from the Devil. Drinking bouts also took place and there was loud laughter whilst, rejecting piety and decency, there was dancing in the presence of friendly death.' Here, as so often later, the traditional form of words was employed. In the year 1009 the Synod of Meeresheim issued new proscriptions against devilish songs and loud laughter at night in the presence of the dead [Balogh]. Bratislav II of Bohemia in 1092 forbade dancing in churchyards and expressly mentioned that masks were worn and demonic conjurations spoken. De Sully, Bishop of Paris, in 1198 and 1199 forbade the Festival of Fools in French churches and referred to similar proscriptions of an earlier date by

Cardinal Pierre. At these festivals the sub-deacons wore masks [du Tilliot].

About 1200 a hitherto indeterminate synod laid down that ring-dances, and shameless and indecent games inciting to vice, must not be permitted in churches and churchyards [Balogh]. Shortly before 1208 the Bishop of Paris forbade dancing in churches, churchyards and processions [Gougaud]. In 1206 the Synod of Cahors threatened with excommunication those who danced inside or in front of churches [Stieren]. In 1207 Pope Innocent III inveighed against the Festival of Fools and the indecent games of priests and sub-deacons [Schrör]. Cambius, Bishop of Paris, in 1208 repeated de Sully's proscription of the Festival of Fools in churches [du Tilliot]. The Council of Avignon in 1209 decreed that 'in night watches for the saints there shall not be performed in churches play-acting, hopping dances, indecent gestures, ring-dances, neither shall there be sung love songs or ditties' [Gougaud]. The Council of Paris, in 1212, and the Synod of Rouen, in 1214 [Hefele], forbade the Festival of Fools in churches and the ring-dances of women in the churchyards. The Council of Trier in 1227 forbade three-step and ring-dances and other worldly games in churchyards and churches [Balogh], and a Council of Rouen in 1231 repeated these proscriptions [Hefele]. The Council of Cognac in 1260 forbade church dances on Innocents' Day, when there was quarrelling and disorder even during divine service. The crowning of 'bishops' was also forbidden [Gougaud]. A Council of Buda, in Hungary, in 1279 exhorted the priests to prevent dancing in churchyards and churches, and this exhortation was reinforced by the Council of Berry in 1286 [Gerbertus]. At the same time, or somewhat earlier, Bar Hebraeus, who died in the same year, inveighed against the pagan practice of women dancing for the dead in churchyards to the music of drums [Quasten]. In 1287 two synods, in Exeter [Chambers] and Liége [Stieren] similarly objected. The Synod of Exeter is of especial interest, for we read, 'It is ordered that there shall be no wrestling, ring-dances or other forbidden games in churchyards, especially at night watches and the festivals of the saints, because by the performance of such play-acting and indecent games the dignity of the Church is dragged through the mire'. In Liége it was only dances in churches, porches and churchyards which were forbidden. This was repeated in the Synod of Tulle in 1298 [Stieren]. The Council of Würzburg [Binterim] in 1298 attacked these dances expressly, threatening heavy punishment and describing them as grievous sin.

In 1300 the Council of Bayeux repeated the decrees, and so did the Council of Tréquier at about the same time [Gougaud]. In 1308 the Bishop of London forbade wrestling, ring-dances and dissolute behaviour in the churchyards of Barking, in connexion with the festivals of St Margaret and St Ethelburga, because they had given rise to disorders, quarrelling and murder [Liebermann]. The Council of Cologne, in 1310 inveighed against all sins committed at funerals: 'No societies, persons in authority or councils shall divert themselves by performing ring-dances or dissolute games or indecencies in churches or churchyards' [Balogh]. In 1318 there were episcopal orders in

Lerida, in northern Spain, against night-watch festivals, and festivals on saints' days and other Church ceremonials, it being forbidden 'to perform in churches and churchyards indecent ring-dances to the singing of songs, with violence, dice games and other forbidden things by which the churches and churchyards are desecrated' [Villanueva]. The Synod of Prague, 1366, warned priests against singing immoral ditties to music or the organ during mass or during the blessing—most probably at the Festival of Fools [Spanke]. A Synod of York, in 1367, forbade wrestling, archery, and games in holy places, at night watches for the saints and at funerals [Chambers]. The Cathedral Chapter of Würzburg in 1377 condemned dancing at the Festival of Fools [Stubenvoll]. In the year 1384 the Bishop of Winchester found himself compelled to forbid the public to 'play with balls or throw stones . . . to execute improper ring-dances or sing ditties, to play indecent games or to perform hop-dances and other shameful games as well as many other kinds of impropriety by which it is feared that the churchyards might be desecrated' [Chambers]. The Synod of Noyon [Naunet], in 1389, inveighed against dancing in churches [du Cange].

At the beginning of the fifteenth century (perhaps somewhat earlier) the Archbishop of Lund complained that at certain festivals, during night watches on the festivals of St John the Baptist and St Botulph (June 17th), in accordance with pagan custom, people performed ring-dances and sang indecent songs in churches and churchyards [Balogh]. The Synod of Langres, 1404, sought to proscribe the Festival of Fools [du Tilliot]. The Council of Paris, in 1429, forbade priests 'for their own pleasure to take part in foolish and shameful games to which they are accustomed—sometimes at their own instigation—at the festivals of the saints' [Gerbertus], which is clearly a reference to the Festival of Fools. The Council of Bâle, in 1435, tried to prohibit ring-dances, three-step dances, plays, loud laughter, bartering and huckstering in markets and in churches and churchyards, forbidding in addition the election of a Fool's Bishop and a Children's Bishop [Binterim]. The circular from the Theological Faculty in Paris, 1444, against the Festival of Fools has already been quoted. The Council of Rouen, 1445, repeated this prohibition, and so did a Council at Sens in 1485 [du Tilliot]. The Council of Soissons, 1456, forbade 'masquerades and play-acting games, ring-dances, buying and selling and such-like things in churches and monasteries as they disturb divine service and reverence for them' [Gougaud].

In the year 1525 were issued the Synodal Statutes of Orléans, in which an attempt was made to abolish all sorts of games, profane songs, plays and feasts in churches and churchyards; while the Council of Sens (held in Paris in 1528) attacked primarily the Festival of Fools and the Children's Festival; the same is true of the Council of Cologne in 1536 [du Tilliot]. The Acts of the Synod of Chartres, 1550, were directed against the Festival of Fools and the Children's Festival [du Tilliot], as also the Council of Narbonne, 1551 [Balogh], which attacked the church dances in the severest terms: 'Since to the dishonour of the Christian name, and in contempt of holy things, there are performed ring-dances and hop-dances and other kinds of three-step dances, as well as other improprieties, the Council desires to root them out entirely, so that henceforth nobody will dare to dance in a holy temple or a churchyard during divine service' [Gougaud]. In the Statues of Ancona of 1560 three-step dances were forbidden 'by day or night in any church of the state or the city of Ancona' [Rodocanachi]. In Compostella there was a Synod in 1565 which forbade dances and plays during mass—but the pro-hibition was soon after withdrawn [Browe]. The Council of Cambrai of the same year advocated strict prohibition of the Festival of Fools, as did the Council of Toledo in 1566, which described it as an infamous abuse and at the same time forbade the election of so-called bishops [du Tilliot]. The Council of Lyons, 1566–67, agreed [Gougaud]. The Synod of Mechlin, 1570, sought to induce the civil authorities to prevent such dances as might seduce the congregation from mass [Gerbertus]. The Synod of s'Hertogenbosch in 1571 [Gerbertus], and that of Chartres, 1575 [du Tilliot] repeated the above, and the latter added a prohibition of the Festival of Fools. These directions were renewed in the Council of Rheims, 1583, in Aix, 1585, and in the Synod of Angers in 1595, which was also directed against the Children's Festival [du Tilliot].

In the year 1617 the Archbishop of Cologne declared, 'Such dance games as are commonly played in churches after the marriage ceremony, when the bridal pair stamp with their feet, must entirely cease. . . . Such a custom conflicts with the dignity and esteem of the Church, the Sacrament and God. The priests must warn their congregations and threaten them with punish-ment and fines, a gold florin in each case, unless they avoid ring-dances and dance games, which are forbidden, and such shameful and indecent dances as the *Kronendanz* or the *Lehenschwinken*, which by this decree we forbid' [Binterim]. In 1644 the Archbishop of Cologne issued an express prohibition of Fools' Festivals with their ring-dances and hopping [Schrör]. But the Synod of Angers inveighed only against the Festival of Fools and its dances outside the churches [du Tilliot].

In 1753 the Bishop of Barcelona sought to stop the eagle dance in churches, and the eagles were forbidden to take part in church processions. A royal decree of Madrid, 1777, sought to prevent all dancing on holy days before the images of the saints, in churches, their porches, or in churchyards. A similar decree of 1780 enacted that, in the churches of the realm, no dances might henceforth be performed; the appearance of giants in the church processions was forbidden [Capmány].

This is an imposing list of proscriptions, but it could probably be much enlarged if the sources were more adequately examined. Some of these proscriptions afford important evidence as to the actual procedure of these church and churchyard dances. But how little did they affect popular custom! Dancing by the clergy was eventually stopped, except certain choristers' dances in Spain; but the Church was never able to suppress the popular church dances. It was only the Reformation, with its highly critical attitude towards traditional church customs and its fight against images and the worship of saints and pilgrimages, which ultimately succeeded in suppressing the church dance, that is, with a very few exceptions, for the Lutheran Church strove more or less in vain against the dance for the dead. One has the impression, however, that the Catholic Church was more or less resigned and contented itself with resisting strongly those dances which by their nature or by their obviously magic character and association with demonology dishonoured the Church. On the other hand, in the Latin countries the popular church dances were simply taken over by the Church and were permitted under its control, and it seems to me extremely interesting that in Spain, where they still flourish most extensively, these dances seem to be quite free at least of any obvious magic significance. These dances are not, for instance, for healing purposes or to secure a better harvest, but are a religious rite and a reverence due to the saints, and so far as one can judge from available accounts they have no magical element, though that element is overwhelmingly apparent in, for example, the Echternach dance. Yet one must not forget that even the Echternach dance was under the control and protection of the Church authorities. Finally we must recognize that the difference is not very great: there is no more magic in seeking a benefit than in seeking to strengthen a prayer by performing simultaneously a reverent and penitential dance. Perhaps it is wrong in such cases as the Echternach dance to describe it as magical, and we ought perhaps to reserve that term for those dances which by their form more or less represent the wish in action. The churchyard dances, however, were to some extent reverent, i.e., in reverence for the dead. But their magical significance cannot be disputed. Thus we come back to the idea concealed behind the action. Possibly we ought to regard the Echternach dance as purely and simply a penitential pilgrimage, with healing as its purpose.

One detail deserves mention. We have frequently found reference to dances performed in the porches of churches or immediately in front of them. As we shall have occasion to note later, the church porch and its precincts constituted an important part of the medieval church: it represents Paradise, whilst the interior of the church is the heavenly temple hall. Even to this day the porch of the cathedral at Aachen is called its 'Paradise'. It is consequently in full agreement with this that the Dance of the Angels is imitated in 'Paradise'. But I am not quite convinced of the correctness of this view, for what is remarkable is the fact that, as the proscriptions so frequently show, people were careful to dance in the porch during the service and so disturbed it with songs and cries, seeming thereby to indicate a more pronounced magical significance in the dance. The dancers must have felt that in performing it during the solemn ritual within the church the effect of the dance would be strengthened and its purpose more easily achieved. Probably the proscriptions are right when they point to pagan prototypes of these dances—not of the dance itself, but as a background to the fact that they took place under such conditions.

As early as the days of the Church Fathers, the Councils were compelled to forbid and to issue warnings against these dances, but to no avail. From the eleventh century the proscriptions became more numerous, being most frequent between 1200 and 1500. The impression is created that dances and processions in churches and churchyards never flourished so much as in the latter part of the Middle Ages and the first centuries of modern times. This may be an illusion, for the numerous proscriptions, warnings and threats, may possibly be due simply to the fact that among the cultured classes within the Church there was a demand that the ritual of the service and Christian standards should be raised to a higher level. The reaction against the all too frequent degeneracy of these dances became stronger and stronger, in spite of the fact that possibly at the same time the hosts of dancers had already begun, for the same reason, to diminish.

One further important conclusion may be drawn. Our survey shows that the Christian religious dances continued from the end of the third century in unbroken succession until our own day. Not a single century is without its proscription. They have not been suppressed and revived in the form of an infection from pagan customs.

X

The Processions of the Flagellants

THE Black Death, which destroyed hundreds of thousands of human beings and laid waste great areas, swept through Europe in 1349, and during that year there appeared a curious religious sect which in its strict asceticism combined moral and religious ideals and a striving for rebirth in religious life. Perhaps we are not justified in attaching to this phenomenon the specific label of heresy, at any rate on its first appearance. It is nevertheless obvious that it soon came to embrace both practical ecclesiastical and religious doctrines which must be described as heretical vis-à-vis the Catholic Church. What especially characterized the flagellants was their endeavour by means of severe asceticism to reconcile themselves and humanity to God, by their own suffering to countervail the sin which had brought the plague as a scourge of God. Flagellation appeared as an essential element of their asceticism, whilst the dance, which was probably performed simultaneously, was only of secondary importance and had only, as it were, a ritual significance. These men were called flagellants or Brethren of the Cross, the latter because they wore a cross on their clothes as a visible symbol, and also because they constituted an organized society or brotherhood.

Various authors have sought to discern in the processions of flagellants a predisposition for the subsequent dance epidemics, especially the extraordinarily widespread epidemic of 1374. But it has never been possible to adduce any real, or even probable, connexion historically between the flagellants and the dancers and it may be asserted definitely that the dance epidemic had no direct connexion with the flagellants' processions. There might, nevertheless, be an indirect connexion, for similar causes may conceivably have given rise to the various methods of seeking deliverance from sickness and suffering. The general affliction of the time, pestilence, ruined harvests and famine, poverty and a high cost of living, constant wars, general ignorance and crass superstition and the general moral degeneracy which was apparent in the fourteenth century—all these are general preconditions and psychological motives which were universal in 1349 and 1374 and which can amply explain a peculiar and confusing reaction. In the one case it found expression in an endeavour, by bodily suffering, by mixing one's own blood with that of Christ, by a strict and ascetic mode of living, by prayer and invocation, to achieve deliverance from a rapid and violent death; in the other case it found expression in an endeavour, by dancing before the saints, to enlist their co-operation in a plea for God's mercy and for deliverance from unbearable bodily pain.

Asceticism has a long ancestry in the Christian church. As early as the third century—that is, in the earliest Christian era—flagellation is represented as an offering acceptable to God [Pfannenschmid]. Many are the theologians and writers who have prescribed bodily pain as a means of suppressing the sinful lusts of the flesh, of conquering sin and of winning God's grace and comfort. Regino of Prüm, at the beginning of the tenth century, ordered flagellation not only for monks, but also for laymen. Burchard from Worms, in the eleventh century, prescribed flagellation as an ascetic treatment for sinners. Thenceforward flagellation was no longer unusual either in religious discipline or as a healing force [Boileau]. When in 1348 the plague reached Avignon and the papal court, Pope Clement IV ordered processions as a protection, and in these processions the participants had to walk barefoot, with ashes in their hair, scourging themselves severely on their bare backs [Runge]. This procession of flagellants has no connexion, however, with the processions of flagellants which we shall here describe; it is only one of many examples of the fact that flagellation and healing processions of flagellants were not at this time unknown to the Catholic Church.

As early as 1260 the first real processions of flagellants moved from Italy over the Alps to various European countries. A Styrian chronicle relates that the flagellants walked naked to the waist and had their heads enveloped in linen cloths. They carried standards, lighted candles and scourges. With the scourges they beat themselves until the blood ran and at the same time they sang spiritual songs. They advanced in procession and stopped at certain places, where they knelt and sang again in their respective languages. In the years 1262 and 1296 there were new processions and the movement flamed up in Italy in 1334 and 1360.

In the year 1347 the plague came from the Levant and spread in the years from 1348 until 1351 over the whole of Europe. The worst year was 1349.

The great processions of flagellants numbering hundreds and even thousands spread in the same year over Austria, Bohemia, Germany, Switzerland, the Rhine province, the Netherlands and England. Men and women, nobles and commoners, priests and monks, even the most exalted personages, attached themselves to these pious pilgrimages [Frédéricq]. Towards the end of 1349 civil and ecclesiastical authorities united—among them were even the King of France and the Pope of Avignon—in their efforts to suppress the processions and to eradicate the flagellants, and on October 20th in that year a Papal Bull was promulgated forbidding the flagellant sects. The Church complained that they had founded a new kind of fraternity without permission, and introduced new forms of divine service, and compared them with heretics. How much truth there is in these complaints is not certain, even if we must admit the great probability that at least some of their circles did not refrain from intimate association with one or other of the numerous sects which, especially in the Rhineland, set their stamp upon the fourteenth century. In any case, as Frédéricq has shown, they sent to the Chapter of Doornik a *Regula Flagellatorum*, which contains an account of their beliefs. In it their submission to the Church and acceptance of its faith and teaching is clearly apparent. They appear as strictly moral and God-fearing. In the Papal Bull they are called devilish flagellants and the priests and monks who follow them are condemned to prison.

Nevertheless the flagellants reappeared between 1351 and 1353. There was a glimpse of them in 1357, but they were soon suppressed—by fire and sword. In the year 1400 the flagellant movement revived for a brief while in Flanders, where the magistrates of Maastricht sought to expel them from the town. Similar measures were also taken in other places in the neighbourhood. They were cast into prison or chased out of the parishes. Both Holland and Italy saw new processions at the beginning of the fifteenth century, also contemporaneously with famine and high mortality. In Sangerhausen in Thuringia they appeared for the last time in 1414 [Spangenberg].

Records of the flagellants' procession of 1349 state that they wore the short pilgrim's pelerine over their shoulders, with red crosses on the front and back. The pelerine could be raised over the head as a sort of capuchon, but above was worn a pointed hat with an upturned brim, also with a red cross before and behind. In their hands they carried pilgrims' staffs [Frédéricq]. There can therefore be no possible doubt that they appear, and must be regarded as, pilgrims engaged on a pilgrimage. The pelerine was black; the lower garment, which extended from the hips to the feet, was

Fig. 57. A Procession of Flagellants at Doornik, 1349. The standard displays two scourges and is followed by two candle bearers and then by the bearer of the crucifix. All the flagellants have scourges with three thongs, each with three knots. Their caps are marked with red crosses; below them, hanging over their shoulders, they wear a capuchon—like a pilgrim's pelerine. The flagellants are naked except for an ankle-length cloth from the waist. All are bare-footed. Contemporary miniature by H. S. van Gilles le Muisis, in the Royal Library, Brussels [Frédéricq].

white, the felt hat grey. The pilgrims marched barefoot [Pfannenschmid].

Three contemporary pictures are preserved, and a fourth which may to some extent be regarded as a part of the living tradition. Unquestionably the most important has been published by Frédéricq. It is a coloured miniature from the middle of the fourteenth century depicting the entrance of the flagellants into Doornik in 1349 (Fig. 57). It is to be found in a manuscript preserved in the Royal Library at Brussels. This manuscript is a chronicle of Egidius Li Muisis, Abbot of the St Martin monastery in Tournai. Li Muisis, however, was blind from 1348, but in 1351 recovered his sight after an operation. Therefore he cannot himself have seen these flagellants, but drew and painted his miniature from the accounts of an eye-witness [Runge]. In this picture the flagellants are in procession, dressed as described above, preceded by a standard bearer with a velvet banner, on which are painted two scourges, further two candle-bearers and one who bears the processional crucifix. All of them carry scourges which are made of short sticks to which are attached three thongs or ropes with three knots and three or four nail-like pieces of metal in the form of a cross. This procession took place on August 15th, the Assumption of the Virgin, and about two hundred persons attended from Bruges.

The second picture is to be found in a Constance chronicle, written at the end of the fourteenth century (Fig. 58). It is possible that these are the flagellants who appeared towards the end of the fourteenth century. They are substantially the same as the others, but the pilgrims' pelerines are doffed, the hats are as usual, and from the waist is suspended the foot-length garment. The flagellation, or a part of it, is in progress and absolution is being given by the following foreman for sins confessed in public.

There is a further miniature to be found in a fifteenth-century manuscript containing St Augustine's work, *Civitas Dei*, preserved in the St Geneviève Library in Paris. It probably represents the flagellants of the early fifteenth century; they are shown inside a church in the act of scourging before a couple of statues raised on pillars. It is not possible to see what these statues are supposed to represent, but most probably they represent Christ and Mary. It was to them that the flagellants addressed themselves. It was

FIG. 58. Absolution of Flagellants. Flagellants, according to a coloured pen-drawing in the Constance chronicle [Cod. Germ. Monac. No. 426]. Fourteenth century. Their heads are covered. All are naked except for a foot-length cloth from the waist [Schultz].

Christ and Mary who were invoked and whose help was implored against the plague. To the right stands a bishop in his robes, who says, in the script: 'They make offerings to the Devil and not to God'. The flagellants are no longer dressed as hitherto but are bare-headed and wear only a girdle round their waists.

In Schedel's world chronicle of the end of the fifteenth century we find a fourth picture (Fig. 59). It may be correct in accordance with surviving tradition. It is noteworthy that both of the flagellants hold a scourge in either hand. In any case these double scourges are known from the processions of 1261 [Spangenberg] and may be supposed to have existed here and there at a later date also. The modern shows, however, seem to be an anachronism in a picture of an ascetic procession for the healing of lowly pilgrims.

When the flagellants approached an inhabited place they went in procession, singing a pilgrim's song (Fig. 60), which was really much older in respect of its general content. It originated in the times of the Crusades, but was revised for the especial purpose of the procession [Runge]. In the Imperial Library of St Petersburg there has been found an old chronicle written by Hugo Spechtshart (died *circa* 1360), called *Hugo von Reutlingen*. It is an account of the processions of flagellants of 1349 and is written in hexameters. It gives all their songs and the melodies to which they were

FIG. 59. Flagellants. Drawn in 1493 by Michael Wohlgemuth. Probably representing flagellants from processions other than 1349 [Schedel].

sung. It was published in 1900 by Runge. On entering a place the flagellants sang this pilgrim's song:

> Now passes the holy host of pilgrims.
> Christ himself rode to Jerusalem.
> He had a cross in his own hand.
> Help us, Holy Ghost.

Sometimes another hymn would be used (Fig. 61) which began:

> Mary, Mother and Maiden pure,
> Have mercy on thy Christendom,
> Have mercy on thy children,
> Living in this evil world.

When they reached an open space, usually the market square of the community or the church itself, they laid aside their cloaks, retaining their other clothes and the pilgrim hat. After various rites had been performed, the scourging took place. It was repeated twice daily except on Fridays when there were three ceremonies. The participants continued the pilgrimage for thirty-three days, recalling our Lord's thirty-three years of life on earth [Sprengel].

On arrival they ranged themselves in a big circle, and then began to move, two by two, round an inner ring of brethren who acted as choir leaders. During this ring-dance the following hymn was sung while the flagellants of the outer ring lashed themselves—

> Who this penance would perform,
> Let him pay and earn release;
> Let him confess and flee from sin,
> He shall then God's mercy win.

Nu ist div betfart so he-re

Crist rait sel-ber gen ie - ru - sa - le - - - - m

FIG. 60. The Pilgrimage Song of the Flagellants, 1349.

A variant of this hymn, which is also supplied by Closener, reads as follows (Fig. 62):

> Who penance will do, let him come forth.
> May we escape the fires of hell.
> Lucifer is a wretched wight,
> He cools with pitch whom he doth capture.
> Bethink thee well and flee his might.

After this they knelt down, stretched out their arms in the form of a cross, and sang more hymns, one falling across another to form a cross as they did so. Then they rose to their feet and walked round in a ring again as first described. Once again they scourged themselves while another hymn was sung (Fig. 62):

> Mary stood in greatest pain;
> As she saw her dear child die
> A sword went through her heart.
> Forget not this thou sinner.
> Mary, Queen, help us now
> That we may have thy son's protection.

Twice they knelt and twice they sang, then followed confession, and after that the absolution, with some final lashes from the leaders.

Other hymns were used on these occasions, but only the first verse of one is quoted here (Fig. 63), and that because it states so plainly the chief object

FIG. 61. Processional Hymn sung by Flagellants in 1349. The flagellants would begin to sing when they reached the market place, churchyard or church where the scourging was to take place [Runge].

of these flagellant bands. While the pilgrims knelt with their arms outflung, or fell to the ground, one across another, they sang:

Now raise we all our hands,
That God may take away the plague,
Now raise we all our arms
That God may have mercy on us.

This, then, is the purpose of the pilgrimage, the object of the self-castigation: that men's souls shall tremble, and their hard hearts may weep in secret, and that God and Christ and Mary may be prevailed on to bring to an end all plague and sudden death, and to guard and protect the pilgrim band.

Frederick Closener, a priest and a writer who was still alive in 1384, com-

168

pleted his chronicle in 1362, and it is still preserved at the Bibliothèque Nationale in Paris. In the course of a detailed description of one of these pilgrimages he makes the significant comment that after the flagellants had formed the ring and the leaders had struck up their hymn, the scourging began, and the pilgrims moved round the circle two by two, while 'the brethren sang just as people still sing for the dance'.

According to the Chronicle of Bern, written by Justinger in 1421, there was a dance-song mentioned by Böhme which practically amounts to a parody of these flagellant-songs and resembles one of them very closely. In

Nu tret her - zuo der bös - se - n we - l - le.
flie-hen von die hai - s - sun he - l - le.
Lu - ci - fer ist bös ge - - - sel - l - e.

Wen er behapt mi - th bech e - r la - pt
dez fliehen wir i - n hab wir den si - n.

Fig. 62. Flagellant Hymn, 1349.

the year 1350, on St Stephen's Day, a number of people left Bern to go to Loubeck and Mannenberg, where they met many others from Frutigen and Thun. The ravages of the Black Death were only just ended, and the people, rejoicing at their deliverance, danced and sang. The song, however, mocked the flagellant bands which had recently passed through that countryside.

> He who will do penance among us,
> Let him take cattle and horses
> And geese and fine fat swine.
> Thus do we repay our wine.

The fact that only a year after these pilgrimages had taken place their songs could be used to accompany dances shows—according to Böhme—that they must have been thus used before the pilgrims adopted them for their own purposes. To me it seems more likely that if the Swiss used these songs for dancing it was because the pilgrims themselves, when they moved in a circle during flagellation, must have been performing some sort of processional dance. This is all the more probable as, on practically every ecclesiastical occasion where a procession took place, movement was in the form of a processional dance, with a 'cadenced' step.

'Plague Dances' are known to have occurred in other places also. The inhabitants of Wertheim danced round a fir tree in the forest until the

169

plague left their city. There were great plague dances in a meadow near the Pratter outside Bâle, a meadow which was popularly supposed to be visited by witches on Walpurgis Night [Böhme].

It therefore seems that in the ritual of the flagellant bands the most important feature, which was the procession of the pilgrims in a ring while they lashed themselves, was really combined with a dance, and that the

Nu heb-ent uf die v - - - wern hend.

daz got daz gro - zze ster - ben wend.

Fig. 63. Flagellant's Hymn for deliverance from the Plague, 1349.

pilgrimages which took place during the year 1349 provide a true example of the religious dance. But it is also clear that this dance was not in itself a particularly prominent item in the ceremony, but was merely a regular and natural accompaniment to some sort of well-established form of religious drama.

XI

The Earliest Dance Epidemics

ONE of the most unusual and remarkable phenomena of the Middle Ages, either from a medical or a religious standpoint, was the so-called Dance Epidemic. Crowds of people, great or small, seemed suddenly to be smitten with a wild fury of dancing, and professed to be suffering great agonies while so engaged. Often they danced themselves to death. Occasionally these epidemics affected many thousands of people, and they gave the impression of being very infectious. From the twelfth century right up to the present day there have been many descriptions of them. Usually they have been treated as miraculous events, and people have been more interested in what happened and how they began than in their fundamental causes. We shall try in the course of this chapter to examine more closely the attitude of various chronicles to these problems. The commonest belief was that it was a question of phenomena of an hysterical kind, nervous disturbances, mental disease and especially fraud. It is obvious that in olden days these dancers were held to have been possessed by evil spirits; such an interpretation of the facts was the only possible one in the existing state of medical knowledge and theological opinion. It must be stated here that the victims of these dance epidemics were seriously affected by physical disease and mental confusion; they suffered from convulsions and violent pains, and not seldom succumbed entirely to this horrible illness. On the other hand these old authors are probably right in saying that among the genuine pathological cases were instances of purely mental disturbance, and even of plain imposture by persons who sought to profit by the alms bestowed on the dancing crowds by the charitable. Many are said to have joined in, in some epidemics at least, to seize the opportunity of leading an immoral life.

I propose to treat the following instances of the earliest dance epidemics: those which took place in the seventh century and at the beginning of the eighth century, and that of the year 1021, the latter being known as 'the banned dance of Kölbigk'; then the Welsh epidemic of about the year 1200, the Children's Dance from Erfurt to Arnstadt in 1237, and finally the dance on the bridge at Maastricht in 1278.

1. The Dance Epidemics of the Seventh and Eighth Centuries

Andoenus of Rouen (609–683) has left us an account of the life of St Eligius (588–659). Bishop Eligius was mentioned before when he commanded some fifty Germans to cease their practice of dancing during the vigil before St Peter's Day. They refused to do so but the story does not end there. On the next occasion, the following June 29th, he once more denounced these church dances; once again he was disregarded and the dances were held with even more enthusiasm. Then St Eligius prayed God to punish these obstinate sinners, and God did punish them, in that they were compelled to continue their frenzied dance for a whole year. Then at last St Eligius released them from their penance [Stieren].

There is one item in this story which is obviously pure legend: the continuance of the dance for a whole year. Clearly, the period must have been very much shorter, probably a week at the most. But the interesting points of the story are the long duration of the dance, and the unwillingness (or perhaps the inability) of the dancers to stop, coupled with the fact that it clearly took place in the churchyard, or perhaps even in the porch of the church. It is therefore not unreasonable to suppose an element of truth in the legend, namely that certain persons, smitten with the 'dancing fever', sought healing from the church and its rites by dancing in the churchyard or in the porch of the church; and that they either could not, or would not, cease dancing. If my supposition is justified, then this is the earliest instance of a dance epidemic that I have been able to find.

At the beginning of the eighth century the Frisian Apostle, St Willibrord, was passing through Waxweiler one day when he came to a church where a service was taking place. But the congregation was for the most part outside the church, that is to say in the churchyard, where they were dancing. Despite his commands they would not stop, so he became angry and bade them continue dancing without end. After three days St Willibrord returned and found them still dancing, and they went on day and night. Their friends and relations besought him to free them, and he granted their request. He released the sufferers from their bondage by sending them to the monastery at Echternach. There they may also have been commanded to dance, but in any case they were soon healed of their ills [Krier].

This account contains hardly any legendary features; all significant details are perfectly plausible and credible. It should always be remembered that the word 'dance' must not be too literally interpreted, for the term must have covered such convulsive movements as we, both laymen and doctors, associate to this day with St Vitus dance, though we know that this is merely a nervous muscular reaction. It is highly probable that in those days persons suffering from fits and convulsions would seek refuge among these semi-ecclesiastical dancers, particularly when the dancing took place in a churchyard, in the hope of regaining their health. The very fact that Willibrord sent his flock—still dancing—to Echternach lends some support to the belief that the dancing festival, which is known to have been an annual event there for many hundreds of years, must have started as early as St Willibrord's own day. From a medical point of view it is quite reasonable to suppose that whereas the 'dancing' in Waxweiler was a symptom of poisoning (as I hope to show later) then this condition would cease when the patients reached Echternach, away from the source of the poison. For various reasons then, we may conclude that the account of this 'Dance Epidemic' may well be true.

The other dance epidemics which I am now about to describe are fairly well known to students of literature. Schröder has written about the literature covering the dance epidemic at Kölbigk in 1021, while Giraldus has described the dance epidemic in Wales in 1200, and there are various chronicles and historical accounts of the Children's Dance from Erfurt to Arnstadt in 1237, and the dance on the bridge at Maastricht in 1278.

2. *The Dance at Kölbigk*, 1021

Kölbigk is a little town in Saxony, which was partly destroyed during a peasant rising. Schröder mentions several manuscripts which describe the miraculous dance that took place there, of which the oldest dates from the early twelfth century. The best accounts all date from that century and are preserved at the Municipal Library at Rheims, the Bibliothèque Royale at Brussels, the Bibliothèque Nationale in Paris, and the Bodleian Library in Oxford. The clearest account of events is given below.

In 1074 Abbot Hartwig commanded one of his monks, Lambert of Hersfeld by name, to write the history of the monastery of Hersfeld, including therein the miracle dance at Kölbigk in 1021. Lambert himself had not witnessed the event, but he heard the story of it from a certain Othbert, who had himself taken part in the famous Christmas Dance, and now twenty-three years later, when he told Lambert about it, was still suffering from nervous tremors. In gratitude for his release from great pain he had devoted himself to his work as a lay servant of the monastery.

It was Christmas Eve in Kölbigk, and outside the church dedicated to St Magnus the Martyr there had gathered fifteen men and three women, among them a son and a daughter of the priest who was to play such a

Fig. 64. The Dance Epidemic of 1021. The dance in the churchyard outside the Church of St Magnus at Kölbigk. After Michael Wohlgemuth in Hartmann Schedel's *Liber Chronicarum Germanice*, Nüremberg, 1493.

fateful part in the story. Instead of attending the Christmas mass they were led by the wiles of the Devil to perform a dance in the churchyard, or, according to another account, in the porch of the church itself. Othbert leading, they clasped each other's hands and began their mad dance, following him round and round. Without ceasing for an instant, they danced on, stamping on the ground, leaping into the air and clapping their hands. As they danced, they sang, and this was the song:

> Bovo rode through the dark green forest
> With him he bore the fair Mersvinden,
> Why do we stay? Why don't we follow?

Bovo and Mersvinden are two of the dancers. Schröder calls this an epic song in ballad form. Presumably the dance was of the kind where the participants form a circle and in the centre one couple dance while the others sing the song; they also clap their hands and jump in the air. With the chorus or refrain they perform the actual ring-dance, probably stamping

FIG. 65. The Dance Epidemic of 1021. The Christmas Eve Dance in Kölbigk churchyard. On the left is the Church of St Magnus; in the centre are the dancers; the man on the left, with his back to the priest, has just pulled off his sister's arm which he is holding in his hand. The spectators join in the clapping. In the background is the charnel house. Copper-plate engraving by Mathew Merian the Elder (after Gottfried).

and leaping wildly at this stage also. In short, it must have been a type of dance closely akin to the group we learned earlier to recognize as characteristically popular ecclesiastical dances.

The dancing and singing disturbed the priest at mass. He went out and bade them cease, or rather to come inside the church and attend the service. They refused to listen and continued to dance and sing and brawl. Once more the priest warned them, and then be bade his son John try to pull his sister away from the ring. John tried, he caught hold of his sister's arm, but it came away in his hand. At this he returned to the church and showed his father what had happened. The arm had come off, but there was no flow of blood. The arm was thereafter preserved in the church as a kind of votive offering, and King Henry II had it mounted and set with fine workmanship in memory of a great miracle. But the priest went out a third time, solemnly excommunicated the dancers, and commanded, in the name of God and St Magnus, that they should not cease from dancing for one whole year. When the year came to an end the ban of excommunication was raised by the Bishop of Cologne. After six months they had tramped down the soil until they were knee-deep in the ground, and after another six months they were hip-deep. During all this time thay had neither eaten nor slept and their clothes were still undamaged. When the ban was lifted, they were brought into church, and before St Magnus' altar once again admitted to the community of Christian people. They then fell into a deep sleep, which lasted for three days. When they awoke the three women died, also one of the men, named John. The survivors returned home but suffered for the rest of their lives from tremors and nervous twitches in their limbs. One version only has nothing to say of these tremors, it merely recounts that when the men woke up they were looked after by friends or relations, and washed and clothed, although they resisted this. Schröder says that this is the oldest and probably the most accurate version.

The Rheims and Brussels manuscripts speak of wandering beggars, epileptics and lunatics as well as plain impostors, who were the Christmas dancers at Kölbigk.

The year 1020 brought many troubles to East Saxony; the winter was very long and severe and claimed many lives; the new year brought more death and suffering and in the autumn both the Weser and the Elbe overflowed their banks.

The events at Kölbigk aroused great interest and have been described over and over again by various writers; they have often been held up as an awful warning. Artists have also been interested, and I myself know of two illustrations of the legend. The oldest one is to be found in Schedels' World Chronicle of 1493, in which there is a wood-cut by Wohlgemuth (Fig. 64). This drawing does not however bear any close resemblance to the legend as known to us; it depicts rather an upper-class dance, with couples in fine clothes and pointed shoes. There are four women taking part, not three; and there are musicians, who appear to have placed themselves on a tomb-stone. There is no sign of church or priest. The second picture is a copper-plate engraving by Mathew Merian I (1593–1650) included in Abelin's *Historical Chronicles*, published in Strassburg in 1630 (Fig. 65). Merian was obviously careful about getting his details right, and the illustration presents the story of the old manuscripts with great accuracy.

There has long been a desire, and particularly since the time of Hecker, to interpret the events at Kölbigk in 1021 as an example of the so-called St Vitus' dance, probably the earliest instance, and Schröder shares this desire. That it was not the earliest instance is however apparent from the Stories of St Eligius (*c.* 650) and St Willibrord (*d.* 700), just described. The dance performed in honour of St Vitus was first mentioned several hundred years later, but the words of contemporary authors must be understood to signify a technical term which can also cover the Kölbigk epidemic, the St Vitus dance being some sort of compulsion to dance or perform dance-like movements. The term understood in this sense is still used by the medical profession today. We must therefore conclude that the Kölbigk dance does belong to the sequence of famous dance epidemics.

In connexion with the 1021 dance epidemic there are certain points that should be borne in mind, namely the circumstances in which it occurred, and some significant details about the performers themselves. We should remember that the epidemic was preceded by an uncommonly long and bitterly cold winter, which caused the death of many people; that a virulent epidemic followed in the spring, while in the latter half of the year there were widespread floods. [Schröder.] Later we shall have occasion to observe that similar circumstances, particularly climatic ones, usually prevail in the months or years before the outbreak of a dance epidemic. So far as the actual accounts of the epidemic are concerned, it is clear that some features are purely legendary, the judgment on the dancers, with a penance of a year's duration for instance, and the manner in which they are supposed to have sunk down to their knees and then their hips, and finally the granting of pardon. Apart from these, however, there is nothing for which a reasonable historical explanation cannot be suggested. The curious passage in which John tried to draw his sister out of the ring, but her arm fell away from her body—either at the shoulder or the elbow—without loss of blood, might be supposed to be merely legendary, but not necessarily. We shall find later a disease, caused by poison, where accounts by doctors of similar happenings are by no means unusual. Another point which interests me particularly is the mention of tremors or tremblings, from which those who took part in the dance are said to have suffered for the rest of their lives. The so-called sleep, which the dancers experienced for three whole days after they had been brought to church is not incredible either. In four cases this sleep became death.

It is extremely likely that among the Kölbigk dancers were very sick people. The twelfth-century manuscripts preserved at Rheims and Brussels both mention specifically that the dancers were such as suffered from nervous diseases and epilepsy, or rather from some disease which one, at that time, must suppose to have been epilepsy. We shall also see, in due course, that there were cases of acute poisoning which caused convulsive movements of various muscles, and affected blood vessels so severely as to cause extremities of the body occasionally to fall off; it clouded the mind, led to fits of an epileptic character, periods of unconsciousness, persistent tremors and various other symptoms.

The Kölbigk dance must be classified as a churchyard dance, in which people hoped, through dancing, to regain their health. As a churchyard dance it was directed towards the dead and the denizens of the underworld, and it is not surprising therefore that the dancers should be considered as 'possessed'. It is even possible that the dance was also directed towards St Magnus, since it took place outside a church dedicated to him, or may even have occurred in the porch or ante-chapel of the church. St Magnus was the Apostle of Allgau, and lived in the eighth century. He is usually depicted with a dragon by his side, which he is threatening with his cross. Legend tells that he killed such a dragon in his own monastery cell. The dragon has a two-fold significance, for the saint is conquering heathendom and also defeating a demon. His power to cast out devils may have been the reason why the sick dancers selected his church and churchyard for their Christmas dance.

3. *The Welsh Dance, circa* 1200

Dr D. Strömbäck has kindly drawn my attention to a remarkable travel journal from thirteenth-century England, namely the *Itinerarium Cambriæ* of Giraldus Cambrensis.

Giraldus was born round about 1150 and wrote his journals at the beginning of the thirteenth century. The events which he describes took place at St Almedha's church in Brecknockshire in South Wales, the account reads as follows:

'The saint's day was celebrated again in the same place where it has been celebrated now for many years. The day was August 1st. Many people came here from distant parts, their bodies weakened by various diseases, hoping to be healed through the merits of the holy maiden. It seemed to me remarkable that the following events actually took place during the celebrations in honour of this maiden. Men and women could be seen in the church and the churchyard, singing and dancing around. Then they would fall suddenly, motionless at first, as in a state of trance, then, as suddenly leap up again, like lunatics, apparently to perform tasks which are forbidden on feast days. They seem to perform these tasks with hands or feet, quite openly, before all the people. One man may have his hands on a plough, another urging on his oxen with a whip. To ease their labours they sing popular songs, but the music is often very untuneful. Here one may be aping a cobbler, another a carpenter, another seems to be carrying a yoke, and yet another drawing out a thread to the full length of his hands and arms, and then, as it were winding it into a skein. One man seems to be walking up and down and trying to make a net with his imaginary thread. Another man you will be surprised to see sitting weaving at an imaginary loom; he casts his shuttle to and from and with little jerks bangs the treadle on to the cloth. Inside the church you will again be amazed to see people handing over their gifts to the altar and then at last waken and recover. The saint, thus, by her heavenly compassion raises up many more than she casts down; and yet to ensure repentance and penitence some punishments there are, that those who come to celebrate this holy day may see and learn.'

These are obviously cases of severe poisoning. The participants in the procession are specifically said to be ill, they move their limbs stiffly and jerkily, and such movements are wrongly interpreted by Giraldus as an attempt to imitate the craftsmen. They fall senseless to the ground and wake with clouded minds, are seized with fury, leap about with wild gesticulations. With their gifts they are taken to the altar, where they gradually recover. It is a churchyard dance which is really being described, with music aimed at expelling demons, though the dance is also directed at St Almedha. Thus we have a typical dance epidemic, and it is the only known British instance to date.

4. *The Children's Dance,* 1237

The Procession of the Dancing Children from Erfurt to Arnstadt in 1237 has long been included among the so-called dance epidemics. Johannes Rothe (1360–1434) was a priest and town notary of Eisenach, and the author of the Thuringian Chronicle, which he completed in 1421. He described in some detail an incident which is supposed to have occurred in 1237. According to Rothe there assembled in Erfurt more than a thousand children; dancing and singing they made their way to Arnstadt, where they stayed the night. Their parents sought them anxiously and when they were found to have arrived at Arnstadt, carts, wagons and sleighs were sent out to bring them home again. None, however, could understand the cause, or what had really happened, and the incident was interpreted as an act of God. The children came home on the Holy Apostles' Day.

There is another account, by Johannes Letzner in the *Chronicles of Corbey*, published in Hamburg in 1390. This contains a passage said to be copied from an old Erfurt chronicle, which describes the children's dance from Erfurt to Arnstadt in 1237. It speaks of a hundred (not a thousand) children, who began to dance in Erfurt, danced out through the gates and all the way to Arnstadt. When they arrived they dropped to the ground, weary and exhausted, and fell asleep where they lay, by the walls and along the streets. Meanwhile the anxious parents sought high and low, but without success, for their children. Then came a message from Arnstadt that the children were there sleeping after the dance. Forthwith the parents fetched them in carts and wagons, but some of the children died, while others had acquired a tremor which remained with them to the end of their lives [Beckmann].

Rothe's description has been used by many historians, including Beckmann and Mencken. Other chronicles, notably that compiled by Stolle round about the end of the fifteenth century, only mention the incident very briefly. Falckenstein also describes it in his lengthy history of Erfurt; he says that more than a thousand children made their way, singing and dancing, through the Lüber gate and along the Steiger road to Arnstadt, where they were tended by the citizens of that town. In other points his account agrees with that of Rothe.

Bechstein used various sources in his *Thuringian Legends*, and in discussing this dance-procession says it took place on June 15th, which again accords with Rothe's account. In other respects also he agrees, but adds that the people of Erfurt were very grateful to the people of Arnstadt, and made a gift to their cathedral. Many of the children, however, remained sick and pale and trembling and were always tired and ailing. The dance was an epidemic illness, says Bechstein, comparing it with the so-called Children's Crusade and the processions of the flagellants.

Some authors have tried to prove that the processional dance of the children to Arnstadt was a kind of festive procession to the convent in that city, where they were celebrating the canonization of St Elizabeth. Elizabeth was the daughter of King Andrew the Second of Hungary, and died at Marburg in 1231, and was canonized in 1235. Relics of this saint were preserved in Marburg. To accept this theory we would have to ignore many elements common to all the other accounts: the general ignorance concerning the whereabouts of the children, the way they were brought home, and the illness from which the children were said to be suffering. Furthermore it is extremely unlikely that two whole years after the proclamation people in Arnstadt should be preparing a celebration of St Elizabeth's canonization. One would probably have to assume that the year 1237 was incorrect. It should also be noted that St Elizabeth's day was November 19th, and not June 15th. We are hardly justified in dealing so cavalierly with ancient records.

It seems to me most reasonable therefore to ascribe the children's dance from Erfurt to Arnstadt in 1237 to just those circumstances which caused so many other dance-processions, and to include it among the instances of medieval dance epidemics. Why they danced to Arnstadt we do not know: there may have been relics there, or some miraculous spring, from which they hoped for healing. It is interesting that in this case, as in the Kölbigk dance of 1021, the writers speak of the children either falling asleep or dying, and that some of them were left with a permanent tremor. We must not, however, exclude the possibility that their imagination may have been at work here, just because the Kölbigk story was so well and widely known.

5. *The Maastricht Dance*, 1278

In 1278 a dancing epidemic occurred, according to various chronicles, in the town of Maastricht. Martin the Minorite [Eccardus] lived until about 1290 and wrote historical accounts which were carried on by Hermann Januensus up to 1346. He describes the incident as follows: 'On the bridge over the Moselle in the city of Maastricht there danced two hundred people on July 15th, anno 1278. They would not cease their dancing when a priest passed by, bearing the Body of Christ, for communion with the sick. As a punishment from heaven the bridge broke, and many of the dancers were drowned.' Nauclerus gives a similar account. Yet another chronicler, Bzovius, whose period runs from 1198–1299, describes the incident in this way: 'In the year 1268, many youths and maidens, men and women, were dancing on the bridge at Maastricht when the blessed sacrament of Christ was carried past. Lost in their vanities they neither knelt, nor bared their heads nor did they cease from dancing. To punish them for their sin the bridge suddenly broke and nearly two hundred of them died. Let men so learn not to mock the divine.' Hondorff, describing the incident in 1278, places it in Utrecht, misunderstanding the ambiguous phrase '*Ultrajectinum*'.

These two chronicles differ on the question of date, and also on the numbers of the dancers; for the rest the accounts are very similar. Bzovius mentions no exact date, but it has been generally held that June 15th, 1278, is the most probable date.

In order that the gravity of the sin that was committed may be realized, it should be noted that the Synod of Paris in 1197 had ordered that all laymen should be frequently admonished, whenever they saw the Body of the Lord (the sacrament) being carried past them, to kneel immediately. Lagergren says in his memoirs that as late as the end of the nineteenth century this custom was very strictly maintained in Spain; as soon as the bell of the choir-boy, escorting the priest and the sacrament to a dying man, could be heard, all persons, wherever they were and whatever they were doing, would kneel and pray for the soul of the dying.

In Schedel's *World Chronicle* for 1493 there is a charming woodcut by Wohlgemuth, who has clearly followed the old account very closely (Fig. 66). The bridge at Maastricht is shown, and on it a group of people dancing and playing, while a priest with the sacrament and a choir-boy with bell and lantern have just passed. The bridge is broken and the drowning people are struggling in the water.

FIG. 66. The Dance Epidemic at Maastricht, 1278. The priest with the sacrament and the choir-boy with bell and burning candle go by, but the dancers do not stop. As a punishment, the bridge collapses. After Michael Wohlgemuth in Hartmann Schedel's *Liber Chronicarum Germanice*, Nüremberg, 1493.

Stieren has produced a number of hitherto unknown stories from old chronicles. One deals with the history of the monastery of St Trond, near Liége, and comes from the second half of the fourteenth century. It speaks of a procession which took place in 1275 in Maastricht, and in which caskets with relics of St Trudo, St Eucherius and St Servatius were carried. The procession was followed by great masses of people, so that the bridge over which they were passing broke, and 300 people were drowned in the river. There was also another chronicle, the so-called Peter's, written in 1276 (though the oldest extant manuscript dates from the fourteenth century), which describes this incident: 'In the same year, 1276, on St Margaret's day (July 20th) in Maastricht, the priest and his parishioners went in solemn procession, and their way lay over the bridge across the river. By the will of God, and the great press of people on it, the bridge collapsed, and about three hundred men and women were drowned.'

Two other fourteenth-century chronicles, the 'Reinhardsbrunn' and the 'Saxon World Chronicle', have little to add and obviously derive most of their information from the Peter's chronicles. Stieren believes that the story of the broken bridge and the drowning people is a historical fact and that it must have occurred during some big religious procession. Among the oldest sources, only Martin the Minorite describes the dance; the others do not mention it at all. It seems that we must assume, as Stieren would have us do, that the dance really happened, in the sense that during this period of the Middle Ages practically every church procession was a kind of dancing procession. It is quite true, and Stieren also makes this point, that bridges at this period were not well or strongly constructed, nor were disasters of this kind uncommon. Thanks to these last chronicles, we now have another date to choose from, namely 1275. It must be admitted that the story of the dancers on the bridge who did not stop when the sacrament went by may well be a later insertion, and not an integral part of the original incident. The significant fact is that there was a procession, probably a dancing procession, across the bridge at Maastricht in 1278, or a little earlier, and that precious relics were carried in this procession. It must therefore have been a 'Mercy' procession, or a 'Litania' undertaken for help against famine or sickness, usually of pestilential or epidemic character. It is quite conceivable, therefore, that the old conception is right, and the dance on the bridge at Maastricht was connected with a dance epidemic, and was intended as a weapon against lies and to heal the sick.

XII

The Children of Hamelin

MANY historians and authors have told the tale of the rat-catcher of Hamelin and the departure and death of its children. There is no agreed interpretation of the old legend, whether it refers to the vague rumours of a participation by the children of Hamelin in the so-called Children's Crusade of 1212, or the part played by the young people in the unhappy battle at Sedemünde in 1259, or whether there was an exodus of children in 1284, or even as late as 1376. The possibilities are numerous. At quite an early date, there appeared the suggestion that it may have been another case of a medieval dance epidemic. Let us now briefly survey the sources.

Hamelin is situated in the province of Hanover, not far from the confluence of the rivers Hamelin and Weser. A picture of the town of Hamelin and its immediate surroundings, printed on a fly-sheet in 1622 (Fig. 67),

FIG. 67. The Rat-catcher and the Children's Exodus from Hamelin, from a fly-sheet of 1622, reproducing the story of how, on June 26th, the rat-catcher led the children away. To the right of the gibbet on the Koppenberg, in the background, the piper can be seen playing to the children. [W = the Koppenberg or Gibbet Hill; R = Bungelosestrasse, leading to the Neue Thor (in the background); G = Town hall (after Joster).]

gives us an idea of what the place looked like. We can see the town wall which surrounds the city, with the New Gate in the middle of the background, while right in front, in the little market square, is the town hall, erected in 1608. In the background outside the city can be seen the gallows on the so-called Koppenberg, or Calvary Hill, which was the site of public executions; on the right stands the rat-catcher, playing his pipe, with the children in front of him. He has just led them out through the New Gate, after proceeding along the Bungelose Street (the street where no drum might be beaten). This street curves round to the right, just inside the wall.

Among the oldest published works which treat of this tale are those of Weier (1566) and Bünting (1586). Weier actually published the first edition of his book in 1563, with a second edition in 1564, but in these the story does not appear. In the third edition he writes as follows: 'a certain flute player was engaged to lure rats away from Hamelin. When his work was done he received only abuse instead of his agreed reward and was displeased. In the year 1284, on June 26th, 130 boys, born in Hamelin, followed this piper, who was clad in multicoloured clothes, to the Calvary Hill, known as the Koppenberg, where they perished. A single lad survived to tell the tale. "Was this piper perchance a wicked demon?"' In the 1577 edition, Weier adds that this story was written in the annals of Hamelin and in its church archives. Bünting, in his chronicle of 1586, treats the incident in greater detail: 'In the year 1282 there occurred in the town of Quernhamelin, by the Weser, a new and wonderful miracle. A man, dressed in garments of many colours, arrived in the city and played on his pipe in its streets; thereupon all the children rushed out to watch the strange spectacle. When by his playing he had gathered together 130 children, he led them out of the city, and the children followed him right into the hill where criminals are put to death, which they call Kopffelberg, and there they were lost. It was said that two children turned back, but one was dumb and the other blind. By signs, however, they gave the people to understand that the Kopffelberg had gaped wide open, and the piper and all the children had gone in.'

Later writers, as Kircher in 1650, Schoockius in 1662 and Meibomius in 1688, give the same account, though Kircher adds a good many elaborate and circumstantial details.

The facts that caused these authors to fix the date of the children's exodus when they did are as follows. A lawyer of Hamelin, named J. D. G. Herr, who died in 1765, had collected a good deal of material about the Hamelin legend. Among other things he made a copy of a *Passionale Sanctorum*, a manuscript which is no longer extant, in which it was written that it was in the year 1284 that the 130 children were swallowed up in the Calvary mountain. For safety's sake the following words were expressly repeated: 'In the year 1284, on the day of SS John and Paul, the people of Hamelin lost the 130 boys who entered the Calvary mountain.' Meinardus says that this would be the oldest version of the story. There are no mysterious details, merely the plain fact that the children 'entered the mountain'. Weier and Meibomius are supposed to have had access to this *Passionale*, said to date from the Middle Ages, possibly the fourteenth century. Unfortunately there is no certain information on this point.

In 1585 the clerk of the council, Friedr. Müller, published a kind of history of Hamelin, incorporating an older work, the so-called *Old Barde*. Here too there was a statement to the effect that on June 26th, the day of SS John and Paul, a piper clad in garments of many colours led one hundred and thirty Hamelin children out of the city, through the East Gate to the Koppenberg and the Calvary (the place of execution), where they disappeared.

An older chronicle of Hamelin, the so-called *Donat*, contained many notes made in 1311, and had various references to events occurring at occasions dated from the exodus of the children, always reckoning that as 1284. These references, however, are later insertions, made in the sixteenth century, a fact which was discovered less than a century later [Meinardus].

When Weier published his book in 1566 he had obviously consulted the *Passionale*, as well as the *Barde* and the *Donat*. It is the latter work which referred to the street by which the boys reached the gate of the city and mentioned that afterwards no drum was ever allowed to be beaten there, nor must there be any dancing (*nec etiam choroae in eadem ducuntur*). Therefore the street was named 'Bungelosestrasse' (the drumless street).

Erich informs us that on the walls of several houses in Hamelin there were carved or painted brief epitaphs referring to the tragedy, all using the date 1284. The most remarkable of these was supposed to be one carved in stone on the town hall (which was not erected till 1608). It read:

> Since the birth of Christ 1284 years had passed
> When into the heart of the Koppenberg there went
> 130 children born in Hamelin town.
> The piper lured them there and they were lost.

In the church there was a painted window which depicted the story. The writing under it was faded but some words were still legible. 'On the day of SS John and Paul, of those born in Hamelin there have two . . . and by . . . altogether to the Koppen . . . Anno 1572.' This date refers to the renovation of the window.

Erich says that in the town journal known as the *Donat*, the following passage was written in red ink. 'In the year of our Lord, 1284, on the day of St John the Baptist, when by old tradition the young people customarily rejoice and celebrate the eve of St John, there strolled up and down the streets a strange and unfamiliar adventurer. He was dressed in curious multi-coloured garments, and he played his pipe and jested and laughed, so that the children followed him, and when at last he left the town he took a hundred and thirty of them with him. Thereafter no one could discover what had happened to the children, or whither they had gone.'

On the outside of the wall, close to the New Gate, a memorial tablet had been inserted at an early date. During the latter part of the nineteenth century it was removed to the crypt of the Cathedral, according to Dörries. There were two pieces to the tablet, the upper one being placed vertically and the lower one horizontally (Fig. 68). The style of lettering shows plainly that the lower stone was newer than the upper. On the upper stone was inscribed in gothic letters, under the Hamelin coat of arms, 'Anno Domini 1500 and 31', the lower tablet 'Anno 1556', and underneath '272 years have passed since a magician led away 130 children from this city, when this gate was built'.

Unfortunately it is very difficult to determine objectively the exact significance of these inscriptions. One may even suspect that it is from this source alone that the date 1284 was arrived at. Is it the upper date 1531, or the lower date 1556 which really marks the building, or perhaps renovation, of the gate. If 272 years are subtracted from 1531, the answer is 1259; if they are subtracted from 1556, we get 1284.

Now there was another important event in the history of Hamelin in 1259, the battle of Sedemünde. This small place is two miles from Hamelin, and on July 28th, 1259, there was a battle there between the citizens of Hamelin and Münden. Münden won, and carried off the men of Hamelin as captives, putting most of them to death. Every year, on July 28th, the day of St Panthaleon, Hamelin thereafter mourned her dead. The events just described are found in the records of the city practically side by side with the account of the children's exodus [Mencken, Fein]. For this reason some people have suggested that the story of the children's exodus from Hamelin is no more than a confusion of the older story, when other young people of Hamelin fell in battle or were put to death.

Most students, however, resist such a suggestion by pointing out that the battle at Sedemünde had never been forgotten, that it was expressly mentioned beside the other account of the children's exodus in the journals of the city, and that it was commanded that every year the memory of the lost battle should be commemorated. These commemorations must have continued until about 1540, for that was the first year in which Hamelin was Lutheran, and with that the commemorations and the singing of Masses for the souls of the departed would also have come to an end [Jostes].

There are other writers who give a totally different date for the children's exodus. Fincelius, in the work which he published in 1566, the same year as Weier, described numerous miracles, among them the legend of the rat-catcher of Hamelin and the children who followed him away. According to him some hundred and eighty years ago, i.e., about 1386, there occurred in Hamelin by the Weser, on the day of Mary Magdalene, the events already familiar to us. The piper, a devil, led the children to a mountain where they disappeared, never to be seen again. Hondorff, in another collection of legends published in 1572, also tells the story, but gives the date as about 190 years earlier, i.e., about 1382. In his version the devil blew his pipe and played tricks with the children, but in other details the account closely resembles that of Fincelius. The latter also refers to the town book of

Hamelin. Pomarius, in his chronicles of Saxony, written in 1588, ascribes the Hamelin story to the year 1376; he describes in detail the gaily clad magician who played a flute or a pipe and presented himself as a rat-catcher. When he had removed the rats he was cheated of his earnings and took his revenge; he led the children to a mountain which swallowed them up. In 1601 Becherer published a chronicle of Thuringia in which he also gives the story with considerable detail, dating it in 1378. Michael Sachsen gives the children's exodus as July 22nd, 1376. Adelarius Erichius, who composed several lengthy chronicles in Hamelin at the begining of the seventeenth century, is supposed, according to his son, to have made a note in a manuscript fixing the Hamelin incident in 1378. An adventurer clad in gay attire was supposed to have wandered round the streets of Hamelin, playing on a flute and drawing all the children after him; some said that he claimed to be a rat-catcher and all the children save two were lost in the mountain. Erichius was quite familiar with the memorial tablets in Hamelin and the relevant passages in the town records, and he states that many people believed the incident to have happened in 1282. The son, Samuel Erichius, in a work published in 1654, agrees with his father.

Fein, building on a theory of Harenberg, suggests that the events in Hamelin may have occurred in 1212, the year of the Children's Crusade from France and Germany to Palestine, but this can be no more than a shot in the dark.

The significant features about this second group of historical theories is that the years which they suggest for the children's exodus fall almost exactly within the period in which the greatest of the medieval dance epidemics occurred, namely from 1374 right into the 1380's.

Bodinus, writing in Bâle in 1581 on the subject of 'possession', considered it quite possible that some, if not all, of the children from Hamelin were suffering from St Vitus' dance, and so severely that no cure was possible. Schoockius, in a thesis on the children's exodus from Hamelin which was published in 1662, also suggested that these boys might have been suffering from a severe attack of St Vitus' dance; after a series of such attacks they might well have thrown themselves into some lake or river, to secure relief. In that case, the piper, Schoockius suggests, might have been trying to soothe and harmonize their disordered movements by his music. Long after him Meinardus seemed to be not unwilling to subscribe to this view that an instance of a 'dance epidemic' may have caused the whole trouble.

To me this explanation seems by far the most likely one for the events in Hamelin, and there is support for this theory in the fact that the *Donat* record stated that after the children's departure no drum should be beaten nor any dance performed in the street along which they walked, which was later called the 'Bungelosestrasse'. In the same source it is also stated that the so-called rat-catcher did not merely blow on his pipe, he also played tricks by which may well be meant a kind of parody of the stamping and gesticulating that accompanied the steps of the dance. Hondorff is the only commentator who notices this point in the *Donat*. These details suggest to me the existence of a faint but definite tradition in the minds of the writers of the *Donat* that the children danced as they made their way through Hamelin and out of its gate.

So far as the date of the tragedy at Hamelin is concerned, I prefer the school of thought that suggests 1382 or any of the years 1376, 1378 or 1386 —that is, after 1374, which was the first year of a period in which dance epidemics, as we shall learn later, ranged far and wide.

We may now ask how this theory fits in with the 'historical' evidence of the town records, the inscriptions and the memorial stone. We have already noted that the inscription on the town hall was probably no earlier than the beginning of the seventeenth century and presumably similar inscriptions on other houses in Hamelin can hardly date further back than the sixteenth century. There is certainly no evidence, and very little likelihood, of their being older. The age of the so-called *Passionale Sanctorum*, which was preserved in the cathedral and then disappeared, is difficult to determine. The two city records, the *Barde* and the *Donat*, are not entirely reliable either: the former is only a copy, dating from 1583, and the text of the latter is certainly corrupt, particularly in the passages relating to the exodus of the children. Convincing proof of the date of this event is not to be found in such sources. We are left then with the original memorial tablet which was let into the wall near the gate.

This memorial tablet (Fig. 68) consists of two stones, the older one dated 1531 with the arms of the city, and a later one dated 1556. On the later one it is stated that the exodus occurred two hundred and seventy-two years before the gate was erected. The question then is if this refers to the year 1531 or 1556. The most reasonable answer is that the gate was erected, or re-erected, in 1556, otherwise this date would have no significance whatever. That it should refer solely to the date of the insertion of the memorial tablet is most unlikely, as it would then flatly contradict the information contained lower down the same stone. We are, however, left with the problem of the significance of the date 1531 inscribed alongside the coat of arms of the city, on the upper or older half of the tablet. We do not know the answer. It is however possible to suppose that it was erected in memory of the battle of Sedemünde; originally there may have been another stone with another inscription which the present lower stone replaced, to the effect that the battle occurred a certain number of years before 1531. Then presumably the year 1556 merely supplies the date of the erection or renovation of the gate. When the old tablet was to be put into the wall a new base and inscription were supplied with the year 1556 on it. Then it would be correct to say that 276 years previously both great events in the town's history had occurred, the battle of Sedemünde, 276 years before 1531, and the exodus of the children before 1556. To speculate further on these lines would be profitless

About 1500 a false tradition about the date of the children's exodus must have begun to crystallize. From it derive the memorial tablets on various houses in the town, the references in the two records and even the dates inscribed on the lower portion of the main tablet we have been considering. Nevertheless it seems to me that this false tradition was never accepted unreservedly; people may have realized that an exodus did take place in the thirteenth century, but that it was not an exodus of children, but of troops marching to the battle of Sedemünde. This uncertainty might well explain the ambiguity of the inscription, making it apply either to 1284 or to 1259,

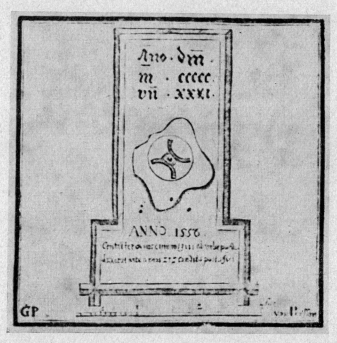

FIG. 68. The Memorial Tablet at Hamelin. Originally situated in the city wall of Hamelin near the New Gate; now preserved in the crypt of the cathedral. In the centre, the coat of arms of the city. Upper text: *anno domini* 1500 *and* 31. Lower text: *anno* 1556. *The magician led away* 130 *children from the town,* 272 *years before this gate was erected* [Fein].

whichever the reader preferred, according to his own interpretation of dates and figures.

For these reasons I am inclined to agree with the sixteenth-century writers who placed the children's exodus from Hamelin in 1374, particularly so if we suppose a dance epidemic to have been the cause of it. We will now examine the legend more closely, but first of all we must have a look at the Calvary mountain or the Koppenberg.

According to Samuel Erich, the Koppenberg was full of skulls, the relics of executed criminals. There was said to have been a fairly deep hollow, overgrown with hawthorn and briar roses, and by the entrance to it two stone crosses more or less in ruins, but with traces still discernible of the roses that had been carved on them: there had also apparently been inscriptions referring to the loss of the children and mentioning the date, 1282. Rethmeier, in a chronicle of 1722, tells the usual story and speaks of the way into the mountain as a sunken hollow, where there were nine stones in the pattern of a cross, 'which must have been set there by the old ones'. Nothing was visible on them except some carved roses. In a remarkable, but on the whole improbable, work concerning the practice of child-sacrifice in the Christian church, Daumer says that on the Koppenberg were two stone crosses, carved with roses, which marked the place where the children entered the mountain. He presumably took his facts from Erich.

Both in the worlds of classical antiquity and of pagan Germany roses had a symbolic connexion with death: the tombs of the early Christians were decked with roses. Roses therefore were the flower of the grave and of resurrection, and even in early Christian times churchyards were often called rose-gardens. Even the porch of a church might be called 'paradise' or the 'rose-garden'. From the thirteenth century comes the legend of St Agnes at the stake, who is granted a foretaste of paradise in that she is able to imagine herself in a rose-garden. In Carinthia, right up to the nineteenth century, it was usual to speak of the churchyard as the rose-garden and the same is true of Silesia and Styria. During the later Middle Ages the symbolism of the rose became more and more associated with the Virgin Mary, who, enthroned in Paradise, was said to be sitting in a rose-garden; in Renaissance pictures of the Madonna this is frequently her setting. The rose-garden remained, however, simultaneously a symbol of the churchyard, of death, and of the paradise achieved through death. The same notion is often found in the inscriptions on tombstones [Jacobs].

> Here I lie in the garden of roses.
> Here I await my wife and children.

Pfannenschmid confirms that pre-Christian graves in Germany, as well as churches and churchyards, used to be known as rose-gardens, the latter, perhaps, because interment often took place in the porch of a church. Roses moreover were planted both on heathen and Christian graves. If then our information concerning the rose-carved crosses by the hollow on the Koppenberg is correct, this must be the place where the children 'disappeared,' that is to say, where they were buried. The oldest version of the story of the children's exodus does not contain that legendary incident of the mountain opening and the children going in and disappearing. It only stated that they disappeared and were never seen again.

If we assume, then, that it was a case of dance epidemic, the story may be interpreted somewhat after this fashion. The children were afflicted just at the time of the year when this disease, for natural reasons, was most prevalent. They moved with convulsive, jerky gestures. They 'danced' as it was said. A musician was found and dressed in gay clothes, and we shall see later that this practice was often resorted to in similar cases, the player, with or without assistants, being brightly dressed, often in red. They played for the sick, or to help them to 'dance', for it was believed—not without reason—that dancing relieved their pain. So they danced along the Bungelose Strasse, out through the New Gate, and along to the Calvary mountain, the Koppenberg, which was the place of execution for criminals, in short, the Gallows Hill. Here the most important part of the dance was to take place. As we shall see later, this sickness was regarded as a kind of 'possession', and we have already noted elsewhere that the dead, and especially the criminal dead, were regarded as particularly dangerous demons who could bring terrible sickness to the living. Here at the Koppenberg many of the children died, perhaps most of them, as in other epidemics and at the 'dances' for the healing of the sick. They were buried at the foot of the Koppenberg, and as a memorial to them and their sad fate stones were placed in the form of crosses carved with roses.

XIII

Dance Epidemics of the Fourteenth Century

DURING the fourteenth century processional dances and religious dances in church, chapel and churchyard raged like wildfire, presenting a picture which has always been regarded with wonder and fear. It is during this century that the dancing epidemics reached a terrifying intensity.

The beginning was quite modest. In the year 1349 the Black Death raged all over Europe, and during this period the flagellants began their processions; singing and lashing themselves, they hoped to avert some of God's anger. In Magdeburg in 1360 there was written a *Schöppenchronik* which describes a dance epidemic in Lusitze in 1349, a little town on the borders of Bohemia, but not at that time part of that country. Here some girls and married women of the neighbourhood began to 'act crazily', dancing and shouting before the image of the Virgin Mary. They claimed that the image spoke to them, and so they went from Torgowe to Interbok by Wittenberg and many followed them in their madness. But Duke Rudolf of Saxony forbade them in his country. 'For the rest, I know of nothing good that came thereof.'

But the great dance epidemic did not start till 1374. There are many references to it in the literature of the period, but all are brief and unclear. Hecker, a German scholar, made the first attempt to describe it properly, but his sources were few; the same was true of Wiechowski and Martin. Dutch sources, as collected and described by Frédéricq, were fuller. Their interpretation, however, was rather fantastic as well as medically improbable, and the final conclusion was merely that hysteria and nervous disorders were partly responsible, while the majority of manifestations were due to fraud. It was also claimed that these 'choreomaniacs', as the dancers were called, were heretics, that is, a Christian sect holding beliefs and opinions contrary to those of the Catholic Church.

During the summer of 1374 great crowds came wandering through Germany to the Rhine and up to Aachen, where they performed a special dance before the altar of the Virgin in the cathedral. Thence they spread to Cologne, up to Holland and westwards to Flanders. Everywhere they danced and sang, usually in the churches, before the images of special saints. Their sufferings were great, and many of them died, even as they danced. We shall now see what information is available in still extant sources about the details of the dances and the behaviour of the dancers. We shall also note what various later writers have been able to contribute to our knowledge of the subject.

The best descriptions come from Flanders, Cologne and Trier.

1. Dutch Chronicles

Petrus de Herenthal, known as the monk van Floreffe, lived until the year 1390. In writing his life of Pope Gregory XI he describes the dances of 1374, though he places them in 1375. There came to Aachen, he says, a curious sect (*mira secta*) of men and women from various regions of Germany, and they penetrated as far as Hennegau and France. 'Persons of both sexes were so tormented by the devil that in markets and churches, as well as in their own homes, they danced, held each others' hands and leaped high in the air. While they danced their minds were no longer clear, and they paid no heed to modesty though bystanders looked on. While they danced they cried out names of demons, such as Friskes and others. Towards the end of the dance they felt such pain that if their friends did not tie linen cloths tightly round their waists, they cried out, like lunatics, that they were dying.

'In Liége rites of exorcism, such as those whereby devils are driven off at baptism, were carried out, and thereby they were freed from their demons. Those who were cured said that it had seemed to them that they were dancing in a river of blood, and therefore they had to leap into the air. But the people of Liége said they were thus plagued because they were not truly baptized, inasmuch as most of the priests associated with whores. For this reason the people (*Vulgus in Leodium—plaga populo contigisset—quod populos male baptizatus erat—proposuerat vulgus*) proposed that they should rise against the priests, murder them and take their wealth. This would indeed have happened had not God prevented it by healing the sick after the exorcism. When the people saw the healing their rage abated so much that the priests were revered even more than before.'

The strong condemnation of the priests of Liége at this time reflects a general lowering of morality among the priests, monks and nuns of the Catholic Church, which was characteristic of the thirteenth and fourteenth centuries. The details of this decadence in Liége are particularly well known. In 1203 the papal legate, William of Palestrina, was compelled to publish once again an edict which had been three times issued by Henry of Albano, namely that all priests must dismiss their concubines. If they refused this time he threatened to cut off all sources of income. Nevertheless the records of the Vatican testify to the fact that the evil continued. Between 1334 and 1352 there are no less than 30 instances in the see of Liége alone of priests who, on being ordained, received dispensation from the section of Canon Law dealing with *defectus natalium*, namely that the candidate was himself the son of a priest. Kurth, whose account we have been following, explains this as the background to the words about priests and their concubines in the dance epidemic of 1374. It should however not be forgotten that during the fourteenth century conditions in Bohemia were very similar, the priests, for exactly the same reasons, being much threatened by the people, sometimes even being set upon and killed [Bachmann].

Petrus de Herenthal adds that the following rhymed chronicle dealing with 'this dance or sect' was current at the time:

> A certain new sect arose at this time.
> With manners and looks ne'er seen before.
> The people danced and leaped violently.
> One lightly touched another's hand, then shrieked.
> '*Frisch, Friskes*', women and men cried it with joy.
> Each one had a towel tied on, and a stave.
> A wreath was set on every head.
> They see the Son of Mary and the Heavens open.
> They fall to the ground. They wail.
> A kick on the stomach cures one forthwith.
> Living comfortably they stroll from place to place.
> They beg what is needful; their own they save.
> The colour of red they hate, also the sight of tears.
> 'Twas to heretic faith that these folk urged each other.
> During the darkness of night these things went on,
> Which surely would be punished down below.
> The priests were hated, ignored were the sacraments.
> Then in Liége they found the cure.
> The trouble, caused by Satan, was overcome.
> The sick man was cured. For this praise be to Christ.

As Petrus de Herenthal more or less admits, the verses are not his own. They come from another's pen and to some extent they conflict with Herenthal's own account. The charge that these people were seeking a life of ease and pleasure is easily refuted. The ordinary man at this period was far too poor to be able to supply these crowds of dancers with the means to a life of ease and luxury. Further, it is only the writer of the verses who claims that the choreomaniacs preached a 'heretic faith' to the people among whom they wandered. Nothing is known of such a tendency. Nor is there any evidence that they abused the sacraments; the very contrary seems to have been true.

FIG. 69. Flagellants and Dancers. Three sacrileges. In a church the naked flagellants are lashing themselves, before the two images perhaps, and the choreomaniacs are dancing; a feast is also being held, probably after a funeral. In the bishop's hand is scroll with the words *Immolaverunt demonis et non deo* ('They sacrifice to demons and not to God'). From a woodcut copied from a miniature in a fifteenth-century manuscript of St Augustine's *Civitas Dei*. In the library of St Geneviève in Paris [after Lacroix].

The poet also states that the dancers hated the priests, thereby directly contradicting the statements of Herenthal. The latter, as we see, distinguishes clearly between *vulgus apud Leodium*, the citizens of Liége, who said that the plague struck the *populo*, the people, because this *populus*, people, had been badly baptized by unworthy priests. It was the *vulgus* who planned to murder the priests, at no time were the sick dancers guilty of criminal conspiracy. This point is of some importance, because attempts have been made from other, even less valid, sources to prove that it was the choreomaniacs who

Fig. 70. Interior of the church of St Mary at Aachen. View of the choir and the altar of Mary. Before this altar the choreomaniacs leaped and danced during the epidemic of 1374. From a painting by Hendrik van Steenwijk the Elder 1573 [after Clemen].

tried to murder the priests of Liége. This is hardly likely to have been the case. Herenthal was definitely an eye-witness, the poet was certainly not.

A deacon in Tongeren, by name Radulphus de Rivo, who died in 1403, wrote a history of the bishops of Liége, wherein he describes how the priests of Liége, Maastricht and Tongeren cured the dancers possessed by devils.

'In the year 1374, in the month of July, on the day of the anniversary of the consecration of the church in Aachen, which is the same day as the Feast of the Apostles (July 15th), there came a curious sect (*admirabilis secta*) of people from the upper regions of Germany; first of all to Aachen, then to Maastricht, and finally in September, to Liége. This is how it happened; persons of both sexes, possessed by devils and half-naked, set wreaths on their heads, and began their dances (*choreas*) and that not only in the market places, but in churches and private houses. They were free of all modesty, and in their songs they uttered the names of devils never before heard of. When the dance was finished the demons would torment their breasts with dreadful pains till they raved and raged and shouted that they would die unless someone bound them firmly and tightly about the waist. From September to October this sect grew until there were several thousands of them (remarkable, but true nevertheless), for, from Germany, as well as from Liége and the neighbourhood, choreomaniacs streamed in every day and many sound

194

and healthy persons were suddenly smitten by the demons, joining their right hands with the choreomaniacs. As an explanation for this devilish sect (*sectae diabolicae*) wise men put forward the gross ignorance of the Faith and of God's Word which prevailed at this time. There were not lacking those who ascribed it to the presence of whores among the priests, for thereby the children were improperly baptized. But in order that the improper baptisms should be no less valid than the proper ones, God sanctified them all and enjoined silence on the backbiters. To the free priests He gave grace through the rites of the Church, and by exorcism the power to drive out the devils and heal the sick; which grace He denied to others, to the priests in service.'

De Rivo gives a very detailed account of the methods used to expel demons from the sick in the churches. He talks of a choir-boy in the Church of the Holy Cross at Liége who one day was seized with a dancing fit during a service, and playfully swung the censer to and fro as he danced and sang unknown songs in many tongues! To free him from the 'possession' from which it was supposed he suffered a priestly stole was hung around his neck, and the conjurations of the church recited, whereby the demon was soon expelled. 'On All Saints' Day in the village of Harstall, which lies barely half a league from Lüttich,' says de Rivo, 'a great number of men and women of this sect determined to go to Lüttich and slay all prelates, canons, vicars—in fact, all the clergy. But through the mercy of God their intentions came to nought. For when they reached Lüttich, and were wisely brought before the priests, they did not seek to kill them, but allowed themselves to be healed, to the downfall of the demons and the glory of the priests.'

Some of these dancers, says de Rivo, were taken to the chapel of St Mary in the convent of St Lambert; there, by the authority of the church and after the reading of the first words of St John's Gospel, they were freed from the tyranny of the demons. Reports of this healing spread far and wide, and many members of 'this sect' were taken to the same place to be cured by the Church's exorcism. Others went to the Church of the Holy Cross, the Church of St Bartholomew, the Church of St Mary and the Church of St Andrew in Liége, where two priests 'carried out their offices without regard to the goodness or wickedness of their patients'.

The rites of exorcism frequently included the first words of the Gospel of St John—'in the beginning was the Word'—and also, according to de Rivo, other accounts from the Gospels of how Jesus healed those who were possessed by devils. In cases that were hard to heal the priests might place the sacrament of Holy Communion, the oblate, on the head of the sufferer, or hold it for him to look upon. Some were given holy water to drink, others water which had been consecrated in some way against demons, and sometimes it had to be forced into an unwilling mouth. Then the priest would cry, 'Get thee hence, unclean spirit', or he might speak the word *Effoeta*, which means 'open', into their mouths and blow into their faces, thereby mocking and weakening the powers of the devil.

To these details de Rivo adds several accounts of actual exorcism and the questions and answers of priests and demons. There was one woman who had to be taken to Aachen when all attempts to cure her in Liége had failed.

FIG. 71. The Virgin Mary with the child Jesus, in the cathedral at Aachen. A painted wood-carving of the early thirteenth century. The Madonna is seated with a lily-wand in one hand. The infant Jesus holds the Gospel. This piece has always stood on the high altar of the cathedral. It was before this image that the choreomaniacs danced when the epidemic swept over Aachen in 1374 [Clemen].

There in the church of St Mary she was clad in the priestly alb and stole and placed in a vessel of holy water which reached right up to her mouth. Then the priest forced the demon to speak. In answer to the question how long he had possessed the woman the demon replied 'two years'. Compelled to tell where he had been on Easter Day, when she was consuming the Host, he replied, 'At that moment I passed into the furthermost toe of her foot, while she was consuming the Host'. Adjured to leave her immediately, he made certain requests which were not granted. In answer to the question whether he

196

could blow a trumpet, he said 'Yes, very well', and blew a loud blast which all around could hear. At last he went out of the woman's mouth with a hissing and whistling sound.

It was also customary for the dancers to fast while the exorcism was going on, for this practice was also required in the gospel. 'By means of this and other ways the church adopted to cure the sick this sect gradually diminished. In one year it had gained possession of many, and for three or four years afterwards many people showed signs of being affected by this devilish mischief. But they could easily be cured by the prayers and exorcisms of the priests, a fact which caused the good repute of the priests and clergy of Liége to be spread far and wide.'

It should be noted that de Rivo makes the point contained in the verses quoted above, that it was the choreomaniacs who wished to murder the priests of Liége. As far as one can see, the versemaker must have used de Rivo's authority on this point. There is one fact which shows that de Rivo was making a mistake, namely that it was not the priests of Liége who had baptized the choreomaniacs, who came mostly from farther afield, witness the words they used, which could not be understood by the bystanders and were interpreted as the names of unknown devils. For this reason greater reliance must be placed on Petrus de Herenthal, who made every effort to distinguish clearly between the ordinary mob in Liége and the choreomaniacs. A summary of de Rivo's account is to be found in Wittius' *History of Westphalia*.

In the days of the Apostles the power of expelling demons was considered as a special gift of the Holy Ghost. It could be granted to anyone, not merely the Church's own people, and was regarded as miraculous. But during the thirteenth century a body of priests grew up in the church, specially trained for expelling evil spirits; to these, at their ordination, the bishop entrusted the formulae of exorcism [Bingham]. Now the early Church regarded as possessed by devils not merely heretics, but all who were not full members of the church. Even catechumens were possessed. Sometimes, however, among heretics or the heathen, sometimes even among Christian men and women, such possession might take a more violent form, which could be clearly recognized by convulsive jerky movements, cramp, attacks of epilepsy, mental aberrations and so on. At this stage the Church stepped in and tried to expel the demons by its own methods and authority; the various methods used had in all probability been handed down from the earliest days of the Christian Church. In common use for this purpose was the Blessed Sacrament, the cross and the sign of the cross, the stole (the broad band, borne over his shoulders by a priest, a symbol of God's yoke); also holy water, holy oil, prayers of all kinds and finally direct speech with and conjuration of the demons. It was also customary, in accordance with the words of St Mark ix, 28, to observe a strict fast: 'This sort (of demons) may only be driven out by prayer and fasting.' As a last step in the exorcism one spoke directly to the demon, exactly as we have seen in the chronicles which describe the healing of the choreomanics. The demon was commanded, in the name of Christ, to ascend from the feet of the sick man to his head, there to speak and answer through his mouth. If the sick man was restless holy water would be cast over him and the sign of the cross made above his head. Little bells would be rung, for Durandus, as early as the thirteenth century, was positive that this helped to drive out the evil spirits. The sick man's cheeks and sides would also be slapped. Sometimes, as happened to the choreomanics, a sick man would be placed in a barrel of holy water up to his neck [Rabelais, *Pantagruel*]. For exorcism and the expulsion of evil spirits, special masses, litanies and benedictions were regularly in use [Neander, Augusti, Binterim].

A chronicle which is in some respects very important is that of Johannes de Beka, written at the end of the fourteenth century. Beka claims to have been living in 1378. Frédéricq knew of this work, but no one else appears to have done so. In any case, no one has drawn any conclusions from the remarkable information which he provides: 'In the same year (1385, *not* 1374) there spread along the Rhine, beginning in the kingdom of Bohemia, a strange plague which reached as far as the district of Maastricht, whereby persons of both sexes, in great crowds, marched here and there bound around with cloths and towels and with wreaths on their heads. They danced and sang, both inside and outside the churches, till they were so weary that they fell to the ground. At last it was determined that they were possessed. The evil spirits were driven out after the customary and proper readings.'

The first question that arises after reading this remarkable account and particularly the statement that the choreomaniacs came from Bohemia is how this can have been possible for persons so obviously and gravely ill. It is also difficult to imagine what reason could have driven them to undertake such a long and difficult journey as that from Bohemia to Flanders and Holland. We shall see, however, that Beka was very probably right; that the journey in question must almost certainly have been one of the Hungarian pilgrimages which took place every seven years. The pilgrims went to Aachen and Cologne, but in 1374 they were stricken with the plague.

There is a sixteenth-century manuscript from the monastery at Gembloux which is preserved in the Royal Library at Brussels, and in which are some passages copied from an earlier chronicle recording events up to 1401. This earlier manuscript was known as the *Liège Chronicle* of 1402; the author was probably a monk, living during the second half of the fourteenth century in the Monastery of St James at Liége [Bacha]. Frédéricq maintains that the author must have used de Rivo as his main source, but this is not necessarily true. Their accounts of the various exorcisms may be similar and yet derived simultaneously from different sources. The most significant part of the chronicle deals with the behaviour of the dancers. 'In the same year (1374), at the feast of the Apostles (July 15th) came dancers of both sexes to Aachen for the feast of the consecration of the church, the Church of Our Lady (the Mary Church). There they danced, leaping high in front of the altar, and dropping down on their feet; those who beheld them were frightened. Then they came to Maastricht, and several citizens of that town fell victim to that same sickness. So they reached Harstall (near by), and the church of the Holy Virgin Mary, where some were cured, leaving behind, as votive offerings to Our Lady, the cloths and towels with which they had been bound. At the Feast of the Cross (September 14th) they came to St Leonard's by Liége, and thence to Liége itself. Daily their number increased, which caused many to fear.' He then describes the exorcism of the possessed in greater detail, and probably more accurately than de Rivo. For instance, the choirboy did not begin to leap and dance until he was leaving the church of the Holy Cross at Liége. Moreover, after the use of the stole and the exorcism, the boy cried out, 'Look, the Evil One makes off, with his short jacket and pointed shoes!' This point of fashion was to play some part in the history of these dance epidemics. Meanwhile the choreomaniacs daily increased in number. 'On their heads they bore a sort of wreath, and as they leaped they cried "Frilis". They went into the churches and danced and leaped before the altars and the images, especially the altar of the Virgin Mary. They were possessed by evil spirits, and when the demon moved into their legs they could not help dancing and leaping; when it moved up into the belly they suffered great pain. For this reason they carried the strips of cloth with which they tightly bound themselves at the navel, and small sticks with which they smote themselves, and begged others to strike their bellies with clenched fists. For these things would somewhat drive away the pain. They tightly twisted the sticks through the cloth, and dreadful was their appearance. At first, when they saw anyone dressed in red they wanted to tear him to pieces or to beat him. When they saw people with long pointed shoes they wanted to tear them apart. For this reason the guild of shoemakers of Liége was forbidden to make pointed shoes.'

The chronicler then proceeds to tell the same story as de Rivo, about the plot of the choreomanics, their entry into Harstall, and their determination to murder the clergy of Liége. Then is described another expulsion of unclean spirits from dancers who danced and leaped high before the altar of St Mary in the chapel at the St Lambert monastery in Liége. The exorcism was wholly successful and was regarded as a miracle. The chapel bell was rung, the sick came from far and near, and were cured in the same way. 'And so there were healed, I believe, some three thousand or more, some very ill, others not so grievously afflicted.' But some were suffocated by the demons and fell dead before the altar in the Lady Chapel. 'The priests then said, exorcizing even them: "Go hence, unclean spirit. Praise the true God, praise the Holy Ghost; get thee hence, thou damned and foredoomed spirit." Speaking thus they placed their fingers, that is, the thumb and forefinger, deep down into their mouths, right into the throat; they could not bite. At their ears they said "*Effeta*", which signifies "Open", and they blew in their faces, as if blowing away the power of the enemy.' But few of the well-to-do had the sickness.

St Nilus lived in Frascati during the tenth century. In 1610 a chapel to St Nilus at Grottaferrata was adorned with frescoes by Domenichino, depicting among other things how St Nilus cured a possessed man with consecrated oil from the lamp hanging by the image of the Virgin Mary. The oil is thrust deep into the throat on a finger. Charcot maintained that the possessed man was suffering from hysteria; in my opinion it is more likely

FIG. 72. The Miracle of St Nilus. The Saint is placing a finger, smeared with consecrated oil, in the mouth of the possessed man. He is in the throes of cramp; probably a case of 'contracting sickness'. From a fresco by Domenico Zampieri, called Domenichino (1582–1641), in the monastery of Grottaferrata [Charcot and Richer].

to have been a genuine case of convulsive cramp. Cramp is visible in the extensor muscles of the back and perhaps in the twisting of the head to the right and in the calf muscles, while the down-pointed toes of both feet are highly typical. It is my belief that this patient should be classified with the large group of illnesses covered by the dance epidemics.

Johan of Leyden is another Belgian chronicler who lived in the fifteenth century and who also described the choreomaniacs. According to him they began to appear in 1374 in Aachen, Cologne and other cities along the Rhine. They danced and leaped and fell to the ground as if unconscious. They continued their leaping and dancing for a long time, but some collapsed completely before the end, and others were tightly bound about the belly to prevent this. They wore a kind of wreath on their heads and as they danced they cried continually: 'Frijsch, Frijsch.' Many men and women who watched them joined their company and were immediately attacked by the same disease. He goes on to give a description of their behaviour similar to that of the Liége chronicle. He adds one detail: sometimes one would rise on to another's shoulder, and claim that he saw wonders in the heavens.

In the Monastery of St Jacob in Liége there lived a monk called Cornelius Zantfliet, who died in 1462 after writing a history of this monastery. He writes of the choreomaniacs that it was said that in the year 1374 demons forced their way into the bodies of many people living in the lower parts of Germany, near the Rhine. 'They cried out with loud voices and began to dance, alone and in circles. After many gestures, and much leaping they would fall to the ground, and unless someone quickly bound them right around the belly with rope and cloth they died in an agony of pain. . . . Above all they hated those who wore red garments or pointed shoes, so much so that shoemakers in the town were forbidden to make any such. When the plague began there were some who thought that it was only a bodily trouble like insanity or epilentia (an error for epilepsy?) or some such illness which the skill of medical art could heal.' They were, however, soon convinced that these were cases of possession. 'Everywhere they went they created disturbances in the churches and the services by their disorderly shouts.' The writer then describes the healing and says that many sick persons were brought to Liége from other places and were cured there.

Jan van Stavelot, another chronicler of the fifteenth century, gives a brief account, substantially the same as that of Zantfliet, mentioning the same year 1374. There is an interesting detail in a fifteenth-century *Flanders Chronicle*, where it says that the choreomaniacs of 1374 seemed to go out of their minds when they danced, and belaboured those bystanders who, willy-nilly, refused to dance with them [Frédéricq]. This suggests that one ought not to take too seriously the suggestion that bystanders were often seized by the same madness and then joined the dance; more often, perhaps, they were simply compelled to do so by the choreomaniacs. There is another point which should not be forgotten: in the account of the dance at Echternach, which is very similar in character, we saw that quite healthy people would often join in a dance to help their sick friends or relations or to protect themselves against the disease.

In the State archives of Hasselt, Frédéricq discovered an edict of November 18th, 1374, directed against the dancers by the magistrates of Maastricht. It proclaimed that no person suffering from this sickness, be he burger or burger's child, might dance in the streets or the churches. However, anyone may dance, with his cloths and attendants, in his own home, though nowhere else.

In an unimportant old Belgian chronicle with brief notes up to 1479 there is a couplet relating to the dancers of 1374,

> *Gens impacata cadit*
> *dudum cruciata salvat.*

This should mean: 'Uneasily the people fall as they recover in their pangs.'

Earlier writers have disregarded this as evidence since the words obviously do not make sense. It has been suggested that '*salvat*' is an error, and that it should read '*salivat*', so that the line would mean '. . . as they foam at the mouth in their pangs'. A more acceptable emendation might be '*saltat*', and then the couplet would mean, 'Uneasily the people fall as they dance in their pangs'. This would accord very well with what in fact happened. I have consulted Professor Joseph Svennung on the point, and he has been good enough to advise me as follows. If the metre in which the couplet is written is taken into consideration it becomes clear that the last word should be trisyllabic. The verse should therefore be

> *Gens impacata cadit*
> *dudum cruciata salivat.*

'Uneasily the people fall, as they foam at the mouth in their pangs.' The chronicle, then, does provide evidence that the choreomaniacs died frothing at the mouth, which points to epileptic attacks.

Frédéricq informs us that the 'memorial book' (*Memorie Boek*) of the town of Ghent contains a reference to October 22nd, 1374, when the dancers came to Ghent. They danced for a whole night, without stopping to eat, drink or sleep. They had thus penetrated far into Belgium.

In 1698 Schiltern made a copy of the *Chronicon Belgicum Magnum*, which is no longer extant, but was probably written in the fifteenth century. In it the dancers are mentioned as having begun to appear on July 15th, and as having subsequently moved on to Maastricht and elsewhere. This 'devilish plague' struck above all at the poor. They wore wreaths on their heads, bound their bellies with a cloth, twisting it tight by means of a staff. After dancing they fell down in great pain, to relieve which they tightened the clothbands still further, or asked their friends to pound their bellies with their fists. They detested pointed shoes and danced in the churches. Then follow descriptions of the exorcisms, which closely follow those of de Rivo and Herenthal. The chronicle speaks of the dancers as a *secta chorisantium*, a sect of dancers.

2. *German Chronicles*

From Aachen, Flanders and Holland the choreomaniacs moved towards southern Germany; they passed through Cologne and, as we shall see, also through Trier. The *Kölner Jahrbücher* and Koelhoff's *Chronicle* speak of their visit to Cologne, but their presence in Trier was not known until recently. The *Year Books of Cologne* spring from the annals of Agrippa; the first part was issued in 1360, they were then continued to 1378 and a third edition to 1398 [Cardanus]. Later they were continued until 1419, and finally brought up to date and re-edited in 1445. The original manuscripts are preserved in the city libraries of Trier and Cologne. In 1499 Johann Koelhoff of Cologne printed his *Chronicle of the Holy City of Cologne*. It is mainly compiled from earlier sources, but he cannot have begun his book before 1490.

Fig. 73. Cologne Cathedral. From an oil painting of 1830. The choir on the left was erected as an imposing chapel for the relics of the Magi. In this choir the choreomaniacs danced in the dance-epidemics of 1374.

The *Kölner Jahrbücher* tell that in 1374 the dancers were in Cologne from August 15th till September 8th. They danced in churches and monasteries and in every sacred place, and they drew great attention to themselves until at last people decided it was all fraud. One of the later manuscripts adds that, as they danced, the performers called out 'Lord St John'. 'As they went, they would lie down on their backs, and be pummelled and kneaded, and would have people to stand on their bellies, and to stamp and dance there; for so they desired. And they did not refrain from much unseemly behaviour.'

Koelhoffs' Chronicle of 1499 goes into greater detail. This remarkable and widespread illness was said by the 'Masters' to be caused by 'natural reasons', and they called it a 'mania, that is, a frenzy or madness'. Many people, men and women, old and young, had the disease; they left house and home, the young left the old; they left relations and friends and the places where they lived. When they were attacked by the disease they 'had a curious feeling in their bodies, and their voices became shrill and fearful. They would suddenly throw themselves to the ground and move along on their backs, and both men and women would ask to be girdled round the belly and that towels and broad strong bands be drawn as tightly as could be. Thus, girded with towels, they danced in churches and monasteries and in all holy places. When they danced they all leaped up and cried:

> Oh Lord St John
> so, so
> Whole and happy,
> Lord St John!

'Those who were really stricken by the disease were usually well again after ten days, but there grew to be much fraud and wickedness at the end; some pretended to be sick that they might beg for alms, others that they might misbehave with women; they went everywhere and did much harm. At last

Fig. 74. Virgin Mary and Infant Jesus from Cologne Cathedral. Known as the 'Mary of Milan'. A wood carving from the Rhineland, dating from about 1330. The choreomaniacs apparently danced before this image when they came to Cologne during the dance-epidemic of 1374 [after *Die Muttergottes Deutsche Bildwerke*].

the evil was made plain and they were driven forth from the lands. These were the dancers who came to Cologne from August 15th to September 8th.'

The last of these Cologne chronicles is the so-called *Limburg Chronicle*. It was first printed in 1617, by Faust von Aschaffenburg at Frankfort and was then lost. For linguistic as well as other reasons it cannot be said to date back further than the beginning of the sixteenth century, and can therefore hardly be regarded as a reliable source. The author says he was born in 1347 and died in 1402. The chronicle does not go further than the year 1398, that is to say the year in which this section of the chronicle was last edited in its original form, which unfortunately we do not possess [Wyss]. The author of the chronicle wrote down his recollections beginning with the year 1377. He first of all describes the great floods which had just occurred, and then goes on to speak of the dancers. He says that in 1347, about midsummer, there happened strange events in Germany, and especially by the Rhine and the Mosel, 'for people began to dance and rage, and they stood two against one, and they danced in one place half a day, and during the dance they fell down on the ground, and let their bellies be stamped on. They believed that thereby they would be cured. And they ran from one place to another, and from one church to the next; and when they could, they accepted alms from the people.' Soon there were no less than five hundred dancers in Cologne. In the end it was discovered that there was much fraud and deception, many things were done merely for money, while some of the women lived disorderly lives. It was discovered in Cologne that more than a hundred women who had no husbands had nevertheless conceived children during the period of the dance epidemic. 'And when they danced they bound and laced themselves around the waist so that they might look smaller. But many of the masters, especially the learned physicians, said that some joined the dance because of their hot natures (*heisser naturen*) as well as for other physical causes. But there were not many of these. The Masters of the Holy Scriptures cursed the dancers, for they held them to be possessed by the Evil One.' It all lasted about sixteen weeks in this region. 'It also appeared as if these dancers, men and women, could not abide the sight of red. It was all fraud, and to my mind a sign of the second coming of Christ.'

It should be noted that the '1347' in the manuscript is an obvious error for 1374. The most interesting point in the chronicle, as I see it, is the reference to the learned physicians who held that the dancing craze was a result of the 'hot nature of men, as well as of other natural physical causes'.

In the city library of Hamburg there is preserved a fifteenth-century manuscript called the *Chronica quorundam regum et imperatorum Romanorum*— 'A Chronicle of Early Roman Kings and Emperors' (*Hist.* 31 *b, Pap. Fol.*). The chronicle is supposed to have been written in 1377 or 1378, but the actual manuscript at Hamburg does not date further back than the first quarter of the fifteenth century [Cardanus]. The existence of the chronicle is well known, but oddly enough, though it is particularly valuable, carefully and well-written, nothing has yet been published from it. I am indebted to the kindness of the director of the city library of Hamburg for a photostatic copy of those portions of the manuscript which deal with the dance-epidemic of 1374. The account reads as follows: 'Frenzy (mania) and madness (insania) have attacked a great number of people. The same year (i.e., 1374) in the months of August, September and October there fell upon men's bodies, far and wide, a violent, rare and strange sickness, which researchers maintain arises from natural causes, and which they call mania, for the sufferers seem to be crazed, uttering confused sounds, with strange movements of their bodies, as if mad. From such a sickness there suffered during these months innumerable people, old and young, men and women, but especially quite young women. Throughout their time of sickness, with intervals of only a few

Fig. 75. The Shrine containing the relics of the Magi at Cologne. A fresco from Cologne Cathedral showing the appearance of the shrine in 1320. Religious dances were performed before this shrine, and probably the choreomaniacs danced round it during the epidemic of 1374 [Clemen].

hours, the strange restlessness of their bodies made an unseemly show for the people, for they left their homes and dwellings, their friends and parents and strolled about the streets and the markets, joining together in groups. They put wreaths and bands on their heads like crowns, and then held hands and danced mightily, like choreomaniacs, throwing their feet in the air. With arms outstretched they clapped their hands above and behind their heads. When they had wearied themselves with leaping and dancing and such like exercises, they suddenly rushed wildly from place to place, screaming fearfully, raging like beasts over the land, and complaining of the most terrible internal pains. Therefore their families or friends tried to keep them shut in, and watched over them as was customary. They would also press their hands or feet with all their weight on the patient's waist or belly, for this particularly was said to ease the pain and heal the sick. And so those who were ill but not actually suffering an attack would always have their waist, stomach and intestines tightly bound with cloth bands and belts, and thus laced up they would go about among the people. Thanks to the great mercy of God very few died of the sickness, but after eight or fifteen days they would return to their senses and recover their health. But, as among men the false is often found side by side with the true, so it happened that even in these terrible times many pretended to be suffering from the sickness, some to obtain the alms which Christians bestowed on the sick, and some from mere folly. Yet others joined their company for the sake of loose living with the women and young girls who shamelessly wandered about in remote places under the cover of night. So they wandered about on saints' days and holy days, when there were big gatherings in public places, and particularly in churches when Mass was being celebrated they would be smitten by the Devil with an attack of frenzy, so that the very service would be disordered. During this time holy men and people in general would perform litanies, and go in procession to churches and sacred shrines so that God's wrath might be averted and the Devil be turned aside. The pestilence had indeed spread far in this short time, and this sad company (*societas*) become numerous, for in one lonely spot in the diocese of Trier, far from the abodes of men, near the ruins of a deserted old chapel, there gathered several thousand members of this company as if to fulfil a sacred vow (*vota sua*). They and others who followed to see the show amounted to some five thousand persons. There they stayed, preparing for themselves a kind of encampment (*statio*): they built huts with leaves and branches from the nearby forest, and food was brought from towns and villages as to a market. At last it befell these people, whose sins the pious thought deserved a harder punishment, that they were possessed by demons and greatly tormented by them. They were brought to churches and shrines, and God in His mercy healed them, after the prayers and alms of the people, by means of the exorcisms of the priests.'

This remarkable description is very valuable for the information it provides about the physical and mental condition of these choreomaniacs. It also gives a full account of their behaviour and way of life. We will now examine these accounts as well as certain other ones.

When the choreomaniacs proceeded to the deserted chapel in the forest, there, as it were, to encamp, to rest, refresh themselves and dance, the place began to resemble a small market town. This incident from the forest of Trier depicted in the chronicle is not an unfamiliar one. It was a very ancient custom to erect small chapels in remote and isolated clearings in the forests. To such a place a bishop or a prelate might retreat for a period of solitary asceticism and spiritual refreshment. Bishop Burchard from Worms (1024) was accustomed to do so, as St Heinrad (1019) and many others who were later

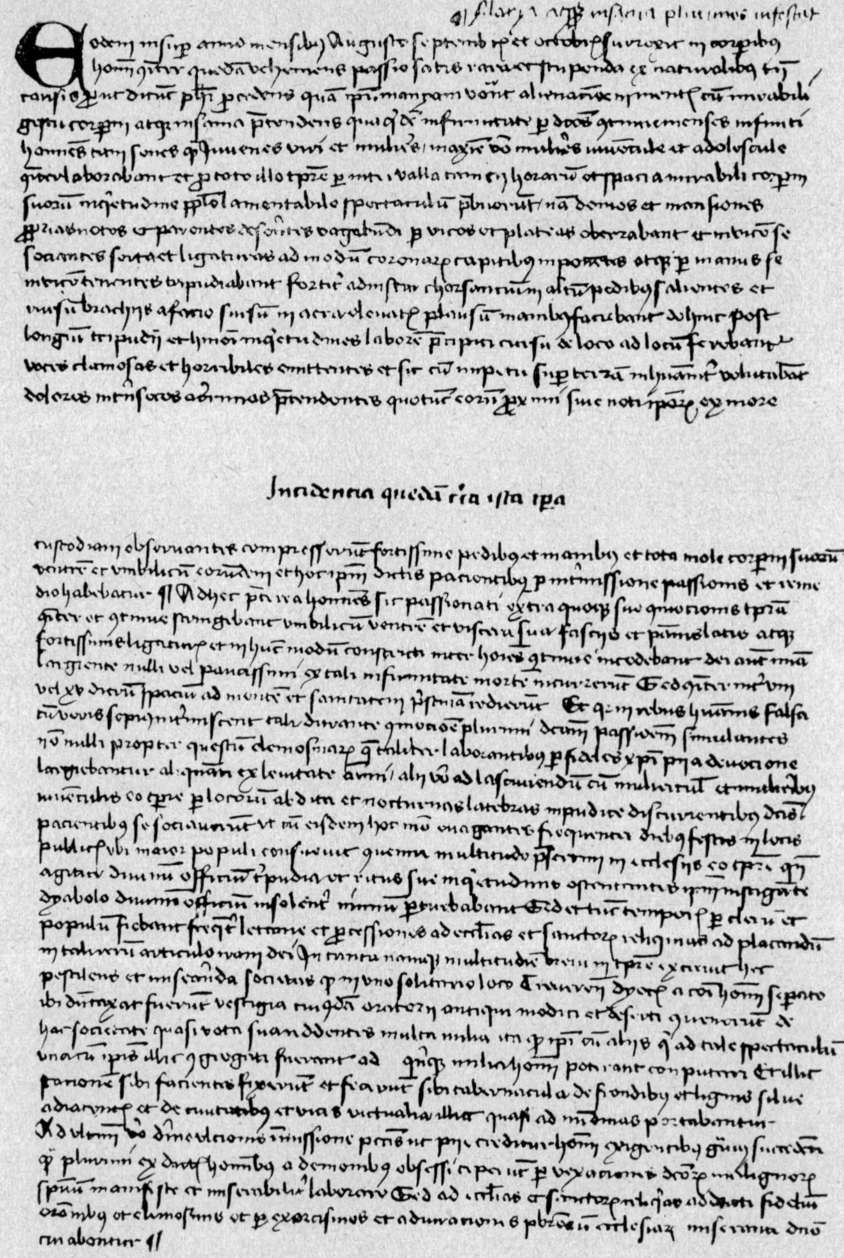

FIG. 76. From the *Chronicle of Early Roman Kings and Emperors*. Hamburg Stadtbibl., *Hist.* 31, b, Pap. Fol. The text describes the dance-epidemic in Trier 1374. The manuscript dates from the first third of the fifteenth century.

called miracle workers and saints. This explains why these forest chapels were regarded with such deep and enduring devotion by the people. Often a

208

nearby tree or spring would be said to have miraculous powers or an image in the chapel would effect miraculous cures. In times of sickness these places would be filled with votive offerings, usually a model of the cured limb, or some object associated with it [Kolbe]. A chapel which had once been the object of pilgrimage was nevertheless subject to the whims of fashion: for a long period it might be in high repute, then it might seem to be more or less forgotten; but, however abandoned it might seem to be, when the day of its patron saint arrived, or when an epidemic began to rage in the surrounding countryside, pilgrims would come from far and near to the little chapel in the wilderness until a small town, complete with market stalls, had grown up, a regular *kirmess* [Andrée].

This, I think, is how we must interpret the passage in the chronicle relating to the visit of the choreomaniacs to the forgotten chapel in the woods. The chronicle does not say to whom the chapel was dedicated, whether to the Virgin Mary, St John the Baptist, or St Anthony. It was to the latter particularly that many of these little chapels out in the country had been dedicated, perhaps because he had been a hermit in the desert. Indeed many of the chapels grew up in places where some hermit had already established himself. On certain occasions, particularly in time of need, the people of the neighbourhood would gather there for a service. The main reason probably was that demons were supposed, by preference, to foregather in such lonely places, as witness St Luke xi, 24, where it is said that when an evil spirit is driven out of a man, it wanders in a desert, seeking rest. Here, then, it would be easy for St Anthony to expel the demons which possessed sick men [Evelt].

Gobelinus, in his *Chronicon Universale*, which records events up to 1418, gives a brief account of this dance epidemic. He says that this strange and unknown disease came to Aachen and Cologne and other parts of the Rhineland. It is interesting to note in his account that the sick fell, as if unconscious, to the ground, and were then wrapped in bands, twisted tight by pieces of wood like a tourniquet. This, however, did not suffice, for bystanders were asked to stamp on the bellies of the fallen, so that every sick man on the ground would have two or three persons stepping on him, which eased the pain in the stomach. Gobelinus also mentions that it was discovered that many of the sick were frauds. 'But whether some of them were really suffering from some sickness or whether they were possessed by unclean spirits, is not certain.' The *Annales Fossenenses*, which go up to 1389, speak of the dancers of Liége and other places as possessed by demons. When they danced in churches and market places they behaved like lunatics. How the priests drove away their evil spirits is then described. Bzovius, in a short note, claims that these events happened because the sick, when they were children, had not been taught the law of God, 'for those were very dark days in Belgium'.

Slichtenhorst writes how in Gelderland, in 1375 and the following year, men and women were smitten by the fantastic frenzy which broke out first in

Gelderland and Jülich (Gulich) and spread to France and Germany. They went in couples, and with every couple was another single person (i.e., two to one); they danced, leaped and sang, and embraced each other in friendly fashion. Most remarkable of all, these strangers were not spoken to, or embraced by other strangers, though they were already suffering from the disease, though they had long known each other and called each other 'brother' and 'sister' [Frédéricq]. If one could rely on this information it would be very significant. For calling one another 'brother' and 'sister' might lend a certain religious tone to the movement, which would accord well with the expressions *secta* and *societas*. But Slichtenhorst's history was not written till the seventeenth century, and is in any case not very reliable. The date, 1375, is certainly wrong, and it is quite out of the question to suppose that the trouble began in Gelderland and Jülich (i.e., South-east Holland and the North-west corner of Germany), and spread thence to Germany and France. Geographically speaking, the exact opposite was the case. It therefore seems reasonable to me to attach weight only to the point that the choreomaniacs were known also in Jülich and Gelderland, a natural supposition in view of other evidence about the spread of the dance-epidemic.

Caspar Hedion, in a chronicle continued until 1509, speaks of the great floods of the Rhine in the spring of 1374 and adds, 'During this year there was a terrible disease, called St John's dance, which attacked many women and girls, men and boys, and caused them to leave their own country. There was also much deception in what happened. Many got much money, and there was much loose living.' This passage is interesting because it confirms positively that the sick had left their own country, an expression that would hardly have been used if they had only come from the regions of the Rhine and of Flanders. It supports Beka's contention that the pilgrimage of the choreomaniacs had originally begun in Bohemia.

Bzovius, in a history of the Church, published 1618, also touches on this point. He speaks of a kind of maniac illness, called St John's Dance, which attacked many people in the year 1374. These men and women, young men and girls, 'were, by their illness, driven into a mad flight from their homes and communities. First of all they fell foaming to the ground; then they got up again and danced themselves to death—if they were not, by others' hands, tightly bound.' From the *Great Belgian Chronicle*, Bzovius quotes this sentence, 'Dancing, they seized churches and churchyards'. His account of the events which actually occurred in the dance does not seem to be quite accurate; times have been altered and he has no good authority for saying that 'first of all' they fell down and foamed or frothed at the mouth. Here again, it is interesting to note the emphasis on the fact that the sick had fled from home and were far from their own country; also that they danced not merely in churches, but also in churchyards. On this point several chronicles agree, namely that there was dancing in churches, chapels and all holy places. In fact Bzovius must have copied this passage from Trithemius, whose *Chronicon Sponheimensis* of 1601 contains the identical words.

3. French Chronicles

The *Chronicle of Metz* was composed in verse towards the end of the four-teenth century; various writers, however, continued it in different copies up to 1583. A first edition was published in 1698 [Molinier] and a number of passages from it were reproduced in a history of Lorraine by Calmet, who recounts that in 1374 certain men and women appeared in Metz, dancing and singing like corybantes. When they met in the streets and one began to dance another would immediately follow suit. The trouble lasted for nine or ten days, sometimes a little longer, and some fifteen hundred souls were thought to have been attacked by the disease. In some parts it was called St John's dance, in others St Guy's or St Vitus', but this was an error. Calmet was writing in 1728, and because of the name he confused the 1374 dance with the Strassburg dance epidemic of 1518. He adds the usual details that the dancers hated red colours and pointed shoes, and that the church's rite of exorcism was used for healing. Some were also cured by having people stamp their feet on them as they lay on the ground, or by tightly binding their bodies at the navel. This madness or illness, which often degen-erated into immorality, spread from Lorraine to the Netherlands, according to Calmet, though in my opinion it moved in exactly the opposite direction. However, it is even more likely that the Metz epidemic was quite distinct from the outbreaks elsewhere.

Calmet then quotes the *Metz Chronicle:*

> St John's dance in the year
> Thirteen hundred and seventy-four,
> When a sad thing happened in Metz;
> For at home, in town and countryside,
> People danced for St John.
> There was distress beyond measure,
> A strange sorrow,
> For those who were most at ease
> Became the most afflicted,
> *Whether sleeping or waking.*
> Whether sick or poor,
> When fate struck home
> Then one must dance.
> The priest performing the Mass,
> The judges who sat in court,
> The labourer at his task.
> Whomsoever the plague did strike,
> He needs must dance for nine or ten days,
> Without eating, without rest,
> For a longer or a shorter time
> According as the trouble did affect,
> They danced for St John in their homes.
> One could not wait for another.
> In the city there were dancers,
> Both great and small, some fifteen hundred.

De Rupelle, in his *Journal de Paris* of 1785, reproduces a part of this chronicle. He suggests that these verses may have been written by the mayor of the city, one Johannes. He is also of the opinion that the rather curious lines about the priest, the judge and the labourer are naturally linked with the Dance of Death which was described earlier and which has been supposed by many to relate in some way to the Black Death and other great epidemics of the fourteenth century, not forgetting the dance-epidemic.

Jean d'Outremeuse (Jean des Preis), who lived in the fourteenth century, wrote a rhymed chronicle, called *La Geste de Liége*, in which he describes the dance-epidemic [Frédéricq]: 'Even so, on the 11th September, 1374, there came from the north to Liége (whence not many people did come) a company of persons who all danced continually. They were linked with cloths, and they jumped and leaped. Around their stomachs the cloth was tightly bound and with a staff they twisted it still tighter. They called loudly on St John the Baptist and fiercely clapped their hands. Such a disturbance did they create that all who heard them were afraid, their hearts trembling with fear, and so they were driven out of Liége. And yet all this did no great harm, through men's faith in God. For the Devil in hell was their master, and he so ordered things that Holy Church could plainly see and understand what was happening. All this is true. The men were all foolish and the women light-witted. All these people from various parts danced with each other. The country was full of them. In the churches they behaved in their usual manner, as also in towns and places round Liége and in the diocese generally. Some of them returned to Liége, shouting and bawling and making such a din that it seemed the world was coming to an end. Pregnant women and others were so distressed that they died and their bodies were carried away. The attacks were such that in their homes and in secret people could not help dancing. All this I saw indeed, and much more also. I was full thirty-six years old at the time.'

The Chronicles and Annals of Flanders [Oudegherst] continue up to 1476, and contain a short reference to the epidemic of 1374. The note reads as follows: 'But on our return we learned that round about the time of the above-mentioned wedding a great host of people in Flanders, France and England, and neighbouring countries left their homes and strolled about through the land. This was because of some strange terror and fear wherewith their hearts seemed smitten though they could not understand the reason or the cause. After three or four months they would return quietly to their homes, and for this period, and a little while before, the whole of Christendom was beset by the strangest pest that had ever been heard of, which first came from India.'

This account is clearly rather confused and unreliable as regards dates. The plague raged in 1349 and the dance-epidemic did not start before 1374. Moreover we know nothing of any dance-epidemic in England during this period. It is nevertheless interesting to note that the sufferers were seized with terror and fear, and also that after the plague had endured for some three or four months they quietly went home again.

4. *Descriptions by later writers*

Browerus, in his seventeenth-century work on Trier, has described the dance-epidemic of 1374 as well as a later one. Concerning the earlier one he says that people flocked together like lunatics, wandering all over the place, even making their way into Flanders; as they went they leaped and danced and sang merry songs. Browerus claims to have discovered that some of them were called St Vitus' dancers, and others St John's (though the former is obviously a mistake). The dancing couples were so placed that one would advance towards the other in an unseemly fashion. There follows a description of how the dancers were laced up, kicked on the stomach and exorcized. 'They indulged in disgraceful immodesty, for many women, during this shameless dance and the mock-bridal singing, bared their bosoms, while others of their own accord offered their virtue.' He ascribes all this to an appalling ignorance of the Word of God, an ignorance which at this time veiled the eyes of sinful men.

In 1381 a new epidemic of dancing broke out in Trier. Many people were attacked, according to Browerus, so that their wits were fuddled; they continually leaped and danced and were unable to give any reason for so doing. To obtain healing from this sickness a pilgrimage was made to St John the Baptist's chapel by the river Gelbim, not far from Kilburg. By reason of the great concourse of people the chapel became famous, was much visited and highly regarded. Kilburg or Kyllburg is a small community, slightly south of Prüm and north of Trier, level with the northern part of Luxembourg, and lying due north-east of Echternachbrück [Wackenroder]. This procession of sufferers from the dancing epidemic to the Chapel of St John took place therefore in a region where the people on all sides were familiar with the religious ceremonies, which incorporated elements of popular dancing. Moreover, during the epidemic of 1374 the choreomaniacs had made their way from Prüm and Echternach into Trier to perform their dances. Kilburg lay in the see of the Archbishop of Trier. Pilgrimages to the Chapel of St John at Kilburg continued, and there was a regular annual one from Trier. Bertelius, according to Krier, speaking of St John's Mount near Düdelingen, said that 'even today' (1638), on the day of St John the Baptist, their patron saint, the people celebrated a feast whose reputation had spread far and wide. Innumerable people from round about assembled there, and many of them were smitten with St John's disease (St John's or St Vitus' dance); they danced to the sound of various musical instruments till they were completely exhausted and fell to the ground as if they were dead, in this way hoping to gain protection and help from the great saint. Bertelius adds that 'even today', i.e., 1638, great hosts of pilgrims came to the little chapel on St John's Mount on the first Sunday after June 14th, on which day there was a church procession to the chapel from the church in Düdelingen.

At this stage it might be interesting to examine certain accounts by doctors which have survived from the end of the sixteenth and beginning of the seventeenth centuries. Here follows a short summary.

Schenck a Grafenberg was the town doctor of Freiburg-im-Breisgau; he was born in 1530 and died in 1598. In his notes he describes for us the extent of medical knowledge at that time concerning the dance epidemic of 1374. He speaks of it as a state of mental aberration and informs us that, unless prevented, these choreomaniacs would continue leaping and dancing to the last gasp. 'Often in their madness they would carry on in such a way that they would do themselves harm if a careful watch were not kept. Some of them were driven by their pain to leap into the Rhine and other rivers, where they drowned.' They shrieked aloud, their faces were wild and terribly contorted and they frothed at the mouth. 'Those who were looking after them used to carry around benches and high chairs with which they would ring them in if they still lived when the dancing was over. In this way their madness was assuaged. Their exhaustion was so great that they would fall to the ground unconscious, helpless, almost to be taken as dead. . . . Those who were rich kept paid attendants to see that they did not hurt themselves or others, and to act as leaders who would guide the crazy band.'

Spangenberg, in *The Mirror of Nobility*, 1591, relates that the dancers of 1373 came from the Rhine and the Mosel into Flanders, and some from Andorff through Hennegau into France. Everywhere they danced, declaring that they could see nothing but blood and that they were dancing in it. Some understood from this that they had not been properly baptized—because of the immorality of the priests; therefore the 'common people' (n.b. not the choreomaniacs then) made a plot to kill all priests.

Philippus Camerarius (1537–1624) was a notable citizen of Nüremberg who published an historical work in 1601. He places the epidemic in 1373 in the Rhineland and Flanders, and by the Mosel. This section, however, consists entirely of extracts from chronicles with which we are already familiar. The only significant information he offers relates to later instances of dance epidemics in the sixteenth century. In a posthumous work on memorable events in medical science, published in 1628, he describes the epidemic of 1374 in greater detail. Like another German doctor, Freigius, he assesses it in the medical terms of that period: 'If it is to be classed as an illness, the only category into which it seems to me to fit is a delirium of melancholia, which has of course quite a wide range. In such cases the mind is entirely disordered.'

Felix Plater, a distinguished Professor of Medicine in Bâle, was born in 1536 and published his *Observations* in 1614. He speaks of the dance as a mad frenzy. 'Some there may have been who pretended, in order to attract more generous alms, or who behaved in this fashion in order that, by presenting a pitiful appearance, they might the more easily prevail on men. There were nevertheless people of both sexes who were indeed attacked by this illness, and whose minds were so confused that they were compelled to leap thus and to dance with each other, without ceasing and without rest, day and night, and not merely for a few days, but for weeks on end.' Plater had noticed in his sources the point that even when they were compelled by hunger or weariness to cease dancing for a few moments, 'they still could not keep their bodies still, but they shook continually, as if they could not help jumping'. When they fell exhausted and had been stamped on so that at last they recovered, they realized their own folly, says Plater.

De Mezeray, in his great History of France, speaks of a great dance epidemic which he places in 1373. He says also that during this year there raged in France, Italy and England both famine and 'Holy Fire', two great afflictions. Meanwhile in the Netherlands there was an outbreak of some mental illness, a kind of madness unknown in previous centuries.

Bonnet tells us, on the authority of another edition of de Mezeray, that the dancers were seized by some crazy madness, a frenzy hitherto unknown. They took off their clothes and went about naked; they put wreaths of flowers on their heads; they held each other in with the bands in their hands, and so they danced through the streets. At last they fell breathless to the ground and swelled up so greatly that they would have burst if one had not bound their bellies tightly. As against this it must be noted that none of the older chronicles confirms the above description, though de Mezeray may have had access to material which has since been lost. The method of keeping together by bands or strips of cloth which all the dancers clasp in their hands is familiar to us from the Echternach dances. A seventeenth-century painting by Hellemont shows that this practice was still customary in his day. The nakedness mentioned by de Mezeray is perhaps confirmed by the repeated stress in the chronicles on the immodesty and shamelessness of the dancers. In actual fact, however, nakedness was by no means rare in the religious pilgrimages of medieval Christendom. We shall return to this point when we consider the practice of magic during the dance epidemics.

5. The Floods of 1374

The various chronicles and many other historical works speak of 1373 and 1374 as years in which there were great floods throughout the Rhineland. The *Chronicle of Liége*, 1402, says that in January 1374, the waters of the Mosel ran so high that in Liége they reached the altars of the churches and filled the streets and market places; indeed people passed through the streets in boats, and into the churches right up to the altars. The *Kölner Jahrbuch* tells how on February 11th, 1374, the Rhine was so high that horses were drowned in the streets, and the water stayed so until Easter. Koelhoffs' Chronicle says that it rose above the city walls of Cologne, and a boat could pass over them. Men travelled round the city in boats and rafts. The *Limburg Chronicle* speaks of floods in Lent in 1373. The Rhine floods were vast, the river rose 26 feet above its normal height due to the great quantities of snow which had fallen, more than had been known for hundreds of years. The *Chronicle of Early Roman Kings and Emperors* also describes this flood.

Here it is said to have occurred in January and February, 1374. The river Rhine is said to have risen thirty-four feet above the normal; in the low-lying parts of Cologne people were transported in boats. The highest level was reached on February 11th, after which the water sank. The *Bishops Chronicle* of Metz, 1530, shifts the date of the floods to 1375, when the rivers at Metz overflowed greatly, forboding misfortune.

In his history of the Bishops of Utrecht, Heda describes this flooding, which brought about the collapse of numerous towns and villages, and which raged for four months. In Holland also there were great floods. Michael Sachsen tells how the waters of the Rhine rose above the town walls and washed away a large part of the town of Bingen.

XIV

The Hungarian Pilgrimages

CERTAIN chronicles describe the participants in the great dance-epidemic of 1374 as pilgrims, as appears clearly in the *Chronicle of the Early Roman Kings and Emperors*, which states that outside Trier these dancers sought to fulfil their sacred votive vows around an ancient and abandoned chapel. This compels us to seek in the pilgrimages to districts of the Rhineland an explanation of the appearance of such numerous hosts of people. Subsequently we shall encounter another dance-epidemic, pictured by Pieter Brueghel the Elder, in which the dancers are expressly depicted as pilgrims.

We know of no other definite pilgrimage to Aachen and Cologne at this time, or of such immense proportions, than that which is called 'The Hungarian Pilgrimage to Relics'. The statement in Beka's chronicle that these dancers originally came from the Kingdom of Bohemia, and indications in various other places that they had abandoned their fatherland, justify the suspicion that a Hungarian pilgrimage was involved.

As early as the eleventh and twelfth centuries pilgrimages to Aachen and Cologne from surrounding districts were known [Beissel]. At this early period they took place annually in the second week in June.

In the year 1052 numerous inhabitants of the Bishopric of Liége, to which Aachen then belonged, emigrated to Hungary as a result of war and famine [Beissel]. During the twelfth century there were also emigrations to Hungary from Siebenbürgen, Bavaria, the Rhine province, Westphalia, the Netherlands, etc., and Germans were predominant [Bachmann]. German colonists

216

were numerous in Hungary, Bohemia and Poland, and constituted the more stable and ordered communities; they retained their connexions with their old homes, the Rhineland and Aachen, and regularly joined in the pilgrimages thither in order to reverence their saints and their relics [Pflugk-Harttung]. Walloon emigrants who settled in Hungary also joined these pilgrimages and gladly went on from Aachen to their old home in Liége [Schreiber], especially because at that time Aachen belonged to the bishopric of Liége [Beissel]. The first important Hungarian pilgrimage to the Rhine province of which we have knowledge was in the year 1221 [Beissel], and thenceforward they seem to have taken place every year, as Elizabeth Thoemmes recounts in her comprehensive description of them. According to legend, a severe famine afflicted Hungary at the beginning of the thirteenth century, and in their misery the people appealed to the Magi, whose relics were preserved in Cologne cathedral, and immediately there was improvement. In their gratitude innumerable pilgrims from Hungary visited the shrine of the Magi every seventh year, for healing and reconciliation. These Hungarian pilgrimages were extended to numerous other places in the Rhine province. They mostly consisted of Germans, Hungarians, Austrians, Czechs from Carinthia, Krain and Styria. They continued throughout the centuries until 1769, which was the last, a ban having been placed on them in 1775.

Thus the pilgrims from Hungary, Bohemia, Austria and Poland and other neighbouring countries assembled and were joined by Germans on the route through Germany. They followed the usual trade routes, and pilgrims came through Aschaffenburg, Miltenberg and Frankfort. Miltenberg was, according to Thoemmes, whose account is here followed, the first place of assembly. Thence the more well-to-do proceeded by boat along the Main and the Rhine to Mainz or Bingen, and thence also by boat along the Rhine to Cologne. But the majority of the pilgrims followed the land route from Miltenberg along the Main to Frankfort, whence they followed the old military road from Frankfort to Aachen, which at Sinzig leaves the banks of the Rhine, turns westward and proceeds via Rheinbach straight to Düren. Along this route there are still various monuments reminiscent of these pilgrimages. At Andernach the pilgrims separated, some going direct to Aachen, whilst the greater part took the route to Cologne along the banks of the Rhine. From Cologne they continued to Düren, which was thus the second place of assembly. Thence they continued to Aachen. But from Aachen the pilgrims went farther: in a northerly direction they proceeded to München-Gladbach and to Duisburg, or south to Trier and to Prüm, Maastricht and Liége [Bock and Willemsen].

The stay in Cologne usually lasted about six weeks and the arrival of the pilgrims was expected about the 15th to the 25th of May. The time of arrival in Aachen is given as the 10th to the 24th of July. The inauguration festival before the Marienkirche was fixed for July 15th [Schiffen].

The pilgrims were hospitably received in the Rhineland. They were given meals in the open air and by way of thanks they danced and hopped

Fig. 77. Pilgrimage of 1519. The pilgrims have reached the 'Schöne Maria' chapel in Regensburg and are entering the chapel in large numbers. The outer walls are hung with votive tablets, mostly of an agricultural character. The procession carries crosses and banners and gigantic processional candles. Individual pilgrims assume the attitude of the Crucifixion [from *Hdb. d. deutsch Volksk.* 1.]

[Thoemmes]. Generally speaking, music and dancing were inseparable from the Hungarian pilgrimages and in these thank-offering dances, as in Aachen, it often happened that persons of standing were seen among the spectators [Thoemmes]. *Das Buch Weinberg* relates how in 1524 the Hungarians brought with them enormous wax candles, which they placed in houses and in the streets and then danced to the music of pipes and drums.

In such high esteem were these pilgrimages held in Aachen that many high-ranking personages from various countries were present in order, together with the hosts of pilgrims, to do reverence to the relics preserved in the church. During the thirteenth and fourteenth centuries, for example, Aachen was visited by, among others, the Markgrave Otto V of Brandenburg; Birgitta of Sweden; a number of Swedish pilgrims; the Empress Elizabeth of Hungary and her large suite, and the Queen of Denmark with numerous Danish followers. In the year 1372 Charles IV of Germany with his wife and an imposing suite came to Aachen, not in connexion with the Hungarian pilgrimage, however, but for political purposes: but the important relics in the cathedral were shown to him [Thoemmes, Beissel]. Arrived in Aachen, Cologne, Trier, etc., the pilgrims arranged processions through the town, singing in their respective languages pious songs in honour of Jesus and Mary.

Even devastating epidemics did not prevent the continuation of these pilgrimages, and when in 1349 the plague raged in Nüremberg, Cologne and

FIG. 78. Exhibition of relics in the Marienkirche at Aachen during a Hungarian pilgrimage in 1622. The four great relics are exhibited in the loggia between the two towers (probably here the dress of the Virgin Mary). Painting of 1622 in the collection of the Aachen Historical Museum [Clemen].

Aachen, one of the most splendid and comprehensive pilgrimages of all time took place. Innumerable pilgrims crowded all the roads to Aachen. In Cologne 20,000 people died of the plague in 1356, but in that very year a great pilgrimage started out in order to combat the sickness. There was a plague also in 1396 and healing processions were therefore organized by the pilgrims [Kessel].

The primary purpose of these pilgrimages was, however, to enable the pilgrims to do reverence and to adore the numerous remarkable and extremely valuable relics which were preserved in the churches. The most remarkable were exhibited every seventh year in association with the Hungarian pilgrimages. This exhibition took place to the accompaniment of

FIG. 79. Exhibition of relics at the Marienkirche at Aachen. The great relics are shown on the balcony of the church tower on the occasion of the pilgrimage to Aachen in 1818. From a contemporary drawing [after Clemen].

great ceremonies and festivals. Such exhibitions occurred in Aachen, Cologne, Maastricht, Tongeren and Trier quite certainly in the fourteenth century and probably a century earlier [Beissel, Bock and Willemsen, Weinsberg].

The four chief relics shown in the Marienkirche at Aachen were robes worn by Mary at the birth of Christ, the swaddling clothes in which Jesus was wrapped as he lay in the manger, the cloak into which the head of St John the Baptist fell when he was executed, and the girdle which Christ wore on the cross. But there was also a reliquary containing earth drenched

FIG. 80. The staff of St Peter. Preserved in Cologne Cathedral since the ninth century, before that in the cathedral of Trier. The staff is enclosed in a richly decorated sheath from the Middle and later Middle Ages. Only the ivory knob belongs to the real staff.

in blood at the stoning of St Stephen, which was so highly esteemed that it formed a part of the so-called coronation treasure placed on the Virgin's altar at the coronation of the Emperor [Beissel]. There were numerous other relics: the nails from the Cross, a piece of the sponge and the lance, pieces of the Cross, and pieces of Christ's loincloth, his sandals, robe, rope with which he was bound, of the post on which he was whipped, etc. There were also pieces of the Baptist's bloodstained clothing, as well as those of various other apostles, martyrs, believers and virgins [Thoemmes]. In the so-called Hungarian chapel there were also preserved, from 1367 and probably earlier, relics of the Hungarian saints, István, László and Imre [Schreiber, Bock].

Cologne Cathedral is dedicated to St Peter. On one side of the choir is an altar to the Virgin, on the other side one to St Peter. There is also a special altar for the Magi. Originally their reliquary was erected in the middle of the choir, with an enormous candelabra above it, and the cathedral was erected principally as a worthy tabernacle for these remains, which were translated here from Milan in 1164.

In *De Admiranda Sacra et Civile Magnitudine Coloniae*, written by Gelenius in Cologne in 1645, we read 'The ritual books in the metropolitan church in Cologne relate "today there is a dance (*tripudium*) around the Magi"' [Schrörs]. It is therefore quite certain that for a long time past there had been dances around the reliquary, which from 1320 was exhibited in the choir. Among the most important relics in the cathedral we note [Clemen, Neu and Witte]: one-half of the staff of St Peter (Fig. 80), three links of his fetters, pieces of the Cross of Christ, of his loincloth, of the crown of thorns, of the whipping post, a nail from the Cross, relics of St Bartholomew and relics of Abbot Antony and of St Ursula and the ten thousand virgins [Beissel]. Other Cologne churches contained further venerable relics, and all were joyfully visited by the Hungarian pilgrims [Clemen].

The cathedral at Trier is the earliest monument of German Christianity. It dates back to the fourth century. The relics still existing there in 1655 were remarkably numerous, and they included the cloak of Jesus (which had been preserved at least since 1105), a large piece of the Cross, a nail from the

Cross, the other half of the staff of St Peter and one of his teeth, relics of the Apostle St Andrew, the head of the Apostle St Matthew, hair of St John the Baptist, and the head of the resurrected Lazarus. In the Church of St Mary was kept the travelling altar of the sainted Willibrord, which he was accustomed to take with him on his missions, pieces of the Cross, of the loincloth, of Mary's robe, and relics of St Stephen, etc.; while in the Church of St

Fig. 81. The Holy Gown of Christ above the altar in Trier Cathedral. It is exhibited every fortieth year, the last time in 1933, when during fifty days more than two million pilgrims offered their reverence and praise [after Pessler].

Matthew the Apostle, St Matthew lay buried and to it, since the twelfth century, there were regular pilgrimages. In this church there is also an altar to St Antony Abbas [Irsch, Beissel].

In the foundation church of Maastricht, there are relics of St Servatius, the patron saint of the city. The church was in fact his burial place. These relics were so highly esteemed that at the coronation of the emperors in Aachen the procession was conducted to Maastricht to do honour to them. In addition, there was a comprehensive collection of relics preserved by emperors, kings and popes. In particular there is to be found a so-called St Peter key (Fig. 82), large and of very artistic design, the upper part fashioned as a sort of reliquary in which small splinters of the chains of St Peter were enclosed. The key itself was regarded as a copy of the one which formerly opened the portals of the St Peter crypt in the St Peter basilica.

The Maastricht key is supposed to derive from the very early Middle Ages. Maastricht also possessed pieces of the Cross of Christ, relics of the apostle Matthew, a part of the whipping post, relics of the apostles Peter, Paul and Thomas, of the saints Valentine and Lambert [Bock and Willemsen]. Originally St Lambert was buried in the Church of St Peter in Maastricht, but the relics were subsequently translated to Liége. To these relics,

FIG. 82. St Peter key in Maastricht Cathedral. It belonged to St Servatius, who received it from Pope Damascus in 1376, and contains—possibly melted into the metal alloy—fragments of St Peter's chains
[after Bock and Willemsen].

FIG. 83. St Peter key in the Church of the Holy Cross, Liége. It was presented to St Hubert on his visit to Rome in 722. The enlarged portion of a reliquary containing pieces of St Peter's chains
[after Bock and Willemsen].

first in Maastricht and then in Liége, there were regular and widely attended pilgrimages [Cabrol and Leclercq].

Liége had exceptionally numerous churches and cloisters and was regarded in this respect as second only to Cologne and Rome. In the crypt of the St Lambert Cathedral its patron lay; the high altar was dedicated to the Virgin Mary and St Lambert. In the Church of the Holy Cross, Liége, we find another St Peter key, the so-called St Hubert key, which he obtained at the beginning of the eighth century during a visit to the Pope in Rome (Fig. 83) [Kurth].

A number of relics are also found in the churches of Prüm. They came for the most part from the reliquaries of Aachen and had been distributed by the beneficence of emperors and kings. Here are relics of Christ, Mary, St Peter, St Paul, St John the Baptist and St Stephen, as well as of a large number of other saints [Schiffers].

The cathedral of Metz was originally very rich in relics, but nearly all its treasures were destroyed, mainly during the French Revolution. As early as the ninth and tenth centuries various bishops had presented crosses and

FIG. 84. Miniature bust in embossed, and later painted, silver, probably originally representing the head of the Baptist on a plate. Preserved since the fourteenth century and belonging to the treasury of Maastricht Cathedral. The choreomaniacs of 1374 probably performed their dances before this bust [Bock and Willemsen].

caskets filled with relics to the church. Thus there were here an arm of St Stephen, the patron saint of the cathedral, taken from Byzantium and concealed in a specially precious reliquary, which was especially reverenced and was called 'St Stephen's hide-out'. The head of the saint, gilded and adorned with precious stones, was preserved in the same reliquary, while in another equally precious reliquary is one of the blood-stained missiles with which the martyr was stoned to death, and some of his hair. A part of our Saviour's praeputium was preserved and placed in the hands of an angel, executed in gold. Bits of the Cross, relics of saints, etc., were among the treasures of the cathedral. Similarly there was an image of Mary in pure gold, which was supposed to have miraculous power [Aubert]. Other churches in Metz were also richly endowed with relics.

The little community of Jülich, near München-Gladbach, belonged from 1356 to a duchy which in reality comprised large parts of the middle Rhine province, including many of the places through which the Hungarian pilgrims passed. The principal church in Jülich was the Marienkirche in which were preserved the relics of Christina of Stumbelen, on the day of whose death, June 22nd, hosts of pilgrims always assembled round the reliquary [v. Stramberg]. Christina of Stumbelen was active during the latter part of the thirteenth century and died in 1312. She was never canonized by the Catholic Church—as is also true of the Three Magi—but was regarded by the people as a saint and was reverenced accordingly.

Beissel in his work on the Aachen pilgrimages relates that King Ludwig I of Hungary and Bohemia and Poland, in the year 1374, together with a large suite, visited Aachen, where on January 5th he signed the founder's letter for the Hungarian chapel in the Marienkirche. Thoemmes makes a similar statement, although she formulates it more cautiously, and adds that according to a manuscript (MS. 261), preserved in the archives of the city of Aachen, the king probably went on his pilgrimage in the year 1374. The chief archivist of Aachen, Prof. Huyskens, writes me that 'the manuscript to which you refer was written by the historian K. Fr. Meyer the Elder, as a still unprinted second part of his history of Aachen, written at the end of the eighteenth century. In this manuscript he mentions that King Ludwig I of Hungary was a zealous supporter of these pilgrimages, and that in 1374 he arrived with a large suite in Aachen, bringing his Hungarians with him, as his predecessors had done, as is shown by an old *Chronicon Manuscriptum* preserved in the archives of the great church in Aachen.' Meanwhile, this manuscript chronicle, as Professor Huyskens informs me, is no longer to be found in the archives; it appears to have disappeared. In all probability it contained only a late tradition. Professor Huyskens, moreover, has closely examined the whole question of this pilgrimage by Ludwig I, but no historical proof has been found. Possibly the accounts rest upon a misunderstanding of an incorrectly formulated memorial tablet of the seventeenth century, which was formerly erected in the Hungarian chapel. This chapel is first mentioned in the records in 1366. The inscription relates that the chapel was donated and provided with valuable ornaments by Ludwig of Hungary, who had it erected and consecrated to the Virgin Mary and to certain Hungarian kings and saints on August 4th, 1374. This we read in the *Chronicon Ungariae et Bonfinius*.

Nevertheless, it seems to me not improbable that the old tradition may be correct; that Ludwig of Hungary may have visited Aachen in the summer of 1374, together with a host of pilgrims from Hungary and the neighbouring countries, and these are my reasons.

We have seen already that the choreomaniacs appeared in Aachen on July 15th. From August 15th to September 8th they were in Cologne. From September 11th to the 14th they are in Maastricht, Harstal, Liége and Tongeren, and as late as October 22nd and October 23rd in Ghent. At some unknown date we find them in Trier. The route is therefore: Aachen, Cologne, Maastrict, Tongeren, Harstal, Liége, Trier, and one which the Hungarian pilgrimages always followed (Fig. 84). Jülich and Gelderland, where the choreomaniacs also appeared, corresponds in the main to the usual route of the Hungarian pilgrimages in the direction of München-Gladbach and Duisburg. This, as well as the fact that the choreomaniacs were so very numerous, many thousands strong, greatly enforces the possibility that it was a Hungarian pilgrimage whose members in this way sickened and suffered.

We have also seen that these Hungarian pilgrimages attracted followers not only from Holland, Belgium and Flanders, but certainly also from Luxembourg and the neighbouring parts of France. This would explain why the hosts of choreomaniacs, at least to some extent, moved up towards Holland and into Flanders and Belgium and down to Northern France, perhaps to Metz. However, the chronicles testify that numerous sick pilgrims streamed eastwards from Brabant to Liége and Maastricht, which is evidence that the causes of the epidemic were to be found not only in the Rhine province, where the plague seems to have begun, but also in Belgium and Flanders. Perhaps also in the Metz district. So it seems to me very probable that if no small portion of these choreomaniacs consisted of Hungarian pilgrims, so also others joined them, natives of these districts, quite naturally overtaken by the same disease. But I find it difficult to believe that there were any Hungarians in the Metz epidemic, because, as we know, it was not their habit to move south to Metz.

De Rivo mentions that, in their dances, the choreomaniacs called out the names of demons never heard before. Herenthal mentions 'friskes', and the rhyming chronicle quoted by him uses the terms 'frisch' and 'friskes'. The *Liége Chronicle* mentions 'frilis' and John of Leyden quotes the term 'frijsh'. These words have been connected with the little song which Koelhoff reproduces and which was sung by the choreomaniacs during their dances in Cologne:

> Here Sent Johan
> So, So.
> Vrisch ind vro
> Here Sent Johan.

It has been thought that these 'names of demons' were mistaken or misunderstood, but such an assumption seems to me in the highest degree unreasonable, for if we suppose that it was the inhabitants of the Rhine and Moselle districts who danced and sang, they certainly all understood what they sang. If, on the other hand, the pilgrims from Hungary, Bohemia and Poland are in question, then the possibility of misunderstanding becomes reasonable and natural. They sang in their own languages and for that reason such words as were yet very like the German were interpreted as peculiar, even as the names of demons.

Frisk. In its various forms this is a distinctly international word, derived possibly from the Latin *friscum* [Diefenbach] or *priscus* [Lexer], and for that reason appearing in almost all Germanic and Romance languages. Medieval German—whether High or Low—possessed this word. Middle High German shows *vrisch* and *vrische* [Lexer], derived from old German *frisch* [Müller, Zarnche]. *Vrische* is also a verb with the meaning 'make whole'. Middle Low

German also has *vrisch* [Schiller and Lübben]. From Middle High German we obtain *vrilich*, with the meaning 'free, unhindered', whilst the word *vraelich* has the meaning 'glad, happy'. Middle Low German shows *vrilik* meaning 'free, fearless, bold', and *vrolich* and *vrolik*, meaning 'smooth'. But there is also a Middle High German word *froelich* meaning 'smooth' [Grimm and Grimm].

Middle Dutch has *vrilike, -lijc, -lic* [Verwijs and Verdam], also *frisch* [Knui-tel]. East Frisian has *frisk*, which means 'healthy, young, unspoiled, lively', and *frisken*, meaning 'to make healthy' [Koolman]. Frisian has *fris(k)*, *frisch* [Dijkstra]. The West Flanders language only has *fritsch* [Priester].

Until the fifteenth century we find the French words *frische, frisque, frisce*, and various others with the customary meaning of 'strong, healthy, quick, lively' [Godefroy, Sainte-Palaye].

There is evidently no difficulty in placing the so-called demon names *Friskes, Frijsch* and *Frilis* in linguistic connexion with Middle High German and Middle Low German and with Dutch. *Friskes* and *Frijsch* are also very near to Frisian and French. But if the choreomaniacs had sung in any of these languages the meaning of their song would certainly not have been so grossly misunderstood. It is more probable that they sang in languages which could not be understood in these districts, so let us consider the Hungarian, Czech, Croatian and Polish forms.

It is well known that Franz Liszt described the two parts of an Hungarian rhapsody (apart from the brief introduction) as *lassan* which meant *andante mesto*, and *friska* which meant *vivace*. Liszt was a Hungarian and grew up in a community which was often visited by itinerant Hungarian gipsy musicians. Liszt's twenty Hungarian rhapsodies have folk-songs as their foundations, taken from Hungarian gipsy music, although he himself called them Hungarian national melodies [Ramann]. The earliest historical record of the penetration of the gipsies into Hungary is in 1219.

From the early Middle Ages the Hungarian language had the word *friss*, meaning 'splendid, gay, quick' [Kötet], and this has been retained [Szamota and Zolnai], but it is pronounced 'frisch'. There is also a word *frissül*, meaning 'grow lively, live'. In the gipsy tongue we find *frischko*, meaning 'healthy, glad', but since it cannot be derived from Sanskrit, it must be a borrowed word [Pott], possibly from Bohemian, which in turn borrowed it from German [Miklosisch, Pott].

The Bohemian language, Czech, has *friský* [Kott]; also *fryžka, fryže, fryž* [Gebaur]. In Croatian we find *fris-ak, friska, frisko*, meaning 'healthy, agile, quick, hasty' [Filipovic].

The Polish language also has *frysz*, with the same meaning. In other Slavonic languages similar words are to be found [Bogumila]. But we have not here been able to find anything corresponding to *Frilis*. So we shall revert to the German of the Middle Ages, where we encounter the word *Vrilisch*, also to be found in medieval Dutch *Vrilijc*; but since *Vrilijc* was not understood, it must have occurred in a language which differed considerably from

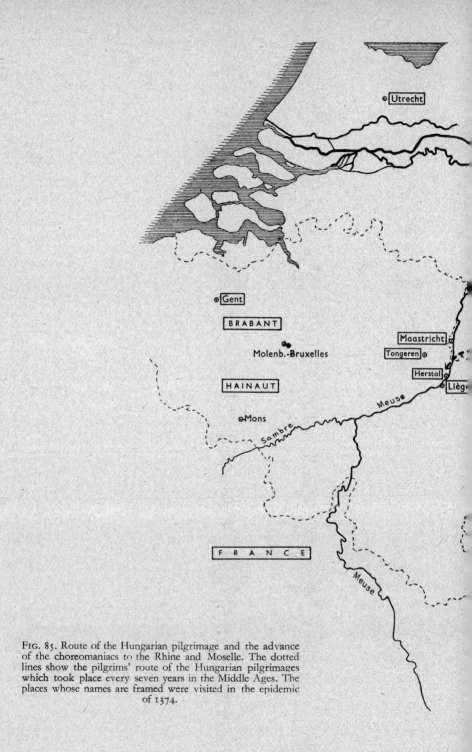

FIG. 85. Route of the Hungarian pilgrimage and the advance
of the choreomaniacs to the Rhine and Moselle. The dotted
lines show the pilgrims' route of the Hungarian pilgrimages
which took place every seven years in the Middle Ages. The
places whose names are framed were visited in the epidemic
of 1374.

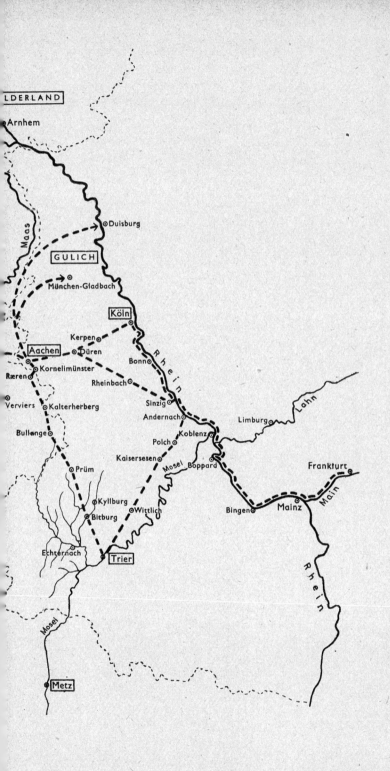

ELDERLAND

Arnhem

Maas

Duisburg

GULICH

München-Gladbach

Köln

Kerpen

Aachen   Düren

Ræren   Kornelimünster

Bonn

Verviers   Kalterherberg

Rheinbach

Bullange

Sinzig

Andernach

Rhein

Lahn

Limburg

Polch

Koblenz

Prüm

Kaisersesen

Mosel   Boppard

Frankfurt

Kyllburg

Wittlich

Main

Bitburg

Bingen   Mainz

Echternach

Trier

Mosel

Rhein

Metz

the languages which were spoken in the Rhine provinces and especially in
Flanders. We then remember the numerous Germans, not least those from
the Rhineland and from the Walloon districts, who in the early Middle Ages
emigrated to Hungary, and who subsequently always appear to have constituted what one might call the kernel of the Hungarian pilgrimages. No full
account has been given as to the construction of the language which the
Germans in Hungary spoke about two hundred years after their emigration.
But we may suppose that they were unable to retain their German language
unchanged, but must to a greater or lesser extent have borrowed words
and have been influenced in their pronunciation by Hungarian, possibly also
by the gipsy language as well as by neighbouring Slavonic languages. We
may be permitted to assume hypothetically that their language was so greatly
changed that they could not readily be understood by the Germans in the
Homeland. A change from *vrilich* to *frilis* with a sharper, more fronted 'ch',
is not inconceivable.

The conclusion is that the dancing epidemic of 1374 comprised a large
number of Hungarian pilgrims who, according to ancient custom, proceeded
to Aachen and Cologne, to N.W. Germany, to Flanders and to the southern
Rhine provinces and Trier. In this pilgrimage there participated, in addition
to Hungarians, also the Germans who had emigrated to Hungary in the
twelfth and thirteenth centuries, principally from the Rhine provinces, as
well as Walloons from the districts around Liège. Croatians, Bohemians
and Poles, also Austrians and Reich Germans, attached themselves to the
pilgrimage, as well as others from Holland, Belgium and France. But as the
hosts of pilgrims passed the most southerly parts of the Rhine provinces
they encountered the infection which caused the grave epidemic, which in its
turn led to attempts at a cure through the church dance for the Virgin Mary
and the Saints, or through churchyard dances. But very many danced
involuntarily, both by day and night, awake or asleep. The proof that the
epidemic of 1347 included especially the Hungarian pilgrims is to be found
in the fact that the dance began at Aachen, often the first town visited by the
pilgrims, and that the epidemic afterwards spread, with constantly increasing
numbers, to Cologne, Maastricht, Tongeren, Liége, up north to Jülich and
Gelderland, and as far as Ghent; in a southerly direction to Hainaut and
finally to Trier. This is essentially the route, and these are the districts which
the Hungarian pilgrims usually visited.

The so-called 'demon' names which, according to certain chroniclers, the
choreomaniacs cried out may most conveniently be interpreted as belonging
to the Hungarian, Bohemian, Croatian and Polish languages, and may
reasonably be associated with the German Hungarians, who always took part
in the pilgrimages.

Beka's statement that during this year (1374) a 'remarkable plague spread
around the Rhine, beginning in the Kingdom of Bohemia', confirms this
interpretation. Further confirmation is to be found in the already mentioned
statements of Hedion that 'they had left their home-land' and of Bzovius

concerning 'fugitive and crazy, away from the home-land and from their own society'.

The enormous extent of the dance epidemic of 1374—incomparably greater and more widespread than any other—also indicates that special circumstances must have existed, and strengthen the probability that it was just the Hungarian participators in the pilgrimages who were to so large an extent stricken by the sickness.

XV

Dance Epidemics of the Fifteenth Century

DURING the year 1418 there were dance epidemics at Zürich, Switzerland, when the sick danced in the so-called Water Church. St Felix and St Regula are revered as the city's patron saints [Buchberger]. They came from Egypt and were relatives and were connected with the Theban legion which fled from the persecution of the Emperor Maximinianus. They followed the route through Wallis, crossed the Furka pass and subsequently worked as missionaries in Urnerland. Eventually they came to Zürich, and suffered martyrdom there about the year 305, at the instigation of Stadtholder Decius and by order of Maximinianus. They were beaten with rods and immersed in boiling oil, but were unscathed, for which reason they were finally beheaded. Their martyrdom took place on a small island in the middle of the River Limmat, which flows through the city of Zürich. Here they had spent the night near a spring. Very soon the memory of the martyrs was honoured by the populace. From near and far the sick hastened to their graves in search of miraculous cures. Their fame was great not only in Switzerland, but also in Germany and Spain [Stadler].

Charlemagne ordered the erection of a chapel on the site of their martyrdom and this was replaced in time by a church, the so-called Water Church, which was completed by the middle of the thirteenth century. Originally the church had two altars, both consecrated to St Felix and St Regula. The earlier of these stood in front of the choir, and was called 'the upper'; the other, 'the lower', stood in the middle of the church, where there was an excavation, a sort of open crypt, about twenty feet deep and surrounded by a wall, which at its northern end was broken by descending steps. Below, in the open crypt, was a large stone slab upon which, according to legend, the martyrs had suffered death, and it was upon this slab that the lower altar stood. There was also a spring or well in the crypt. The roof of the church was originally painted blue and strewn with golden stars.

In the course of time, however, more and more altars were erected in the Water Church. Altars to the Magi, to St Stephen and St Lawrence were added in the fourteenth century, and as late as 1441 an altar was erected to the Holy Cross, and one in 1467 to St Anthony.

The dance epidemic of which there is some mention in the records was known and described by Martin, amongst others. Thanks to the great courtesy of the director of the State archives in the canton of Zürich, it has been possible to obtain copies of the minutes of the Court and Council [Erste Hälfte 1418, B, vol. VI, 204 Bl. 137 and ditto 1452, B, vol. VI, 218, Bl. 90], which describe the two epidemics now under consideration.

In 1418 a certain butcher named Heini Murer reported that he was standing in the Water Church, looking at the wretched women dancing there, when there came the harness-smith, Heini, who wished to make more room for the women so that they might have more air, whereupon he pushed people behind him.

This statement, in spite of its brevity, is of very great interest. It shows that the women were very sick and it seems to me to show, above all, that they were breathless and had difficulty in breathing, since Heini wanted to give them more room, in order that more air could reach them. We do not know exactly where in the church the dance took place, but since no altar is mentioned the upper part of the church and near to the spring is the most probable place.

The most remarkable thing about this dance is the selection of the Water Church as the scene. It is reached by a bridge spanning the Limmat river and leading direct to the main porch, so that it is necessary first to pass over running water. Then the dance was performed beside or near this remarkable spring in the open crypt. This spring, says Vögelin, early stood in high esteem because in some miraculous way it bestowed health and strength, whether one bathed in it or drank its waters. It seems to me beyond doubt that these two circumstances were of influence when the sick women chose to dance in the Water Church.

Daumer relates, after Hottinger, another case of dancing sickness, which took place in the week after the festival of St Vitus, i.e., June 23rd, in the cloister of St Agnes at Schaffhausen. A monk of particularly distinguished origin danced himself to death. It may be assumed that the 'dance' began just before the St Vitus festival, 1442, June 15th, and grew steadily worse until June 23rd. Possibly the sick man danced, in the real sense, in order to find release from his suffering.

From the minutes of the Court and Council of the city of Zürich of 1452 we take an account of a third case. There we learn that on St Vitus' day,

FIG. 86. The Water Church at Zürich. The depression in front of the altar is the scene of the martyrdom of St Felix and St Regula. The spring is there too. Dancing took place in this church in 1418 and 1451 [from an oil painting of the sixteenth century, reproduced by Vögelin].

June 15th, a poor creature danced in the Helmet House of the Water Church, a sort of covered way protecting the passage between the bridge and the main entrance to the church. The roof elevation resembled a pointed hood or helmet, hence the name [Vögelin]. On this occasion the armourer Hanns had stood near and watched the spectacle. The wretched dancer had then called out to Hanns that he 'should help him in his need and come to his assistance'. And Hanns, for the love of God and His Beloved Mother (Mary), did so;

233

and when he had helped the sick man and danced with him, four workmen began to laugh at him. A quarrel and a fight ensued, as a result of which one of the workmen brought an action in the courts. This workman stated that during the dance Hanns made such extraordinary gestures that he could not help laughing (*und habe also wunderliche geberde gehept, das er sin lachen must*). During the subsequent quarrel Hanns had called down on him the curse of epilepsy.

The atrium of a church, its outbuilding, was sometimes in the form of a hall of pillars and was called 'Paradise' in Germany, Westphalia and France [Pfannenschmid]. According to Jacobs it was the outbuildings of the old foundation churches which were called 'Paradise' or 'the Rose-garden'. In a record of 1340 in connexion with the cathedral of Speier, reference is made to the place called Paradise, 'where the bodies of the dead were given up for church burial'. When churches began to have towers the nave stretched out as a sort of independent outbuilding and the 'Helmet House', which was erected in front of this outbuilding, was similarly known as Paradise [Pfannenschmid]. The Helmet House thus belongs to the consecrated ground of the church and to dance in it was therefore equivalent to dancing within the church, so the sick dancer danced in a symbolic mystic sense in Paradise. If this is correct, we have found a further instance of the dance of the angels being imitated in 'Paradise'. Just as the heavenly paradise knows nothing of imperfection or suffering, so the sufferer shall, as far as possible, participate in this joy and in the bodily well-being which he so eagerly seeks in his imitation of the dance of the angels.

But the fact that the sufferer had to pass over running water to perform his dance may play an equal or even greater role. Also remarkable is the fact that spectators took part and were implored by the dancers to assist. When they did so it cannot have been merely for the sake of the dance; the sufferer was probably unable to stand on his own feet or to move his limbs. But the dance seems to have been in some way peculiar; the helpers made such strange gestures that they provoked laughter. This may mean merely that they had difficulty in keeping the sufferers upright and in inducing them to participate. Not altogether without significance is the fact that Hanns cursed the scoffers with epilepsy. Such curses were common enough at the end of the Middle Ages [Böhme], including the curse of St Vitus' dance and St Anthony's fire, but the fact that epilepsy was named may possible indicate that the sufferer's malady was similar to that disease.

XVI

Dance Epidemics of the Sixteenth Century

IN the year 1518 a great epidemic of dancing broke out in Strassburg. For a long time it was not clear in which century this epidemic raged. The year 1418 was usually named, yet as early as 1879 the psychiatrist Witkowski furnished indisputable proof that this was no less than a century in error. The mistake goes back to Schiltern's report of 1698, which twice gave the date as 1418, so that other authors derived from him their incorrect information. Witkowski referred to Kleinlavveln's chronicle of 1625, to Goldmeyer's *Strassburg Chronicle* of 1636, to Osea Schad's notes of the seventeenth century, to Sebastian Brant's annals of the period before 1521, and to Imlin's family chronicle in the Strassburg archives, all of which give 1518 as the year of the epidemic. In addition, Witkowski referred to a number of documents in the Strassburg city archives which further confirm that the epidemic occurred in 1518. Subsequently Martin confirmed Witkowski's conclusions in every respect.

The architect Daniel Specklin was born in Strassburg in 1536 and died there in 1589. About 1587 he began to write his *Strassburg Chronicle*. His manuscript was burnt in the library fire during the Franco-German War of 1870, but during the seventeenth century Osea Schad, and André Silbermann in the nineteenth century, made copious extracts from the manuscript; similarly there are in Schiltern's work numerous notes derived from it. There are similar notes in a manuscript of Schneegans. It has thus been possible to reconstruct the Specklin chronicles in their main outlines.

Specklin relates that in the year 1518 young and old began to dance in Strassburg; they danced night and day until they fell to the ground. More than a hundred danced at a time. At first they were allowed to dance in the halls of the various guilds, but subsequently arrangements were made for them to dance in two market places, and persons were specially appointed to dance with them for payment, to the music of drums and pipes. But all this was of no avail, and many danced themselves to death. Then they were sent to St Vitus, to Hohlenstein, quite near Zabern. There they were given small crosses and *red shoes** and a mass was held for them. On the uppers and soles of the shoes crosses were drawn in consecrated oil and in the name of St Vitus they were sprinkled with holy water. This helped all of them. Hither came also numerous others afflicted with St Vitus' dance. But there was much imposture. [Mitt. Ges. für Erh. d. Gesch. Denkm. im Elsass, 15.]

Before the fire of 1870 there existed in the city archives of Strassburg a manuscript entitled *Sebastian Brant's Annals*. This Sebastian Brant was appointed secretary of the council of Strassburg in 1503. He died in 1521. These annals were copied by Jacques Wencker (1668–1743). They are founded partly on the minutes of the council of Strassburg, and partly on authentic notes of Sebastian Brant [Mitt. Gesch. Denkm. Elsass 15]. The minutes themselves were lost long ago.

One report in this chronicle bears the title: 'A marvellous cure for St Vitus' dance in the year 1517.' There follow similar reports from Specklin, as mentioned above, in which it is said that the sufferers were sent to Zabern and Hellensteg, whither many others hastened of their own accord. Here the dancers prostrated themselves before the image and the priest held mass for them. Thereupon they were given small crosses and red shoes, on the uppers and soles of which crosses had been drawn with consecrated oil and which had been sprinkled with holy water in the name of St Vitus. This helped many and led to great offerings. It is for this reason that the affliction is named after St Vitus.

In 1518 there arrived many sufferers from this sickness, though many pretenders joined them. Wencker adds, mainly from the minutes of the council and Brant's annals, that on July 22nd, 1518, began the terrible sickness known as St Vitus' dance. More than fifty persons were afflicted and danced day and night in a distressing manner. All were cared for at the expense of the town and were taken to the shrine of the holy St Vitus at Hohlenstein near Zabern, where they were almost cured. But then a decree was issued forbidding music, except at weddings and at the first mass celebrated by a newly inducted priest. On August 10th it was decreed that every person must take care of his own people and that the various guilds should examine their members and send those who were ailing to St Vitus. When, subsequently, a number of women and boys performed the 'evil' dance, the people were advised to play for them in their homes. Later the city authorities sent the sufferers to the hospitals, though they continued to send others to St Vitus' chapel, to which the city also sent valuable gifts.

Imlin's family chronicle from Strassburg, which goes back to the sixteenth century, relates that a week before the festival of St Mary Magdalene,

---

* The red dancing shoes reappear later as a familiar saga motif in the story of Snow-White, by the brothers Grimm. The cruel stepmother forces Snow-White to put on red-hot iron slippers in which she was compelled to dance until she fell dead. In Hans Andersen's story there is a little girl who is given red dancing shoes and who was forced to dance without stopping until she was released by having her feet chopped off.

236

July 14th, 1518, a woman began to dance and continued for six days. Then the city council had her conducted to St Vitus near Zabern, and there she was cured. But many others began to dance, and thirty-four men and women were involved within four days. Then drummers and pipers were forbidden to play and some of the dancers were conducted to the halls of the guilds. Finally they were taken all together to St Vitus. But in spite of all this more than four hundred persons were afflicted within four weeks.

Duntzenheim's chronicle (*Fragments de Diverses Vieilles Chroniques*) relates that the madness originated with a woman who began by dancing for four days at a stretch, and that only a few days later thirty-four persons were dancing and by the fourth week the number had risen to two hundred.

·But as the epidemic continued to spread the city authorities issued stricter regulations, which prescribed that the guilds must take charge of their own sick, '*das die nyder getuschet*', or send them to St Vitus and take care that they did not run about the streets. Meanwhile, the disease proved obstinate and it was consequently decreed that the sufferers must be kept indoors and that the guilds likewise should care for their sick and take them to St Vitus, or *to a saint of their own choice*, so that they might not dance publicly on the streets to the discomfort of the public [Martin].

Schiltern quotes from the minutes of the council with regard to the regulations for the care of the sick. When they were sent to the chapel of St Vitus, they were divided into three groups and conducted by specially appointed guardians. A number of priests were encouraged to attend the chapel. There they held a mass for each group and the sufferers were led round the altar and made a small money offering. Offerings were occasionally made by others attending. Thereupon the poor were given alms. Relatives complained of the difficulty of keeping the sick at home. One man even suggested that his wife had been seized by St Martzolff's disease and that he had in consequence arched her body and engaged a piper to play for her. The sufferers were driven out to Zabern in three-horse waggons at the expense of the city.

Schiltern quotes a poem from a Chron. MS. Argent, long since lost:

> Many hundreds in Strassburg began
> To dance and hop, women and men,
> In the public market, in alleys and streets,
> Day and night; and many of them ate nothing
> Until at last the sickness left them.
> This affliction was called St Vitus' dance.

This dance was regarded by some people, says Schiltern, as a special form of cramp and was due to natural causes, like tarantism. But others attributed the disease to supernatural causes and employed spiritual cures.

Kleinlavveln published in 1625 a *Strassburg Chronicle* in which, on the authority of Königshoffen, Brant and various other chroniclers, he briefly describes the epidemic of 1518.

> 1518.   Counting fifteen hundred years
> And eighteen more . . .
> A remarkable disease spread
> At this time among the people.
> Then many in their madness
> Began to dance,
> Which they did day and night
> And without interruption
> Until they fell down unconscious.
> Many died in consequence.

An astrological chronicle for Strassburg was published in 1636 by Goldmeyer. In it we read: 'In the year 1518 A.D., when the procession entered into the twentieth degree of the Virgin in opposition to the head of Medusa, and when Mars was in the ascendant, together with Capricorn, there occurred among men a remarkable and terrible disease called St Vitus' dance, in which men in their madness began to dance day and night until finally they fell down unconscious and succumbed to death. This disease was caused by opposition to the head of Medusa.'

Wencker's, Brant's and Specklin's annals relate that the epidemic began during a period of acute famine, ruined harvests and general want. The summer of 1515 was unusually dry and was accompanied by high prices. During the year 1516 there was extreme cold so that the grain and the wine harvests were frozen. There was severe famine and widespread disease. These conditions prevailed until as late as 1518 [Trausch's Chronicle, Mitt. Gesch. Denkm. Elsass, 15]. Wencker confirms that in 1517 there was severe famine, that the harvests had failed three years in succession, and that prices ran high. In 1518 the city was compelled to throw open its granaries to the people. After the dry summer of 1517 there followed a severe and cold winter, with the result that many lay in the hospitals and leprosy homes. Specklin also relates that during this difficult and costly year of 1518 the clergy would not help the poor because the latter were suspected of leanings to the Lutheran heresy. In protest against this, Luther's articles were affixed to the churches and the houses of the clergy.

This statement should be read in combination with the report already mentioned that the city council finally abandoned its previous view that the sufferers must be sent to St Vitus and agreed instead that they might be sent to the shrine of any desired saint. It is difficult to reconcile this with Catholic doctrine, but it may be explained by the fact that—as the chroniclers frequently declare—about this time Luther's tenets were beginning to be openly exhibited and that the plundering of churches and chapels, the destruction of images and the looting of monasteries were rife. The certainty that the epidemic in Strassburg really occurred in 1518 and not a century earlier is thereby established.

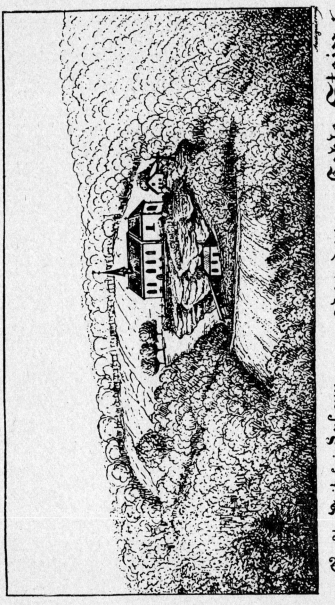

Sankt Veit bei Zabern   oder der   Hohle Stein :
Die Beiden Kapellen und das Bruderhaus, vor 1792.
(Obere Kapelle, L des Schiffs – 16.ᴹ 06 ; Br. 9.ᴹ 99 ; L. des Chors – 9.ᴹ 45 ; Br. 8.ᴹ 38).

Fig. 87. Zabern and the Chapel of St Vitus. Directly below it is the lower chapel, which partially conceals the entrance to the grotto of Hohlenstein. Here occurred the dance-epidemic of 1518 [Adam].

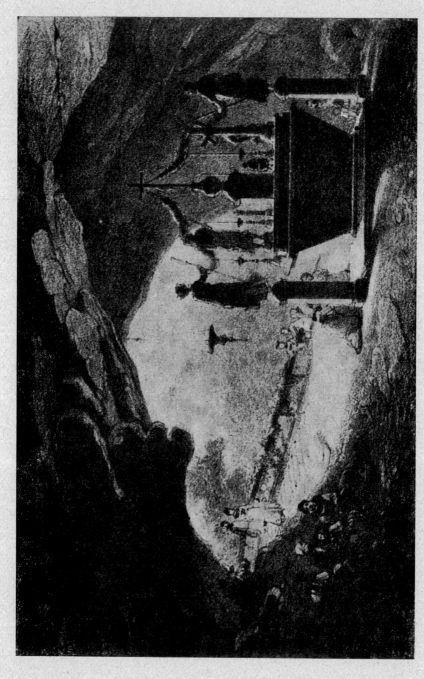

FIG. 88. The St Vitus Grotto of Hohlenstein. View over the mountain slopes near Zabern, south of Strassburg. On the altar stands St Vitus in his cauldron, St Sebastian and possibly St Christopher. To the left, in the background, the grave-stones of two hermits and the steps up to the chapel of St Vitus [from a drawing by E. Laville in Klein].

Zabern lies in a district abounding in cliffs and crags. Just to the west lies the St Vitus mountain, also called la Vixberg. About half way up is a grotto called Hohlenstein. It is about twelve feet high, twenty feet wide and forty feet long [Fischer]. At the top of the mountain is a chapel dedicated to St Vitus (Fig. 87). Up the mountainside are steps to the grotto and thence to the chapel. It was primarily to the chapel of St Vitus at the top of the mountain that the sick of Strassburg were conducted in 1518, but it is not at all impossible that they also visited the grotto and there held divine service.

Phot. A. Merckling
Zabern
HOLZGRUPPE AUS DER EHM! ST VEITS-KAPELLE:
ANFANG DES XVI JAHRH.º __ ZABERNER-MUSEUM.

FIG. 89. Group of Saints at the St Vitus Chapel at Zabern dates from the beginning of the sixteenth century. Represents the Virgin and Child, St Vitus in the cauldron, and Pope Marcellus. Dancing took place before the image in the epidemic of 1518 [Adam].

From ancient times the grotto had also played a religious role (Fig. 88). It was inhabited by a hermit and just in the entrance there are two gravestones with inscriptions concerning two hermits who had had charge of the grotto and who had died, the one in 1651, the other in 1702 [Rothmüller]. Among other things they were the guardians of the chapel of St Vitus on the mountain [Klein].

In the museum in Zabern there is a wood-carving representing the Mother of God and the infant Jesus with, on her right, Pope Marcellus, and, on her left, St Vitus (Fig. 89). It is a work dating from about the end of the fifteenth century and was originally placed either in the chapel of St Vitus or in the grotto. Pope Marcellus was approximately contemporary with St Vitus; he became Pope in 308 and he is invoked with St Vitus in the consecration of St Vitus' water. The formula of consecration includes the wish that God might make the water holy 'so that it might prove a health-bringing cure for mankind and that in the name of the Lord and with His blessing and with the help of St Vitus and St Marcellus everybody sprinkled with it or everybody drinking it might recover bodily health and spiritual safety' [Adam].

This little chapel possessed relics of St Vitus, wrought in silver, and on the evangelical side of the altar was placed a small image of St Vitus. On both sides of the altar stood two statues of the apostles Phillip and Jacob, erected as late as the nineteenth century. On this altar there were also two smaller statues of St Christopher and St Sebastian. The two latter can be traced to the year 1605, when, although already very old, they were re-silvered, regilded and repainted. Just in front of the grotto there is also a small chapel dating back to at least 1554—existing records do not go back further. It was, however, at that time consecrated to St Trilgen [Adam].

It would seem that pilgrimages to the chapel of St Vitus were continued century after century until the nineteenth century. Fischer relates that on Easter Monday and on June 15th, when the church in Strassburg celebrates the memorial festival of St Vitus, numerous pilgrims used to visit the St Vitus mountain; the inhabitants of the surrounding parishes came with processional cross and banners to Hohlenstein and everybody laid his offering on the altar or in the poor box in the chapel. Until the beginning of the nineteenth century pilgrimages thither were undertaken by people suffering from epilepsy or St Vitus' dance.

St Vitus was reverenced during the 1850's in numerous places in Alsace and especially in Zabern and the Hohlenstein grottoes. All who suffered from epilepsy made a pilgrimage there. After they had prayed in the grotto chapel and made their offerings, they placed their pilgrim's staffs against some tree in the belief that whoever afterwards took it would also take the sickness away [Stoeber]. Hysterical and barren women offered iron toads to the saint; Adam, Rothmüller and Klein all mention this fact, and the last of these authors adds that women other than hysterical offered iron toads. In the Zabern museum seven iron toads are preserved which have been taken from the grotto, but they are not older than the 1850's, one or two perhaps from the end of the eighteenth century [Glöckler].

During the year 1758 Cardinal Louis de Rohan made a church visitation which included the St Vitus chapel at Hohlenstein. On this occasion he issued the following order: 'We expressly forbid henceforth the placing in this chapel of iron toads, distorted images of human beings (*des marmousets d'hommes*—actually small dolls in human form) or other superstitious images' [Adam]. Nevertheless the pilgrimages continued and in spite of the Cardinal's order iron toads were still offered even as late as 1868, according to Fischer. In our chapter on the magic ritual of the dancing epidemic we shall explain the meaning of the iron toads in their medico-symbolic sense.

In his collection of remarkable stories published in 1572, Hondorff describes certain dance-epidemics which occurred in the year 1551. His description is derived from Fincelius, and it is also to be found in Beckmann's history of the principality of Anhalt, published in 1710, where the same epidemic occurred. On Palm Sunday, 1551, in a family three children, aged between seven and thirteen, had begun to dance and hop in a mysterious way and continued to do so day after day for eight hours, also at night. They leapt and hopped hither and thither in the room as well as in the open air. During the dance they twisted their bodies and made such leaps that they were completely exhausted; they snorted and panted and lay down on the ground, twisting their bodies, 'as if they wanted to dance on their heads'. Sometimes they fell to the ground and lay motionless as if dead, and then they would fall asleep for some time. On awakening they would eat and then begin to dance again. They spoke little, but laughed a great deal. A priest took care of them, and treated them—probably by means of exorcisms—but without result.

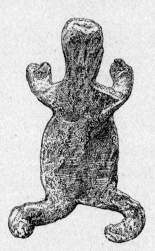

FIG. 90. One of the votive offerings, an iron toad, found in the St Vitus grotto at Hohlenstein, near Zabern. In the museum at Mülhausen [Andrée].

From about the same time, the middle of the sixteenth century, Felix Plater describes another case. He writes that when he was a boy—he was born in 1536—he saw in Bâle a woman who danced continuously in a public place for a whole month. The magistrate hastened to direct two strong men to dance with her in turn and to help her. In the first edition of Plater's *Observations on Human Diseases*, which was published in 1614, it is stated [Beckmann] that these men were dressed in red clothes, with white feathers in their hats. After dancing for a month the skin on the woman's feet wore out. When she was forced from weariness to sit down or sleep for a while her body still continued to leap until at last she was unable to keep it upright. Then she was taken to hospital, where in the course of time she recovered her health. Plater also describes another case: a prelate first of all had cramps, succeeded by mental disturbances, during which his body moved as if in a dance, though he also danced in the literal sense. More and more exhausted, his body still moved and he tried to induce others to help him in his dance. Finally, he died.

From the latter part of the sixteenth century Camerarius describes fresh

FIG. 91. Dance Epidemic of 1564. Pieter Brueghel the Elder: 'The Dancing Pilgrims at Muelebeek, 1564'. Pen drawing with white superimposed, signed and dated: 'bruegel. M. ccccc.lxiiij'. In the Albertina Collection of Vienna [Romdahl].

cases of choreomania. He relates that near the Swabian city of Regensburg people like to show the mountain that is named after St Vitus. Not long before (the work was published in 1601 and Camerarius was born in 1537) a number of dancers used to congregate here in order, by dancing, to pay tribute to the saint and with his help to become whole. But when access to the mountain was forbidden and the chapel was turned to other uses the gatherings ceased.

Pieter Brueghel (1528–69) has illustrated a dance epidemic of 1564 at Moelenbeek Sint Jans, now a part of Brussels (Figs. 91–98). This pen-drawing is to be found in the Albertina Collection in Vienna and is reproduced by several writers, including Romdahl (Fig. 91). It has frequently been mis-understood, as, for example, by Charcot and Richer, who believed that it represented the dance procession at Echternach. It is, however, signed and dated by Brüeghel and bears his note: 'These are the pilgrims who were to dance on St John's day at Muelebeek outside Brussels, and when they have danced over a bridge and hopped a great deal they will be cleansed for a whole year of St John's disease.' But there exists another drawing, also signed by Brueghel, but dated 1569, i.e., the year of his death (Fig. 92); it is preserved in the copper-plate cabinet of the Rijksmuseum in Amsterdam. It also carries a text which is exactly the same as that on the former one, with the exception of minor details in spelling (even of the painter's name)—this point should be emphasized, because it has been argued by Martin that it does not refer to Moelenbeek. Comparison shows that the two pictures are

244

FIG. 92. The Dance Epidemic of 1564–69. Pieter Brueghel the Elder: 'The Dancing Pilgrims at Muelebeek'. Pencil drawing signed and dated 'bruegel, 69'. Copper-plate collection in Amsterdam [Meige].

not absolutely identical: the Amsterdam picture is not as elegantly executed, the movements are not rendered in such a masterly fashion, and it gives a somewhat tired impression. It has also been suggested that it may be a forgery and that the drawing in the Albertina Collection is the genuine one. This view may appear to be supported by the fact that the date of the Amsterdam drawing is different, i.e., 1569 instead of 1564. But it is possible that it is a copy by the master himself, and would have been made just before the death of the master, when his powers and his memory were failing. I myself can see no real objective reason for denying its authenticity. These drawings of Brueghel are from the medical point of view of the utmost value, because they give us what is in all probability a perfectly correct picture of the manner of these processions, whilst at the same time they make it possible to understand something of the symptoms which the choreomaniacs displayed.

We will remember from the descriptions of the pilgrimages and the popular church dances at Moelenbeek that it was there a small healing spring, dedicated to St Gertrude. The little stream which is seen in the middleground of the drawing may be regarded as having its source in the spring. To the left a small bridge spans the stream. In the background we glimpse trees and among them to the right we see the faint outlines of a church—the church of St John in Moelenbeek. In the foreground moves a procession, consisting of four women, each of whom is supported and helped by two men, one on each side. The dancers are thus grouped exactly as in the descriptions of the dance epidemics of 1374: two and one—a form of dance which was, moreover, very common in those days, as appears from the paintings of various masters. The dancers range into two groups on either side of the musicians, two bagpipers. The latter, too, are, so to speak, classic for the music of the dance epidemics. In the background we see a fifth woman who, supported by two men, is just dancing over the little bridge. On the other side of the stream yet another woman sits on the bank bent double in a state of collapse. On the evidence of Brueghel's drawing it was essential to hop and dance over the little bridge. This woman, therefore, has completed the dance. Still more remote in the background appears a woman, or perhaps a man, watching the dance, supported on two sticks. We may perhaps assume that when the dance is finished the performers continue dancing in the church of St John. In the middle distance we see yet another man and woman hastening from the left towards the bridge, carrying jars in their hands. The men assisting the dancing women evidently take part in the dance also, as can be seen in the last group, which executes a stamping or hopping dance—which is just as it should be, from all we have learnt. The men clearly exert themselves to the utmost, especially in the first two groups and still more so in the second to the left. Here the men attempt with all their strength to support and lift the women up.

FIG. 93. The Choreomaniacs of 1564.
Details of Fig. 91.

We shall now look more closely at the women in the dance procession. The first to the left (Fig. 93) shows cramp in left neck muscles, with the result that the head is twisted to the right. There is also cramp in the extensor muscles of the thigh and the muscles of the calf. The second woman (Fig. 94) shows cramp in the extensor muscles of the back, in the muscles of the neck and possibly there is also cramp in the extensor muscles of the thigh and certainly in the muscles of the calf, as is shown by the down-pointed foot characteristic of such cramp. Perhaps the extensor muscles of the right arm and hand are also cramped. The third woman from the left (Fig. 95) shows cramp in the extensor muscles of the back and neck, of the arms and hands and possibly of the thigh and calves. We also have the impression that she is crying out in pain. The fourth woman on the extreme right (Fig. 96) shows cramp in the extensor muscles of the back, the arms, forearms, hand and thigh, as also in the muscles of the calf. She too shows signs of the down-pointed foot. The fifth woman (Fig. 97), who

246

is dancing across the bridge, shows cramp in the flexor muscles of the back and arm. The sixth woman (Fig. 98), sitting in the background by the stream, gives the impression of being completely exhausted, in a state of collapse and without any interest in her surroundings.

It has been thought [Richer] that this picture affords proof of the suggestion that the choreomaniacs of the 1374 epidemic had become obscene. In this case it must be the first group on the extreme left which is meant. At first glance the man on the woman's left might appear to be kissing her hand. This

FIG. 94. The Choreomaniacs of 1564. FIG. 95. The Choreomaniacs of 1564.
Details of Fig. 91.   Details of Fig. 91.

is by no means certain. Either cramp or an occasional shifting of the balance may have caused her to raise her hand towards the man's head. From the appearance of the man and his expression I cannot see anything but an honest attempt to help and support the women with all his strength and to share in the dance. The appearance and behaviour of the men also seems to me to reveal deep sympathy with these very sick and tormented women.

Thanks to Pieter Brueghel we have preserved what is most probably a very reliable picture of the choreomaniacs; we can almost see their torment and we can without hesitation diagnose the presence of severe cramp. But his picture is also a remarkable presentation of the hopping and stamping movements of the dance epidemic. Moreover, we find a water course and a bridge, both of which play an important role in the dance cure.

We have already heard of Moelenbeek as the occasional destination of vast processions of dancers on the eve of St John. Sometimes they proceeded to St Gertrude's spring and sometimes to St John's church. We do not know whether the dance procession depicted by Brueghel was the first of its kind to Moelenbeek or whether it was only one of a long, perhaps century-old, succession of similar dance processions on Midsummer eve. Possibly the legend of the miracle by which in 1399, on the occasion of an 'infectious disease in which the sufferers fell into a torpor', may suggest that the procession which

FIG. 96. The Choreomaniacs of 1564.
Details of Fig. 91.

FIG. 97. The Choreomaniacs of 1564.
Details of Fig. 91.

was then, and thereafter, organized around the church was the origin of subsequent processions. In any case they continued into the nineteenth century.

At a later date Hendrik Hondius, who lived between 1573 and 1610, etched in copper and on a much larger scale Pieter Brueghel's picture of the dance epidemic of 1564 at Moelenbeek (Figs. 99–100). In it he divided the procession into three parts. The middle one contained the two bagpipers. The two others represent partly the dancing group to the left and partly the groups to the right. In the former one sees also the group dancing over the bridge and the exhausted woman by the stream. In the latter there is to the right, in the far background, a glimpse of what is perhaps the church and its tower. In all of them he has greatly changed the background, filled it out with trees and bushes, and given glimpses of houses in the distance. The figures are very much coarser, but the ensemble is constructed with greater decorative effect, certainly in the case of the dancing group on the left.

248

Brueghel's drawing gave rise to yet another copperplate engraving. In Stenström's work *The Dance* appears an engraving without indication of date or origin; it is reproduced here (Fig. 101). It may perhaps be attributed to the latter half of the seventeenth century. It shows the four groups in the foreground of Brueghel's drawing, but completely disregards the remainder. The anonymous etcher may never have seen Brueghel's picture but only the three Hondius engravings, since he appears not to have known

FIG. 98. The Choreomaniacs of 1564.
Details of Fig. 91.

where in his composition to place the single musician whom he incorporates. He has also provided hats for the men who help the women to dance, whereas in Brueghel's picture they dance either bareheaded or in caps. The head-dress of the women is also changed. Beneath his etching this copyist has inscribed some verses which show that he did not know or understand the real meaning of the picture:

Here are madmen hopping, as peasants do,
Anyone half dead might laugh himself to life again.
They set their jaws, and make gestures
As if the dance had driven them mad.
The piper blows the tune as if he would quicken the pace.
The best are those who pretend to be most mad.

FIG. 100. The Dance Epidemic of 1564. Hendrik Hondius (1573–1610): 'Pilgrims at Moelenbeek near Brussels on Midsummer Eve'. Engraving after Pieter Brueghel's drawing [Hovorka and Kronfeld]

FIG. 99. The Dance Epidemic of 1564. Hendrik Hondius (1573–1610): 'Pilgrims at Moelenbeek near Brussels on Midsummer Eve'. Copperplate engraving after Pieter Brueghel's drawing [Richer].

250

Wer sieht man toll springen bey sauren Begehren machen
Ein halb machtlosus sist, durch sich selbst suchen

Zur eisten Mandig auff, und machen solch Gebærden.
Die wollen sich dem Tantz mit gleichsam zu seyn werden.

Die Plauste haßt im Zwol. Jahr. Es dauren nicht sonsten
(Das sind die höste. He: nerisen se diser Hilder.)

Fig. 101. The Dance Epidemic of 1564. Anonymous copper etching of the latter part of the seventeenth
century. All the men and women are taken from Pieter Brueghel's drawing of 1564; the women for the most part
unchanged, the men dressed in hats. Everything is coarsened. The composition is in some respects changed and
the situation completely misunderstood. The verses are derisive [after Stenström].

XVII

Dance Epidemics of the Seventeenth Century

IN the literature of medicine there are only a couple of references to the dance epidemics of the seventeenth century.

Schenk à Grafenberg published in 1609 his *Observations on Medical Phenomena*, in which he describes with considerable detail the great dance epidemic of 1374, though he adds features from later epidemics. He describes the choreomaniacs as driven by the terrible frenzy of the hop-dance and as in the grip of mental confusion. Then he describes some recent occurrences: 'You can still see pregnant women—a remarkable recent case—urged and incited by the same madness, tied round their waists and swollen bellies with broad sashes, so that their pregnant condition may not be noticeable. They leap around among the crowd. It would scarcely be possible to believe, if it were not confirmed by recent cases. . . . Those in our own Breisgau and neighbouring districts who were smitten by this madness arrived every year on the festival of St John the Baptist at two chapels: one in Biessen, dedicated to St Vitus and situated in Breisach, and the other nearer Wasenweiler, but on this side of the Rhine and dedicated to St John the Baptist and belonging to the German Order. These assemblies took place either for the fulfilment of promises (votives) or in the hope that the saints in question would grant deliverance from the madness. What is remarkable is that during the whole of the month preceding the festival of St John they went about sad, shy, depressed and anxious, whilst all the time feeling stabbing and jumping pains in their bodies, just as if premonitory of the disease, and renewed festering evil. They were convinced that they could never again be still or be delivered from the evil until they had danced before the chapel of the saints and thus driven out the madness, and results showed that in many cases they were right. After these carefully executed annual dances, which usually continued for three hours, they regarded themselves protected from the madness for a year to come.'

The detailed account left by Schenk à Grafenberg is of special importance from the point of view of medicine, because it tells us of the so-called premonitory symptoms which appeared before the actual disease set in. Later on we shall have an opportunlty of analysing further the significance of these symptoms.

Philipp Camerarius published in 1628 his collection of memorable medical cases. In it he describes, with quotations from Plater and Horstius, the old epidemics. With the support of a letter from Thomas Freigius he gives an account of two girls 'of the neighbourhood', that is, probably in the district of Nüremburg, who, by continuous dancing, almost danced themselves to death, and he thinks it must have been due to the malady which is generally called St Vitus' dance. Freigius' letter runs as follows: 'In Southern Germany as a rule nobody went mad from black gall, but from the blood, and this madness was called by the people St Vitus' disease, referring to the epidemics of 1374 and 1518. If it is to be related to any particular disease I think it can only be placed in the group of deliria, on the ground of the melancholy, which malady may vary very much. In it the mind is usually completely obscured. But during the dance both of the girls prayed and their prayers were well spoken. From this I conclude that these unusual symptoms cannot be unnatural or diseased or supernatural or divine or demonic . . . For natural sickness one should use natural cures, for unnatural diseases unnatural remedies, for divine sickness divine means.' Scholzius also repeats the report concerning the two girls and Freigius' speculations, but puts the date in the 1570's.

Horstius in his work on medicine, published after 1625, gives an account of the dance epidemic in progress at that time. 'I remember,' he says, 'that I talked during the spring with several people who every year used to visit the chapel of St Vitus near Geisling and Weissenstein in the administrative area of Reichsberg, in order there, in their delirium, to hop and dance day and night until they fell down as if in ecstasy. In this way they seem to have been cured to the extent that for a year following they felt little or nothing of the malady. But in the month of May in the following year the discomfort in their limbs began to torment them to such an extent that they were forced in the period before the festival of St Vitus (June 15th) to hasten to the above-mentioned places in order to dance and hop. One woman was reported to have danced and hopped there annually for twenty years and another for thirty years. Apart from superstition there is no probable or natural reason why just at the beginning of the spring such cramps should develop in the limbs as might be dispersed by dancing and simultaneous excitement and hope of restoration through St Vitus. Then the sufferers can look forward for a year to restored strength and freedom from attack. For some weeks before arrival at the chapel of St Vitus they suffer from cramp in all their limbs, from a feeling of tiredness and of heaviness in the head. They remain in this condition until they arrive at the usual place for dancing and hopping. When they hear the musical instruments played for their benefit they are driven to dance and hop, whilst their minds become more and more confused.'

This gives us an excellent picture of the general premonitory symptoms of the disease and helps to clarify its real nature. I can see no objection to the assumption that the district from which the women came was more than usually infected by the poison which appeared every year and produced preliminary symptoms in those who, owing to previous poisoning, were unduly sensitive to it. When they arrived at the scene of the dance they recovered because they had escaped from the source of the poisoning. On their return its effectiveness had more or less disappeared. They were restored for a year to come.

XVIII

Dance Epidemics of the Eighteenth and Nineteenth Centuries

THE older literature and the various chroniclers contain, so far as I know, no accounts of dance epidemics during the eighteenth century or of disease of obviously the same kind. This may be due to the fact that the sufferers who in earlier times had recourse mainly to the religious dance as a means of deliverance from the evil, or who were regarded and treated as if they were possessed, were now subject to a quite different kind of diagnosis and to quite different treatment. In other words we must seek such sufferers in groups which belong to a quite different category of disease. The causes which gave rise to the so-called dance epidemics certainly existed in the eighteenth and nineteenth centuries. Even in the eighteenth century there were probably isolated sufferers who sought healing from this source more or less simultaneously with proper medical treatment, and took part in dance processions in order to regain their health.

During the eighteenth century there were no less than five different, annual dance processions from which sufferers from the old 'dance disease' could choose. In all of them the sufferers found companions among epileptics and among those who suffered from cramp-like maladies or from possession by demons. Thus there continued, and continues into our own time, the great dance procession at Echternach, the procession of the hopping saints. There was also an identical procession at Prüm, which continued until 1777. In Liége, until the end of the eighteenth century, Gontran's dance procession took place, the demons being exorcized with noise, with hopping and with distortions of the limbs. At Moelenbeek near Brussels there were annual

FIG. 102. The Dance Epidemic of 1829. Section of a coloured lithograph of about 1840. The sufferers from cramp are dressed as pilgrims to Santiago de Compostela, dancing the St Vitus' dance before the image of St James [Meige].

processions which sometimes attracted great numbers and continued into the nineteenth century. To Hohlenstein near Zabern there were pilgrimages of those who suffered from epilepsy, St Vitus' dance and other cramps in order to find a cure.

Meige published in 1904 a coloured lithograph which he found in an *album comique* dating from the middle of the nineteenth century (Fig. 102). He interprets it as a representation of a group of peasants dressed in pilgrim's attire decorated with large shells, carrying pilgrims' staffs and purses. Meige recognizes the shells as typical St James shells, but thinks that the saint before which they dance is St Vitus or, in French, St Guy, because of the inscription on the statue, *La danse de Saint-Guy*. In a later statement Meige maintains that St Guy is also called St Willibrord—an obvious confusion. Quite rightly he confirms that the dancers show signs of cramp and thinks that they have been seized either by some hysterical dance disease, Brissaud's disease or Huntington's disease. We shall now examine the picture more closely.

There are three men and a woman. The man to the left has cramp in the muscles of the right calf and the typical down-pointed foot; possibly cramp also in the flexor of the right elbow. The second from the left has cramp in the muscles of the face, the third in the muscles of the arm and of the fingers, and in the flexor of the left lower leg. The woman has cramp in the left flexor of the head, possibly also in the calf muscles, with down-pointed foot. They dance before a statue placed in a niche. It represents an elderly, bearded man in an ankle-length robe and a cape, his left hand extended in the attitude of an orator. The dancers are dressed as pilgrims; they wear the short pilgrim's pelerine and at least two of them have large shells of a flattened type embroidered thereon. They are scallop shells, the pilgrim's scallop. The woman has a pilgrim's staff, from which hangs a purse, the pilgrim's purse, contain-

FIG. 103. Symbols of Completed Pilgrimages. Pilgrim with shell and crossed keys of St Peter as proof of a pilgrimage to Santiago de Compostela and to the tomb of St Peter in Rome. Panel-section of a larger picture, belonging probably to the school of Filippo Lippi, at the beginning of the sixteenth century.

ing her offering to the saint. But our view of the saint's identity is quite different from that of Meige.

Both the costumes and the emblems of a pilgrim showed conclusively that a pilgrimage had been undertaken. The pilgrim's costume was a brown or grey cape or mantle with a hood or hat, preferably broad-brimmed. This hat was adorned with shells or with a band of shells, in which case they were of the smaller kind, with inturned edges. On the long, consecrated staff, which usually terminated in a knob, there usually hung a purse. As a rule a pouch was worn at the belt for provisions and a calabash for water. But if the pilgrimage had been to some famous shrine the pilgrims had the right, in memory and proof of the pilgrimage, to wear special emblems on their cos-

256

tumes. After an ordinary pilgrimage they wore two crossed staffs, after a pilgrimage to Palestine two crossed palms, after a pilgrimage to the tomb of St Peter the crossed keys of St Peter, after a pilgrimage to Mont St Michel a picture of the Archangel Michael, and after a pilgrimage to St James of

FIG. 104. St James the Elder, dressed as a pilgrim with staff, purse and rosary. Two pilgrims kneel before him. On his hat the large flat shell consecrated to the apostle, the symbol of pilgrimages to his tomb in Compostela. Wood-carving of the fifteenth century in the church of St Nicholas, Cologne [Veit].

Compostela the emblem of St James, the large flat shell [Franz, Buchberger]. I reproduce a picture of a pilgrim of the early sixteenth century, or possibly of the late fifteenth, from a panel which is quite certainly only a small part of a larger painting, and which I found in an art dealer's in Stockholm (Fig. 103). The pilgrim in this picture wears on his dress both the crossed keys of St Peter and the St James's shell, thus showing that he had visited both Rome and Santiago de Compostela.

257

The figure of the saint can in no circumstances be that of the boy Vitus, who suffered a martyr's death at the age of eight. In all probability it represents St James the Elder, who is usually depicted as a still vigorous old man, in the costume of a pilgrim with staff and calabash, preferably preaching [Stadler]. Here we may appropriately give another picture of St James, sitting on a chair with an enormous shell on his head-dress (Fig. 104). He is also the protector of pilgrims [Buchberger]. Various hospitals have been dedicated to him.

The riddle of the lithograph is now in the main solved. A number of sufferers from cramp-like maladies have assumed the dress of St James' pilgrims and execute a St Vitus's dance before his statue. The name *La danse de St Guy* is only of medical importance as a *terminus technicus*, i.e., St Vitus' dance, though it is performed before St James.

Thus it is clear from the picture that as late as the nineteenth century the old methods of treatment for St Vitus' dance were by no means forgotten. This view is strengthened in a statement by Gurdon of the English Folklore Society that at the beginning of the nineteenth century a woman suffered from St Vitus's dance and that, in order to cure her, the Suffolk band used often to play to her in her own home.

XIX

The Saints Invoked

IN the preceding pages we have seen how during the epidemics the sufferers danced before certain definite saints or were conducted to the churches of certain saints, and also how in all probability they visited, or were conducted to, famous or treasured relics in order to pray for them for help and healing. It would be worth while to investigate how far the healing powers which from olden times were attributed to particular saints may throw any light on the symptoms revealed by the choreomaniacs.

The dance in the churchyard at Kolbigk in 1021 took place in front of the church dedicated to St Magnus. He was, as has been said already, the apostle of Allgau; he died in 655 (Fig. 105). It is told of him that in his cell at Kempten he slew a dragon with his staff. He is therefore preferably depicted with a dragon, snakes and other dragon-like creatures around him [Stadler, Doyé]. The dragon has a double meaning: on the one hand it suggests that the person depicted was a missionary to the heathens and had victoriously overcome heathendom; alternatively it means that the person depicted has power to defeat the devil and to drive out demons. But these two meanings are basically identical in so far as the heathen, like the Katechumens of the old church, was regarded as possessed, in whom still prevailed the spirit of unbelief, denial and evil. He who converts the heathen, defeats the demons and overcomes the dragon [Augusti].

The holy Magnus became the patron saint against worm as a disease, but by this far more was meant in the early Middle Ages than later, for the ancient symbol, inherited from Egypt, of the canker indicated a disease in which the sufferer was possessed. At an early stage much reverence was paid to St Magnus; his prayers were supposed to possess special powers; pilgrimages were made to his grave, to his churches and altars. His worship spread to the whole of South Germany and Switzerland [Stadler]. It therefore seems probable that the choreomaniacs visited the church of St Magnus in 1021 because they thought themselves possessed.

It is quite true that in the Middle Ages and late into modern times both the medical men and the general public considered most diseases as of demonic origin or due to possession by disease demons or to their influence from without. But there were very special types of sickness which both the learned and the lay considered as typical cases of possession. Such maladies as caused the sufferer to be cast down as if by invisible forces and forced them into cramp-like contortions, or attacks of frenzy and screaming, grimacing and 'wild' shouting, that made them throw themselves upon the spectators—such maladies were regarded as of unquestionable demonic origin and the victims were regarded as possessed [Taczak].

FIG. 105. St Magnus, the Apostle of Allgau; died 655. One of the fourteen helpers. Wood-carving from the sixteenth century. Upper Bavaria [Künstle].

For this belief in the reality of possession, and its incredible significance as the cause of serious sickness, there was convincing support in the declarations of various fathers of the Church, such as Justin, Tertullian, Chrysostom, Cyril and others, as well as in the Bible and the Evangelists [Tylor]. It was the devil who caused such bodily suffering, usually in the form of violent activity; this was evangelical as well as early Christian belief. So there arose even in the early Christian Church a long service devoted to the expulsion of devils, which was later taken over by a special *Ordo Exorcistatus*, a special section of the priesthood which devoted itself to exorcisms and the driving out of devils, similar in detail to that which we discovered in the treatment of the 1374 choreomaniacs [Taczak].

The probable conclusion is, then, that the dancers of the year 1021 not only considered themselves as possessed, but as suffering from cramps and even from epileptic fits combined with mental aberration.

The dance procession over the bridge at Maastricht in the year 1278 took place during the commemoration of the Saints Trudo, Eucherius and Servatius, and their relics were certainly borne in the procession. St Trudo was a priest at St Truyden in Belgium, and died in the year 695, but he was not associated with any particular sickness. The same is true of St Eucherius, a Bishop of Orleans, who was transferred to Cologne and then to Liége; he died in the year 738 in the monastery of St Truyden. St Servatius, the patron saint of Maastricht, was the first bishop of Tongeren and died in 384 in Maastricht; he was preferably depicted with a dying dragon at his feet, thus signifying his successful struggle against heretical Aryanism. In addition he drove out demons. He was invoked to bring success to any undertaking— such as a pilgrimage for the recovery of health. He was also invoked against sickness and pains in the feet, against fever, lameness and the fear of death. One feels inclined to surmise that since sick persons participated in the great dance procession they suffered from some severe illness which produced a painful condition of lameness of the feet, such as tonic cramp, in which the muscles were severely and painfully hardened and constricted, a feverish condition with sensations of heat and burning, which often ended in death.

During the great dance epidemics of 1374 at Cologne and Metz, and those of 1381 at Killburg, and 1564 at Moelenbeek, as also in Breisgau at the beginning of the seventeenth century, St John the Baptist was invoked in the songs which were sung. St John the Baptist is the saint invoked against epilepsy, cramps, vertigo and choreomania, the last because it was Salome's dance which cost him his life [Doyé]. A medieval legend recounts that St John the Baptist asked of God that he might be allowed to see the lightning; in spite of warnings he persisted in his wish, but when he saw it he was blinded and cast to the ground. This, it is said, was the origin of St John's disease, epilepsy [Cock]. As the patron saint against this sickness he is invoked especially in the churches which possess his relics and which for that reason are the objective of many pilgrimages [Reinsberg—Düringsfeld]. When the choreomaniacs danced before St John or invoked him during their dance, we may be sure that they had cramps, vertigo and attacks or symptoms of epilepsy.

In the epidemic of 1374 many of them danced in churches before the most sacred image of the Virgin Mary. She protects against sicknesses of every kind. The invocation of the Virgin, therefore, in this connexion meant nothing more than that the dancers were very ill and tormented.

But the sufferers of 1374 on their own initiative visited or were conducted to the St Lambert monastery and to the churches dedicated to St Bartholomew and St Andrew. They also visited Jülich and its churches, which contained the relics of Christina of Stumbelen, who was regarded by the people as a saint. Whether their dances really were intended for the above-mentioned saints we do not know; in any case they danced here also before the Virgin Mary, though the chroniclers report that they danced before many other saints also.

St Lambert (Fig. 106) was bishop of Maastricht and suffered a martyr's death in Liége in 705 or 706. He is represented in episcopal robes, bearing a

FIG. 106. St Lambert, Bishop of Maastricht. Died at Liége 705–6. The bust, which is a relic, is an extremely valuable specimen of the goldsmith's art of the year 1512 [Künstle].

glowing coal. He is a patron saint against diseases of the kidneys and eyes. We shall learn later that eye diseases also afflicted the choreomaniacs. St Bartholomew was one of the Apostles; he cured the daughter of the King of Armenia, who was possessed of demons, and for that reason became the saint invoked against nervous maladies, cramps, convulsions and possession. His festival was celebrated on August 24 and 25. St Andrew was also one of the Apostles and was celebrated on November 30th; he was invoked in cases of gouty afflictions [Doyé, Buchberger, Kerler].

If these saints were invoked by the choreomaniacs, it may be assumed that they suffered from eye diseases, cramps, convulsions, gouty pains and possession.

What is more certain is that the dancers, when visiting Jülich, paid reverence to the relics of Christina of Stumbelen. A Swedish Dominican, Peter de Dacia, who visited Cologne in the 1260's, belonged to her circle and wrote her life history, which is preserved in a fourteenth-century manuscript in a church at Jülich. She lived in the village of Stumbelen, just outside Cologne.

Schück quotes from Peter de Dacia: 'A devil took possession of her and cast her backwards and knocked her head so hard against the wall that it was injured.' The devil threw her down several times with great violence so that she was marked by haemorrhage of the feet, etc. Her first attack was regarded as epileptic, but was afterwards considered as a proof of the special grace of Providence. She also suffered from hallucinations. During her attacks her senses were benumbed and her body motionless. When she awoke she was dazed. She died in 1312. The probable diagnosis is epilepsy, although other symptoms are visible. She was therefore invoked by others for help when suffering from epilepsy-like afflictions, and the visit of the choreomaniacs to Jülich consequently shows that many of them were subject to such attacks.

When the choreomaniacs came to Cologne in 1374 they found there a collection of valuable relics of those who especially attracted the admiration and reverence of the pilgrims. They were the relics of the Magi and of the Saints Peter, Bartholomew, Andrew and Ursula.

From 1134 the Magi were honoured by the people as saints, though the Catholic Church never recognized them as such. Legend gives them the names Caspar, Melchior and Balthazar. Their remains came, through the Empress Helena, to Constantinople, and thence in the fourth century, possibly at the beginning of the fifth, to Milan. In the year 1162 they fell into the hands of the Emperor Barbarossa and were presented and translated in the year 1164 to the church of St Peter in Cologne. They are the patrons of pilgrims seeking an easy death, and they protect against magic and sores, but especially are they the patrons of epileptics, because they fell down and prayed to the Christ child [Buchberger]. Bernard de Gordon, who died as a professor in Montpelier in 1318, when dealing with epilepsy in his book, *Lilium Medicinae*, proposes that one should whisper in the ear of the sufferer, three times during an attack, the words:

Caspar brought myrrh,
Melchior incense,
Balthazar gold.
He who has within him the name of the Magi
Shall be cured, by the grace of Christ, of epilepsy.   [Segange]

St Peter, first of the Apostles, is among the most highly esteemed protectors of the sick, He is invoked against possession, hydrophobia, foot diseases and fever, as well as against early death. Yet one must not forget that hydrophobia and its violent cramps could not be diagnosed at that time, but was regarded as a sort of possession, like dancing frenzy, and we shall find that cases of hydrophobia were included in the category of St Vitus' dances. Of a certain interest is the staff of St Peter, the two halves of which are preserved in the cathedrals of Cologne and Trier, as well as the iron fetters of St Peter, fragments of which were found in the two keys preserved in Maastricht and Liége. Legend relates that the holy Maternus, bishop of Cologne, Trier and Tongeren, died in Elegia in Alsace on the very day that nuncios arrived there from Rome. Much perturbed, they returned to Rome and prayed to

St Peter to awaken St Maternus. They then received the staff of St Peter and returned to Elegia, touched the dead bishop with it and thereby recalled him to life [Doyé].

St Bartholomew's relation to the sick has already been told. St Antony Abbas, or the Hermit, will be described in greater detail later; he was the protector against the holy fire, against epilepsy and possession in general, as also against the plague. St Ursula, who, together with her ten thousand murdered virgins, is one of the treasures of the Cologne cathedral, was invoked only to help to make death easy and good.

If we now reconstruct the picture of the diseases which are indicated by the saints and relics invoked and worshipped by the hosts of pilgrims visiting Cologne, we find once again: possession and magic, epileptic conditions, choreomania, cramps and convulsions, fever and premature death; finally, also, the holy fire.

When the choreomaniacs visited Trier they were ranged in front of the relics of the Saints, Peter, Andrew, Matthew, John the Baptist, and Stephen, as also before the mantle of Christ.

It was the Apostle Matthew who, by the drawing of lots, completed the circle of Apostles after Judas Iscariot and who subsequently suffered death by the axe. His relics were divided by the Empress Helena between Rome and Trier. His tomb in the cathedral of Trier has been highly revered since the eleventh century. As a patron of medicine he appears only in connexion with pox—a sickness completely excluded from this survey.

St Stephen, the protomartyr, is described in the Acts of the Apostles, as is also his death by stoning. In the year 415 his grave was found in Jerusalem. His relics were distributed among various churches in Europe and Africa. The day of the finding of the relics, August 3rd, has since been kept as a holiday. He is patron both of Alsace and of the city of Metz. He is a helper and protector in cases of stitch and headache and ensures the blessing of a peaceful death. When in 1374 the dancers came to Maastricht they were placed before the relics of Saints Servatius, Peter, Matthew, Paul, Thomas, Lambert and Valentine. New names here are those of Paul, Thomas and Valentine. But the keys of St Peter deserve mention, for they contained small filings of the chains of St Peter's captivity and were themselves imitations of the key which opened the grave of St Peter in the old St Peter basilica. It is the Bollandists who in their *Acta Sanctorum* recount the legend of these keys: an angel had revealed himself to Pope Sylvester and directed him to have made and to bless a key which would resemble the key of Paradise, which the Lord Jesus Christ himself gave to St Peter. For this reason, and certainly also because of the relics of St Peter which it contains, it can be laid upon those possessed to drive out the demons and bring healing [Segange].

The Apostle Paul protects against snake-bite and cramp diseases. This is associated with the fact that, as recounted in his letters, in his wanderings to Damascus he was suddenly thrown backwards, as if by some magic power. Segange thinks this means that he was seized by a violent cramp.

The Apostle Thomas nowhere appears as an active patron in matters of disease.

St Valentine (Fig. 107) was Bishop of Terni in Umbria and died a martyr's death about 273. During a visit to Rome he cured a cripple. For this reason he is usually represented with a crippled boy at his feet [Doyé]. According to others the boy suffers from epileptic cramp [Buchberger]. Frequently there is a cock at his side. He protects against epilepsy, cramp, fainting and pestilential sickness. Epilepsy is also known as St Valentine's disease. There is, however, another Valentine, also a consecrated saint, of interest in this connexion: the Apostle of Rhaetia, who died in the middle of the fifth century and was Bishop of Passau. He was invoked against epilepsy.

FIG. 107. St Valentine, Bishop of Terni in Umbria. At his feet a child in an epileptic fit. Wooden statue of the fifteenth century, preserved in the Kaiser Friedrich Museum in Berlin [Künstle].

In Liége the choreomaniacs of 1374 were placed before the relics of St Lambert, St Peter and the Virgin Mary. It was here that yet another St Peter's key was preserved. In Prüm they made their reverence before relics of the Virgin Mary, St Peter, St Paul, St John the Baptist and St Stephen. In Metz they beheld the relics of St Stephen and the miracle-working image of the Virgin; in Aachen of St John the Baptist also.

The holy martyrs Felix and Regula, who were frequently invoked on the pilgrimages to the Water Church at Zürich, do not appear as patrons in respect of any definite sickness. At that time there were altars in the church also to the Magi, St Stephen and St Lawrence. This last was a Roman deacon who, during the Valerian persecution of 258, was condemned to death on a red-hot grid. He is the protector against the fires of purgatory, against the powers of Hell, against burns and itches, kidney troubles and leprosy [Segange]. The women who danced within the church in 1418 may also be supposed to have danced before the altars of the three saints who were patrons of medicine. Whichever one chooses, one is forced to the conclusion that it was a sickness accompanied either by a pronounced burning in the skin or by cramps and attacks of an epileptic character. The male dancers in the helmet house of the church seem to have danced rather with the symbol of 'running water and a bridge' than with the saints.

The great Strassburg dance epidemic of 1518 seems to have been in honour of a single named saint, St Vitus (in German St Veit, and in French

St Guy). The choreomaniacs at the beginning of the seventeenth century did the same when they danced in Breisgau [Schenk] and at Geislingen [Horstius]. In the Strassburg records it is mentioned that a married man declared that his wife was '*von Sanct Martzolff beladen*'. Probably this refers to the St Martial who was Bishop of Limoges and lived in the middle of the third century, and is the patron and protector in general misfortune, plague and epidemics.

St Vitus is the saint who, besides St John the Baptist, was extremely important in dance epidemics. Whereas before 1518, and only in a few isolated cases afterwards, was the dance epidemic called 'St John's dance', after 1518 'St Vitus' dance' has been by far the commonest name. On the other hand I would like to emphasize that I have not been able to find one single record in which before 1518 choreomania was called St Vitus' dance, or any single record before 1518 in which the dancers invoked St Vitus.

St Vitus (Figs. 108–111) was one of the fourteen helpers. As a seven-year-old or, as some say, a twelve-year-old boy he suffered a martyr's death during the Diocletian persecution in Lucania, Southern Italy. His father tried to induce him by force to abandon his Christian faith, but he refused and, even when his father locked him up with seductive female dancers, he could not be tempted to renounce his faith. He fled with his nurse Crescentia and his teacher Modestus to Rome, where he drove off the demons which possessed

FIG. 108. St Vitus in the cauldron. On the cauldron is inscribed SANGTUS. FI. TUS. The martyr is represented with the bird (a cock). Wood-carving from the beginning of the sixteenth century from the chapel of St Michael in Schwaz, Tyrol.

the Emperor's son. But the Emperor had him cast into a cauldron filled with boiling tar and lead, from which he arose unscathed. A lion was let loose upon him but did not hurt him. An angel then delivered him from torture and led him to the south of Italy, where he and his two disciples died. These legends go back to the fourth century [Pfleiderer]. According to Agricola there is an ancient fable which tells that St Vitus prayed to God that He would protect and preserve from St Vitus' dance all those who fasted on his holy day and celebrated it. Immediately a voice from Heaven was heard, saying, 'Vitus, thy prayer is granted' [Förstemann]. His relics were taken to Corvey in 823 and spread from there to numerous other places where he was revered. He became the patron saint of Saxony, and many churches were built in his honour, among others in Cologne and Prague [Kessel]. He is usually represented as standing in a cauldron [Fig. 108] over a fire, with eyes and hand directed towards heaven in prayer; beside him, or in the cauldron, stand Crescentia and Modestus with palms in their hands. Frequently St Vitus carries a book on which sits a bird, usually regarded as a cock. He has also been represented as a child holding a burning dish, or an open bowl, in his hands (the cauldron of martyrdom). Sometimes he is depicted as a knight or prince [Pfleiderer, Kessel]. The pictures of St Vitus given here are of the sixteenth century.

We are reminded of the sculpture in the chapel of St Vitus in Hohlenstein near Zabern, and possibly later in the grotto there, depicting St Vitus as a boy standing naked in a cauldron, with hands clasped in prayer, beside the

FIG. 109. St Vitus suffers martyrdom in a cauldron filled with boiling tar and lead, watched by the tormentors' servants. The flames are painted red. From the town church of Schwaigern, about 1529, and now in Stuttgart Museum [Baum].

Virgin Mary. It was before this very image, and round the altar on which it was placed, that the choreomaniacs, wearing red shoes, performed their dances in 1518.

Another wood-carving shows the classical representation. St Vitus stands naked in his cauldron, above a fire, painted red, so that there be no mistake (Fig. 109). His hands are clasped in prayer and he is watched on both sides by the servants of the tormentors. The sculpture is from 1520 and from South Germany [Baum]. There is also a third sculpture of *Sanctus Fitus* (Fig. 108). It too is painted red; the saint stands naked in the cauldron. At his right hand sits the cock. The sculpture is from the Tyrol [Andrée]. The fourth St Vitus image (Fig. 110) is from Junkenhofen and represents him in a somewhat later form with the instruments of martyrdom in his hand. His head-dress is crowned with the cross of suffering and victory [Künstle].

I should like to reproduce one further picture of St Vitus. It is a painting executed at the beginning of the sixteenth century by the German painter Bernhard Striegel (Fig. 111). The saint is here depicted as much older; in his right hand he carries the green palms of victory and everlasting life, in the other hand the instrument of his martyrdom, the cauldron. But what is

remarkable is that this cauldron is inscribed with an alphabet and consequently belongs to the so-called ABCD magic [Gemälde Gall., Berlin].

St Vitus is the patron of sufferers from epilepsy, madness, hydrophobia,
snake-bite and possession. Epilepsy was also a St Vitus disease [Höfler]. The
alphabet around the cauldron reveals what an import-
ant role St Vitus must have played as an expeller of
demons. Dornseiff mentions that the custom of
attributing magical power and the means to drive
out demons to the alphabet originates in the early
Middle Ages. It was the duty of the priest when
consecrating a church to trace the Latin and the Greek
alphabet in the ashes which, in the form of St
Andrew's cross, were strewn on the floor of the
church. The alphabet is also engraved on early Christian tombstones and church bells as a device for
driving out devils.

The invocation of St Vitus indicates that the sick
suffered from epileptic conditions, mental confusion
and attacks of madness, and regarded themselves,
and were regarded by others, as possessed of devils.

St Gertrude, who died in 659 as Abbess of Nivelles,
just outside Brussels, was the patroness of travellers
and pilgrims and especially of the souls which she
sheltered on the first day after death (Fig. 112). She
was invoked against fever because a spring in the
crypt of a monastery at Nivelles had proved a cure
for fever. Various springs were subsequently found
and reputed to have healing powers and were therefore consecrated to St Gertrude. During a sea voyage,
according to legend, a storm arose and the vessel was
threatened by a fabulous sea monster, but when St
Gertrude's name was spoken it disappeared. She also
protected against rats and mice and is frequently
depicted with the lily of maidenhood in one hand

Fig. 110. St Vitus carries
the instrument of martyr-
dom in miniature. Wood-
carving from the latter half
of the sixteenth century,
Junkenhofen [Künstle].

and a rat in the other, or else surrounded by rats and mice. These signify
[Stadler] both the temptation of the devil which she has overcome in life
and also those whom she has helped us humans to subdue. We must therefore designate St Gertrude as one of the great expellers of demons, who can
be invoked in all maladies which are caused by possession by demons.

If it was really true that the visit of the choreomaniacs to Moelenbeek in
1564 was connected not only with St John the Baptist, because they danced
on Midsummer Eve, but also with St Gertrude, because the dance had to be
executed beside and over the little stream which had its source in the St
Gertrude spring, then we are justified in assuming that the sufferers regarded
themselves as possessed and as tormented by rats and mice, which may be

267

interpreted as peculiar sensations in the skin, as also of fever, or, more correctly, a sensation of burning. The invocation of St John the Baptist shows that they also suffered from cramps, spasms and attacks of an epileptic nature. The invocation of both of these saints seems to indicate that the malady was regarded as due to possession by demons.

FIG. 111. St Vitus holds the instrument of martyrdom in the one hand, the palm of victory in the other. Painting by Bernhard Striegel, 1460–1528 [Gemälde gal. St. Mus. Berlin].

The Welsh choreomaniacs of about the year 1200 danced to St Almedha who was not canonized and is not known as a patron saint.

The curious lithograph discovered by Meige, which seems to represent a dance epidemic between 1820 and 1830, probably 1829, depicted the dancers as St James' pilgrims, dancing before an image of St James. St James the Elder was the first of the apostles to suffer a martyr's death. He was the apostle of Spain, but when he returned to the Holy Land he was condemned to death by Herod. His body was taken later to Compostela in Spain, where his relics are preserved. He is the patron saint of all in need on land or sea [Stadler]. Since the twelfth century he was most frequently represented as a pilgrim with the typical shell and long pilgrim's staff. In art he is occasionally permitted to perform one of his miracles, such as bring a roasted cock back to life [Buchberger]. When the sick danced before him in 1829 we can only conclude that they regarded themselves as being in dire distress, though possibly they relied on the powers of the saint to heal those who were sorely tormented by a sickness in which at least one of the symptoms was a sensation of burning and fever.

If we now summarize the conclusions which with some degree of probability we can reach regarding the symptoms which the choreomaniacs
displayed and their relation to the saints whom they invoked and reverenced,
we find the following picture. In Kölbigk in 1021
they suffered from cramps, spasms and epileptic
attacks, which were thought to be due to possession by demons. In Maastricht in 1278 they showed
a painful condition of the feet, with lameness
(possibly cramped and contracted toes, perhaps
cramp of the calf muscles, with down-pointed
feet), as well as a feverish condition. In the Rhine
province and Flanders in 1574, they thought they
suffered from the influence of magic and from
possession by demons; they regarded their malady
as due to a pestilential sickness and had eye trouble,
cramps, convulsions and an epileptic condition,
as well as attacks of fainting, gout, fever and a
sensation of burning. Sometimes they were tormented by the holy fire and sores. In Zürich in
1418 the symptoms were of burning as well as
cramps and attacks of an epileptic nature. In
Strassburg in 1518 the dancers suffered from
mental confusion, attacks of madness and of an
epileptic nature, and they regarded themselves as
possessed. In Moelenbeek in 1564 they felt a curious stinging of the skin and a sensation of intense
heat. They also had cramps, spasms and epileptic
attacks; they thought themselves possessed. In
Breisgau and in Geislingen at the beginning of
the seventeenth century they suffered from mental
confusion, possession, cramp and epileptic attacks.
In France in 1829, in addition to the symptoms seen
in the picture, they probably also suffered from
a sensation of burning as if from fire.

Fig. 112. St Gertrude, Abbess
in South Brabant; died 659.
Wood-carving from the Cologne district of the fourteenth
century. The saint holds a rat
in the right hand [Künstle].

Broadly speaking these symptoms agree very
closely with those which the surviving chronicles
describe as characterizing the choreomaniacs, but
in some respects they complete them. In a more
specific medical analysis we shall find a quite remarkable correspondence
between, on the one hand, the symptoms described in the chronicles or
shown in the carvings, etc., and the indirect conclusions from invocations
to the saints, and, on the other hand, the symptomology which marks the
poisoned condition upon which, in my opinion, the epidemics depended:
at one and the same time symptom and cure.

XX

Choreomaniac Magic

THE various dance epidemics have revealed that in order to recover their health the choreomaniacs made use of obviously magic means as well as dancing.

1. *The Churchyard*

The proscribed dancers at the St Magnus church in Kölbigk in 1021 danced above all in the churchyard, but probably also in the porch of the church. So also did the sick in Wales at the beginning of the thirteenth century. In the great epidemic of 1374 the choreomaniacs danced not only in churches and chapels, on the streets and in the market place, but also in churchyards. The symbolism of the churchyard dance has already been explained. Here we would only emphasize that it shows that the sufferers considered themselves possessed, that the symptoms are due to magic and possession by the demons of death and by the dead themselves. It is at one and the same time a dance of the angels and a dance of resurrection which they execute for the dead, in order to bring them peace, to propitiate them, and avert their anger.

2. *Paradise*

At Kölbigk in 1021, and at Zürich in 1452, they danced in the church porch or in the helmet-house. Earlier we pointed out that these were commonly called 'Paradise', and that the nave and choir must have been thought to represent the heavenly temple and God's dwelling. We also saw how, during the earliest Christian era, members of the congregation not infrequently danced in the church porch. Time after time the Fathers complained of the practice. We saw how it persisted in the Basque provinces until our own time and how people danced in the porch—certainly with the church doors open—whilst the congregation sang the Magnificat in honour of the Virgin Mary. It can scarcely be disputed that when the choreomaniacs danced in the porch or helmet-house it was the old dance of the angels that they danced. They are in Paradise and do as the angels do: they dance. Thereby they give expression to their desire and to their faith that they too could be healed, happy and blessed. By the imitative, sympathetic powers of magic they will recover their health.

Fig. 113. Peasant dance from the latter part of the fifteenth century. Couples dancing round a tree. Four dancers wear floral wreaths. One half of a drawing in Weimar Museum [after Schultz].

3. Music

Often the choreomaniacs sang their own songs to their own dances, as at Kölbigk in 1021, in Wales in 1200, and during the great epidemic of 1374. In any case the children who danced from Erfurt to Arnstadt must have done so to the accompaniment of singing. Otherwise the dancers usually performed to music, like the magician who played the flute or the pipe at the exodus of the children from Hamelin in 1376. During the Strassburg epidemic pipers and drummers were engaged by the city council and musicians were also sent to play in the homes of the sick. At Moelenbeek in 1564 the musicians were bagpipers; at Geislingen in the seventeenth century, and in Suffolk at the beginning of the nineteenth century, it is merely stated that music was played. But in earlier times wind instruments and drums were principally used. In early Roman times music, especially that of the flute and cymbals, was thought to have the power of banishing magic and driving out demons; but it also had power to invoke the beneficent gods. Music had a double effect. It came to play an important role in the religious rites of purification and protection. Early Christianity regarded death as a deliverance, though St Chrysostom regarded music as something which rejoiced the dead. According to Basileios this music was made by flutes, zithers and timbals; but Tertullian voiced the opinion that music—of the trumpet—disturbed the dead [Quasten].

Yet whether music rejoiced or disturbed the dead, it came to have a protective significance in relation to the dead and to demons. For this reason popular magic held that wind instruments, shouting and singing (especially spiritual songs) could drive out spirits and ghosts [Bâchthold-Stüabli].

Fig. 114. Peasant dance from the latter part of the fifteenth century. A dance partly in couples and partly processional. Three dancers wear wreaths. The second half of a drawing in the Weimar Museum [after Schultz].

Popular belief preserved until our own time customs based on this conception. In the Tyrol on Walpurgis Night people sought to drive out evil spirits by making as much noise as possible with all sorts of bells and tin cans. In Bohemia witches were driven out by creating as much noise as possible at a cross-road with the help of boards [Semter].

The little song sung by the choreomaniacs in Cologne in 1374, and also in Flanders, must be regarded as having some magic content. It is addressed to St John the Baptist and contains the exclamation 'So, so—healthy and happy'. This can only mean that 'so, so' was sung or shouted just at the moment of the high leap into the air and is a demonstration to the saints of the freedom and agility which they wished to obtain.

4. Wreaths

During the dance epidemic of 1374 the choreomaniacs wore a certain kind of wreath on their heads; in Trier it is reported that these wreaths were provided with a ribbon. Did these wreaths have any independent meaning? Wreaths on the head have been familiar since the days of antiquity, and they were worn both at festivals and for magic rites. This is true also of the Middle Ages. At confirmations, communions, baptisms and weddings, girls wore wreaths, and after the wedding ceremony newly married couples received wreaths from the priest, to wear as they left the church [Martene]. So also in church processions and dance festivals wreaths were worn on the head. Such was the case at the Festival of Fools, at which specially invited guests wore wreaths; similarly, the Corpus Christi festival in Nüremburg in 1442 [Bächthold-Stüabli].

On the three days on which, during the Middle Ages, the great litanies were celebrated, by papal ordination, at various places in Franconia processions gathered with cross and standard; all the participants adorned their heads with wreaths and held willow staffs in their hands. Thus equipped they entered the churches to take part in the mass [Schultz]. We have also seen that recently in Spain floral wreaths have been worn in many dance processions.

FIG. 115. Dance and floral wreaths. Hans Sebald Beham (1500–1559): 'Peasant Dance'. Signed and dated 1546 [Sachs].

Two other dance pictures (Figs. 115, 116), reproduced by Hans Sebald Beham, 1546, show the more clumsy, grotesque, hopping and stamping peasant dance; one man and one woman wear wreaths of leaves on their heads. Life in the spas, with their miracle-working springs, was very free in the Middle Ages, and priests and clerics often shared it. Wreaths were often worn on the head [Schultz].

It is also a very old custom on the Eve of St John to carry certain herbs in the hand or to hang them on the body or to plait them in wreaths for the head. Bock mentions that in German lands in 1539 people gathered St John's wort and laurel on that day for protection against fever or to hang on their bodies and, after dancing round the St John fire, threw them, together with all evil, into the fire, whilst pronouncing exorcisms. Brunfels relates that in 1532 in many places in Germany people collected wormwood and made wreaths for their heads or garlands for their bodies and then, at the end of the dance on Midsummer Eve, cast them into the fire.

Sebastian Franck, in his *Weltbuch* of 1534, relates that on Midsummer Day people used to carry crosses of wormwood and laurel, as well as larkspur, and threw them into the fire after the dance, so that for another year they might be free from evil. On casting them into the fire they uttered the formula:

> Go thy way, thou my misery,
> And be thou burned with this herb.

The Devil cannot hurt him who has wormwood in his house. If wormwood hangs over the door, no evil can touch the home. On Midsummer Day people gird themselves with wormwood—St John's girdle—or bind it in a wreath and wear it on their heads. After the dance it is cast in the fire, and with it all the ills from which they suffer [Grimm]. Bock adds that this magic was more widespread among the clergy than among laymen [Marzell].

Fig. 116. Dance with wreaths of flowers. Hans Sebald Beham: 'Peasant Dance' [Sachs].

When Petrarch visited Cologne on Midsummer Eve in the year 1330, he found the banks of the Rhine crowded with women adorned with chains of aromatic herbs. Just at sunset they dipped their arms and hands in the water and washed them to the accompaniment of certain words in order to wash away all manner of evil for a year to come. Frequently they also hung such wreaths and garlands of greenery and flowers over the streets of the towns in the Rhine province and in Flanders in order that the children might dance under them [Reinsberg—Düringsfeld]. But it was principally St John's wort and wormwood that they wore on their heads as they danced round the fire and it is especially noteworthy that both of these plants were regarded as a specific against epilepsy [Hovorka and Kronfeld], or more properly that they expelled demons.

From the world of antiquity, and especially from Greece, the chief heritage was the idea of the demon-expelling and repelling powers of the wreath. Since the various chronicles are at pains to emphasize that the choreomaniacs of the year 1374 wore 'a certain kind of wreath' on their heads and since wreaths in themselves are not in any way remarkable while dancing, then it must be that the wreaths of the choreomaniacs were especially remarkable. We learn also from Trier that the wreaths were bound with ribbons, which probably hung down from the sides of the wreaths. The wreaths of the choreomaniacs were therefore not purely ornamental; they had some magical significance and were supposed to assist in the expulsion of evil.

FIG. 117. 'Two and One' Dance. David Teniers the Younger (1610–1696): 'Village Carnival'. Section. In the centre, *Zwei g'en ein*. Kunstmuseum, Vienna [Gluck].

Although nothing is said of the flowers which made up the wreaths, we may guess that they consisted of St John's wort, laurel, wormwood and larkspur.

5. Hopping

The forms of dance employed were evidently very varied. At Kölbigk in 1021 we have seen a ring-dance with a couple in the middle, all under a leader. In the year 1374 there were line dances and perhaps ring-dances. A miniature from the beginning of the fifteenth century shows, it is true, a ring-dance but in other places during the same epidemic we hear of 'two and one', as was also the case in 1518 and 1520. This form, 'two and one', is also a common form of folk dance. A characteristic dance of this type is shown in the 'Village Carnival' of David Teniers the Younger, painted about 1650 (Fig. 117).

A typical ring-dance from the fourteenth century is preserved in a mural painting in Runkelstein castle (Fig. 118). It shows the dancers holding each other by the hand. Sometimes however, in order to make the dance more elastic, they linked themselves with green branches, wreaths, cloths or pieces of cloth—as is also shown in an earlier illustration.

But the dance which the choreomaniacs performed was by no means 'courtly'. Quite apart from the fact that contemporary chroniclers describe it as indecent and shameless—whatever that may mean—it certainly was characterized by violent hopping. They hopped in front of the altar, sometimes to the top of the altar. In other words, they sought to hop as high as possible. They hopped before the image of the Virgin Mary and before the images of the saints. This hopping characterizes all the dance epidemics after 1021, when we first have information concerning the nature of the dance. We have already described in another connexion the magical significance of hopping. We encountered it in the popular church dances of the early Christian era. But we can scarcely associate harvests and fertility with the hopping of the choreomaniacs, and must therefore regard it rather as demonstrative magic aimed at restoring free and easy movement of the

FIG. 118. Courtly Line Dance. Mural painting of the fourteenth century in Runkelstein Castle [Sachs].

limbs by imitative means. But at the same time this hopping shows that the sufferers had symptoms of restricted movement in the lower extremities, perhaps also of marked bodily weakness. This view is supported by the numerous cases in which other, healthy, bystanders were obliged to assist them in their dancing.

6. Hand Clapping

It is reported both of the dance in Kölbigk in 1021 and of the dances in the Rhine province and Flanders in 1374, that the sufferers clapped their hands during the dance. We have seen also that in the earliest Christian Church the dance was performed to the accompaniment of hand clapping, the admonition of Ezekiel was followed: 'stamp the feet; clap the hands'. . . . And later on, in the profane dance, nothing was more common than for the time to be beaten out in dance and song by hand-clapping, which still applies to folk dances in our own day. It is thus quite possible that in the churchyard dance outside the St Magnus church in Kölbigk the hand clapping had no other function than this; and yet it seems to me quite as possible that there was another significance, since the narrator, who was also leader of the dance, so strongly emphasized it. If we refer to the already quoted poem in Balde on

Fig. 119. The Dance as a 'Devil's Procession'. Peter Paul Rubens (1577–1640): 'Flemish Carnival'. Louvre, Paris [Burckardt].

the manner of the churchyard dance, then it becomes still more probable that demon-exorcizing magic was involved, for in Balde this purpose is clearly manifest. If we turn to the dance epidemic of 1374 in Trier there can be no doubt whatever that the clapping of hands had an exorcizing significance. Here the chronicler describes how the dancers stretched up their arms and clapped their hands behind and above their head. Such a peculiar and detailed technique, so completely unlike the normal procedure, must have had a special meaning.

Similarly, sagas and legends tell of hand-clapping as a means of exorcizing demons; perhaps it derives its power not only from the noise created— together with the music and the general din—but also because the demons, too, clap their hands. Thus it is told in the fairy tale that the water nymphs and the mermaids clap their hands and laugh for joy when anybody crosses a bridge [Grimm]. In that case the clapping of hands is a sort of homeopathic sympathetic magic: by imitating the demons they are driven out, just in the same way as the Devil was thought to flee from his own image on Gothic churches.

7. Poulaines

During the dance epidemic of 1374 the choreomaniacs showed their detestation of a foolish fashion of the day, the so-called poulaines, and often broke out into such violence against them and their wearers that the magistrates of Liége were compelled to forbid shoemakers to make them. It has been argued in this connexion that the choreomaniacs were posing as reformers for a simplification of dress and fashion. But such a view cannot be reconciled with their behaviour in all other respects. Let us therefore inquire whether there is another and simpler explanation. John Hus (1369–1415) also agitated against these poulaines and Geiler von Kaisersberg was compelled at his Magister examination to swear on oath that he would not wear them. The Limburg Chronicle states that they first appeared in 1350, yet this cannot be quite correct, because poulaines seem to have been worn since the eleventh century [Scherr]. At the beginning of the fifteenth century these shoes were a yard long and sharply pointed. There were also similar shoes, equally long, made of wood. It seems certain that poulaines made of cloth or leather must have had some sort of wooden or metal frame in order to control the long-drawn tips. They were first forbidden in 1252 in Leipzig, and in 1460 throughout Saxony. But in 1452 they appeared in Strassburg. Between 1470 and 1480 they had finally passed out of use [Schulz].

Now many of the older chroniclers describe how the choreomaniacs begged the onlookers to kick them or to trample on their stomachs, in order that they might thereby find relief from severe pains; they often declared themselves cured as a result. There is reason to suppose, therefore, that their furious agitation against the poulaines was only due to the pain, and even injury, which they suffered from sharply pointed shoes in the course of this grotesque treatment. There is no question of magic, no agitation against a contemporary fashion, but only an effort at self-defence.

8. *The hatred of red*

The chroniclers record of the 1374 choreomaniacs that they loathed red; they even hastened to tear to pieces the clothes of any man dressed in red as soon as they caught sight of him. But in the Strassburg epidemic of 1518 the sufferers wore red shoes in which they danced before the image of St Vitus and round the altar. We are reminded of the account of a woman who danced in Bâle, about the year 1550, supported and assisted by two men who were placed at her disposal by the city authorities and at their expense, and who were dressed in red clothes. Until 1634 the relics of St Vitus were preserved in the cathedral of Corvey, where his anniversary was celebrated with great solemnity. After a magnificent service in the cathedral a great procession was formed which proceeded round the parish bearing the relics of the saint, and those who bore the baldequin over the reliquary wore a red costume with silver borders [Kampschulte]. This reminds us of the popular church dance of the hopping saints at Echternach, in which the sextons and beadles appeared in ankle-length red costumes.

Red must therefore have a meaning, but it is clear that in the epidemic of 1374 its significance to the choreomaniacs must have been quite different from what it was later. We shall now make a brief survey of the symbolic meaning of this colour and then consider its relation to the epidemics.

Even in antiquity it was thought that red had some protective power against evil. In the festivals of the Cabiri in Lemnos, Thebes, Phrygia, Imbros and Samothrace the initiates were given a purple-red ribbon which they always had to wear as a protection against all dangers [Seligmann]. Both Greeks and Romans wore a woollen thread round their necks as an active protection against evil [Scheftelowitz]. The early Christians inherited similar ideas and the Fathers of the Church, Saint Chrysostom and Saint Clement of Alexandria, condemned the use of red wool in amulets [Wunderlich]. The Church declared that red symbolized the blood of Christ; it is the colour of fire and of blood and it signified the flame of warm love, sacrificial love, which conquers death. For this reason red became the colour of the liturgical decorations, as also of the festivals of the martyrs [Bächthold-Stüabli].

But as we shall later relate, St Anthony the Hermit became the dispenser of the holy fire, which by God's command he sent down among men to plague and consume them as a punishment and a discipline. This brings an affliction which we shall encounter later as St Anthony's fire. It raged widely for many centuries and brought a horribly petrified death to thousands. Those who escaped with their lives were always crippled, because whole limbs, or parts of them, fell off. The Catholic Church, in whose hands the care of the sick was mainly placed in the Middle Ages, hastened to establish special hospitals, the so-called St Anthony hospitals, which devoted themselves exclusively to the care of those who suffered from this fire. But the Middle Ages had no methods for its medical treatment. Practically nothing was known of its causes and nature and the only relief which the monks of St Anthony could offer was amputation, and all who entered a St Anthony's hospital knew that they would never leave it except dead or crippled. These hospitals had their outer walls and door-posts painted red as a symbol of the holy St Anthony's fire, against the ravages of which they offered care and assistance. Thus, in the story of Pantagruel, Rabelais says that down in hell Epistemon had seen the Inquisitor of heretics, who met an acquaintance who was urinating against a wall on which was painted St Anthony's fire.

Barger relates that one of the St Anthony's hospitals in Lyons was called *Domus contractoria*, the home of sufferers from cramp, and was painted red.

In the fifteenth century, and probably even earlier, the custom prevailed in France and Italy of painting mortuary chapels red, of using red bier cloths and of dressing the coffin bearers in red. To some extent this custom has survived to the present day [Wunderlich]. The same custom was also found in respect of the supreme head of the Catholic Church: the dead Pope, lying on his bier, was covered with a red silk cloth before the procession started and the inside of the coffin was lined with crimson velvet [Sonny]. It is not merely a custom of antiquity to paint the graves of the dead red; it is prehistoric [G. Backman]. One may say that it symbolizes that just as in death man must pour out the last drop of his blood, so also he may hope that beyond the portals of death he will enter into the real and everlasting life. The red colour is therefore the symbol not only of that which has been poured out and lost, but also of that which has been conquered and gained. Red is associated with death in yet another way: the medieval execution block was covered with scarlet cloth and the executioner was dressed in a scarlet costume, while the judge who delivered sentence wore a red mantle [Wunderlich]. As late as 1802 criminals were executed in the red shirt of the 'poor sinner' [Bächthold-Stüabli].

Evil is red. The Devil is dressed in a red mantle and a red cap; he wears a red beard. Elfs, goblins, dwarfs, water sprites, etc., all wore red breeches, red stockings, or the red cap of invisibility [Bächthold-Stüabli]. The denizens of the Underworld also wear the red cap as a sign of their fellowship with the Devil, the Red [Duhn].

The ancient custom of driving out disease by using red continued throughout the centuries, even to our own time. The Jewish Talmud commands the faithful to bind red cords and knots round the necks of children as a protection against illness, and the Slavonic Jews regarded a red wire round the wrist as protection against the evil eye. This idea spread throughout the whole of Central Europe [Scheftelowitz]. In the Jewish synagogues the trees placed at the entrance were often protected by a red covering. At the end of the nineteenth century children in Germany, Switzerland, Hungary and Bohemia wore red ribbons round their necks or wrists as a protection against evil [Seligmann]. A similar custom also existed in France, where a red cloth was laid over a sick person [Wunderlich]. Broberg describes similar customs in the north. In Norway red woollen yarn had the power to drive out sickness.

Red therefore drove out demons and disease, and the explanation is to be found in homeopathic, sympathetic magic. Red things on earth and red dress in the Underworld. The North-Germanic heathens therefore said:

> Then leap the dead
> For cocks red.   [Broberg].

Why did the choreomaniacs of 1374 hate this colour? Obviously, not because red had the power to drive out demons and sickness. Possibly they recoiled from red because it reminded them of death and destruction, of the coffin and the grave, of the execution block and the executioner? Perhaps these grievously sick and tormented persons were so vividly reminded of the death they feared. Or did they see in a man's red clothes a representative of the Underworld and of its demons by which they were possessed and tormented? Perhaps there is yet another motive, that experience had taught the choreomaniacs that their sickness sometimes brought on symptoms which compelled a visit to one of the St Anthony hospitals, leading them to believe that it sometimes ended in the holy fire. But the holy fire was red, the St Anthony hospital was painted red, and the holy fire was, if possible, more terrible than choreomania.

It is probable that there were several motives for their hatred of red and I think it is most probable that the real motive was the conception of red as a symbol of spilled blood, of death and burial, and the risk that sickness might be combined with the holy fire. We shall see later that in the fifteenth century the sufferers directed their prayers and paid their reverence to St Anthony the Hermit.

Nevertheless, after 1518, as we have seen, red appears as a contributory element in the healing of the dancing sickness. Evidently, then, it had by this time acquired the simple significance of an expeller of demons and disease, compelling the demons to flee, and possibly even imparting to the feet and legs the power to resist their influence.

9. *The Cross*

In the dance epidemic of 1518 the sick were given small crosses to carry in their hands and crosses were painted in consecrated oil on the uppers and the soles of the dancers' shoes. The power of the cross to expel demons is well known and is clear from the very beginning of Christianity. What an immense number of legends tell of the holy men who by the cross or the sign of the cross have driven out the devil and his demons and have conquered the infernal powers. The symbolism is evident: the cross is the symbol of suffering and triumph, by which Christ conquered death and the devil, was able to descend into hell, to deliver its captives and lead them forth in a jubilant procession. It was early conceived as a symbol of protection. The Fathers of the Church advise the regular use of the sign of the cross on the bodies of those possessed. During the Middle Ages the sick and the possessed were healed by the sign of the cross and in exorcisms the possessed made the sign of the cross or else a cross was carried before them. The words of the exorcism were always accompanied by a laying on of the hands and the sign of the cross. The significance of the sign of the cross should be seen against the background of the utterance of the patriarch Origenes: 'the demons fear the sign of the cross, the cross of Christ; and become afraid when they see the sign of the cross and our complete faith' [Franz].

10. *Consecrated Oil*

We have seen examples of the power of consecrated oil to drive out sickness, especially in the epidemic of 1518, when crosses were painted with oil on the red shoes. We saw also the miracle of St Nilus when he inserted a finger dipped in consecrated oil into the mouth of the possessed youth. The Ambrosian formula for the consecration of the oil contains directions for the managing or the coating of oil on the sick. Here it is said that this oil expels all discomforts, all sicknesses and all attacks of the Devil. And we are assured in this formula that the oil is a specific against diseases of all kinds [Franz]. The consecrated oil—which was also used in church lamps—has been employed to an unimagined extent in medicine for the cure of diseases, used both internally and externally. Just this quality of being consecrated, together with the rôle it played among the dying for the expulsion of demons and for protection against demons, was the cause of its high esteem among the clergy and the public. St Mark (vi, 13) relates how the Apostles drove out devils, anointed many of the sick with oil and cured them. James' letter (v, 14) directs that when anyone falls sick the eldest of the community shall be summoned to pray for him and to anoint him with oil in the name of the Lord [Achelis].

11. *Consecrated Water*

In the dance epidemic of 1374 the sick were completely immersed in consecrated water. This treatment is well known from other sources as an expeller of demons [Franz]. We learn of the epidemic in Strassburg in 1518 that the choreomaniacs and their red shoes were sprinkled with St Vitus' water, that is to say, water which had been especially consecrated to St Vitus. Consecrated water played as important a rôle in the healing of sickness as did consecrated oil, and this has been so since the early days of the Christian Church. By degrees, however, the water which was consecrated in memory of a particular saint, with special prayers, came to be considered as more effective. For this reason water was consecrated to St Stephen, St Anthony, St Blasius, St Vitus, etc., and with it the monks and priests could perform miracles of healing. The sick were healed, demons were expelled, the fertility of the fields was increased and noxious insects were driven away. According to St Thomas Aquinas, Durandus and others, this consecrated water served to exorcize the evil spirit and to protect against disease and the plague [Franz]. We have already seen in the treatment of the choreomaniacs in the chapel at Hohlenstein the significance of the benediction of this St Vitus' water. It was also effective against dancing sickness, but in that case there was also a St Willibrord water against epilepsy, spasms, etc., a so-called St Valentine water against epilepsy and a St Anthony water against the holy fire, etc. [Geiler v. Kaisersberg].

12. *The Altar*

In the St Vitus chapel at Hohlenstein near Zabern the priests allowed the choreomaniacs of the 1518 epidemic to dance before the St Vitus image and to be led, most probably dancing, round the altar. This circuit round the altar has a very old and magic significance. Already in the world of antiquity there existed the custom of leading any offering round the altar. The trinity was above all the divine symbol, the number three was the divine number, the number of perfection, the number of the present and the future. This circuit dance magnified its purifying and defensive, its protective and consecrating powers. According to Eitrem a straight dance was performed round the altar in the cult of Artemis, Dionysius, etc. In the Greek orthodox church a newly baptized child was formerly conducted round the font; nowadays the priest and the godfather walk round it instead. During the Litany for offerings the priest with the censer and the deacon with a lighted candle walk round the altar before the offering is laid on the offertory table.

In Jylland, as late as the end of the nineteenth century, a body was borne three times round the grave or three times round the church, a custom deriving from Nordic-Germanic heathendom. In medicine, too, the circuiting was often performed; the cures which drove out sickness were borne three times round the patient or the sick-bed, or the patient himself was carried three times round the church [Eitrem].

This dance round the altar of St Vitus near Zabern signifies not only a circuit but also the closure of a ring. According to Eitrem this means that the person so borne is consecrated and sanctified, purified from any taint or evil. The circle is magical and protects against demons and danger. Whoever completes the circle and stands within it is protected and defended; whoever stands outside it is warded off and driven away.

Circuiting has played an important rôle in all popular magic: how often has a man not circled churches, altars, the images of saints, the fields, his own home and hearth in order to drive away evil, to regain health or improve the harvest?

The dance of the choreomaniacs round the altar of St Vitus is an attempt by the postulants to cleanse themselves of demons, to consecrate themselves and to prepare themselves for the exorcisms which really expel the demons, and to protect themselves against the demons of disease.

13. Bridges and Running Water

In Zürich in 1452 the choreomaniacs first crossed a bridge above running water before they danced in the helmet house of the church. In Moelenbeek in 1564 the sick had to dance over a bridge across a little stream before they could be sure of being cured of their sickness for a year to come. We have previously quite briefly indicated the great importance attributed to springs in expelling sickness. We shall now examine the rôle of running water in the same connexion. Water is the enemy of evil spirits [Goldziher]. Just as with water one washes the dirt from one's body so also can one wash away the diseases of the body and the filth of the demons by the same means. Every kind of sorcery can be counteracted if it is possible to bring running water between us and the sorcerer. On certain days, Maundy Thursday, Easter and Midsummer Eve all water has healing powers, and whoever bathes in running water will be whole for a year to come [Seligmann].

As early as the twelfth century the Church was active in preventing attempts to find help in springs and waters during epidemics and when in distress. Grohmann relates how women on Easter Monday visited running waters at sunrise in order there to wash themselves and so preserve their health for a year.

This running water can drive out demons and is a protection against them. It is the living water in which, in early Christianity, baptisms took place.

The Greek Hades, like the Germanic Hell, is surrounded by a river which is crossed either by a ferry or a bridge and Kleinpaul points out that in various countries, for example, Egypt and Scandinavia, there is evidence of the custom that the dead were conveyed over a bridge to their final rest and hence also to the new life. The road to Nifelheim leads through dark valleys down to the abyss. Over thorny heaths and over swamps the wanderer must pass through the eternal darkness to reach the roaring stream which is spanned by the Gjallar bridge. On the other side is hell. According to Germanic sagas the infernal denizens also pass over this bridge when they are compelled to release humans [Mannhardt].

In England there was a custom on the night of December 31st to January 1st, after the stroke of twelve, of carrying water under a bridge, which then was able for a whole year to protect one against evil spirits, witches and the evil eye [Seligmann]. According to Bâchthold-Stüabli certain legal transaction and magical performances had to be executed on or near a bridge. There also were set up images of the saints (e.g., St Nepomuk) instead of the old river gods. Bridges were at the same time regarded as being especially beloved by the demons. They willingly stayed there in order to capture, to plague or possess, those who crossed the bridges.

Bridges over running water are therefore of special significance for protection against and expulsion of demons. The passage over the water to the other side assures the sufferer liberation, more especially if the river or stream has its source in healing or medicinal springs as was the case both in Zürich (St Felix and St Regula springs), and in Moelenbeek (St Gertrude springs). But we have seen how in the popular church dancing processions the bridge, river or spring have quite evidently played a significant rôle in the ritual. In the sacred hop-dance of the saints at Echternach, the participators assembled outside the city on the farther side of the bridge and the dancing procession had first to pass over it. In the Croix de Verviers procession at Liége the procession, when passing over the bridge, was obliged to perform a special dancing ceremony upon it; and after the end of divine service and at the end of the dance ceremony the final dancing rites were performed on another bridge, together with an offering to the river. The procession at Prüm danced three times round a spring. The dance epidemic in Maastricht had its scene on a bridge.

It seems to me not inconceivable that the original magic ceremonies which were obligatorily executed near running water and on a bridge may really have been associated with some conception of the waters of death which encompass the infernal regions and of a bridge which the Saviour crossed. In popular magic we should therefore see an effort to leave running waters behind, pass across the waters of death, with all their demons, and to pass across the bridge which, although it led to the world of demons, yet also led away from it. It is thus a flight from the demons, an escape from the world of demons, in which one is captive and possessed. For this reason Brueghel was able to write on his drawing that when the pilgrims had danced over the bridge and hopped violently, they were cured for another year. The bridge played an important and inescapable rôle.

14. *Nakedness*

In the dance epidemic of 1374 the choreomaniacs probably appeared more or less naked. The fact that, according to various chroniclers, they had to be tightly laced or bound round the stomach at the end of the dance, or during the intervals between the attacks, and went about bound in this manner, seems to indicate that they were at least half naked. This would seem to explain de Herenthal's statement that in their dance they observed no modesty in the presence of spectators. But de Rivo maintains that they were half-naked and without any shame and de Mezeray describes them as stark naked, except that they were dressed like the flagellants, who during the flogging and the attendant ceremonies were also naked but for the cloth that hung from their waists to their feet. The choreomaniacs, however, can scarcely have worn a foot-length cloth. It must have been much shorter, because dancing and hopping was a part of their religio-medical ceremony—and it is therefore intelligible that their dance might be described as immodest by the spectators. But de Mezeray may be right: in certain cases they possibly appeared quite naked, with the exception of the loin-cloth and the wreath of flowers on the head. It may, therefore be supposed that this nakedness was caused not only by important considerations of comfort, but also by some magical significance. Let us glance at the religio-symbolic significance of nakedness.

In an earlier work I have described the magic role of nakedness [Backman, Alvablåst]. From the very earliest times nakedness has been prescribed as a part of magical or religious rites. Even among the Babylonians nakedness formed a part of the customary ceremonies for the driving out of demons and the protection of the sick. In the mysteries, the Greek and Roman, nakedness was more or less a constant rule for initiation. In baptism in the earliest Christian church the baptized, when renouncing the devil and in the subsequent proceedings, had to be naked [Hechenbach]. From the Bible we only learn, concerning nakedness, that the man who is filled with the Holy Ghost must cast off his clothing. Such was the case with Saul (1 Samuel xix, 23), who went to Najot and there beheld Samuel and the prophets in a trance; then God's spirit descended upon Saul and when he arrived at Najot he fell into a trance and cast off his clothes and lay there naked all day. Therefore as we are told, one is accustomed to say—'Is Saul also one of the prophets?'

Nakedness has played a very important role in popular medicine and folk customs. As late as 1790 naked girls danced around the flax fields in order that the flax might grow as high as possible [Mannhardt]. In Bohemia there was a similar custom. In the same century sterile women danced naked at midsummer in order to regain their fecundity. From France we know that during the seventeenth century women and girls prayed quite naked at sunrise to Our Father and to Mary to be delivered from their fever. Many sicknesses were cured by rolling naked in the morning dew, especially at Mid-

FIG. 120. Nakedness in a Pilgrimage. At the healing well of St Florian in Austria. The first woman and boy on one of the steps are naked, except for their shirts. From a painting by Albrecht Altdorfer (1480–1558) [Hdb. d. Deutsch. Volksk.].

summer, or by crawling naked between two trees, etc. [Weinhold]. The Southern Slavs drove out the spirits of disease by exposing themselves to the spirits naked. In the year 1602 the Wendish peasants adopted a cure against the plague in which six naked virgins, guided by a peasant, pulled a plough in a wide circle and all were preceded by a naked widow [Bächthold-Stüabli]. Many such cures are to be found in Scandinavia, in which complete or partial nakedness is prescribed for the success of the cure [Backman].

The popular church pilgrimages also prescribed nakedness for the more certain achievement of their eager purpose (Fig. 120). Various healing processions were undertaken with bare feet [Moleon] and in 1523 the Archbishop of Besançon granted the small cloister chapel of Sulz in Upper Alsace the privilege of granting absolution to those suppliants who visited the shrines half-naked or bare-footed. Several such pilgrimages to Aachen took place [Pfleger]. In a healing procession in Paris in 1224 all taking part were barefoot and clad in shirts; some of them were naked. In the procession which set out from Paris to St Denis in 1315 there were those, though not women, who marched quite naked. In a procession in 1589 many men and women were quite naked and one of the priestly participators wore only a narrow linen cloth. So also in Germany men went on pilgrimages naked, as for example in 1588 and 1589; they also marched with their arms stretched outwards, representing the sign of the cross. As late as 1797 individuals made pilgrimages completely naked [Bächthold-Stüabli]. In the fifteenth century such pilgrimages were made naked with arms stretched sideways or upwards, when the pilgrims suffered from severe sickness; also when they were acting as deputies for sick persons. This seems to have been the case especially in Bavaria and Austria [Zoepfl].

What then was the meaning of this nakedness on pilgrimage? Was it merely by nakedness to humiliate oneself, as Zoepfl thinks? This seems to me very improbable. The role of nakedness elsewhere in the world of antiquity, in the account of Saul and in popular medicine, all seems to show that nakedness originally had its own magical significance in healing processions and pilgrimages. Ultimately this nakedness is the same thing as the possession of Saul by a divine spirit and can only be interpreted according to Genesis i, 27, 'And God created man in his own image'. Because naked man is God's image the devils flee from him and avoid his body. For this reason nakedness is a powerful force in expelling the demons which plague and torture man.

15. Toads and Puppets

In the little chapel at the Hohlenstein grotto and in the grotto itself the pilgrims offered, in the eighteenth century and very probably much earlier, toads and small doll-like figures. These were offered not only by hysterical and sterile women but also by those who believed themselves to be affected by St Vitus' dance, dancing sickness or epilepsy.

We do not know how far back this practice goes, but when Cardinal de Rohan forbade it in 1758 we can be quite sure that it was old. *Les marmousets d'hommes*, of which the Cardinal speaks, are usually rendered in translation as 'grotesque figures', but they are also something else. *Marmouset* is a small doll, a grotesque figure, a kind of idol. According to Godefroy it is a madman or a little pet and it is only in modern French that it comes to mean a grotesque figure, more or less grimacing. It seems to me therefore to be more correct to interpret marmouset as a small doll-like image of man, a puppet. This meaning is also given by Angé.

From earliest antiquity comes the custom by which the sick offered to the gods representations of diseased limbs, of hands and feet, of various organs or even of the whole body. This custom was taken over by the Christian Church at a very early stage, and continues to this day. These votive gifts were offered before the miracle-working images and they were wrought in wax, wood, metal or other material. Of special interest in this connexion is the offering of puppets; they have been found in various churches in different European countries [Hermann, Weber, Sauer, Blind, Andree]. Frequently these small human figures had their hands clasped or raised as if in prayer; they are to be found in nearly all the pilgrimage churches, and they were left partly in gratitude for recovered health, and partly to make clear to the saint the purpose of the supplicant's prayers [Weber]. In my account of St Anthony's fire and its devastations in Europe I reproduce two remarkable engravings which show how people buried models of their diseased limbs in the St Anthony churches or chapels, and sometimes as votive gifts the limbs which had fallen off during the terrible ravages of the epidemic. According to Fragoso, in various St Anthony hospitals in Spain there were still preserved in 1590 arms and legs which had fallen from the sick. And yet there had been no holy fire in Spain since the mid-fifteenth century. As late as 1702 similar relics were still to be found in the monastery church of Vienna [Fuchs]. As to the tiny images of human beings, it seems to me improbable that these were offered by those who had suffered from the holy fire, but by those suffering from St Vitus's dance, the dance epidemic, because among those who prayed to St Anthony we find some which show a marked condition of cramp. The magical belief was that what happened to the image would by resemblance also happen to the person represented by the image; by sympathetic magic the sick recovered their health.

More remarkable and more difficult to interpret is the offering of iron toads. Many writers have been satisfied that the toad signifies the womb of a woman. This was true in classical antiquity. It was also thought that the womb was the cause of female hysteria, a view which was also found in formal medicine. It is certain that toads were offered by hysterical women as well as by sterile women and by those who suffered from diseases of the womb [Bächthold-Stäubli]. But earlier accounts complete the picture of offerings. During the seventeenth century the 'womb' was the seat of colic pains in general and even a man was said 'to have been violently seized in his womb' [Füstenfeld Miracle 1605—Panzer]. This womb was represented by a toad. During the sixteenth century 'womb' in no way signified only the female organ, but rather the source of stomach-ache or colic. Both men and women can be affected by the womb. In v. Megenberg's *Buche der Natur*, of the fifteenth century, we read that blood and excreta of wolves are good for pains in the stomach, 'what is called the womb'. The custom of offering toads as votive gifts probably arose more from the resemblance of the toad to the womb than because of its old appearance as a demonic animal [Kriss]. Such votive gifts were made not only to St Vitus, but also the Virgin Mary, St Leonard, St Pancras, St Erhard, St Kümmerniss and Christ. However, it may well be objected that the toad as a votive gift for men suffering from stomach pains can scarcely be connected with the female womb, and since by far the great majority, perhaps all, were at that time considered to be the result of possession, it is more probable that the toad represented demons who plagued the sick and from which the sick sought deliverance through the intervention of the saints. The toad was, after the worm, the commonest symbol of the demon which caused disease. It lay like the nightmare of a toad in the pregnant womb, like a toad in the heart, like a toad under the tongue of a cretin. All the infernal beings may appear in the shape of a toad; it is a refuge which they often preferred. For this reason the toad has come in folklore to signify various bodily abnormalities [Höfler, Handelmann].

I, therefore, take the offering of iron toads to St Vitus at Zabern as proof that those who suffered from St Vitus's illness or from epileptic conditions, regarded themselves as possessed and therefore offered to the saint an image of the devil in order to make clear to him their wish to be freed and healed by his power to expel demons. It is perhaps not quite without significance that the toad was made of iron, because iron is also a symbol of the underworld. We read in Solomon's Ode, a Christian Gnostic hymnary of the second century, that on Christ's journey to the underworld they opened the closed doors and burst open the iron bolts. The dwellers in the infernal regions are surrounded by walls of iron; the infernal powers have laid iron fetters upon mankind, therefore the spirits of the churchyard in Balde's death song danced in rust-coloured mantles.

16. *Immorality*

In the 1374 dance epidemic the choreomaniacs are accused by nearly all the chroniclers, as also in the lampoons, of having lapsed into immorality. We know very well that depravity had a magic significance in various popular rites for the recovery of health and other purposes. We are therefore tempted to assume a further magic in these chronicler's accounts of the choreomaniacs. But it is far from certain that the chroniclers are right. Such accusations were very common when it was a question of attacking popular movements of which the Church or the civil authorities did not approve. Moreover it is clear that the interpretations of certain chroniclers of the binding by the choreomaniacs of their bellies with cloths and ribbons is unreasonable. It cannot possibly have been for the purpose of concealing incipient pregnancy. In this case the prejudice of the accusation is quite clear. Moreover, it seems unreasonable that these extremely sick and tortured beings, many of whom died during the dance, should have abandoned themselves to sexual dissipation. But we have learnt from *The Chronicles of the Early Roman Kings and Emperors* that numerous others were attracted to the choreomaniacs who followed them into the woods of Trier as spectators and perhaps also to some extent as participants. It would appear from this chronicle as if it were these who were guilty of immorality. But other chroniclers emphasize especially that it was against the choreomaniacs that the accusation was directed.

One should remember that immorality during the period now under consideration was both general and important. Immorality was rife, not only among men of the church, and certainly still more so among laymen. All descriptions of contemporary life confirm this. In this respect the profane dances leave nothing to be described; frequently they danced more than half naked, the manner of dancing was crude and indecent, and both civil and ecclesiastical authorities fought energetically against this evil. There was really convincing evidence for the view of the leaders of the mystics during the fourteenth century that dancing was an invention of the devil.

One may concede that conditions were different in the various places where the choreomaniacs appeared. Possibly the indecent excesses occurred principally in Cologne, Trier and Flanders, though not in other places. Possibly these excesses were especially in evidence where the adhesion of choreomaniacs from Polish and Slavonic countries was great. These dances were especially wild, with violent distortions of the body, with stamping and leaping and grimacing [Anton]. But more remarkable is it that the medieval chroniclers describe the Czechs and Bohemians as conspicuous in a high degree for their immoral behaviour. Cosmas of Prague describes conditions in the eleventh century as those of general prostitution. A monk in the Russian monastery at Eleaser, named Pamphilius, who lived in the sixteenth century, declares that this prostitution still continued among the Bohemians; there were annual festivals during which complete sexual freedom was the order of the day, such dancing festivals being held on the banks of the river, especially on Midsummer Eve, together with general prostitution. It was towards the end of this century that the church in Bohemia seriously sought to cope with these conditions [Kowalewsky]. In such circumstances one might be inclined to see a possible explanation of the immorality of which the choreomaniacs are accused by so many contemporary chroniclers. It would then be in accord with the habits and customs of the choreomaniacs coming from their homeland in Bohemia and other Slavonic countries. It is quite possible that these customs ultimately had a magical impulse for the preservation or recovery of health.

XXI

Choreomania and Heresy

HERE and there in the literature of the subject one finds that the 1374 choreomaniacs constituted a mystic-spiritual movement which was in opposition to the Church. Hahn, in his history of the medieval heretical sects, mentions that the choreomaniacs might to this extent be equivalent to the flagellants, who also strove for another church, a church of the spirit, but that they never made up their minds how to bring about such a rebirth of the church. However, Hahn never adduced any evidence in support of his view, neither has any of his successors.

If we turn to the old chroniclers, it cannot be denied that there is certain evidence in support of the view that the choreomaniacs constituted a special sect whose wild dancing not only purposed healing but was also a kind of expression of their godly life. The lampoons quoted by Petrus de Herenthal call the choreomaniacs *a certain new sect* and adds, 'these people stimulate heretical faith', that they hated priests and cared little for the sacrament. But the lampoons are not reliable in so far as their reference to the hatred of the choreomaniacs for the priests contradicts Herenthal's description of events in Liége, where it was the local inhabitants who turned against the priests because of the dances. And the expression 'heretical faith' cannot be meant in a general sense, for the Church in no wise intervened in respect of their faith but treated them merely as possessed by demons.

De Rivo calls the dancers 'a curious sect' and also 'a devilish sect', though none of the other chroniclers has a similar expression. In Beka, John of Leyden, Zantfliet, Jean d'Outremeuse, and Koelhoff, and in the chronicles of Liége, Limburg and Cologne, as well as in the 'Great Belgian Chronicle', the choreomaniacs are everywhere called a plague, a cloud, a frenzy, a devilish pest. In all of them the element of sickness is emphasized. Only in the last-named chronicle are they referred to as 'a miserable society', a name which, about 25 years earlier, is applied to the flagellants.

Slichtenhorst, in his account of 1654, is able to relate that the choreomaniacs of 1374 embraced each other when they assembled and called each other brother and sister, whether they knew each other or not. If this is true then it is strong evidence of a marked mystical tendency. But Slichtenhorst does not tell us whence he derived this information and not one of the known chroniclers, many of whom were contemporary with the dance epidemics, affords us any such information. For that reason I think we must doubt it. Moreover Slichtenhorst's brief references are certainly very misleading in other respects. The real dance epidemic did not occur in 1375 and 1376 but in 1374, and quite certainly it did not begin in Jülich and Gelderland but in Aachen, and arrived much later in the Jülich and Netherland districts.

If one is to weigh the truth of these earlier assertions of Herenthal, de Rivo and the lampoons, that the choreomaniacs constituted a sect which despised the sacrament and hated the priesthood, one may perhaps find some guidance by a glance at the more important church sects which flourished in the Rhine province in the latter part of the fourteenth century.

The Beguines and the Beghards appeared in these districts of the Rhine as early as the eleventh century. Originally they consisted of a sort of association which devoted itself to a pious life without cloistral discipline. They multiplied in the thirteenth century and sought a nearer approach to the so-called third order of Franciscans and Dominicans. They then began a wandering life as beggars and mixed with vagrants of various heretical sects and even more directly attached themselves to the latter. For that reason the persecution by the Church of the Beguines and Beghards was in full swing in the fourteenth century. In the latter half of that century these associations appear to have assimilated the Fratricelli and the Lollards, also the 'Brothers and Sisters of the Free Spirit'. The headquarters of this movement were in Cologne. Numerous persecutions and proscriptions against the Beguines took place in the fourteenth century, and in 1374—the year of the great dance epidemic—they were burnt at the stake in Berne [Gieseler].

It has been maintained by Hahn that the Lollards and the 'Brothers and Sisters of the Free Spirit' should be regarded merely as two main tendencies of the Beghards and Beguines. They appear as quite distinct heretical sects. What is interesting in this connexion is primarily that they thought they might do anything without sin, because they manifested the spirit of God working through perfected man. They called the Catholic Church false and simple because perfect man was free from anything associated with the observation of church decrees. They rejected the priesthood, they despised the saints and are said to have had pronounced sensual leanings [Hahn]. Unlike the Lollards, the Brothers and Sisters of the Free Spirit were characterized by a general gnostic outlook; their pantheism was evident and they may be regarded as sympathetic to Platonic thought [Herkless]. They too despised the sacrament, regarded it as worthless and in general expressed views resembling those of the Lollards. Members of both schools were frequent victims of the Inquisition during the fourteenth century. The Bull of Clement V in 1311 confirms that, as has been said, they rejected the saints and refused to do reverence to the sacrament. They are said to have adopted a special costume and a special way of life [Hahn]. During the thirteenth century and until the end of the fourteenth century, there appeared a pronounced gnostic sect, the so-called Cathars, who were numerous in certain tracts of Hungary [Döllinger], and may be described as a sort of revival of the old Manichaeans; in any case their gnosticism is clear. They derived their impulse mainly from the Spanish Jews, who in turn received them fron neo-Platonic writings. They were numerous in Bohemia, Austria and Thuringia in the fourteenth century, and in the latter half of the fourteenth century they went over more and more to the Beghards. In their hearts they seem to have hated the Church and all its ordinances. They despised all of them and fought against the sacrament and its cult. They rejected the patriarchs and the tradition of the saints and refused any participation in pilgrimages. They refused to obey the Church authorities [Hahn]. They also rejected the altar and refused to recognize it as of importance in religion; they rejected the consecrated oil and dismissed all outer forms and ceremonies as useless [Marx].

Towards the end of the twelfth century the Waldenses began to spread in the Rhine province. About the same time arrived the Albigenses or, as they were called, 'the poor from Lyons'. They did not form themselves into congregations, and might perhaps be compared with the itinerant preachers, who resembled the Apostles in the proclamation of the Word and in their choice of poverty. They wandered from place to place, teaching, praying, taking confession and giving absolution and accepting the alms of the faithful. At any rate, during the early fourteenth century, they wore a special dress and peculiar sandals. They refused to believe in the intercession of the saints, they disbelieved in their miracles and would not honour their relics. Persecution compelled them outwardly to observe the saints' days, the vigils and the fasts of the Church, but they did this only as the worship of God [Müller]. The Waldenses were indifferent to the Church and regarded the saints as false gods, whilst denying the value and meaning of the Cross. Both the Waldenses and Albigenses repudiated pilgrimage. Yet no sect raged so furiously against dancing as did the Waldenses and Albigenses. They described it as a procession of the Devil; its participants entered the train of the Devil, who as leader was the aim and purpose of the dance. By as many steps as a man takes in this dance, by just so many steps he hastens towards hell. They also scorned the songs of the Church and refused to take part in them.

There was in Austria and Bohemia yet another heretical people, called the Adamites, who flourished in the first half of the fourteenth century. We know little about them, but it would appear that they had Manichaean tendencies and possibly formed associations of members with the Brothers and Sisters of the Free Spirit [Hahn].

The Amalricians came to the Rhine province from France and spread first in the bishopric of Trier during the thirteenth century. But they appear very soon to have merged with the Free Spirit movement. Their attitude to the Church was similar; they rejected the sacraments, described the cult of the saints as idolatry and reverence for relics as a masquerade [Delacroix].

At the end of the thirteenth century began the movement later called the Friends of God, to which so many eminent religious personalities belonged. Men and women, laymen, monks, nuns and priests joined the movement, whose purpose it was to deepen the knowledge of the Bible, to absorb the teaching of divine wisdom, to practise virtue, to flee from vice, to bear suffering with patience and steadfastness, and to practise charity. Under the influence of the great misfortunes which befell the districts round the Rhine and Moselle in the fourteenth century this movement grew in strength; converts were numerous and its religious attitude acquired more and more the stamp of mysticism. The chief centres of the Friends of God were Strassburg, Bâle and Cologne. In every respect they associated themselves with the forms and doctrines of the Church and won the confidence and admiration of both the Church and laity [Neander]. Some sections of the Friends of God movement appear to have called themselves 'Brothers and Sisters of the Communal Life'. They adopted a monkish manner of life, but with the monkish discipline of hard work, translating the Bible and the works of the Patriarchs, etc. In their general life they refused all kinds of begging for alms [Preger]. Their organization was intimately bound up with the discipline of the Church. Some of these associations bore other names such as 'Brethren of Good Will' of 'The Brethren of the Capuche' (because they wore a special dress), and 'The Brethren of Hieronymus' (because of their diligence in copying books). Their costume was of black or grey with a black capuche on their heads.

This brief survey of heretical sects which flourished along the Rhine in the fourteenth century shows that if the choreomaniacs really were a separate sect they cannot have belonged to any of the known sects. These choreomaniacs did of their own volition visit the Maria church in Aachen, where they danced and sang in full vigour before the altar; they visited other churches and chapels, where they similarly danced in front of the altar of the Virgin or the images of other saints, and they allowed themselves to be conducted without demur to the relics. They invoked St John the Baptist, danced in his honour, sang a song to him, etc. Thereby they proved that they were in no way opposed to the dance, which they evidently regarded as worthy and as a humble offering to the saints. They joyously reverenced the images of the saints and their relics, and called upon the saints for aid and deliverance. They were led to the priest and to the exorcisms, but many of the sick ran there of their own initiative and submitted gladly and in true faith to the exorcisms. The chroniclers have nothing to relate of the choreomaniacs denying or seriously interfering with the priests when the sacrament was laid upon their heads, when consecrated oil or water was placed in their mouths, when the stole was hung about their shoulders, when the exorcisms were read and prayers were uttered, etc. One has the impression that the great majority submitted to the exorcism of devils and the methods of the Church, and the choreomaniacs revealed nothing which could be regarded as hostile to the Church, the priests or the sacrament.

We must therefore reject all ideas that the choreomaniacs constituted any sort of heretical sect. They were only very sick people who, in accordance with their Catholic faith, sought out the Church and the saints, in order, through them and their own dancing and all other magic means to gain deliverance from their evil and from possession by demons.

In the literature of the nineteenth century it is sometimes stated that the Catholic Church proceeded against the choreomaniacs as against all other heretics; that they were persecuted by the Church and were even burned at the stake. But all the existing chronicles and accounts show not the slightest sign of such persecution. These assertions have no support whatsoever, and probably have their origin in Schnurrer's chronicle of epidemics, written in 1823. He describes the epidemic of 1374 and says that there were many, during the succeeding years, who pretended to be seized with ecstasy in places of pilgrimage in the hope that they would meet a devout company and that they tried by the violence of their movements to draw attention to themselves. The Beghards especially were blamed for such attempts, and in

Augsburg in 1381 two of them were burned at the stake, as well as a barefooted monk, because it had been proved that their ecstasy was false. However, there is no single chronicle which in any way connects the dancing epidemic with the Beghards.

But how are we to interpret 'a certain sect' or 'a devilish sect'? The letter to the Galatians mentions among the evils of the flesh *secta*, which was translated as 'division of parties'. In the old ecclesiastical language the word retains the meaning of 'heretic', a confession of faith which departs from the teaching of the Church. But in the early Middle Ages, and later, the meaning of the word *secta* was extended, so that it no longer meant only 'heretic' and 'false doctrine', but rather merely 'an outward fellowship'. And instead, the words 'heresy' and 'schism' were preferred to designate a heretic. Only after the coming of Protestantism did the word *secta* revert to its original meaning [Weber, Corradini].

This was the secret of the problem: an expression commonly misunderstood by later authors when they found it among the older chroniclers, who, by describing the choreomaniacs as 'a certain kind of sect, a curious or devilish sect', only meant 'a curious and remarkable fellowship'. But from all appearances the choreomaniacs never preached any heretical doctrines; neither did they strive to deepen or spiritualize the Godly life or the Christian attitude towards life. They never sought a new church without first knowing the way they should go. They only sought in their own way and in the manner of their time to find deliverance from a grave sickness. And the Church never treated the choreomaniacs as heretics. The Inquisition was not interested in them; on the contrary, the Church authorities regarded them as possessed of devils, as grave sufferers, and hastened to employ all the means of the Church, preserved from the earliest Christian times, for the expulsion of devils.

XXII

St Anthony's Fire

AS early as Greek and Roman times we find the medical term *ignis sacer*, 'the holy fire', for external ills with a pronounced burning sensation. How far was included under this heading the serious sickness which later acquired this name is uncertain. What we call *ignis sacer* occurs first in the ninth century. The winter of 857 was very cold and dry on the Rhine, and the following year there raged a severe epidemic with blisters on the skin, passing over into mortification, so that the rotting limbs fell off before death. In the tenth century there were several similar epidemics, e.g., in 994 in France, in Aquitania and Limousine, in which more than 40,000 died. An invisible fire, it is said, consumed the bodies and parted the affected limbs from the body. Many of the sufferers recovered when sprinkled with holy water and the plague departed when the Bishops of Aquitania carried St Martial's relics in solemn procession through the land [Fuchs].

Similar epidemics raged in the eleventh century, principally in France, Lorraine and Flanders. In 1042 the disease disappeared from Verdun after St Vitonus had been invoked. In the year 1089 there was a severe epidemic of holy fire in Lorraine and Flanders [Fuchs]. But the disease had two forms. In some patients the nervous system was attacked and they suffered from cramps and curious distortion of the limbs, with associated symptoms of ecstasy and somnambulism; other patients showed symptoms of the typical holy fire, with scorched limbs, blackening to the colour of coal, the limbs sometimes falling off [Schnurrer]. The epidemic spread to France also and chroniclers relate that the bread 'bled'. These epidemics continued one after another for centuries. In the years 1128–29 the holy fire killed no less than 14,000 in Paris alone, and on that occasion the fire was accompanied by cramps; the Virgin Mary and St Geneviève were invoked. As early as the epidemic of 945 the sick had betaken themselves to the church of Nôtre Dame, in Paris, where they were fed by Duke Hugo and where many were healed. But many patients who believed themselves cured returned to their native villages and were again stricken by the fire [Ehlers]. For this reason the sick-

FIG. 121. St Geneviève, 422–502. Healer of the holy fire, protector against war and famine, she is the patron saint of Paris. As a helper in the struggle against fire she carried a wax candle in her hands. Wood-carving of 1490 from Altsimonswald, Baden [Künstle].

ness was then called St Mary's Sickness or Our Lady's Sickness. In Arras in 1105 there was introduced a method of healing the sickness with water into which had been dropped pieces of wax from candles burned to the Virgin, in consequence of a revelation made by her [Vloberg]. The sickness was also named Our Lady's Fire [Fuchs].

In the year 1129 we first encounter St Geneviève (Fig. 121) as a protector against the holy fire or 'the burning evil' (*mal des ardents*), as the sickness is also called. The saint was born in 422, saved Paris in 451 from the ravages of Attila, and succeeded in a great famine in providing bread for the population. She died in 502 and is the patron saint of Paris.

A church—Ste Geneviève des Ardents—was erected to preserve her relics which finally, together with the church, were burnt during the Revolution in 1793. On the site of the church the Pantheon now stands. She is represented with a wax candle in her hands and the Devil at her feet. She is the protrectress against eye diseases, leprosy, the holy fire, the plague and famine. When the holy fire raged in 1129 the relics of the saint were borne in procession from her burial church to Nôtre-Dame, in which the sick had been previously assembled. All were healed except three, who had not sufficient faith [Buchberger, Segange]. In a Paris missal of 1602 there is a prayer to St Geneviève, imploring her that those suffering from the horrible fever might be protected from Gehenna [Segange]. Durandus quotes a thirteenth century hymn to St Geneviève, as follows:

> She cools the holy fire,
> She who by her virtues lives after death.
> Over death, sickness and devils,
> As over the elements, she holds sway.
>   [Segange]

In the year 1180 a plague-like epidemic of holy fire came again to Lorraine. The afflicted showed gangrenous symptoms of the skin and their limbs fell off; but in some cases they also had convulsions. They filled the streets and the market places with their wailings [Schnurrer].

In England too the holy fire made its appearance; for example, in 1354 and 1373. It appeared repeatedly in Spain until 1400 [Fuchs]. During the thirteenth and fourteenth centuries it recurred in France. Almost without exception the epidemic seems to have occurred in years of terrible famine, ruined harvest, heavy rainfall, etc. [Ehlers]. Boucher has left an account of the epidemics of gangrenous holy fire in Lille and Flanders in the years 1749 and 1750. He recounts how in numerous cases limbs or parts of limbs might fall off when touched. In this epidemic the sickness began with violent painful cramp in the muscles of the arms and legs, and sometimes there were violent contractions of the flexor muscles. The burning sensation was very pronounced in the affected limbs. One might see a foot suddenly part from the body, although the manifest changes and severe pains which preceded this auto-amputation had not lasted more than a day. Many of those whose limbs had fallen away lived, nevertheless, for many years after.

In Normandy the sickness was called St Laurence's Fire, primarily because this martyr's death was by grilling on a grid. But the name which in time became the most common was St Anthony's Fire. One of the most severe epidemics occurred in France between the years 1090 and 1100 when the whole country, but especially the Dauphiné, was ravaged by *ignis sacer*. The relics of St Anthony had been transferred in 1070 from Constantinople to

Dauphiné. In 1093 a son of the Count de la Motte-Saint Didier, who defrayed the costs, was smitten by the holy fire but was treated by the relics of St Anthony. This happened in St Didier de la Motte. Soon afterwards, in 1095, Pope Urban II founded the order of St Anthony with the function of taking care, in the name of the saint, of those afflicted by the fire. From this time the sickness is known more and more by the name of St Anthony's Fire.

FIG. 122. St Anthony Abbas the Hermit. Drawing by P. de Franchis, Venice, 1496. Clothed in the habit of the order with a T-cross, pilgrim's staff and bell. To the right the swine. In the left hand burns the holy fire [Rodenkirchen].

Anthony the Hermit (Figs. 122–124) was born in Egypt about the year 251 and went out while young into the desert, where he lived as a hermit, a teacher of theology and a worker of miracles. He was also one of the Christian founders of the monastic system. During his life in the desert he was exposed to numerous temptations by devils and demons, over all of which he triumphed. These temptations subsequently became the subject of reproduction in the pictures of many artists. Thanks to his steadfastness and his triumph St Anthony the Hermit, or the Abbas as he is also called, is the most prominent of the demon-expelling Catholic saints. The Catholic Church preserves numerous hymns and songs addressed to St Anthony. Some of them may be quoted here, as they are of interest for the medical problems under consideration.

From the year 1331 we have a hymn in which a dance to St Anthony is suggested [*Anal. Hymn.* 55, 69]:

> On this happy pleasant day
> The choristers sing and dance (*tripudio*);
> On this day of triumph
> They bring in special prayer,
> Their praise of St Anthony.
> He who is destroyed by fires of Hell
> Is saved by the virtues of the Saint.

A hymn of the fourteenth century [*Anal. Hymn.* 55, 70]:

> Bringing to the sorrowful,
> To those destroyed by fire,
> The longed-for happiness.
> He conquers devils
> And forces them always
> To be subjects of Christ.

A remarkable hymn which was written at the end of the fourteenth century or the beginning of the fifteenth is of interest because it seems to me to show that St Anthony was invoked not only against the fire, but also against cramp [*Anal. Hymn.* 9, 132]:

> Come, father Anthony,
> And send us a ray
> Of heavenly favour!
> Come, Father of the poor,
> Give healing to the flesh
> And to the wounds of the heart!
> Thou, supreme Comforter,
> Thou drivest away the fire
> By giving coldness;
> The heat in which re-animation
> Is not, is lessened
> By thy grace.
> Make thou the stiffness bend (*morbum rigidum*),
> Transform heat to cold,
> Chasten what is wrong.

It is just these words, *Make thou the stiffness bend* and *Chasten what is wrong*, which I find remarkable. They can scarcely refer to anything but those cramp-like convulsive forms of the sickness in which the tonic and clonic cramps induced stiffness. We shall find that other circumstances support this interpretation.

The holy St Anthony not only freed victims from the fire, he also sent it. According to the teaching of the Church this saint had been entrusted with the care of certain of God's scourges and on His behalf and by His command inflicted punishment. But he was also empowered to mitigate the sentences and to renounce punishment. In 1466 there was an epidemic of the holy fire in Strassburg and neighbourhood [Specklini Collect. No. 2093]. It is stated [*Fragments div. vieilles chron.* No. 4217] that more offerings than usual were made to St Anthony, because he was angry.

During the sixteenth century a hymn was sung to St Anthony [*Anal. Hymn.* 44, 49] as follows:

> To thee the whole earth shall cry out,
> Thou shalt be invoked to expel
> The fiery sickness,
> In order that we may not be consumed
> By the terrible infernal death!
> Stretch out thy hand, guard us against the fiery sickness!

St Anthony the Hermit was usually represented as dressed in the costume of the order of St Anthony, with blue T-cross on his cloak, in his hand a pilgrim's staff, crowned with a similar cross hung with bells, with a pig at his side. Often enough a bell hangs from the head of the pig. Sometimes we see the saint with his herdsman's staff in hand while great flames issue from his feet (Fig. 124). The symbols of St Anthony have been misinterpreted with remarkable frequency in a superficial and stupid manner, and should therefore be explained. It has been said [Segange] that the flames at his feet are the flames of lust, which he so victoriously extinguished by his ascetism;

FIG. 123. Abbot St Anthony the Hermit. From Gersdorff: *Feldtbuch d. Wundarztney*, Strassburg, 1535. Pilgrim's staff, crowned with a T cross and hanging bells. Habit of the order with T cross, the pig at his side. He is invoked by a sufferer from the holy fire, already crippled, from whose left hand flames appear [Ehlers].

that the pig was a symbol of sin, of impure and carnal pleasure, also successfully overcome by the saint, and that it symbolized the right of the members of the Order of St Anthony to have swine feeding around their hospitals and monasteries. There may be some truth in this; but the original meaning is different.

According to the history of the saints by Molanus, published in 1594, St Anthony bears this T cross because he was an Egyptian. Among that people the Christian cross very often assumed the T form. The cross on his staff therefore indicates not only his Egyptian origin but also his rank within the Church and his power to expel demons. This is still further emphasized by the pig. Molanus points out that the pig has the most intimate association with devils, in the sense of the Evangelists when they recount how Christ drove out the evil spirits from those possessed and collected them in a herd of swine. This beast therefore emphasizes that St Anthony has the very special power of expelling devils from the possessed. In the *Acta Sanctorum* it is said, 'For the devils are always symbolized by the swine'. The bells on St Anthony's staff also symbolized his power of exorcizing devils. We may here quote Durandus' explanation from the thirteenth century: 'So we ring the bells, so that the fruits of the earth, just like the soul and the body of the faithful, may be protected and saved; in order that the hosts of the Devil and the attacks of all the demons may be revealed and driven away.' That the flames at the feet of St Anthony really signified the holy fire will be confirmed by the illustrations in this work. St Thomas Aquinas—as early as the thirteenth century—declared that these flames symbolized St Anthony's protection against fire, because to him had been given the patronage of the infernal regions [Segange].

The fire which St Anthony emitted and which ravages mankind so terribly is still called *ignis sacer*, 'the holy fire', sometimes *ignis divina*, 'the divine fire', and sometimes *ignis infernalis*, 'the infernal fire' [Fuchs], sometimes *ignis Gehennae*, 'hell fire' [Evelt, and the above-quoted hymns]. One may wonder how this fire could have acquired such different names. It seems to me that the question can be satisfactorily answered by reference to Edsman's extraordinary dissertation on the baptism of fire. Both the Old and New Testaments, as well as some of the Apocrypha, describe fire as belonging to Paradise. God's dwelling is of fire, the heavenly Temple is aflame with fire, the angels are clothed in fire and every person entering Heaven must be so clothed. Paradise is encompassed by a river of fire and on the last day the whole of creation shall be conducted through this penal, purifying and sanctifying fire in order to behold the glory of God [Peter 3, 7, 10, 12, 13]. The church writer Origenes (quoted from Edsman) explains that 'the Lord Jesus Christ shall then stand in the river of fire amid the flames so that everybody who, after life, wishes to enter into Paradise and needs purification, him He will baptize in the river and send him forth into the future'. It is the same thought as we find in Paul in *Corinthians i*, 3, 13: 'Every man's work shall be made manifest: for the day shall declare it because it shall be revealed by fire, and the fire shall try every man's work of what sort it is.'

One may be saved, but only by fire. Origenes here adds, 'In my opinion we must all ultimately come to this fire. Both Peter and Paul and whosoever it may be, must all come to the fire. But they shall hear the Words: Even though thou dost pass through the fire, the flames shall not burn thee.' These words are from Isaiah 43, 2, 'And thus said the Lord: if thou must pass through the fire thou shalt not be burned and the flames shall not consume thee.'

The Catholic Church has never forgotten the divine fire, which tests, purifies and saves whilst punishing, torturing and consuming evil. This fire has even been presented dramatically. The fire has been made to flame up at the font and it has been even more strongly dramatized at the Whitsun festival. Then, on the reading of the account of the pouring out of the Holy Ghost upon the Apostles, the choristers from the balconies in the church let

FIG. 124. St Anthony Abbas the Hermit. Miniature from *Les Heures d'Anne de Bretagne*. The T-cross on the mantle, th e pig in the background to the right. Great flames rise from the lower folds of the habit of the Order [Mâle].

fall bunches of burning shavings so that they formed a ring of fire round the altar, while the priests seemed to stand in a sea of fire [Veit]. G. F. Young, in his work on the Medici, describes a similar ceremony in Florence: during the Whitsun festival in 1471 a miracle play was performed in the old church of Santo Spirito; fires were kindled round the altar as a symbol of the descent of the Holy Ghost to the Apostles. Unluckily the church was burned to the ground.

This idea of baptism in fire on the last day is also found in the strange sequence of the death mass which was created in the thirteenth century by

Thomas of Celano, *Dies irae, dies illa, solvet saeclum in favilla*, which we find again in our own Book of Psalms.

> The day of wrath and doom impending
> Heaven and earth in ashes ending.
> Worthless are my prayers and sighing
> Yet good Lord, in grace complying
> Rescue me from fires undying.

According to the Apocalypse of Peter—from the beginning of the third century—when man passes through the fire the righteous shall not be harmed. But the unrighteous shall remain in the inferno, where fire shall be their punishment. From the writings of Ephraim Syrian the following may, according to Edsman, be quoted: 'they pass through this fire, which tests the righteous and the sinners, who are there judged. The righteous pass through and the fire cools; when the sinner approaches it flares up.'

In some cases Origenes prefers to describe this heavenly fire primarily as a penal and disciplinary force. When he explains Luke iii, 16 on baptism by fire and water he regards the former as a punishment and a torture. He writes, 'Unhappy will he be, and weep bitterly, who after baptism of the spirit must be baptized in fire'. God is said to be a fire for sinners but a light to the holy (at that time a technical term for Christian). 'But if anyone is spared the second resurrection, then is he a sinner who requires baptism in fire and purification by burning, so that whatever he has of wood, hay and straw may be consumed.'

Thus St Anthony's Fire and all its apparently contradictory appellations are fully explained. It is this heavenly fire, the fire which is a part of God's dwelling and abode, which surrounds Paradise like a river, which St Anthony has been commanded to some extent to control. It is this fire which he sends forth as a trial and a punishment to man. He is able in response to the prayers of the sufferers to lessen or cool the fire, but against the sinner he grows angry and inflames it. For that reason the fire is both holy and divine, and of course invisible, but this fire is at the same time the punishment and discipline of the infernal regions and of hell.

In the year 1597 the medical faculty of Marburg was able to confirm that St Anthony's Fire was caused by seed infected by yarrow [Fletcher]. This is true in so far as the infected seed really was the cause of the holy fire, but it was a different kind of infection. In 1630 Sully's personal physician, Thuillier the Elder, witnessed the ravages of St Anthony's Fire in France. Attention had already been directed to the appearance of ergot in the seed and on the invitation of the French Academy of Science, Thuillier undertook dietetic experiments on hens and was able to prove change in the comb [Ehlers, Barger]. This was further confirmed by the researches of the Medical Academy in Paris [Fletcher].

Ergot is a fungus at a low stage of development, which develops on all sorts of grain but especially on rye (Figs. 125–126). It fastens itself on an ear of rye, like a single dark violet, somewhat bent and oblong in shape. In the Middle Ages the bread which was principally eaten by the poor consisted of rye, or wheat and rye. Until the end of the eighteenth century rye was the principal food in France, Germany and other countries. The first time ergot is mentioned is by Lonicer in his herb book of 1587, where it is recommended for sicknesses of the womb [Barger]. Even today it has its medical uses to

FIG. 125. Ergot on an ear of rye. Consists of the mycelium of the fungus *claviceps purpurea*. It is in this form that it bears the name ergot. *Secale cornutum* [Eberle].

hasten and accentuate pains in the pregnant womb and to stop bleeding after delivery. In districts of France the quantity of ergot present in grain, as late as 1814, was from 33 per cent to 56 per cent, and in the ergot epidemics in Germany in the eighteenth century as high as 33–40 per cent [Barger]. What this means will be understood from the fact that about 0.05 per cent is sufficient to produce symptoms of poisoning.

Ergot is botanically a very remarkable fungus. One might even assert that no other plant or part of a plant is so incredibly potent in highly poisonous elements. Especially is it rich in peculiar alkaloids, which have a paralysing influence on the motor nerves of the sympathetic nerve system, with the result that adrenalin, the secretion which is obtained from the marrow of the kidneys, acquires entirely new powers. Normally it occasions a violent constriction of the blood vessels by a contraction of their walls and thereby causes a rise in blood pressure; under the effect of ergot it is transformed into

304

a substance expanding the blood vessels, with a consequent lowering of the blood pressure. Especially does ergot affect the blood vessels of the stomach, which in turn are the principal regulators of the blood pressure. But the various alkaloids and other substances contained in ergot have other effects also. Some of them cause cramp in the muscles of the smaller blood vessels and induce a tendency in slow moving blood to solidify and cause throm-

FIG. 126. Ergot on ears of rye [Eberle].

bosis. The result is that certain areas of circulation, such as fingers or toes, hands or feet are choked or sealed off, which causes mortification and the shedding of the affected part. One part of the ergot alkaloids paralyses a very important reflex group at the junction of the throat arteries (cârotis-sinus reflex), and by this paralysis the regulation of the blood pressure, which should take place on bodily movement, is impeded. This group of alkaloids also produces a constriction of the delicate muscular system of the respiratory channels, leading to asthmatic conditions and acute shortage of breath. It has not been possible to induce these cramp conditions in animals by ergot poisoning but there is no doubt about its effects on human beings.

They cause the so-called clonic cramps, consisting of swift lightning-like spasms as well as tonic cramps, i.e., persistent violent muscular contractions [Barger, 1938].

It is very curious that ergot poisoning in France and Spain was the principal cause of these gangrenic epidemics, the holy fire, whereas in Germany, Sweden and elsewhere it led to cramps. But no strict schematic division is possible. The cramp epidemics in Germany were not infrequently associated with gangrenous changes and not infrequently in France the holy fire produced characteristic symptoms of cramp. But there is an evident difference, which can be fully explained by the consideration that the plants in question developed differences in the percentage content of ergot poison according to climatic and botanical variations, as also in the presence of alkaloids. Thus ergot in some countries contains alkaloids which in other countries are missing. Different years also yield different and varying composition of the chemical constituents of ergot.

St Anthony's Fire was nothing but ergot poisoning. Ergot flourished best in rainy summers preceded by severe winters. This explains why St Anthony's Fire occurred during such years. Four months after harvesting ergot is much less poisonous, after another four months it is practically innocuous.

XXIII

Dance Epidemics and Ergotism

THE first description of ergotism—convulsive ergotism—is afforded, according to Berger, by Balde Ronsseus, who in his medical letters of 1590 described a new and hitherto unknown disease which occurred in 1581 in the Duchy of Lüneberg. Somewhat later there is an account of convulsive disease occurring in the years 1587–88 in Silesia, a typical ergotism which is described as *das Kromme*, i.e., 'the crooked'. On the other hand the epidemic in Westphalia, Hesse and Cologne in 1596 was called *Kriebelkrankheit*, which points to the initial symptoms of crawling sensation and of itching hands. The disease was also called cramp, ergotism, pestilential cramp, etc. The cause was already supposed to be infected bread or hunger [Hecker]. This ergotism, like gangrene, first attacked the poor, nearly always during years of heavy rainfall when famine was also rife. As a rule the epidemic broke out in August and September and never lasted more than a year [Hecker, Hoven, Sprengel]. Haase relates that this disease appeared as early as 1577 in Hessen and was recognized as such.

It was at this time—the last quarter of the sixteenth century—that the real dance epidemics completely ceased. Only isolated cases, with one or two participants, are found thereafter. The great epidemic dances disappear from the accounts of chroniclers and medical writers, and the reason must be that medical men had begun to understand that the phenomenon was caused by some special diseased condition and to realize where the cause was to be found. They therefore devoted special medical care to the sick, so far as this was possible with the existing knowledge of diseases and their cures. The patients were no longer regarded as 'dancing night and day'; they were sick with cramp convulsions and they no longer turned to the religious dance or invoked the help of the saints in driving out evil or sought by an imitation of the heavenly dance to expel the devil-inspired dance of the demons. Neither must we forget that in the second decade of the sixteenth century Luther's Protestant theses were nailed to the doors of churches in the Rhine province. The opposition to the Catholic Church flamed up just in these areas, where the ground had been so well and so long prepared both by the mystics and pietists within the Church and by the numerous heretical sects, which had so gladly raised the banner of revolt. Churches were stormed, monks and nuns expelled, paintings in the churches were destroyed and images of saints smashed to pieces, etc. The Reformation grew and spread, and the old faith in the saints and relics in many places weakened. As a result of all these circumstances the diseased condition which had hitherto appeared in the form of a dance epidemic was now diagnosed in medical terms and was left more and more to the care of the doctors.

Let us now look at the symptoms which characterize ergotism, the disease which in my opinion was the chief cause of the dance epidemics. We ought to pay special attention to the early medical accounts of the symptoms of the sickness, because three doctors had the opportunity to observe the symptoms of a severe form of poisoning which, when the danger of the ergot became known, no one could observe again. But we should remember that from the middle of the sixteenth century St Vitus' dance included various kinds of sickness giving rise to constrictions and cramps, so that the diagnosis of the causes of St Vitus' dance becomes much more difficult and confused. It seems to have been Gesnerus who started the confusion when in 1551 he declared that the bite of a mad dog was the cause.

We shall now briefly describe the symptoms of ergotism before surveying the symptoms of the St Anthony and the St Vitus dances.

In his book *On Fevers*, 1658, Sennert writes fully on ergotism. It begins, he says, with twitches and a feeling of numbness of the hands and feet, followed suddenly by violent cramps, first in the fingers and toes, then in the arms, knees, shoulder muscles and the whole body. The patient falls down, folds up the whole body and then stretches out on the floor. All this is accompanied by excruciating pain, loud cries and screams. The illness continues for days or weeks. Some become epileptic and after their attack are as if dead for six or eight hours; others are dazed, sleepy and sluggish; others again become dizzy. Some become blind, deaf or lame. According to Hecker, Sennert's account of the sickness follows the account of the great ergotism epidemic published by the medical faculty of Marburg in 1597.

In the years 1770 and 1771, in the Duchy of Lüneberg, there was a very serious epidemic of ergotism which was also the subject of several medical reports. According to Taube it began at the end of August. The illness lasted with some patients for a fortnight and with others for six months. In its milder form the patient felt heavy in arms and legs as if numb for several days, strength declined and the sense of depression was severe. There was a creeping sensation in the skin, a form of irritation of the sensitory nerves. In the muscles there were rapid twitches which after some days

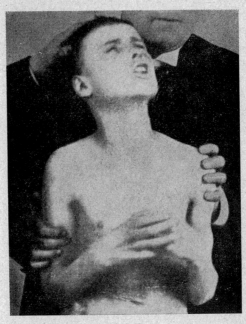

FIG. 127. Ergotism. Hungary, early twentieth century. Cramp in the muscles of the face, neck, arms and hands [Barger, 1931]

became more severe. Then came dizziness and discomfort in the region of the heart. The cramps became more violent, and twitchings and constrictions of the face muscles accompanied them. The patients grimaced. In this epidemic the patients broke out into a sweat. Upon this followed coma. In severe cases came cramp; the muscles remained contracted, fingers or toes bent, hands clenched or elbow joints bent, feet were outstretched or pointed down, etc. The patients could not walk on their heels, but only on their toes. Any violent sensation intensified the cramps. If occasionally the cramp relaxed a new attack followed upon any form of excitement. The psychic symptoms were increased irritability, sensory instability and quarrelsomeness. During periods when the sickness receded and relative calm prevailed there remained a trembling and shaking of all the limbs. This condition might persist for weeks after the twitchings had disappeared. In this toxic condition real epilepsy might ensue and one of the most serious consequences of the disease was madness. It set in when the cramp gave way. This mental confusion might persist from four to six weeks and yet be cured. In many cases idiocy remained as an after-effect of poisoning. In serious cases ergotism might lead to mortification, with gangrenous blisters on the body, especially on hands and toes. Large areas of skin might peel off, muscles and sinews be exposed. Wichmann adds, concerning this epidemic, that the stomach was sometimes swollen and he describes how by changes in the cramped condition of the muscles the patients made slow movements and contortions of the body. The kind of epilepsy which ensued was not, however, typical; the

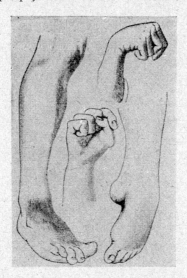

FIG. 128. Cramps in ergotism. Oberhessen, mid-nineteenth century. Cramp of the muscles of the feet, toes, hands and fingers. Especially characteristic is the cramp in the muscles of the calf, which forces the foot to point downwards [Barger, 1931].

attacks were especially violent, with frenzy and pronounced psychic obfuscation. From the account of the ergotism epidemic in Marburg in 1597 he also relates how the sick cried aloud and wailed in their cramps, and complained of the icy cold which they suffered in spite of the burning heat which tortured them.

There is anonymous evidence that in 1770–71 the sick also suffered from cramp of the chest muscles; the chest was contracted, the stomach swollen and they complained of shortage of breath. Another anonymous source relates that the epidemic really began in 1767 and continued until 1770. To all the other symptoms he adds a pronounced asthma. When the sickness was prolonged, blindness and deafness ensued; others 'suffered the evil which is called St Vitus' dance'. Frequently all these symptoms were accompanied by a violent fever, from which the patient usually died. Mortality was considerable and death usually occurred as a result of the frequent convulsions.

In Sweden, too, ergotism has a long history. There are accounts of its appearance especially in the eighteenth century. Ilmoni has collected a considerable amount of material relating to ergotism epidemics in Northern Sweden. The disease appeared in Sweden in 1741; in 1745 it was found in Älvsborg county, in 1746 in Västergötland, Småland and Blekinge, in 1747 again in Älvsborg, in 1754 in the greater part of Southern Sweden, in 1756 in Östergötland, in 1763 in Jönköping county, in 1765 in Småland, in 1769 again in Jönköping, etc. Only in so far as in certain of these epidemics the disease was accompanied by a burning of the skin is there any suggestion of a connexion with the holy fire. But if we go back to the Middle Ages we can safely assert that the holy fire already existed in Sweden. Hedqvist relates that the St Anthony order established its hospitals in Sweden in which the sufferers were tended by the monks, called Tonnisherrar in Sweden. During the epidemic of 1754 it happened that the sufferers, because of extreme heat, attempted to throw themselves into the water, or else, because of the icy cold, into the fire. These details are given by Rothman, who adds that cramps might attack the chest muscles and impair breathing, that the sufferers wished to die. This epidemic affected Småland and Blekinge and returned in 1755. One of the symptoms was a malodorous perspiration, reminiscent of the English sweat. Heiligtag describes a similar epidemic in 1745 in Älvsborg county. The sickness began when people first ate the new bread of the year, i.e., at the end of August, and the beginning of September. The sufferers threw themselves on the ground in convulsions and were mentally confused; they tried to throw themselves into fire or water or against the walls of their houses.

Perhaps the last epidemic of ergotism occurred in 1841 in a couple of Småland parishes. Sondén rightly refers to it as the medieval St Vitus' dance. It began with sudden cramps in various parts of the body, especially the arms and shoulders, and with a kind of suffocation that developed into a violent gasping for breath. Thereafter the cramp recurred daily. Sköldberg mentions that the cramp also attacked the muscles of the throat and vocal chords. Contrary to the medical opinion of the time, people in the vicinity rightly thought that this was ergotism. The sufferers became mentally confused, dizzy and torpid. This mental confusion, combined with certain historical circumstances, led to the belief that these hallucinations had a religious content, that the activation of their thought related to ultimate things, penal sentences, etc., which enabled the sufferers to preach, for which reason the disease also acquired the name 'Preacher's Disease'. During an attack the victims experienced great pain; the twitchings were violent and were accompanied by grotesque distortions and contortions of the face, stomach and extremities. Frequently they leapt and hopped so violently that they could not remain seated or in their bed. *Anything which disturbed the mind or imagination of the sufferers induced and greatly intensified these spasms.* The victims frequently spoke of visions of heaven and hell and of the angels. Sometimes they had longer or shorter periods of prophetic vision, with a strong sense of anguish and unrest, heaviness and pain in the head and limbs, difficult breathing, soreness and burning in the chest, etc. Billengren, the provincial doctor in Ljungby, says that the attacks resembled epilepsy and consisted of violent bodily contortions. Curiously the preaching of the sufferers was directed against shallowness and vanity, with disapproval of fine clothes, buttons, mother-of-pearl, glass, red clothing and brandy. It is confirmed that during this epidemic the grain was more than usually rich in ergot. As much as 25 per cent was found in certain samples.

Hecker gives a comprehensive survey of ergotism symptoms. It is founded on the eighteenth-century epidemics. Wherever the disease was more or less general practically all the inhabitants of a village were attacked. They all began with the peculiar sensation already described, creeping in the skin, numbness and narcosis. In some the disease stopped at this stage and an improvement set in. With others there was a sensation of cold, twitches and sweating, extremely painful cramp in the limbs, especially in the reflex muscles, and vomiting. The attack continued for some hours, after which the sufferers were exhausted, quiet and calm, but with a frenzied increase of sensitiveness. They could now work, but were soon subject to new attacks. The fingers and toes were dead. Nothing but hard work, which put the blood into more rapid circulation, improved their condition. Epileptic symptoms soon appeared. Then the sufferers became confused; their speech was scarcely intelligible owing to cramp in the muscles of the tongue, followed by twitchings and cramp-like contortions of the body. Vomiting and diarrhoea ensued; the intestines showed rapid signs of gangrenous decay.

During the last years of the sixteenth century it was thought, as has already been said, that the cause of *ignis sacer* was to be found in impure bread and in hunger. During the eighteenth century proof accumulated that ergotism, gangrene and the holy fire were due to ergot. But there were many other guesses; for example, the cause was sought in the composition of the air or in the combinations of grain with various weeds, etc. Most people were agreed, however, that the cause of the disease lay in the grain. Linnaeus, with all his authority, was of the opinion that it was a combination with Raphanus, turnip radish, which caused ergotism, and for this reason the disease was for a long time called Raphania [Rothman].

Modern accounts of ergotism and its causes are to be found in Barger, though he has of course not much to add to what the eighteenth-century writers told us. Blindness or affected eyesight sometimes produced by the poison was due to cataract, i.e., opacity of the lens. He emphasizes that the two forms—holy fire and ergotism—were not so very different in their symptoms, but that they frequently revealed more or less similar ones, and that typical blending also occurred. It has, however, been insisted that ergot alone cannot produce the cramp conditions of ergotism but that there must also have been a lack of certain vitamins, supposedly vitamin A. The investigations do not appear convincing and other investigators have insisted that in normal cases there might be some poison in the rye which might produce such changes in the central system as to explain the cramps.

311

But these investigations are not fully satisfactory either. It may be imagined that lack of vitamin B especially, and possibly of other vitamins, could have contributed to the incidence of ergotism, for it is clear that it only appeared in those years in which, owing to climatic conditions, the harvests were ruined and hunger and famine afflicted the population. What is certain, however, is that ergot, even as regards ergotism, was the most important cause.

In the early summers of 1828 and 1829 there occurred in France, especially in Paris, epidemics which ended each autumn or mid-winter. It revealed disturbances in the intestinal canal but more especially nervous and skin symptoms. After the preliminary period of eight or ten days the symptoms of nervous disease appeared. There were contractions of groups of muscles, combined with severe pains. Breathing became difficult and elderly patients relapsed into intense diarrhoea and sweating. This disease has been called acrodynia because it mainly attacked hands and feet. Numerous patients flocked to the hospitals, suffering severe pains in their hands and still more in their feet. The skin was very red [Littré]. *La grande Encyclopédie* relates that the year 1828 was very rainy and that the grain harvest was poor. If one compares this brief account of the symptoms of acrodynia with the Meige picture already referred to, where the pilgrim sufferers danced before St James, then I think we may venture the guess that the acrodynia of 1828 was also an ergotism epidemic. And the remarkable thing is that they tried to cure ergotism, ergot poisoning, in the old way—by dancing before the image of a saint.

One of the most recent epidemics occurred in 1880 in Frankenberg [Jahrmärker]. It was principally of the cramp type, but gangrene also occurred. The sufferers had attacks resembling epilepsy and occasionally made movements like those of the choreomaniacs. Most of them showed great weakness in the lower extremities; they were unable to stand upright. Cramp in the vocal chords, with changes in the general character of the voice, also appeared. Sometimes cramp in the breathing muscles was observed, and in the muscles of the waist and the stomach. The great majority of the sufferers revealed mental disturbances, with unrest and anxiety.

In the foregoing we have seen varying evidence of the conceptions of the old chroniclers and medical writers regarding the medical character of the dance epidemics. Nevertheless, they did not get beyond the names, mania, madness, mental aberration and so on. We find also the name epilentia, which is probably a mis-spelling of 'epilepsia', i.e., epilepsy. Freigius thought that the epidemic of 1374 was not caused by black gall but by the blood. Plater reminds us that some Arabian physicians described the disease as a 'disposition of the limbs to dance', and thought that it must be regarded as a kind of convulsion, but he thinks that it is from the mental confusion that the primary urge to the dance arises, 'except in so far', he adds, 'as this disorderly hopping is not in some way implanted by the Devil and with God's permission has been inflicted as a punishment for man because he has sinned by dancing'. Sennert describes St Vitus' dance as delirium and madness, and as due to natural causes and diseased bodily fluids. But he admits the possibility that it may also be due to devils 'with God's approval'. Willis thinks that by dancing the sufferers succeeded in avoiding serious consequences, but testifies that both the people and worthy upholders of the Faith believe that sorcery could produce such effects. Profius thinks that it is the animal soul which, by influencing the limbs, compelled this dancing and hopping. Dolaeus, who in 1685 had under observation for seven years in the district of Nürnberg those who suffered from St Vitus' dance, tells the physicians that the sickness was vermicular. Bodinus says quite simply that it were best to let the dance continue. Zwingerus shares the view that St Vitus' dance was the result of some mental desire to dance; but he also thinks that this desire was caused by an irritation of the nerves of the brain. The desire was a sort of mental confusion and dancing was of the real nature of this disease. Ultimately it was conditioned by the volatile salt which had entered the blood, and this salt came from diseased grain; alternatively the disease was caused by something supernatural having entered the blood, or by sorcery or exorcisms. Tulpius likens St Vitus' dance to both hydrophobia (he agrees there with the view of Gesnerus, expressed a century earlier) and Italian tarantism. Junckerus denies this resemblance and is of opinion that St Vitus' dance—or, as some call it, St Modestus' dance, after St Vitus' teacher and fellow martyr—was a convulsive disease of a special kind.

But most significant in the earlier literature, something which is reflected in the writers just quoted, is the explanation given of St Vitus' dance by Aureolus Philippus Theophrastus Bombastus von Hohenheim, called Paracelsus. He was opposed to the general conception of epilepsy as being caused by devils and sought the causes in the brain, heart, liver, intestines and limbs (*de morbis amentium*). Mania and insanity are only a change in the mind and senses, and it may disappear of itself and allow reason to return. In his book, *On the Art of Healing*, he devoted a chapter to St Vitus' dance, and expressed the view that the saints had nothing at all to do with sickness. Behind such a belief there was only faith but no observation. He therefore described St Vitus' dance as a sort of *chorea lasciva*, or as *æstimativa*, a light-headed dance, with its cause in imagination and feeling. But there was a further cause in the 'laughing arteries', from which arose an irresistible laughter. But St Vitus had not sent this plague; it arose from the levity of the victims' senses and the weakness of their wills. But there was also an enforced dance (*chorea coacta*) which had its origin in human nature. As to the means of curing St Vitus' dance, Paracelsus fell back upon the ancient magic of the earliest periods of human history, Babylonian, Egyptian, Greek and Roman. His advice was this: the patient should make an image of himself in wax or resin; he must with the help of his own thought transfer to the image all his conceptions, thoughts and feelings and then cast the image in the fire and let it burn. Nothing must be left of the image. With the image would also be destroyed all the harmful thoughts and feelings of the sufferer. But if the dance were due to some inner levity, then the dancer must be confined in darkness and fast on bread and water for a longer period in an unpleasant place and without receiving any pity. Thereby he would be changed in his nature and his thoughts; the unchaste thoughts would vanish, the blood would circulate again, the mind would be calmed and through sorrow and depression the laughter would cease, and with it the dancing. Paracelsus was not opposed to physical force but he thought it better to throw the patients into cold water. The dance, which results from nature itself (*chorea naturalis*), or the laughing blood vessels, should be treated with such medicines as fluid gold, precious stones, the quintessence of mandragora, oil and water in which real pearls have been steeped, the quintessence of opium, the water of life (essence of spirits from precious stones), etc.

In the year 1526 Paracelsus was in Strassburg [Sticker]. As we may remember, in 1518 the great dancing epidemic raged there and excited much surprise and terror. It is very probable that Paracelsus shared that experience. Moreover in his father's library at Einsiedeln he possessed Trithemius' writings with their accounts of the epidemic of 1374. From Strassburg Paracelsus went back to Bâle, but afterwards he revisited Alsace shortly before 1529. The two books from which we now quote are *Volumen Paramirium* and *Opus Paramirium*, which were published by Paracelsus in 1526 and 1531 respectively.

In the *Volumen Paramirium* he intensified his magic-mystical views of the image and its effects. If an image were made and buried and covered with stones, then the person must carry a heavy burden. And this burden he will feel just in the places where the stones were especially heavy and that person would not live long. When the image had been finally destroyed then his life would be ended too. But if a bone of the image were broken then the person represented would suffer a broken bone. This is true also of pricks and the like. 'Therefore it is also possible for me by my own will to force myself into the spirit of my enemy and then to break him or tame him as I wish in my image.' In the same way it was possible to lay a curse on images, so that they were seized with disease, fever, epilepsy, paralysis, etc. He thought the same applied to paintings.

These early sixteenth-century theories have a special interest with reference to all the votive gifts of which we have already spoken, which at Zabern were offered by the choreomaniacs in the shape of small human figures, and which we shall encounter as offerings to St Anthony by those suffering from the holy fire or from ergotism or St Vitus' dance. The influence which the saint exercised over the image would reach the sufferer by the mysterious magic which Paracelsus, in spite of all his talk of objective natural science, described with sympathetic approval.

In his *Opus Paramirium* Paracelsus described the origin and cause of St Vitus' dance, i.e., the Strassburg dance. 'Mistress Trophaca was the first to suffer from this disease. She was peculiarly loud voiced. Once when in anger she quarrelled with her husband, when he asked something of her which she did not want to do, then she behaved as if she were ill and pretended an illness which suited her. She began to dance and pretended that she must dance whatever happened, because nothing annoyed her husband more than just dancing. In order to make the deception as perfect as possible and really give the impression of illness she hopped and sang, which was all most distasteful to her husband. When she had ceased dancing she fell to the ground, which terrified her husband; then she twitched and fell asleep. This she declared to be her illness and carefully concealed the fact that she was making a fool of her husband. Then other women began to do the same thing, informing each other of the trick. Then finally the public came to believe that this sickness was a punishment from heaven. Owing to the symptoms of the sickness people began to look for the causes in order to drive it out. At first the faithful believed that it was Mager, a pagan spirit, which was the cause of this disease. But faith soon endowed St Vitus with the spirit which caused the sickness. He became an idol and after him the sickness was called St Vitus' dance.' If one disregards the scorn and mockery, the deliberately ridiculous embroideries and foolish assertions, then the accounts of the woman's dance symptoms—cramp followed by epileptic-like attacks and sleep—show extremely well what really happened. We remember that according to Imlins and Duntzenheim's chronicles the sickness really did begin with one single woman.

At the beginning of the nineteenth century we glimpse the correct solution of the problem of the dancing epidemics. But the problem is very confused because for centuries people had defined almost anything as St Vitus' dance, and not least the disease which nowadays we call choreomania and which has nothing whatever in common with St Vitus' dance. In this connexion, however, what is most interesting is what the writers say about the old St Vitus' dance. These writers are guilty of a curious mistake when, in agreement with Hoven (in his handbook of practical medicine), they say that Bzovius had stated that the sufferers in the epidemic of 1374 were conducted to St Vitus in the monastery of Korbey. There is no such statement in Bzovius nor in any single one of the old chronicles. St Vitus as a protecting saint against dancing frenzy appears for the first time in connexion with the epidemic in Strassburg in 1518. Until then, in so far as the dance had any specific name at all, it was called St John's dance. So when Hoven institutes a comparison between choreomania (*chorea minor*) and the original St Vitus' dance he advances as the most important differential diagnostic fact that the dancing sickness was never epidemic and did not continue during sleep, whilst the exact opposite was the case in the epidemics. It is also emphasized that the former did not cause death, though the latter frequently did so. For this reason Hoven thinks that these epidemics were perhaps ergotism, caused by ergot, Raphanus (turnip radish), Loleum, Agrostemma, Nigella, etc. But he does not fully accept this view. His opinions are repeated later by Sprengel, Bernt, Haase and Richter. Both Richter and Haase point out that in severe cases of ergotism the blood vessels of the stomach are filled with a

315

blackish blood and the stomach itself filled more or less with an evil-smelling serum. Wilhelm rejects the theory of a connexion between the old dance epidemics and ergotism and thinks that the cause is to be found rather in psychic conditions, that it was some psychic infection. Other writers in the early eighteenth century surmised epilepsy, convulsions, laming by hydrophobia, etc. [Wilhelm]. Boersch also was of the opinion that the dance was due to psychological causes, nervous disturbances of a convulsive kind and imitative infection. 'They were regarded as possessed of devils and in order to deliver mankind from them they were publicly burned at the stake, for the true edification of the faithful'—an elaborate untruth. Krauss included St Vitus' dance among the neurotic diseases.

In the year 1832 Hecker published the first scientific work entirely devoted to choreomania as a medieval disease. It was very highly esteemed and was translated into various languages. And yet he did not attempt any explanation of the deeper nature of the phenomenon. He seemed to regard it as hysteria, mental derangement and imposture. Wicke subsequently added a many-sided account in continuation of Hecker's works, but he was unable to separate the dance epidemics from a number of other diseases with cramp-like symptoms, so that he was forced to reject any idea of the old dance epidemics being identical with ergotism. He also considered that the epidemics were in part caused by deception and partly by madness induced by superstition. Haeser thought that the epidemics were partly ordinary St Vitus' dance, and partly the psychic ecstasy which occurred in periods of famine and disease. Mysticism and religious fanaticism also contributed. Further, he shared the view that the choreomaniacs and the flagellants were to that extent peculiar, that they were a religious sect opposed to the clergy and the Church, considering themselves 'threatened with a descent into the abyss of their sins, into the abyss of their blood-burdened conscience'.

In more modern times it is Martin who has sought the solution of this old riddle. He has left a detailed account of the dance epidemics as revealed by the chronicles and the earliest writers on medicine. Martin was the first to see clearly that dancing was not only a disease but also a means of curing disease. The dance was an attempt at healing. But he described this dance sickness as hysteria and explained that the insane also took part. It must have been maniacs and incurably mad people, mad youths of the katatone type, as well as ordinary choreomaniacs and epileptics who made up the hosts of the dance epidemics. Martin interprets Brueghel's picture of the choreomaniacs at Moelenbeek as showing an epileptic-like cramp of an hysterical kind. In his view the St John's dance or the St Vitus' dance, on their respective festivals, arose from the false idea that dance sickness in the broadest sense could be cured by dancing. Some superstitious people found themselves compelled to dance every year, believing that otherwise they would be smitten with the dance disease and the spiritually weak could, weeks beforehand, sense certain premonitory symptoms in their limbs.

316

Let us now survey the essential symptoms of the epidemic dancers as described by the chroniclers and early writers.

In the epidemic of 1021 part of a dancer's arm fell off, apparently without any bleeding. At the end of the dance the dancers fell into a prolonged and apparent coma, in which four persons died, whilst the others for the rest of their lives were plagued with tremors and shudders. In Wales in 1237, 1,200 persons afflicted with bodily disease took part in the dance; they suddenly collapsed and were seized with madness and cramp-like movements of the arms and legs.

The children who danced from Erfurt to Arnstadt in 1237 were exhausted on arrival, collapsed into sleep and were plagued for the rest of their lives by tremors.

The dancers in the epidemic of 1374 were no longer fully conscious during the dance; towards its end they were afflicted with pain and discomfort in the chest; they had hallucinations and howled. When the dance was over they collapsed upon the ground [Herenthal], crying out that they were going to die, because they felt horrible pains [de Rivo]. When the demon arose in their stomachs they suffered painfully and had terrible expressions on their faces [*Liége Chronicle*]. During the dancing and hopping they fell unconscious after hallucinations [John of Leyden]. When, after hopping, they fell headlong to the ground they suffered the most violent pains. On their visit to the church they raised inarticulate cries. Possibly it was a case of madness or epilentia [Zanfliet]. During the dance they seemed out of their senses [*Flemish Chronicle*]. They collapsed foaming at the mouth [*Old Belgian Chronicle*]. After the dance they fell to the ground and grovelled on their backs; they had to be massaged and the spectators had to stand on their stomachs and dance and trample on them [*Cologne Annals*]. When the sickness first came upon them they had a curious feeling in the body. They screamed in a terrifying way. During the dance they would suddenly throw themselves to the ground and grovelled on their backs. As a rule they recovered in ten days [Koelhoff]. They suffered from confusion, madness and frenzy and made strange movements of the body and displayed in church the strange unrest of their bodies. They raised wild and terrible howls and wailed over their internal pains, even when not dancing. According to ancient custom people compressed their stomachs and midriff with hands and feet and with all the weight of their bodies. After eight to ten days they recovered their health, but many died. [*The Chronicles of the Early Roman Kings and Emperors*.] They fell to the ground as if out of their senses [Gobelinus]. They appeared like madmen [*Annales Fossenenses*]. First they fell down frothing; then they danced [Bzovius]. Whether asleep or awake, when the moment came they had to dance. The disease lasted nine or ten days [*Metz Chronicle*]. In the beginning they were alarmed and terrified and the heart was affected in a curious way, though they could not understand the cause [*Flemish Chronicle* and *Annals*]. They were seized with mental aberration and threw themselves into the Rhine or other rivers in their frenzy. They had a terrifying appearance. They foamed at the mouth and threw themselves to the ground [Schenk à Grafenberg]. They suffered from delirium and mania [Camerarius]. It was a mad frenzy and their minds were confused; even during sleep the movements of the body continued; they trembled and all the time seemed as if compelled to continue hopping [Plater]. The suffering was a maniacal obfuscation. The sufferers fell down breathless and the stomach was distended [Mezeray].

The complex of symptoms is so great, so embroidered and so characteristic that there is no need to make a comparison with the symptoms of ergotism already described in detail, or with those of the holy fire. The similarity is overwhelming and the only possible diagnosis is this: *the victims of the dance epidemics were poisoned by ergot*. It was also extremely probable that it was ergot which caused the hitherto so mysterious 'English sweat' or *sudor anglicus*. This latter appeared in England and Germany in 1517–18, but also in other countries. It raged in Strassburg in 1517. There was a famine at the same time [*Fragments div. vielles Cron*. No. 3977]. Fincelius mentions that in 1518 this English sweating sickness ravaged Germany and especially Brabant. Four hundred persons died of it in Antdorff in three days. And the sickness was of long duration. Ergot has played a fateful and terrifying rôle in human history and has caused the most severe epidemic diseases, including the holy fire, dance epidemics, English sweat and ergotism, and the mortality was at times enormous.

The story from Kölbigk in 1021, according to which part of an arm fell from a woman and was later preserved in the St Magnus church, is clearly not unreasonable. Descriptions of the holy fire often afford information concerning extremities, fingers or toes, falling off unnoticed, and without bleeding. The blood vessels were in part very much contracted and in part to a great extent choked by clots of blood. We have also seen from other, earlier, accounts how, as a sort of offering and recognition of a life saved, parts of limbs which had fallen off were hung upon the images of saints. The apparently pronounced legendary character of the account from Kölbigk is therefore, from a medical point of view, quite reasonable in this curious detail.

The accounts of how in the epidemic of 1374 the dancers let the spectators strike their stomachs with clenched fists or kick them with their feet, or trample on their stomachs when they fell down, aroused wonder at the time and still does so. The sufferers complained during the dance, still more when it was finished, of violent internal pains; they had to be laced with broad ribbons and cloths round the stomach. In order to tighten these bindings a wooden pin or stick was inserted in the knots and twisted. It was these cloths and sticks which they left behind in the churches as votive offerings when they were cured. They used also to scream that if they were not helped in this bandaging they felt they would die. The explanation is to be found in the manner in which several of the ergot poisons work. The pronounced stagnation of the blood vessels of the stomach, with subsequent distension, which, as has been said, has been confirmed by post-mortems, causes a

318

lowering of the blood pressure. The ergot poisons also cause a contraction of the small muscles of the throat, so that a kind of asthma ensues. These two circumstances, low blood pressure and contraction of the throat muscles, cause a shortage of breath with all its consequences of anxiety and malaise in the region of the heart. Nowadays we know also that in muscular exertion and all bodily effort an increased quantity of adrenalin is given off by the gland, which in combination with other factors induces contraction of the muscles in the major blood vessel areas and then a raising of the blood pressure. But in ergot poisoning the reaction is not the same. The adrenalin no longer has its normal effect, but causes instead a distension of the vessels and a lowering of the blood pressure. Our experience of ergotism has shown us that muscular effort, at any rate for the moment, improves the subjective condition of the patient. We may therefore assume that the 1374 choreomaniacs really made the observation that bodily effort improved the subjective condition and for *that reason found in dancing the means which would obviously cause an improvement*, and perhaps a cure. Simultaneously, however, the blood pressure fell violently, the blood vessels of the stomach were filled with blood in quantities which interrupted the normal circulation; as a result the heart pumped insufficient blood, the tissues received too little oxygen and a sense of suffocation became pronounced. In these various ways there must have occurred a very distinct shortage of breath, a sensation of suffocation and of great pain in the region of the heart. All these symptoms, which the chroniclers described in connexion with the dance, especially at its conclusion, are very easily explained by the direct and indirect effects of ergot poisoning. The lowered blood pressure could then be raised in two ways. By moderate blows on the stomach a reflex mechanism affected a raising of the blood pressure, which was, however, transitory. The second method, according to which spectators danced or trampled on the stomach of the sufferer was more effective, but the binding of the stomach with bands and cloths must have been an especially effective means of improving the condition of the patient. Tight bandages round the stomach, with bending and pressing, forced the blood back into circulation. The blood pressure rose—very considerably—the action of the heart improved, the supply of oxygen was increased and the sensation of suffocation, anxiety and dizziness was removed.

When the sufferers fell down or threw themselves to the ground, clearly they were often more or less unconscious, suffered violent pains and 'crawled on their backs'. In the process they often foamed at the mouth and sometimes, perhaps, the stomach was distended—quite in accord with the observed symptoms of both ergotism and holy fire. Sometimes, no doubt, they foamed at the mouth before falling down. This no doubt varied from time to time. Their crawling on their backs can scarcely mean anything else but that they were seized with cramps, both spasms and contractions, very like epilepsy.

Their wild, terrifying expressions may perhaps indicate cramp in the muscles of the face, combined with contortions ... made wild and horrifying shouts, and inarticulate scream... ... as of the description of ergotism in which the ergot poisons reached the tongue and vocal chords. They could not bear to see weeping, and sufferers from ergotism also found their conditions worsened by mental strain.

The sufferers had certain premonitory symptoms of their sickness: curious bodily sensations, a sense of fright, fear and anxiety, all in accord with the pre-symptoms of ergotism with its creeping sensation, the feeling of numbness in the limbs, anxiety, depression and unrest.

The choreomaniacs made strange bodily movements, expressive of a curious bodily discomfort. Whether awake or asleep they were driven to dance. The bodily movements continued during sleep and the sufferers trembled incessantly, as if forced to hop. All this is typical of ergot poisoning and its cramp-like twitchings, especially the symptoms during sleep. The mental confusion and madness is depicted by all as an especially typical feature, and this psychic fog led to pronounced hallucinations: the sufferers saw marvels in heaven, they say heaven open, and the Son of Mary; they imagined themselves wading in blood. Mental derangement and hallucinations are characteristic of advanced ergot poisoning.

Very remarkable is the statement by Schenk à Grafenberg that the sufferers in their dementia sought to cast themselves into the Rhine and other rivers. It is by no means unreasonable to suppose that this happened; the history of ergotism, not least in Sweden, confirms that such things might happen to the sufferers. But this information has another and a greater interest: it shows with a high degree of probability that the sufferers experienced an intense feeling of fever, as of a fire burning in the skin. This is a symptom of ergotism, but also, though in a higher degree, of the holy fire. We have seen already that these two forms of ergot poisoning may pass over to the other, or that both may occur in one and the same person. We shall soon notice quite credible evidence in support of the view that the dancers really did have these symptoms and that they feared that their sickness might become that of the holy fire.

Concerning the Zürich epidemic of 1418 we learn only that the women wanted 'more air', which seems to point to a pronounced shortness of breath. During the epidemic in the same city in 1452 the helper of the dancing sufferer invoked the curse of epilepsy on the jeering spectators. It seems probable that he would scarcely have invoked just this curse—there were many others—if he had not considered that it was a case of epilepsy; it was obvious that he wished to call down on the spectators the same evil as that from which the dancer suffered.

We are informed that in the Strassburg epidemic of 1518 the sufferers danced in their madness day and night until they fell down prostrate [Klein-lavveln]; that they suffered from a special kind of cramp [Schiltern]; that they were insensate and that they were bent double [city minutes].

Of the middle and end of the sixteenth century it is related that the sufferers hopped and danced in a peculiar way, contorting their bodies whilst snorting and gasping. They lay down on the ground, contorted their bodies and sometimes were quite motionless in prolonged sleep [Fincelius]. The woman who danced in Bâle about 1550 went on hopping even in sleep and the prelate who fell sick revealed psychic obfuscation and cramps; his body moved as if dancing [Plater].

Peter Brueghel's paintings of the epidemic in Moelenbeek in 1564 afford us valuable information concerning the cramps of the sufferers. We have already analysed them, and it is evident that these cramp symptoms accord very closely with those of ergotism; especially important is the down-pointed foot caused by cramp in the muscles of the calf.

In the Breisgau epidemic of the seventeenth century the women dancers were mad and had shown premonitory symptoms, such as anxiety, shyness and pricking and shooting pains in the body [Schenk à Grafenberg]. In Geislingen the dancers were demented, had cramp-like movements of the limbs, and fell down during the dance. The premonitory symptoms were heaviness in the head, a tired feeling and cramp in the limbs [Horstius].

The illustration of the dance epidemic in the Paris district, probably in 1829, shows cramps in the body muscles, the muscles of the face and the down-pointed foot.

The conclusion seems to me inevitable: the dance epidemics were caused by ergot poisoning, arising from its frequent appearance in immoderate quantities in grain.

The question may now arise whether in reality these mortally sick and poisoned sufferers never—except in the Kölbigk epidemic in 1021—revealed symptoms of the holy fire or St Anthony's Fire, as it was then called. We have already voiced the suspicion that such was the case, despite the fact that the chroniclers are silent on the subject. After all, only a few of the frequent ergot poisonings of an ergotic character were mentioned in literature in those centuries. But the curious horror and fear of red which sufferers felt in the epidemic of 1374, and which later on disappeared, seems to me to indicate a fear on the part of the sufferers that they would be taken to a St Anthony hospital, a fear that their illness might turn to gangrene. We are reminded that these St Anthony hospitals, which only received those who were seized by St Anthony's Fire, had their outer walls and doorposts painted red as a symbol of the fire which it was their function to combat. Of the greatest interest is Barger's statement that the St Anthony Hospital in Lyons not only had its walls painted red, as was usual, but was also called the *domus contractoria*, i.e., the home of cramp sufferers. This must mean that in some epidemics of the holy fire the cramp symptoms, which were most pronounced in ergotism and the dancing epidemics, were predominant. It is also possible to prove conclusively that the choreomaniacs must have sought help from St Anthony, just as if they suffered from St Anthony's Fire.

In Fig. 129 we reproduce an illustration from 1440–50 from Swabia. St Anthony sits on an abbot's stool, clad in the robes of the St Anthony

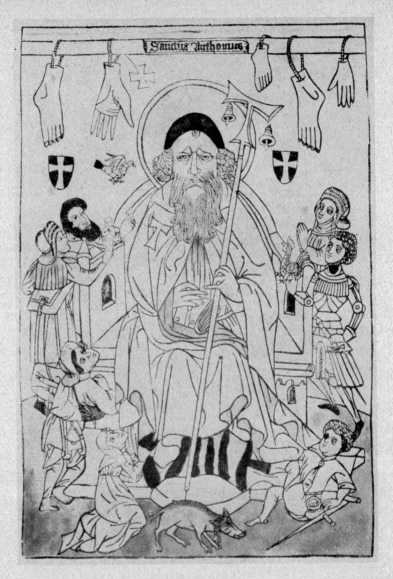

FIG. 129. St Anthony Abbas the Hermit, in the robes of his order, with T cross and bells, swine and bell. Great flames rise at the feet of the saint. To the left a woman burns her hands, and to the right a man burns his foot in the holy fire. In the middle distance a woman suffering from cramp; in the background gifts are offered. On the wall are votive gifts, probably representing limbs attacked by the fire. Woodcut from Swabia, 1440–50 [Schreiber].

order of monks, with the T sign on his mantle and in his left hand the pilgrim's staff with the T cross and bells. Flames rise about his feet. In front of him is the swine with a small bell around its neck. In the foreground, to the left, is a woman with one hand stretched into the flames and to the right a man stretching one foot into them, thus showing in which part of the body the fire rages. To the left, in the middle distance, a woman stands on the saint's right, her head bent sideways and backwards in cramp, with the left arm and left leg contracted. In my opinion she is suffering from St John's dance, from ergotism. The picture is of especial interest in other respects. The two couples in the middle distance, on either side of the saint, appear to bear votive gifts, a cock and a human doll. In the background other votive gifts are hung up, hands and feet of adults and children.

FIG. 130. St Anthony the Hermit, with T cross, swine and bells. Behind him a St Anthony chapel with a T cross on the roof. To the right a crippled man suffering from *ignis sacer*; to the left a woman in a somewhat contorted posture possibly with ergotism. On the chapel are suspended numerous votive gifts: lower extremities, hands and puppets. In the window a puppet and a hand. Copperplate of the fifteenth century [Rodenkirchen].

Their schematic appearance seems to indicate that they are made of wood, wax or other crude material. Of course, they represent limbs afflicted by the fire which the saint will heal.

Another picture (Fig. 130) is from a copperplate of the end of the fifteenth century. We stand outside a St Anthony's chapel, recognizable by the T cross erected at the top of the façade. In the foreground is St Anthony, clad as a monk and carrying the T-crowned pilgrim's staff. From his left hand hangs a bell; on his right side is the swine led by a chain. To the left of the saint a man kneels and stretches out his hand towards the saint. From this hand rise great flames, showing clearly that this is the source of the fire. He carries a crutch; he has already—either in this or some preceding epidemic—been crippled by the fire. To the right of the saint is a woman with a somewhat contorted body, with a pronounced backwards and sideways bending; possibly she suffers from cramp, i.e., from the dancing sickness of that day and the ergotism of later days. Of very special interest are the votive gifts suspended along the outer cornice of the St Anthony chapel and the window balustrade. We see hands and feet, and especially a pair of lower legs in which the painting gives such precise details that one wonders whether these are artificial limbs or limbs which had actually fallen off as a result of gangrene, which seems to me most probable, because this would accord best with what happened in the Kölbigk case in 1021 and with what we know of the offering of sundered limbs during epidemics of St Anthony's Fire. There

Fig. 131. St Anthony Abbas the Hermit. Sufferers from the 'Holy Fire', more or less crippled, supplicate St Anthony, who here wears the Patriarchal Cross (Cross of the Holy Ghost). *Fresco* in the St Anthony chapel in Waltalingen, Switzerland. Fifteenth century [Durrer].

is one other noteworthy detail in this picture: two small dolls, one in the corner and one on the window balustrade. I venture to think that these are *marmousets d'hommes*, the figures which, according to Cardinal de Rohan, in the eighteenth century, and probably long before, were offered by pilgrims to the Hohlenstein grotto at Zabern in honour of St Vitus, especially by those suffering from the dancing sickness or similar sicknesses.

Durrer reproduced certain pictures with St Anthony as the principal figure and Barger interpreted them as relating partly to St Anthony's Fire and partly also, in all probability, to the symptoms of ergotism. In the village of Waltalingen part of the chapel dates from the thirteenth century and the church, as the records show, was in full use in the fifteenth century. On the internal walls of the church there is a series of pictures illustrating episodes in the life of St Anthony. St Anthony wears the violet robes of the order and in some of the pictures there is the blue T cross on the right-hand side of the mantle. Durrer is of opinion that these paintings are of the fifteenth century. In one of the pictures St Anthony carries the so-called patriarchal cross (the Cross of the Holy Ghost) instead of the more correct T cross (Fig. 131). The saint is surrounded by various sufferers from the holy fire who extend their crippled limbs towards him. Administering the blessing with his right hand he assents to the supplications of the sick for mercy. Another picture from Waltalingen represents St Anthony as a hermit in the desert just emerging from his cave (Fig. 132). He is invoked by a number of the sick suffering from cramped contortions and contractions of the limbs. There is a host of

FIG. 132. St Anthony the Hermit. Sufferers from ergotism, more or less crippled, invoke St Anthony coming out from the desert grotto, leaning on his T-formed staff. Fresco in the St Anthony Chapel, Waltalingen, Switzerland, of the fifteenth century [Durrer].

ergot poisoned victims of dancing sickness and ergotism—whichever name one prefers to use—who ask St Anthony for mercy and help.

One might be inclined to assume that these sufferers from cramp were invoking St Anthony only because he was the great exorcizer of devils, cramp being regarded above all other conditions as the work of devils. But the fact that the artist has represented both the sufferer from the holy fire and the sufferer from cramp, while St Anthony is also represented in one of the pictures as the sender of fire, seems to me to support the assumption that it was well known at the time that the one disease might pass over into the other and that they were in some way connected. Especially it must have been clear that the condition of cramp which we call ergotism and which was formerly called dancing sickness might lead to or be combined with the holy fire. Then the fear and loathing with which the choreomaniacs of 1374 regarded the colour of red appears reasonable, the fear of having become afflicted with the holy fire and of possibly being taken to one of the red-painted St Anthony hospitals, with all their misery, crippling and death.

FIG. 133. St Anthony as the expeller of demons, on his saintly throne under a richly carved Gothic baldequin. In the right foreground the swine. The saint is supplicated for mercy by two sufferers from fire. Flames leap from the already consumed hands of the one on the left and from the other they leap from a hand which has already lost some of its fingers. In the background are devils assisting, with God's permission, the ravages of the fire. They are exorcized by the prayer. Woodcut from the Upper Rhine or Swabia, 1440–50 [Schreiber].

We must never forget, when the old chronicles speak of the dance epidemics of the Middle Ages and early modern times—of dancing, incessant dancing, of dancing asleep or awake, for days and weeks—that people of those times did not mean by dancing what we mean today. For them any twitching of the muscles or bending of the limbs was a dance. Technical medical terminology retains certain names even today of various diseases, all of which have their origin in the diagnoses of the Middle Ages and the early sixteenth century, e.g., *St Johannis Chorea* and *St Viti Chorea*. The word 'chorea' is the Greek and Latin word for dance. But the sufferers in the dance epidemics not only showed symptoms of dancing sickness, but they also danced in the real sense. Quite certainly it was the sufferers from ergotism, those poisoned by ergot, who made up the hosts of dancers. So much is clear from the violent and painful symptoms and the high mortality among the dancers. But among them were very probably others, not least those suffering from epilepsy and similar diseases, as well as those mentally deranged and *malades imaginaires*. That such was the case is confirmed by the Echternach dance, in which the dancing host consisted of various kinds of sufferers, though principally epileptics. The great majority, however, suffered from *St Johannis* or *St Viti chorea*, and this word *chorea* has become a technical term in medicine in our own days, comprising very different diseases. This is partly due to the growing confusion in modern times as to what the St Vitus' dance exactly was. In modern technical terminology we find *Sydenham's Chorea* for dancing sickness among the young and adolescent, a *Huntington's Chorea* for certain advanced nervous diseases, a *Pregnancy Chorea* for the dreaded eclampsia, a *Chorea Senilis* for tremors among the aged, etc.

It is now possible to draw one further conclusion concerning the dance and the dance epidemics. The sufferers must themselves have regarded their cramp and contortions as a 'dance', as also did the spectators. They must have thought that although they performed their dances in honour of the Virgin Mary or the saints in order to win their sympathy and their mercy and thereby to obtain some alleviation of their severe suffering, yet at the same time they found in the muscular exertion of the dance a more direct assuagement of their pain. The most important conclusion seems to me the one which is now obvious: when they regarded cramp as a dance, they must have sought in the dance a sympathetic and active cure. The violent hopping and leaping would, with the help of the saints, drive out the devil-inspired 'dance' in their arms and legs and tortured bodies. The heavenly Dance of the Angels would, by its magic power, expel the hellish and devil-inspired dance.

XXIV

Summary

THE dance is a part of all developed religions. In the divine services during classical times as well as in the numerous mystic religions the dance had an important ritual significance. The Jewish religion in no wise constituted an exception to this universal rule. Expanding Christianity had its main inheritance from the Jews and based itself on the Old Testament and the Jewish cult dances, and on some of its teachings as a support for its own ritual dances and ceremonies of divine service and even as a direct command to praise God in the dance. Similarly, certain passages in the New Testament and in the Epistles of St Paul have been adduced as partial motives for the introduction and preservation of the religious dance. The dance in the Christian church began in the latter part of the third century and continued throughout the centuries to our own time. But it is highly probable that the religious dance among the Germanic, Slavonic and Romanic nations, among whom the Church proselytized, occasionally stimulated the resurgence of the inherited dance within Christian circles.

Even in pre-Christian times the dance was a means of influencing the invisible powers and of establishing contact with them. This was also the fundamental belief of the Christian Church.

In the second century Christianity already declared that there was dancing in Heaven. The Fathers of the Church declared that the blessed and the angels dance a perpetual dance, and in such a manner that when the dwellers in heaven reveal themselves to the faithful they do so dancing. Ultimately this view goes back to Plato and to the mysteries of antiquity.

St Clement of Alexandria described the dance as a part of the inauguration festivals of the Church mysteries. There was a dance of the angels, and the church dance is an imitation of that dance. One wanted thus to display at the end of prayer the physical desire to enter into heaven. According to St Ambrose the person to be baptized must approach the font dancing. The reverent church dance, in fear of God, was, in the mysteries, an approach to God, at the same time representing the revealed mysteries of the Resurrection. The dance was a reanimation of him for whom it is performed.

The churchyard dances for the martyrs were an act of grace and signified a triumph, and the dance was still allied to faith. The churchyard festivals of song and dance for the martyrs involved, according to Gregory of Nazianzus, a threefold benefit: the suppression of the devils, avoidance of disease and knowledge of things to come.

The types of dance varied even in the earliest Church. Frequently there seems to have been a question of round dances, usually with stamping and hopping, but always with clapping of hands and a certain rhythm. Sometimes the dance was a solo dance and in such cases it appears to have been a typical pirouette.

The idea of the Dance of the Angels persisted throughout the centuries until our own times. Medieval dance hymns often described this dance as characteristic of the bliss of paradise. But more often it was added that the dance was for the dead, exorcizing the king of the Underworld. Another hymn declared that in this heavenly dance the vices were trampled underfoot. All this connects with the statement of St Ambrose that the dance— the imitation by the faithful of the Dance of the Angels—was a part of the revealed mysteries of the Resurrection. This heavenly dance exorcized the powers of death and the Underworld, hastened and facilitated the deliverance of captive souls from the kingdom of the dead and assisted their triumphal processional dance into Paradise. The Dance of the Angels in heaven trampled under footthe devils of the Underworld and all their evil.

As early as the fourth century church dances began to show signs of degeneration. Women began to take a more active part; men and women began to dance together. Drinking and loose living crept into the Church festivals. The dance became increasingly indecent and immoral. In the middle of the fourth century Bishop Epiphanius began a cautious and dubious struggle with the church dance; he sought if possible to spiritualize it and to make it signify the dance before the Lord of Good Deeds and Christian Faith. The Fathers of the Church followed him, but concerned themselves mainly with the degradation of the dance and its abortions. Even St Augustine, who so often and so strictly rejected the dance in the Christian church, shrank from completely forbidding it. It was impossible for him to escape the generally accepted interpretation of Matthew xi, 17, and Luke vii, 32, and St Augustine was therefore obliged to let wisdom speak: 'he who would dance may dance'.

The Festival of Fools, or the Festival of the Ass, arose in the sixth century, perhaps considerably earlier. In my opinion they have no direct connexion with pagan festivals. It is not possible to point to any which have such a character. It seems to have been Alcwyn, or whoever hides behind his name, who first put forward the essentially unreasonable view that the Festival of Fools within the Church derived from the Janus festivals of antiquity. As early as the sixth century Caesarius referred to a Christian festival which he strongly condemned as the 'Mules' festival. Other names were the 'Little Hind' or the 'Little Hart'. The earliest proscriptions of these festivals do not suggest that the latter were taken over from the heathen. For this reason it seems to me probable that they arose independently among Christians as a sort of memorial festival for the ass which, according to the Gospels, played so important a part in Christ's life on earth. It was organized as a memorial from created animals to the ass and the mule. As a festival of the animals it consequently became burlesque and grotesque and finally even blasphemous. Certain unimportant details were taken perhaps from pagan rites but not necessarily. This is especially true of the important detail that the lowest priests became, in the festival, the highest. Such ideas were derived directly and literally from the Virgin Mary's song of praise in Luke i, 52, 'he hath cast down the mighty from their thrones and . . .', etc. Then came the climax of the festival—the handing over of the staff—just when this song of praise, the 'Magnificat', was sung. The prototype of the dicing is the division of Christ's clothes.

The ball dance and the pelota in Auxerres cathedral constituted a mystery play. The dance symbolized the joyous and triumphal journey after the Resurrection from the labyrinthine kingdom of the dead. The great ball was the Sun of Resurrection and Righteousness, i.e., the resurrected and victorious Christ. The bergerette was also in the nature of a mystery play. It may be regarded as having been celebrated as the heavenly dance, in which Christians might take part when, after resurrection and baptism in fire, they have been cleansed and sanctified and taken up into the flock of heavenly lambs on the meadows of Paradise.

The choristers of Seville, dancing before the high altar of the cathedral on certain Church festivals, were in the fifteenth century dressed as angels and proved thereby that the Church still cherished the old idea that the sacral-church dance primarily imitated the Dance of the Angels.

The Church processions during the Middle Ages, as late as the seventeenth century, were quite certainly dance processions. Possibly this may have been because the heavenly hosts of angels were regarded as being present and assisting at Church ceremonies; they of course continued the heavenly dance, which was never-ending.

The popular church-dance processions have continued from the early Middle Ages to our own time, and are still extensively performed. Most frequently they have been associated with magical conceptions, in so far as the participators believed that the dance in honour of the saints would bring a cure for illness or promote abundant harvest. In particular features they have preserved ritual details which remind us of similar ones in the earliest Christian church-dance ceremonies. The Spanish popular church-dances seem to lack this magic significance and seem to have preserved more of the original pure character of reverence and devotion to the saints.

The dances for the dead, the dances in the churchyards, have the same meaning as they had in the early Church at the graves of the martyrs: one comforts the dead, one dances for their resurrection, one demonstrates their physical resurrection and their participation in the Dance of the Angels. But the dance is simultaneously a protection against evil spirits and against the dead as demons.

The idea behind the dance of death is that the dead become devils who seek to inflict disease and misfortune on the living in order thereby to drag them down to an early grave. By the dance for the dead they are forced to help in driving out illness, to assuage suffering and to reveal the future. Everything is preserved from the motives of the Christian dance festivals at the graves of the martyrs.

From the fourth to the end of the eighteenth century ecclesiastical and lay authorities issued one prohibition after another against dancing in churches and church porches, in churchyards and for the dead. Every century, without exception, has such prohibitions: by Fathers of the Church, popes, archbishops, bishops, missionaries, councils, synods and state authorites. They were most frequent at the end of the Middle Ages and the beginning of modern times. They are directed mainly against the debasement of the dance, against the participation of women and against crude magical churchyard dances. But the desire to dance was strong and the dance ritual was supported by the books of the Bible, by the Evangelists and the writings of the Fathers of the Church. So the prohibitions had little success and the Church hastened to bring the religious dance under its protective wing.

The vast processions of flagellators in the plague year of 1349 were common in various European countries and developed a number of ritual ceremonies in connexion with flagellation. These occurred during the progress of the procession around the leaders, when songs were sung to tunes which accompanied the dance, both before and after. Since all religious processions, at that time and much later, were dance processions, it seems probable that the flagellants in certain ceremonies also used the rhythmic dancing step. But the flagellants' dance cannot claim any independent role in the ceremonies.

We have been able to trace the history of dance epidemics as far back as A.D. 650 or 700. The account of the banned dances at Kölbigk in 1021 affords a number of details of valuable medical interest, and so does the dance in Wales at the beginning of the thirteenth century. It is to some extent true, too, of the children's dance between Erfurt and Arnstadt in 1237. The exodus of the children from Hamelin should apparently, in accordance with the evidence of various chroniclers of the sixteenth century, be dated around 1374, i.e., the period of the greatest epidemic in Germany and Flanders; the dance led the children to the gallows hill and represented protection against possession by the demons of dead criminals. The dancers collapsed during their dance and as a memorial there was erected in the burial grounds the old symbol of a rose-wreathed stone cross.

The dance epidemic of 1374 afflicted the Hungarian pilgrimage which took place about every seventh year to Aachen, Cologne, Trier and Flanders. The pilgrims came, according to Beka's chronicle, from Bohemia, but also from Hungary, Poland, Carinthia, Austria and Germany. Great hosts from the Netherlands and France joined them. On the journey to Aachen and the visit to the Rhine province these pilgrims were sorely afflicted with ergot poisoning and consequent cramps, epileptic fits, mental confusion, hallucinations, etc. Their clonic cramps were at that time described as a 'dance', but they sought in actual dancing a relief from their pains and deliverance from their ills. They regarded themselves, and were regarded by others, as possessed. A hitherto unpublished work, *The Early Roman Kings and Emperors*, a chronicle from the fifteenth century, furnished a large number of important and hitherto unknown details concerning the choreomaniacs.

The Hungarian pilgrimages to the Rhine province have already been described. The route was essentially the same as that of the choreomaniacs, as were the churches and cities which they visited. The hitherto 'unknown and never heard of demon name' which the chronicles say that the choreomaniacs called out can be identified as Hungarian, Polish, Bohemian and German-Hungarian words, probably a translation of the light dancing song which the German choreomaniacs sang in Cologne. The conclusion therefore is that it was a Hungarian pilgrimage to the Rhine province which in 1374 came to disaster in a dance epidemic. An ancient tradition relates that just in that year Ludwig I of Hungary, together with his Hungarian subjects, were pilgrims to Aachen.

The occurrence of dance epidemics in Zürich in the fifteenth century shows that in the popular treatment of this demon-caused sickness a bridge and running water sometimes played a rôle, as had for long been the case in other medically significant popular church dances and processions. In the epidemic of the sixteenth century outside Brussels this becomes manifest. The great epidemic in Strassburg must now be dated 1518, not a century earlier, as has been maintained. It coincides in time with the publication there of Luther's articles.

Pieter Brueghel's picture of the sick dancers at Moelenbeek Sint Jans in the year 1564, on close examination gives extremely important information from both the medical point of view and that of popular magic. Brueghel's drawing is one of the most valuable medical memorials of the medieval dance epidemics. For the second time we encounter the bridge and the running water as of importance in the proper observance of the ritual.

In the last quarter of the sixteenth century the dance epidemics ceased. There were one or two outbreaks during that century but epidemics did not occur. There was also an outbreak in 1829. The reason why the epidemics ceased in the sixteenth century was to be found in the circumstances that about that time it was becoming understood that the 'dance' was caused by some sort of poisoning connected with impurities in grain. Then there appeared a new sickness, the so-called 'Kriebel sickness', ergotism, and all those who were formerly supposed to be possessed and suffering from choreomania were now supposed to suffer from the new disease.

The victims danced for the Virgin Mary, St John the Baptist, St Vitus and other saints; they visited certain churches dedicated to these saints, also their precious relics, which were later the most valuable possessions of the churches to which the pilgrims went in procession. The saints known to have been invoked, as well as those who were most probably invoked, around whom the dance was performed, and the more important relics which were exhibited in the churches to the sick choreomaniacs, afford some information on the more pronounced symptoms which the dancers may have shown. The dancers regarded themselves as possessed by devils and believed that their sufferings were caused either by demons or by sorcery. They turned to the saints and relics which were supposed to have special remedies for or protection against cramp, convulsions, spasms, epileptic symptoms, painful laming of the feet, gouty pains, eye and skin troubles, sores, burning sensations and fevers, the holy fire, obfuscation and mortal suffering. All of these symptoms noted indirectly, though with some uncertainty, agree with those described by the chroniclers.

The dancers did not seek merely by magical imitation to overcome the dance caused by the devil which possessed them. They sought at the same time to reveal to the Virgin Mary and the saints how they wished to recover full freedom of movement. Therefore they jumped as high as they could, sometimes to the very level of the altar table. Therefore they shouted 'So, so!' thereby indicating how they wished to become. But we are probably quite right in assuming that the dance which the choreomaniacs performed in the churches in front of the images of the saints was in imitation of the Dance of the Angels in honour and refreshment of the saints. At the same time it was a variation of the thought that this Dance of the Angels by sympathetic magic and by its paradaisical nature and mysteries would drive out and destroy the devils' dance, which the choreomaniacs, tortured in their bodies by those devils, were compelled to perform.

The choreomaniacs tried to cure themselves by a large number of magic rites in addition to their magic dances. These varied in different epidemics, but some were normal right through the centuries. They all of them have deep roots in the customs and ideas of bygone ages. It is the choreomaniacs who attract the greatest interest by their hatred of poulaines, red clothing, and their offerings of dolls and iron toads. The choreomaniacs of 1374 were by no means an heretical sect; they were not interested in religious or church subjects. They were just very sick people who regarded themselves as possessed by devils and were so regarded by others. The Church took care of them and endeavoured by its own methods of devil expulsion to bring them healing. When they are described by the chroniclers as a 'sect' this only meant in medieval language that they formed a sort of association. The meaning of 'heretic' in a church or religious sense is not part of the meaning of 'sect' in medieval speech.

St Anthony controls the holy fire which surrounds the heavenly Paradise like a river or a sea. It is in this river that on the Last Day the baptism is a sanctification; for the unrighteous the consuming fire flames up and the heat is intensified for punishment, cleansing or consumption. St Anthony has the power to send this fire down among men as a punishment and discipline, but he can be moved to assuage his anger and permit the fire to be reduced or extinguished. This so-called St Anthony's Fire, the holy fire, was caused by the poisoning of grain by ergot. But frequently the fire was combined with cramps, and ergotic symptoms of a cramp-like character were associated with the fire. For this reason St Anthony was invoked by the sufferers both as the wielder of the fire and as the mighty expeller of demons in those afflicted with ergotism, the 'possessed'. The medieval hymns in honour of St Anthony show that he was invoked precisely against cramps and spasms, which at that time were commonly considered as caused by devils. Around his images assembled both those who suffered from the fire and those who were considered to be epidemic dancers, who were compelled to attend, and this the more so since the two sicknesses merged into each other more or less.

A detailed comparison of the various symptoms of the dance epidemics and the symptoms of ergot poisoning and ergotism reveals an extra-ordinary and exact correspondence. The conclusion is irresistible: the dance epidemics were caused by ergot poisoning of grain and bread. Ergot poisons have the power to develop in human beings, possibly in combination with severe famine and lack of vitamins, muscular spasms and bodily contortions which in those days were considered as a 'dance'. Herein is the explanation of the belief that the sufferers could without interruption dance day and night, for days and weeks.

The medieval church hymns, the wood-cuts of the Middle Ages and church paintings prove that the choreomaniacs also invoked the wielder of the holy fire, St Anthony. These circumstances and their fear of red may be connected with the fact that the St Anthony hospitals were painted red. We are therefore forced to suspect that the choreomaniacs hated red principally because they feared that their possession by devils might ultimately pass over into the 'holy fire', also called 'the devil's fire' or 'Gehenna's fire'.

The religious Church dances still exist extensively today. As late as the first World War the hopping dance of the saints continued in Echternach in Luxembourg, so did Church dances in honour of the Virgin Mary in the Basque provinces. There are also various dances, mainly processional dances, in association with Church festivals in Spain and South American republics; and there is a comprehensive ceremony in the Coptic Christian Church in Abyssinia. There are relics of the Church dance in the Greek Orthodox Church, too; these religious dances are performed in honour of God and Christ, for the glorification of Mary and the consolation of the saints and martyrs, in honour of the angels and the comfort and joy of the dead.

A not inconsiderable number of the melodies by which the religious dances were accompanied in medieval and modern times have been col-lected. It is clear that they can be grouped in three main divisions; i.e., Church hymns, such as psalms or sequences, church songs of a character expressly adapted for the dance, and profane melodies.

To the Church hymns belong *Veni Sancte Spiritus*, *Victimae Paschali Laudes* and the *Magnificat*. They are not characterized by decided rhythm. Of Church songs adapted for dancing there are *Mos Florentis Venustatis* in four-four tempo, the song of the Ass Festival and Fools Festival, *Gregis Pastor Tityrus* in two-four tempo, and the two choristers' song from Seville, *Al Regio Banquete* and *Quiem me Diera*, both in three-four tempo, and *Resonet in Laudibus* in three-four tempo. Among profane melodies we may include the Echternach Jubilee song, *Adam had Seven Sons* in two-four tempo, the funeral dance from Bailleul, *In Heaven there is a Dance*, in six-eight tempo, the burial waltz from Norrland in three-four, and the Rakoczi march in four-four tempo, sung to a funeral dance in Hungary.

This survey shows that in the choice of melodies for religious dances no strict religious principles were followed. They seem to have taken some well-known melody of which the verbal text was suitable to the festival which was solemnized with dancing. Sometimes, however, as in the choristers' dance in Seville, special music was composed and a suitable text written for it. This was also done at other festivals, such as the children's festivals and at the pilgrims' dances in Montserrat. In yet other cases popular music was employed if suitable to the character of the dance, as at Echternach and in Hungary, or otherwise appropriate to its function, as in Norrland.

What a mighty rôle the dance has played in the Christian religion and in medicine! This is of course quite obvious when one remembers how closely associated have been religion and medicine from the earliest times, in Babylon, Egypt, Greece and Rome, and throughout the Middle Ages and until the first centuries of modern times. During the earliest millenia the 'physicians' were in part priests of the temple. Subsequently medicine was very closely associated with religion, and during practically the whole of the Middle Ages it was primarily an activity of the Catholic Church, which by its monks and nuns, its monasteries and hospitals sought to preserve the ancient art of healing and its ideal of mercy for the sick and suffering [Backman]. The connexion between religion and medicine is of the most intimate kind and finds ample support in the Bible. It is quite natural that such an important act as the religious dance, which imitates a supernatural mystery, must be taken into the service of healing medicine in the expulsion of devils. And just as the early Christians danced at the graves of the martyrs in order to regain health and to move them to drive out the secret cause of their sickness, so also did the dancers in the epidemics. Such were the hopes of the choreomaniacs when they danced before the Virgin Mary in the churches or before the images of the saints.

Similar thoughts inspired all those who danced and mumbled their incantations in the churchyards throughout the night. Such is the thought also of the thousands taking part even today in the hopping-dance procession at Echternach, when they dance around the tomb of the saint in the church and around the graves outside.

BIBLIOGRAPHY

Achelis, H.: Das Christentum in den ersten drei Jahrhunderten. Leipzig, 1925
Acta Sanctorum: Venetiis-Bruxelles. 1910
Adam, A.: Sankt Veit bei Zabern oder der Hohle Stein. Strassburg, 1897
Alkuin (attributed to): On Kalendis Januarii. *Migne:* P.L. 101, col. 1177. Paris, 1851
Aldén, G. A.: I Getapulien. Stockholm, 1883
Alin, J.: Labyrinterna på Onsalalandet. Halländsk Bygdekultur, p. 50. Göteborg, 1925
Ambrosius: Commentary on the Gospel of St Luke. Lib. VI. *Migne:* P.L. 15, col. 1670, 1679. Paris, 1845
— Commentary on Ps. 118. Ib. col. 1290
— On repentance. II:6:42. Ib. 16, col. 1180. Paris, 1845
— Speech. Ib. col. 1180
— Speech 42. Ib. 17, col. 688. Paris, 1845
— Letter 22: 2, 17. *Migne:* P.L. 16, col. 1019. Paris, 1845
— Letter 26: 16. Ib. col. 1024
Analecta Hymnica, herausgegeb. von *Dreves* and others 1–50. Leipzig, 1890–1906
Andersson, N.: Svenska Låtar. Västergötland. Stockholm, 1932
Andree, R.: Votive und Weihegaben des katholischen Volks in Süddeutschland. Braunschweig, 1904
Andrews: Folklore. 8:8, 1897
Angé, Cl.: Nouveau Larousse illustré. Marmouset. Paris, s.a.
Annales Fossenenses. 1123–1389. In *Pertz:* Monumenta Germ. Hist. scr. 4, 35. Hannover, 1841.
Anonymous: Nachricht von der Kriebelkrankheit welche in dem Herzogthum Lüneburg in den Jahren 1770 und 1771 grasiret. Zelle, 1771
— Berichte und Bedenken die Kriebelkrankheit betreffend. Kopenhagen, 1772
— Liturgical Dances. The Sacristy. A Quarterly Review of Ecclesiastical Art and Litt. I, 63. London, 1871
— En märklig trefaldighetskälla. Fataburen, p. 155. 1908
Anstein, H.: Die abessinische Kirche. Stuttgart, 1935
Anton, K. G.: Erste Linien eines Versuches über der Alten Slawen Ursprung, Sitten, Gebräuche, Meinungen und Kenntnisse. Leipzig, 1873
Aubé, B.: Homélie inédite en append. à Polyeucte dans l'histoire. P. 79. Paris, 1882
Aubert, M.: La Cathédrale de Metz. p. 281. Paris, 1931
Augusti, J. Ch. W.: Denkwürdigkeiten aus der christlichen Archäologie. 7, 204. Leipzig, 1825. 10, 130, 1829
Augustinus: Letter to bishop Alypius. *Migne:* P.L. 33, col. 119. Paris, 1845
— Speech 323. Ib. 38, col. 1446. Paris, 1845
— Speech 326 : I. The executed Martyrs hasten to bliss. Ib. 38, col. 1449
— Speech 311. Ib. 38, col. 1415
— Speech 265 (nowadays attributed to *Cesarius*). Ib. 39, col. 2239. Paris, 1845
— The City of God. Ib. 41, col. 255, 761. Paris, 1845
Aurelius, E.: Föreställningen i Israel om de döda och tillståndet efter döden. Akad. avh. Upsala, 1907

Baas, J. H.: Die geschichtliche Entwicklung des ärztlichen Standes und der medizinischen Wissenschaften. Berlin, 1896

Bachmann, A.: Geschichte Böhmens. I–II. Gotha, 1899

Backman, Gaston: Människans förhistoria. I. Den äldre stenåldern. Stockholm, 1911

Backman, E. Louis: Om den äldsta svenska farmakopén, dess medicinskt-historiska bakgrund och dess ställning till folkmedicinen. Upsala Läkaref. Förh. 29, 63, 1924

—Älvablåst och de folkmedicinska riterna vid helbrägdagörandet. Upsala Universitets Årsskr. Progr. 5. Upsala, 1927

— Den historiska innebörden i benämningarna hospital och lasarett. Kungl. Vetenskapssocietetens Årsbok, 1941

Backman, V.: Likdansen. Landsmålsarkivet, Hälsingland, Bjuråkers sn. 3257: 3. Upsala, 1931

Balde, J.: /e Soc. Jesu/ Lyricorum Libri IV. Od. 33: choreae mortuales. Colon., 1645

Balogh, J.: Tänze in Kirchen und auf Kirchhöfen. Niederdeutsche Z. f. Volksk. 6, I, 126. 1928

Balsamon: In can. 63 conc. in Trullo. *Migne:* P.G. 137, col. 731. Paris, 1865

Barger, G.: Zur Geschichte des Mutterkorns. Verh. d. Deutsch. Pharm. Ges. p. 105. Leipzig, 1928

— Ergot and Ergotism. London, 1931

— The Alkaloids of Ergot, Hdb. d. exp. Pharm. Erg.-Werk. 6, 84. Berlin, 1938

Baronius, C.: Annales Ecclesiastici. I. 338, A. Venetiis, 1600

Bartsch, K.: Mittelniederdeutsche Osterlieder. Jahrb. d. Ver. f. nieder-deutsche Sprachforsch. p. 49, 1880

Basileios: Sermon on drunkenness. Num. I. *Migne:* P.G. 31, col. 446, 459. Paris, 1857

— Epist. ad I: 2. Ib. 32, col. 226. Paris, 1857

— Epist. 46. Ib. 32, col. 371. Paris, 1857

Batillard, Ch.: Les Anes légendaires. Mém. de l'Acad. Nat. des sc. arts et belles-lettres de Caen. p. 238. Caen, 1873

Baum, I.: Deutsche Bildwerke des 10. bis 18. Jahrhunderts. Stuttgart, 1917

Beckmann, J. Chr.: Historia des Fürstenthums Anhalt. III: 4. cap. 4, § 3. p. 467. Zerbst, 1710

Becherer, J.: Newe Thüringische Chronica. p. 272, 366. Mülhausen, 1601

Bechstein, L.: Thüringer Sagenbuch. I-II, Leipzig, 1885

— Der Sagenschatz und die Sagenkreise des Thüringerlandes. Bd. III. Meiningen, 1837

Beka, Joannes de: Canonicus Ultrajectinus et *Heda, Wilhelmus,* Praepositus Arnhemensis: De episcopis ultraiectinis, recogniti. Append. ad Chron. I. Bekae ex M. S:to Codice *Gisb. Lappii* a Waveren. p. 124. Ultrajecti, 1643

Beissel, St: Die Verehrung der Heiligen und ihre Reliquien in Deutschland bis zum Beginne des 13. Jahrhunderts. Stimmen aus Maria-Laach. XII Erg.-Bd. H. 47. Freiburg im Br., 1890

— Die Verehrung der Heiligen und ihrer Reliquien in Deutschland während der zweiten Hälfte des Mittelalters. Stimmen aus Maris-Laach. XIV Erg.-Bd. H. 54. Freiburg im Br., 1892

— Die Aachenfahrt. Verehrung der Aachener Heiligtümer seit den Tagen Karls des Grossen bis in unsere Zeit. Erg. H. 82 zu den Stimmen aus Maria-Laach. Freiburg im Br., 1902

Belethus, Joh.: Rat. divin. off. c. 120. *Migne:* P.L. 96, col. 123. Paris, 1851

Bérenger, Féraud, L.-J., B.: Réminiscences populaires de la Provence. p. 337. Paris, 1885
— Superstitions et survivances étudiées au point de vue de leur origine et de leurs transformations. 3, 407. Paris, 1896
Bergstrand, C.-M.: Kulturbilder från 1700-talets Västergötland. Göteborg, 1933
Berlière, U.: Les processions des croix banales. Bull. de la Cl. des Lettres et des sc. mor. et pol. Acad. R. de Belgique. Sér. 5. T. 8, p. 419. 1922
Bernt, J.: Monographia Choreae Sti Viti. Diss. Prague, 1810
Bertelius, Jo.: Historia Luxemburgensis seu Commentarius. Coloniae, 1638
Besseler, H.: Die Musik des Mittelalters und der Renaissance. Potsdam, 1931
Billengren: Cf. Sondén
Bingham, J.: The Works. I. Origines ecclesiasticae. p. 112. London, 1726
Binterim, A. J.: Die vorzüglichsten Denkwürdigkeiten der Christ-Katholischen Kirche. II: 2. p. 80. Mainz, 1838
Blind, E.: Gynäkologisch interessante 'Ex-voto'. Globus, 82, 69. 1902
Bloch, J.: Der deutsche Volkstanz der Gegenwart. I. Hess. Bl. f. Volksk. 25, 124. 1926
Blondez: Aux Auteurs du Journal. Journal de Paris. No. 263, p. 1084. Paris, 1785
Blümmel, E. K.: Germanische Totenlieder. Arch. f. Anthropol. 5, 149. 1906
Bock, Fr.: Der Reliquienschatz des Liebfrauen-Münsters zu Aachen zur Erinnerung a. d. Heiligthumsfahrt i. Jahre d. Heils 1860. Aachen, 1860
Bock, Fr. u. Willemsen, M.: Die Mittelalterlichen Kunst- und Reliquienschätze zu Maestricht. Köln u. Neuss, 1872
Bodinus, J.: Daemonomania oder ausführliche Erzehlung des wutenden Teuffels (in seinen dahmaligen rasenden Hexen und Hexenmeistern). Hamburg, 1698
Boehn, M. v.: Guido Reni. Bielefeld, 1910
Boemus, J.: Omnium Gentium Mores, Leges et Ritus, fol. 58 b. Aug. Vind., 1520
Boersch, Ch.: Essai sur la mortalité à Strasbourg. Thèse de Strasbourg, 1836
Bogumia, L. S.: Slownik Jezyka Polskiego. Warszawa, 1900
Boilean: Histoire des Flagellants. Amsterdam, 1701
Bonnet, M.: Histoire générale de la Danse sacrée et prophane, ses progrès et ses révolutions, depuis son origine jusqu'à présent. Paris, 1724
Bonnet, B.: Acta Apostol. apocr. II: I. p. 54. Martyrium Andreae Prius, 13. Lipsiae, 1898
Booch-Arkossy, F.: Neues vollst. Polnisch-Deutsches Wörterbuch. Leipzig, s.a.
Boucher, M.: Sur la Gangrène épidémique, qui a régné dans les environs de Lille, en Flandres, dans les années 1749 et 1750. Journ. de Méd., Chir. et Pharm. 17, 327, 1762
Brant, Seb.: Cf. Chron. Strasbourg
Broberg, J. V.: Bidrag från vår Folkmedicins Vidskepelser till kännedom om våra äldsta tider. Stockholm, 1878
Browe, S. J. P.: Die Verehrung der Eucharistie im Mittelalter. München, 1933
Browerus, Christ. et Masenius, Jac.: Antiquitatum et Annalium Trevirensium. Libri XXV. T. II.: p. 149, 161, 220, 244, 250, Index 31. Leodii, 1670
Das Bruegel-Buch: Wien, 1936
Brömel, Chr. H.: Fest-Täntze der ersten Christen und darauf erfolgte alte und neue Missbräuche bey den S. Johannis, Veitz, Elisabeths etc. Täntzen. Jena, 1701
Buber, M.: Ekstatische Konfessionen. Leipzig, 1923
Buchheit, G.: Der Totentanz, seine Entstehung und Entwicklung. Berlin, 1926
Bueno, J. J.: Los Españoles pintados por si mismos. I–II. p. 257. Madrid, 1844

Buchberger, M.: Lexikon f. Theol. u. Kirche. Freiburg, 1934

Burchard from Worms: Decret. libri. Lib. 19: On the magic art. *Migne:* P.L. 140, col. 960. Paris, 1853

Burchardt, J.: Rubens. Salzburg, s.a.

Burdach, K.: Der Gral. Forschungen über seinen Ursprung und seinen Zusammenhang mit der Longinuslegende. Stuttgart, 1938

Buschan, G.: Die Sitten der Völker. III, 343. Stuttgart, 1916

Bünting, M. H.: Braunschweigische und Lüneburgische Chronica. Magdeburg, II:50 b. 1856

Bzovius, Abr.: Annalium ecclesiasticorum. T. XIII. Lib. XIII: 781, XIV: 1468, 1501. Colon. Agripp., 1616

Bächthold-Stäubli, H.: Handwörterb. d. deutsch. Aberglaubens. Berlin, 1927–1936

Böhme, Fr. M.: Geschichte des Tanzes in Deutschland. I–II. Leipzig, 1886

Cabrol, F. et Leclercq, H.: Dict. d'Archéol. chrét. et de liturgie. Paris, 1921

Cahusac, M. de: La Danse ancienne et moderne ou traité historique de la Danse. I–III. La Haye, 1754

Calmet, Aug.: Histoire ecclésiastique et civile de Lorraine. II. p. 567, p. cxxij, cxxxij. Nancy, 1728

Calvisius, S.: Opus chronologicum. Ed. quarta. p. 823, 857. Francofurti a. M. 1650

Cambry: Voyage dans le Finistere en 1794, p. 216. Brest, 1835. Cf. *Gougaud*

Camerarius, Ph.: Operae horarum subcisivarum siue Meditationes Historicae. Cent. alt. p. 462. Francofurti, 1601

Camerarius, Ph.: Sylloges memorabilium medicinae et mirabilium naturae arcanorum. Cent. XI, p. 201. Silberdinae, 1628

Cange, du: Glossarium mediae et infimae Latinitatis. Niort, 1887, Cervulus. Chorea. Kalendae. Festum stultorum

Cantón, Sanchon: Spanien, p. 108. Madrid, 1933

Capmány, A.: El Baile y la Danza. Folklore y Costumbres de España. I–II. Barcelona, 1931

Cardanus, H.: Zur Geschichte und Verfassung der Stadt (Cöln) und Übersicht der Geschichtsschreibung. Die Chroniken der nieder-rheinischen Städte. I, p. I, LIV. Leipzig, 1875

Casel, O.: Die Liturgie als Mysterienfeier. Ecclesia orans, v. *I. Herwegen.* Freiburg im Br., 1923

Caspari, C. P.: Dicta abbatis Pirminii. Kirchenhist. Anecdota. p. 176, 188. Christiania, 1883

Castil-Blaze: La Danse et les Ballets. Paris, 1832

Chambers, E. K.: The Medieval Stage, I–II. Oxford, 1903

Charcot, J.-M. et Richer, P.: Les démoniaques dans l'art. Paris, 1887

Chevalier, U.: Repertorium Hymnologicum. I–III. Louvain, 1897

Childebert: I *Migne:* P.L. 72, col. 1122. Paris, 1849

Chronicon Bekae. Cf. *Beka*

Chronicon Belgicum. Cf. *Leydis, Johan a.*

Chronicon Belgicum magnum. Cf. *Schiltern*

Chronicon vetus belgicum. Ex schedis Petr. Scriverii. In: *Matthaeus, A.:* Veteris aevi analecta seu vetera aliquot Monumenta. I. p. 73. Lugduni Batav., 1698

Chronica Braunschweigische und Lüneburgische. Cf. *Bünting,* also *Rehtmeier*

Chronica Fr. Closener. Die Chroniken der oberrheinischen Städte. Strassburg. I. Leipzig, 1870

Chronik Düringische. Cf. *Rothe*

Chronicon comitum Flandrensium. Cf. *Frédéricque*. Corpus, 2, p. 147

Chronica Newe Keyser. Cf. *Sachsen*

Chronik v. Koelhoff. Cf. *Koelhoff*

La Chronique Liégeoise de 1402. Called *Chronicon Gemblacense*. Publ. by E. *Bacha*. Bruxelles, 1900

Chronica episcoporum Metensium 1260–1376 (1530). Published by G. *Wolfram*. Jahrbuch d. Ges. f. Lothring. Gesch. u. Altert. 10, 296. 1898

Chronik des Johan Oldecop. Published by v. *Karl Enling*. Tübingen, 1891

Cronica S. Petri Erfordensis Moderna. Mon. Germ. Hist. Scr. 30: I, p. 411., Hannover, 1896

Cronica Reinharsbrunnensis. Mon. Germ. Hist. Scr. 30: I, p. 628. Hannover, 1896

Chronik, Schöppen v. Magdeburg. Cf. *Schöppen-Chronik*

Chronik der Seuchen. Cf. *Schnurrer*

Chronica Sponheimensis. Cf. *Trithemius*

Chronica, von Stavelot. Cf. *Stavelot*

Chronik, Sächsische Welt-. Cf. *Sächsische Welt-Chronik*

La Chronique strasbourgeoise de *Jacques Trausch* et de *Jean Wencker*. Annales de *Sébastian Brant*. Mitt. d. Ges. f. Erh. d. Geschichtl. Denkm. im Elsass. 15. 1890–92

Chronica, Newe Thüringische. Cf. *Becherer*

Chroniques, fragments de diverses vieilles. Mitt. d. Ges. f. Erhalt. d. Geschichtl. Denkm. im Elsass. II. Folge. 18. 1897

Chronicon Cornelii Zantfliet. I: *Martène et Durand*: Amplissima collectio. V, blz. 301, 302. After *Frédéricq*: Corpus

Chrysostomos, Joh.: On the resurrection of Lazarus. I. *Migne*: P. Gr. 48, col. 963. Paris, 1859

— Speech on the holy martyrs. Ib. 50, col. 648. Paris, 1859

— On St Julian the Martyr. Ib. 50, col. 669. Paris, 1859

— Hom. ad Agricolas. Cf. *Brömel*

— Commentary on the Gospel of St Matthew 48. Ib. 58, col. 492. Paris, 1860

— Sermon on marriage. Ib. 60, col. 300. Paris, 1859

Clemen, P.: Die Kunstdenkmäler der Stadt Köln. I: Die Kunst-Denkmäler d. Rheinprovinz. 7: 3. Erg.-Bd. Düsseldorf, 1937

— Belgische Kunstdenkmäler. Vol. 2. Monaco, 1923

— *Neu, H. u. Witte, Fr.*: Der Dom zu Köln. Ib. I: 3. Düsseldorf, 1937

Clemen, C.: Die Reste der primitiven Religion im ältesten Christentum. Giessen, 1916

Clement of Alexandria: Exhortation to the heathen. 12: 119 (1–2), 120(1). *Migne*. P. Gr. 8, col. 239. Paris, 1857

— Stromatum. Lib. VII, *Migne*: P. Gr. 9, col. 455. Paris, 1857

Clément, F.: Histoire générale de la musique religieuse. Paris, 1860

Closener. See *Chronica Fr. Closener*

Cock, A. de: Volksgeneeskunde in Vlanderen. Gent, 1891

Commitorium cujusque episc. anonymi. Saec. VIII. *Migne*: P.L. 96, col. 1378 Paris, 1851

Copia cujusdam Epistolae a venerabili Fac. Theol. studii Paris. *Migne*: P.L. 207, col. 1169. Paris, 1855

Corpus documentorium Inquisitionis haereticae pravitatis Neerlandicae. Publ. by P. *Frédéricq*. I–III. Gent, 1896

Corradini, Fr.: Lexicon totius latinitatis. Patavii, 1871

Cosmas, v. Prag: Die Chronik der Böhmen. Mon. Gern. Hist. Scr. Rer. germ. N.S. 2. Berlin, 1923

Coussemaker, C. de: Chants populaires des Flamands de France. Gand, 1856

Cuendias, M. de et Fereal, V. de: L'Espagne pittoresque, artistique et monumental. Paris, Libr. Ethnogr., s.a.

Czerwinski, A.: Geschichte der Tanzkunst bei den cultivierten Völkern von den ersten Anfängen bis auf die gegenwärtige Zeit. Leipzig, 1862

Caesarius: Sermo 265. Dancing before the saints' churches. *Migne:* P. L. 39, col. 2239. Paris, 1845

Cölner Jahrbücher des 14. und 15. Jahrhunderts. Die Chroniken der niederrhein. Städte. 13. Cöln, Bd 2. Leipzig, 1876

Dahlgren, L.: Några anteckningar om Bengt Gustaf Geijer d. ä. och hans söner. Stockholm, 1916

Damascenus, Johannes: Barlaams and Joasaphs life. *Migne:* P. Gr. 96, col. 971. Paris, 1860

Danza: Encyclopedia Universal Ill. Evropeo-Americana. 17, 694. Barcelona, s.a.

Davillier, Ch.: L'Espagne. Ill. par G. Doré. Paris, 1874

Daumer, G. Fr.: Die Geheimnisse des christlichen Alterthumes. Hamburg, 1847

Delacroix, H.: Essai sur le mysticisme spéculatif en Allemagne au quatorzième siècle. Thèse. Paris, 1899

Delehaye, H.: Les origines du culte des martyrs. Bruxelles, 1912

Dict. d'Archéol. chrét. et de liturgie. See *Cabrol et Leclercq*

Dict. of Christ Antiq. Martyrs. London, 1880

Diderot et d'Alambert: Encyclopédie. VI, 575. Paris, 1756

Dierbach, J. H.: Flora Mythologica. Frankfurt a. M., 1833

Dijkstra, W.: Friesch Woordenboek. Leeuwarden, 1900

Dionysios Areopagita: Über die beiden Hierarchien. Bibl. d. Kirchenväter. Kempten, 1911

Diurklou, G.: Gunnarsboarnas seder och lif efter Lasses i Lassaberg anteckningar. Sörby, 1874

Dolaeus, J.: Observatio de Epilepsia Saltatoria. Decuriae ann. sec. Miscell. med.-phys. Annus tert. Norimbergae, 1685

Dornseiff, Fr.: Das Alphabet in Mystik und Magie. Stoikeia. H. 7. Leipzig, 1925

Doyé, Fr. v. Sales: Heilige und Selige der Römisch-katholischen Kirche. I–II. Leipzig, 1926–30

Dreves, G. M.: Zur Geschichte der fête des fous. Stimmen aus Maria-Laach. III. F. 47; 571. 1894

Duhm, H.: Die bösen Geister im Alten Testament. Tübingen, 1904

Duhn, Fr. v.: Rot und Tot. Arch. f. Relig.-Wiss. 9: I, 1906

Duntzenheim. Cf. Chroniques fragments de div. vieilles.

Durandus, G.: Rational ou manuel des divins offices. Tr. par. Ch. Barthélémy. Paris, 1854

Durrer, R.: Der mittelalterliche Bilderschmuck der Kapelle zu Waltalingen bei Stammheim. Mitt. d. Antiq. Ges. Zürich. 24, 233. 1898

Dölger, Fr. J.: Die Sonne der Gerechtigkeit und der Schwarze. Liturgiegesch, Fosch. H. 2. Münster, 1919

— Sol salutis. Liturgiegesch. Forsch. H. 4-5. Münster, 1920

Döllinger, I. v.: Beiträge zur Sektengeschichte des Mittelalters. I–II. München, 1890

Dörries, L. Cf. *Herr*

Eberle, G.: Mutterkorn. Natur und Volk. 69, 417. 1939

Eccardus, J. G.: Corpus Historicum medii aevi sive scriptores res in orbe universae praecipue in Germania. Here is quoted: *Martini Minoriten:* Flores temporum. col. 1632. T. I. Lipsiae, 1723

Edling, E.: Priscillianus och den äldre priscillianismen. Diss. Upsala, 1902

Edsman, C.-M.: Le Baptême de Feu. Diss. Upsala, 1940

Ehlers, E.: Ignis sacer et Sancti Antonii. Köpenhamn, 1895

Eitrem, S.: Opferritus und Voropfer der Griechen und Römer. Vidensk.-S. Skr. II. Hist.-Fil. Kl. 1914, N:o I. Oslo, 1915

— Mysterie-Religioner i Antikken. Oslo, 1942

Elliot, V.: Dansextas inför den heliga señoran i Andacollo. Nya Dagl. Alleh. 3/4 1927

Encyklopédie La Grande. Acrodynie. T. I. Paris, s.a.

Engnell, I.: Studies in Divine Kingship in the Ancient Near East. Diss. Upsala, 1943

Epifanios: Sermon on the Palm Festival. *Migne:* P. Gr. 43, col. 427. Paris, 1858

Erens, M. A.: Sint Willibrord, Apostel der Nederlanden. Tongerloo, 1939

Erich, S.: Exodus Hamelensis. Wallensen, 1690

Erman, A.: Ægypten. Tübingen, 1885-87

Eusebios: Church History. X: 9. *Migne:* P. Gr. 20, col. 903. Paris, 1857

— History of Constantine. Lib. II. *Migne:* P. Gr. 20, col. 998. Paris, 1857

Evelt, J.: Die Verehrung des heiligen Antonius Abbas im Mittelalter. Zeitschr. f. väterländ. Gesch. u. Alterthumsk. IV F. 3, 4. 1875

Faerster, W.: De Tumbeor Nostre-Dame. Romania, II, 316. 1873

Falckenstein, J. Fr. v.: Civitatis Erffurtensis Historia Critica et Diplomatica. Erffurt, 1739

Fehse, W.: Das Totentanzproblem. Z. f. Deutsche Philol. 42, 261. 1910

Feilberg, H. F.: Dansk Bondeliv saaledes som det i Mands Minde førtes navnlig i Vestjylland. I: 404, II: 111. København, 1922

Fein, E. F.: Die entlarvte Fabel vom Ausgange der Hämelischen Kinder. Hannover, 1749

Filipovic: J.: Neues Wörterbuch der kroatischen und deutschen Sprache. Agram, 1875

Filon. See *Philo Judaeus*

Fincelius, J.: Wunderzeichen. Warhafftige Beschreibung und gründlich verzeichnus schrecklicher Wunderzeichen und geschichten die von dem Jar ab M. D. XVIj. bis auff jetziger Jar M. D. LVj geschehen und ergangen sind nach der Jarzal. Frankfurt a. M., 1566

Fischer, F.: Das alte Zabern archeologisch und topographisch. Zabern, 1868

Flentzberg: Fataburen, 1909

Fletcher, R.: On some diseases bearing names of saints. Bristol Med. Chir. Journ. 30, 295. 1912

Franz, L.: Totenglaube und Totenbrauch. Zeitschr. f. Vor.- u. Frühgesch. 3, 165. 1927

— Alt-Europäische Tänze. Mitt. d. Anthrop. Ges. in Wien. 63, 186. 1933

Franz, Ad.: Die kirchlichen Benedictionen im Mittelalter. I–II. Freiburg, 1909

Frédéricq, P.: Corpus Documentorum Inquis. haeret. pravit. Neerland. I–V. Gent, 1889

— De secten der Geeselaars en der Dansers in de Nederlanden tijdens de 14:
de Eeuw. Mém. de l'Acad. des Sc. des Lettres et de Beaux-Arts de Belgique.
53. 1895–98

Freigius, J. Th.: Questiones physicae. Lib. 24, p. 592. Basileae, 1579

Frazer: The Golden Bough. III. The Dying God. London, 1919

— The Golden Bough. IV. Adonis, Attis, Osiris. London, 1919

Fuchs, C. H.: Das heilige Feuer des Mittelalters. Wissenschaftl. Ann. d. ges. Heilk.
v. Hecker, 28, I. 1834

Funke, A.: Brasilien im 20. Jahrhundert. p. 59. Berlin, 1927

Förstemann, E. G.: Versuch einer Geschichte der christlichen Geisslergesellschaf-
ten. . . . . nebst einen Anhange über einige mit den Geisslern verwechselte
Gesellschaften. Arch. f. alte u. neue Kirchengesch. v. Stäublin u. Tzschirner.
3, 117. 1817. Also separately: Halle, 1828

Gagnér, A.: Gammal folktro från Gagnef i Dalarne. Malmö, 1918

Gebauer, J.: Slovník Staroceský. Praze, 1903

Geiler, J. v. Kaisersberg: Zur Geschichte des Volksaberglaubes im Anfange des
XIV Jahrhunderts. Aus Eneis. herausgegeb. v. A. Stöber. Basel, 1856. Orig.
Ausg. Strassburg, 1517

Die Gemälde-Galerie. Staatl. Museen Berlin. Die deutschen Meister. Berlin, 1929

Gerbertus, M.: De Cantu et Musica Sacra a prima Ecclesiae aetate usque ad praesens
tempus. I–II. Typ. S.-Blasianis, 1774

Gesnerus, C.: Historiae Animalium. Lib. I. c. 197: 40. Tiguri, 1551

Gieseler, J. C. L.: Lehrbuch der Kirchengeschichte. II–III. p. 293. Bonn, 1848

Giraldus Cambriensis: Itinerarium Cambriæ. Op. VI. Lib. I, cap. 2, p. 32. Chronicles
and Mem. of Great Brit. 21, 1861

Glück, G.: Gemäldegalerie Wien. p. 112, 1923

Glöckler, I. G.: Geschichte des Bisthums Strassburg. Strassburg, 1879

Gobelinus, Persona: Cosmodromium hoc est Chronicon Universale. Francofurti,
1599

Godefroy, Fr.: Dictionnaire de l'anc. langue française. Paris, 1888

Goldmeyer, Andr.: Strassburgische Chronica astrologisch beschrieben. Strassburg,
1636

Goldziher, I.: Wasser als Dämonen abwehrendes Mittel. Arch. f. Relig.-Wiss. 13,
20. 1910

Gottfridus, J. L.: Historische Chronika. (Merian.) 1674

Gougaud, L.: La Danse dans les Églises. Revue d'histoire eccles. 15, 5: 229. 1914

Gregory the Great: Letter II: 3. Sermon 23. *Migne:* P. L. 76, col. 1182. Paris 1849

Gregorios of Nazianzus: Speech 24. *Migne:* P. Gr. 35, col. 1191. Paris, 1857

— Against Julianus II: 171. Ib. col. 710

— Speech 33. Against the Aryans. Ib. 36, col. 215. Paris, 1857

— Speech 40. Against women. Quoted after *Brömel*

— Speech II to Gregory of Nyssa. Ib. 35, col. 838. Paris, 1857

Gregory of Nyssa: Speech on the Martyr S. Theodorus. *Migne:* P. Gr. 46, col. 745,
758. Paris, 1858

— On the forty Martyrs. *Migne:* P. Gr. 46, col. 784. Paris, 1858

Gregory the Wonder-worker: Four sermons. I. *Migne:* P. Gr. 10, col. 1146, 1154.
Paris, 1857

Grimm, J.: Deutsche Mythologie. I–III. Berlin, 1878

— *u. Grimm, W.:* Deutsches Wörterbuch. Leipzig, 1878

Grohmann, J. V.: Aberglauben und Gebräuche aus Böhmen und Mähren. Prag, 1864

Grundtvig, S.: Danske Folkeminder, Viser, Sagn og Æventyr levende i Folke- munde. III, 173. Kjöbenhavn, 1861

Grönfeld, A.: Beiträge zur Kenntnis der Mutterkornwirkung. Arb. d. Pharm. Inst. zu Dorpat. 8, 108. 1892

Gurdon, E. C.: County Folk-Lore. The Folk-Lore Soc. Print. Extr. N:o 2, Suffolk. London, 1893

Götlind, J.: Saga, Sägen och Folkliv i Västergötland. Upsala, 1926

Haase, W. A.: Über die Erkenntniss und Cur der chronischen Krankheiten des menschlichen Organismus. T. 2. p. 208. Leipzig, 1820

Haeser, H.: Lehrbuch der Geschichte der Medicin und der epidemischen Krank- heiten. T. 3, p. 89, 190. Jena, 1882

— Lehrbuch der Geschichte der Medicin und der Volkskrankheiten. Jena, 1845

Hagberg, Louise: Gammal tro och sed i Sveriges bygder. Påskhögtiden. p. 129. Råsunda, 1920

— När döden gästar. Svenska folkseder och svensk folktro i samband med död och begravning. Stockholm ,1937

Hahn, Chr. U.: Geschichte der neu-manichäischen Ketzer. I–III. Stuttgart, 1845

— Geschichte der Ketzer im Mittelalter, besonders im 11., 12, und 13. Jahr- hundert. T. II. München, 1847

Hahn, J.: Les Croix de Verviers. Bull. pér. de la Soc. Verviét. d'Archéol. et. d'hist. N:o 9. 0. 209. 1899

Halldén, N.: Begravningsvals från Norrland. I: Valentin, K.: Svensk Sång. p. 79. Stockholm, 1900

Handelmann: Der Krötenaberglauben und die Krötenfibeln. Verh. d. Berl. Ges. f. Anthrop., Ethnol. u. Urgesch. p. 22. 1882

Harispe, P.: Le Pays Basque, p. 221. Paris, 1929

Harvey, S.: Brethren of the common life. Cf. Hastings, J.: Encyclop. of Relig. a. Ethics. II, 839. Edinburgh, 1909

Hechenbach, J.: De nuditate sacra sacrisque vinculis. Giessen, 1911

Hecker, J. F. C.: Die Tanzwuth, eine Volkskrankheit im Mittelalter. Berlin, 1832

— Geschichte der neueren Heilkunde. Berlin, 1839

— Die grossen Volkskrankheiten des Mittelalters. Historisch-pathologische Untersuchungen. Berlin, 1865

Heda, W.: Historia Episcoporum ultraiectensium. p. 258. Ultraiecti, 1642

Hedion, Caspar: Ein Ausserlessne Chronik von anfang der Welt bis auff das iar nach Christi unsers eynigen Heylands Gepurt M. D. vliij. Strassburg, 1543

Hedqvist, V.: Den kristna kärleksverksamheten i Sverige under medeltiden. Diss. Strengnäs, 1893

Hefele, C. J.: Conciliengeschichte. Freiburg, 1855

Heiligtag, J. B.: Diss. inaug. med. de Morbo Spasmodico convulsivo epidemico. Lund, 1749

Helmbold: Johannes Rothe und die Eisenacher Chronicken des 15. Jahrhunderts. Zeitschr. d. Ver. f. Thüring. Gesch. u. Altertumsk. N. F. 21. 393. 1913

Henne-Am-Rhyn, O.: Deutsche Volkssagen. Leipzig, 1878

Hennecke, E.: Neutestamentliche Apokryphen. Tübingen, 1924

Herenthal, Petrus de: Vita Gregorii XI. Cf. Baluzius, S.: Vitae Paparum avenionen- sium. N. edit. T. I. p. 466. 1916

344

Herkless, J.: Brethren of the free Spirit. See *Hastings, J.:* Encycl. of Relig. a. Ethics, II, 842. Edinburgh, 1909

Herr, J. D. G.: Collectanea, p. 658 (died 1765). Cf. *Dörries, L.:* Der Rattenfänger von Hameln. Zeitschr. d. hist. Ver. f. Niedersachsen, p. 169. 1880

Herrmann, F.: Silbervotive aus Venezuela. Jahrb. f. Volkskunde. I, 278. 1936

Hieronymus, E.: Transl. Homil. Origenis in Jeremiam. Hom. 14. *Migne:* P. L. 25, col. 686. Paris, 1845

Historia Westphalica von den Benedictiner Bernardus Wittius. Munster, 1778. Cit. efter *Frédéricq:* Corpus

Hiärne, U.: Een uthförlig Berättelse om the nyys opfundne Suurbrunnar widh Medewij uthi Ostergöthland. Stockholm, 1680

Hondorff, A.: Promptuarium exemplorum. p. 48 a, 79, 185 b. Leipzig, 1572

Honorius: Gemma animae: *On dancing.* cap. 139. *Migne:* P. L. 172, col. 587. Paris, 1854

Horstius, Gr.: Operum medicorum. T. II. p. 119. Norimbergae, 1660

Hoven, Fr. W. v.: Handbuch der praktischen Heilkunde. T. 2, p. 135. Heilbronn, 1805

Hovorka, O. v. u. Kronfeld, A.: Vergleichende Volksmedizin. I–II. Stuttgart, 1909

Hyltén-Cavallius, G. O.: Wärend och Wirdarna. I–II. Stockholm, 1863–68

Hyginus, Fr. P.: Die letzte Chronik der Benediktiner-Abtei Prüm in der Eifel. Stud. u. Mitt. aus d. Benedikt.–u. d. Cisterciens.–Orden. 28, 618. 1907

Höfler, M.: Altgermanische Heilkunde. p. 456
— Deutsches Krankheitsnamen-Buch. München, 1899
— Krankheits-Dämonen. Arch. f. Relig.-Wiss. I, 100. 1898

Ilmoni, I.: Bidrag till Nordens Sjukdoms-Historia. Helsingfors, 1853

Irsch, N.: Der Dom zu Trier. In *Clemen, P.:* Die Kunstdenkmäler der Rheinprovinz. I: 1, Düsseldorf, 1931

Isidorus: On divine service. Lib. I. *Migne:* P. L. 83. col. 775. Paris, 1850

Isensee, E.: Die Geschichte der Medizin und ihrer Hülfswissenschaften. I–II, p. 260. Berlin, 1840

Jacobs, E.: Rosengarten im deutschen Lied, Land und Brauch. Neujahrsbl. Hist. Komm. Prov. Sachsen. H. 21. Halle, 1897

Jacobsen, J. P.: La comédie en France au moyen age. Revue de Philol. Fr. et de Litt. 23, 182. 1909

Jahrmärker: Zur Frankenberger Ergotismusepidemie und über bleibende Folgen des Ergotismus für das Centralnervensystem. Arch f. Psychiatr. 35, 109. 1902

Jeremias, A.: Das Alte Testament im Lichte des Alten Orients. Leipzig, 1916

Jewish Encyclopedia (The). New York, 1903

Jostes, Fr.: Der Rattenfänger von Hameln. Bonn, 1895

Junk, V.: Handbuch des Tanzes. Stuttgart, 1930

Junckerus, J.: Conspectus Physiologiae Medicae et Hygienes in forma tabularum. Halae-Magdeburg, 1735

Justinus Martyrus: Quaestion. et resp. ad Orthodoxos. Cf. after *Gerbertus*

Kampschulte: Die Feier des Vitus-Festes in alter Corvey'scher Zeit. Zeitschr. f. vaterl. Gesch. u. Alterthumsk. III. F. 10, 155. 1872

Kaufmann, C. M.: Handbuch der altchristlichen Epigraphik. p. 199. Freiburg, 1917

Kautzsch, E.: Die Apokryphen und Pseudepigraphen des Alten Testaments. Tübingen, 1900

Kelle, J.: Geschichte der Deutschen Literatur von der ältesten Zeit bis zur Mitte des elften Jahrhunderts. Berlin, 1892

345

Kemp, P.: Healing ritual. Studies in the technique and tradition of the southern slavs. London, 1928

Kerler, D. H.: Die Patronate der Heiligen. Ulm, 1905

Kessel, J. H.: Wie wurden es früher in Epidemie—und Kriegsjahren mit der Feier der siebenjährigen Heiligthumsfahrt gehalten? Zeitschr. d. Aachener Geschichtsvereins. 3, 267. 1881

Kessel, J. H.: S-t Veit. Jahrb. d. Ver. v. Alterthumsfr. im Rheinlande. H. 43, p. 152. 1867

Kinch, J.: Ribe Bys Historie og Beskrivelse. II, p. 895. Odder, 1884

Kircherus, Athanasius: Musurgia universalis sive ars magna consoni et dissoni. II, 232. Romae, 1650

Klein, Ch. G.: Saverne et ses environs. III. par E. Laville. p. 170. Strasbourg, 1849

Kleinlavveln, M.: Strassburgische Chronick /Oder Kurze Beschreibung von ankunfft/ Erbaw und Erweiterung der Statt Strassburg. p. 130. Strassburg, 1625

Kleinpaul, R.: Die Lebendigen und die Toten. Leipzig, 1898

Kmosko, M.: De apocrypha quadam dominici baptismi descriptione corollarium. Oriens Christianus IV. 195. 1904

Knuitel, J. A. N.: Woordenboek der Nederlandsche Taal. 's-Gravenhage. 1920

Koch, H.: Pseudo-Dionysius Areopagita in seinen Beziehungen zum Neuplatonismus und Mysterienwesen. p. 170. Mainz, 1900

Koelhoff's Chronik 1499. Die Chroniken der deutschen Städte. 14. Die Chroniken der niederrheinischen Städte. Cöln, T. 3. Leipzig, 1877

Kolbe, W.: Hessische Volks-Sitten und Gebräuche im Lichte der heidnischen Vorzeit. Marburg, 1888

Koolman, J. u. Doornkaat: Wörterbuch der Ostfriesischen Sprache. Norden, 1879

Kott, Fr. St.: Česko-Německý Slovník. Praze, 1878

Kowalewsky, M.: Marriage among the early slavs. Folk-Lore. I, 463. 1890

Kozáky, St: Anfänge der Darstellungen des Vergänglichkeitsproblemes. Bibliotheca Humanitatis Hist. Budapest, 1936

Krauss, Fr. S.: Slavische Volksforschungen. p. 110. Leipzig, 1908

Krier, J. B.: Die Springprozession und die Wallfahrt zum Grabe des heiligen Willibrord in Echternach. Luxembourg, 1871

Kriss, R.: Das Gebärmuttervotiv. I: Das Volkswerk. Beitr. z. Volkskunst u. Volkskunde. Diss. Augsburg, 1929

Kristensen, W. Brede-: Livet fra døden. Studier over ægyptisk og gammel græsk religion. Oslo, 1925

Kurth, M. G.: La procession dansante d'Echternach. Rev. Gén. 24, 240, 1876

— La Cité de Liége au Moyen-Age. II, 243. Bruxelles, 1910

Kuylenstierna, Kr.: Mediceerna. p. 115. Stockholm, 1939

Künstle, K.: Ikonographie der Heiligen. Freiburg, 1926

Köhler, R.: Der Spruch der Todten an die Lebenden. Germania, Vierteljahrsschr. f. Deutsche Alterthumsk. 5, 220. 1860

Kötet, E.: Magyar Nyelvtörténeti Szótár. Budapest, 1890

Lacroix, P.: Vie militaire et religieuse au Moyen Age et à l'Epoque de la Renaissance. p. 451. Paris, 1873

Lagergren, Cl.: Mitt livs minnen. III. p. 326, 467. Stockholm, 1924

Lamprecht, K.: Deutsches Wirtschaftsleben im Mittelalter. II. Leipzig, 1885

Launay, R. de: Les fallacieux détours du Labyrinthe. Revue Archéol. 2, 114, 348; 1915. 3, 116, 295, 387; 1916. 4, 119, 287, 415; 1916

Lebeuf: Mémoires concernant l'histoire ecclésiastique et civile d'Auxerre. I: 596; II: 323. Paris, 1743

Lexer, M.: Mittelhochdeutsches Handwörterbuch. Leipzig, 1878

Leydis, Joh. a.: Chronicon Belgicum. In *Frédéricq:* Corpus

Liebermann, F.: Englische Vergnügungen auf Kirchhöfen. Arch. f. d. Studium d. neueren Sprachen u. Litt. 65, 180. 1911

Limburger Chronik, des Johannes. Ann. d. Ver. f. Nassauische Alterthumsk. u. Gesch-Forsch. 6, Wiesbaden, 1860. And: Mon. Germ. Hist. IV: I. Hannover, 1883

Liszt, Fr.: Die Zigeuner und ihre Musik in Ungern. Leipzig, 1883

Littman, E.: Abessinien. p. 68. Hamburg, 1935

Littré, E.: Des grandes Epidémies. Revue des Deux-Mondes. 5, 220, 1836

Lloyd, E.: Peasant life in Sweden. p. 112. London, 1870

Lossius, Lucas: Hameliae in ripis jacet urbs celebrata Visurgis. Cf. *Schoockius.* Poem from 16th century

Lucius, E.: Die Anfänge des Heiligenkults. Tübingen, 1904

Lukianos: Œuvres. Tr. par *Massieu.* T. 6, p. 263. Paris, 1787

Lübeck, K. L.: Die Krankheitsdämonen der Balkanvölker. Zeitschr. d. Ver. f. Folksk. 9, 295. 1899

v. Lüpke, T.: Profan- und Kultbauten Nordabessiniens. T. III, p. 97. Berlin, 1913

Mac Creagh, G.: The Last of free Africa. p. 329. New York, 1928

Mâle, E.: L'Art réligieux de la fin du moyen âge en France. Paris, 1908

Mannhardt, W.: Germanische Mythen. Berlin, 1858

— Die Götter der deutschen und nordischen Völker. Berlin, 1860

— Wald- und Feldkulte. I–II. Berlin, 1875

Martene, E.: De antiquis Ecclesiae ritibus. III, col. 547; II, 560. Antuerpiae, 1736

Martin, A.: Geschichte der Tanzkrankheit in Deutschland. Zeitschr. d. Ver. f. Volksk. 24, 113, 225. 1914

— Die Tanzkrankheit in der Schweiz. Med. Wochenschr. 4, 470. 1923

Marx, J.: Das Wallfahrten in der katholischen Kirche. Trier, 1842

Marzell, H.: Volkskundliches aus den Kräuterbüchern des 16. Jahrhunderts. Zeitschr. d. Ver. f. Volkskunde. 24, I. 1924

Massmann, H. F.: Explication de la Danse des Morts. Serapeum, 8, 129. 1847

Mathiessen, H.: Bøddel og Galgfugl. Et kulturhistorisk Forsøg. Köpenhamn, 1910

Matthew, W. H.: Mazes and Labyrinths. London, 1922

Meibomius, H.: Bardevicum sive Historia urbis istius, omnium Germanicarum antiquissimae. T. III, p. 80. Helmstadii, 1688

Meier, J.: Zu dem Aufsatz: "Tänze in Kirchen und auf den Kirchhöfen" von J. Balogh. Niederdeutsche Zeitschr. f. Volksk. 6, 112. 1928

Meige, H.: La Procession dansante d'Echternach. Nouv. Iconogr. de la Salp. 17, 248, 1904

— Documents figurée sur les tics et les chorées. Bull. de al Soc. Fr. d'hist. de la Méd. 2, 506. 1908

Meinardus, G.: Der Historische Kern der Hameler Rattenfängersage. Zeitschr. d. hist. Ver. f. Niedersachsen. p. 256. 1882

Memorieboek der stad Ghent. I. blz. 98 en 99. In *Frédéricq:* Corpus

Menckenius, J. B.: Scriptores rerum germanicarum praecipue saxonicarum. col. 1553. T. II, p. 1712. Lipsiae, 1728

Ménestrier, C. F.: Des ballets anciens et modernes. Paris, 1682. Cf. from *Castil-Blaze*

Mercure de France: Lettre écrite d'Auxerre touchant une ancienne danse Ecclesiastique. May, p. 911. Paris, 1726

Merian, Matth. d. ä.: Todten-Tantz /Wie derselbe in der löblichen und weitberühmten Statt Basel /Als ein Spiegel Menschlicher Beschaffenheit/ gantz künstlich gemahlet zu sehen ist. Franckfurt, 1649. La Danse des Morts. Basle, 1744

Mering, F. C. v.: Die Bischöfe und Erzbischöfe von Köln. Köln, 1844

Mezeray, de: Abrégé chronologique de l'histoire de France. II, 435. Amsterdam. 1740. First ed. Paris, 1643

Michel, Fr.: Le Pays basque. Paris, 1857

Miklosisch, Fr.: Über die Mundarten und die Wanderungen der Zigeuner Europas. Denkschr. d. Phil.-Hist. Cl. d. Kais. Akad. d. Wiss. Wien, 1872

Molanus, J.: De historia S. S. Imaginum et picturarum pro vero earum usu contra abusus. p. 113. Lovanii, 1594

Molbech, Chr.: Uddrag af Biskop Jens Bircherods historisk-biographiske Dagboger for Aarene 1658–1708. p. 94. København, 1846

Moleon, de: Votyage liturgiques de France. Paris, 1718

Molinier, A: Les Sources de l'histoire de France. I. Paris, 1901

Die Muttergottes Deutsche Bildwerke. Insel-Bücherei N:o 517. Leipzig, 1941

Müller, D. K.: Die Waldenser und ihre einzelnen Gruppen bis zum Anfang des 14. Jahrhunderts. Gotha, 1886

Müller, M. Fr.: Sur l'origine d'un Pélerinage qui se fait en dansant, appelé, en allemand, der springenden heiligen, en usage dans la ville d'Echternach. Mém. de l'Acad. celtique. III, 454. 1809

Müller, W. u. Zarncke, Fr.: Mittelhochdeutsches Wörterbuch. Leipzig, 1854

National Gallery. Illustr. I. Italian Schools. London, 1930

Nauclerus, J.: Chronica succinctim copraehendentia res memorabiles seculorum omnium ac gentium ab initio mundi uscq. ad annum Christi nati M.CCCC. fol. 862. Coloniae, 1544

Neander, A.: Allgemeine Geschichte der christlichen Religion und Kirche. 5: 2; 6: 504. Hamburg, 1845–52

Nehring, A.: Seele und Seelenkult bei Griechen, Italikern und Germanen. Diss. Breslau, 1917

Neujahrsblatt v. d. Stadtbibliothek in Zürich. See *Vögelin*

Nilsson, M. P.:son: Årets Folkliga Fester. Stockholm, 1936

Nordlander, J.: Om trolldom, vidskepelse och vantro hos allmogen i Norrland. Sv. Fornminnesför. Tidskr. 4, 113. 1878–80

Norlind, T.: Svenska allmogens lif i folksed, folktro och folk-diktning. p. 489, 628. Stockholm, 1912

Noyen, A.: De l'Origine et du But véritable de la Procession dansante d'Echternach. Bull. de l'Inst. archéol. Liégeois. 15, 223. 1880

Oldecop. See Chronik des Johan Oldecop

Oesterley, W. O. E.: The sacred dance. A Study in comparative Folklore. Cambridge, 1923

Palamedes: Religious Dancing. Notes and Queries. Ser. 8. Vol. 10. p. 202. 1896. Vol. 11, p. 29, 511. 1897

Panzer, Fr.: Bayerische Sagen und Bräuche. Beitrag der deutschen Mythologie. T. 2. p. 43. München, 1848–55

Paracelsus: Sämtliche Werke. T. I. Volumen Paramirum. Opus Paramirum. Herausgegeb. v. B. Aschner. Jena, 1926

348

Paracelsus, Aureolus Philippus Theophrastus Bombastus von Hohenheim: des Edlen /Hochgelehrten/ Fürtrefflichsten /Weitberühmtesten Philosophi und Medici Opera. Strassburg, 1603. Das sibende Buch in der Artzney/ De Morbis Amentium. p. 486.—Das Dritte Capitel. Von S. Veits Tanz. p. 491.—Das Dritte Capitel. De Cura Vitiste. p. 501.

Pauly, A.: Real-Encyclopädie d. cl. Alterthumswissenschaft. Stuttgart, 1846

Pereira, J.: Handbuch der Heilmittellehre. I–II. Leipzig, 1848

Pessler, W.: Handbuch der deutschen Volkskunde. Bd. I, p. 274. Potsdam, s.a.

Pfannenschmid, H.: Die Geissler des Jahres 1349 in Deutschland und den Niederlanden mit besonderer Beziehung auf ihre Lieder. In *Runge, P.* Die Lieder und Melodien der Geissler. Leipzig, 1900

— Das Weihwasser im heidnischen und christlichen Cultus. Hannover, 1869

Pfleger, L.: Sühnewallfahrten und öffentliche Kirchenbusse im Elsass im späten Mittelalter und in der Neuzeit. T. 8, p. 127. 1933

Pfleiderer, R.: Die Attribute der Heiligen. Ulm, 1920

Pflugk-Harttung, J. v.: Weltgeschichte. Mittelalter. p. 229. Berlin, 1909

Philo Judaeus: Om Essaeerne, Therapeuterne och Therapeutriderne. Övers. av I. Berggren, Söderköping, 1853

Piae cantiones: A Collection of Church and School Song, chiefly Ancient Swedish, orig. published in A.D. 1582. Plainsong and Medieval Music Soc. London, 1910

Pirminius: Dicta. Cf. *Caspari, C.P.:* Kirchenhist. Anecdota. p.176,188. Christiania, 1883

Plater, F.: Praxeos Medicae, p. 88. Basileae, 1656

— Observationum in hominis affectibus. Basel, 1641

Platon: Koch, H.: Pseudo-Dionysius. Mainz, 1900

Plotinos: Ennéades. Coll. des Univ. de France. 6: 9(8). p. 183. Paris, 1938

Polda, J. de: Chronica Ecclesiae Hamelensis. Anno MCCCLXXIV conscriptum. See *Menckenius, J.:* Script. Rer. Germ. praecipue Sax. T. 3, c. 819. Lipsiae, 1730

Polyeuctes. Cf. *Aubé*

Pott, A. F.: Die Zigeuner in Europa aud Asien. II. p. 394. Halle, 1845

Preger, W.: Beiträge zur Geschichte der religiösen Bewegung in den Niederlanden in der 2. Hälfte des 14. Jahrhunderts. Abh. d. Hist. Cl. d. Kgl. Bayer. Akad. d. Wiss. 2, I. 1895–98

Preller, L.: Griechische Mythologie. T. 2, p. 551. Berlin, 1894

Priester, L.-L.: Westvlaamisch Idioticon. Gent, 1892

Profius, G.: Diss. med. inaug. de Chorea S. Viti. Jena, 1682

Quasten, J.: Musik und Gesang in den Kulten der heidnischen Antike und christlichen Frühzeit. Liturgiegesch. Quellen u. Forsch. H. 25. Münster, 1930

Raabe, W.: Sämtliche Werke. Serie I. Bd. 6. p. 171. Die Hämelschen Kinder. Berlin, 1921

Rabelais, Fr.: Les œuvres de Maistre François Rabelais. Edit. by Chr. Marty-Laveaux. T. I, p. 369. Paris, 1868

— Gargantua et Pantagruel. Texte transcrit par H. Clouzot. Pantagruel, p. 31. Paris, 1913

Ramann, L.: Franz Liszt. I–II. Leipzig, 1880

Rats- und Richtbücher der Stadt Zürich, erste Hälfte 1418. B VI 204, Bl. 137; erste Hälfte 1452, B VI 218, Bl. 90. Copies.

Regino: In *Migne:* P. L. 132, col. 243. Paris, 1853

Rehtmeier, Ph. J.: Braunschweig-Lüneburgische Chronica. T. I, p. 498, 521. Braunschweig, 1722

Reichborn-Kjennerud, I.: Vår gamle Trolldomsmedisin. I: 135. Oslo, 1928

Reichhardt, R.: Hochzeit und Tod im deutschen Volksbrauch und Volksglauben. Jena, 1913

Reimer, L.: Seder och bruk i Albo härad i början of 1880–talet. Fataburen, p. 208. 1908

Reimers, A.: Die Springprozession zu Echternach. Frankfurter zeitgem. Broschüren. N.F. 5, 240. 1884

Reinsberg-Düringsfeld, O. de: Calendrier belge. Fêtes religieuses et civiles. I–II. Bruxelles, 1860

— Das festliche Jahr in Sitten, Gebräuchen, Aberglauben, und Festen der Germanischen Völker. Leipzig, 1898

Rey, C. F.: The real Abyssinia. p. 190. London, s.a.

Richer, O.: Etudes cliniques sur la grande Hysterie ou Hystéro-Epilepsie. Paris, 1885

Richer, P.: L'Art et la médecine. Paris, s.a.

Richter, A. G.: Die chronischen Krankheiten. Abth. 5. Die specielle Therapie. T. 7, p. 725. Berlin, 1820

Riser, A.: Volksbrauch und Volksglauben aus dem Emmental. Schweiz. Arch. f. Volksk. 24, 61. 1923

Rivo, Radulpho de: Decani Tongrensis: Gesta pontificium Leodiensium ab anno tertio Engelberti a Marcka usque ad Joannem a Bauaria. In Frédéricq: Corpus

Rodenkirchen, N.: Den heliga elden. Terap. Tidskr. 4, 149. 1941

Rodocanachi, E.: La Danse en Italie du XVe au XVIIIe siècle. Revue des Etudes hist. 71, 585. 1905

Rohde, Erw.: Psyche. Seelencult und Unsterblichkeitsglaube der Griechen. I–II. Tübingen, 1925

Romdahl, A. L.: Pieter Brueghel der Ältere und sein Kunstschaffen. Jahrb. d. Kunsthist. Samml. d. allerh. Kaiserh. 25, 136, Taf. 21. Wien, 1905

Rosa, y López, Don Simon de la: Los Seises de la Catedral de Sevilla. Sevilla, 1904

Rothe, Johan: Düringische Chronik. Herausgegb. v. R. v. Liliencron. Jena, 1859

Rothman, G.: De Raphania. Diss. med. Upsaliae, 1763

Rothmüller, J.: Vues pittoresques des Chateaux, Monuments et Sites remarquables de l'Alsace. Publ. par Hahn et Vix. Colmar, 1836

Runge, P.: Die Lieder und Melodien der Geissler des Jahres 1349 nach der Aufzeichnung Hugos von Reutlingen. Leipzig, 1900

Rupelle, de: Aux auteurs du Journal. Journal de Paris. N:o 242. p. 1001. Paris, 1785

Rääf, L. F.: Svenska Skråck och Signerier. 1–7. 1863. Vitt. Hist o. Ant.-Akad. Bibl. Handskr.

Røstad, A.: Frå Gamal Tid. Folkeminne frå Verdal. Oslo, 1931

Sachs. C.: Eine Weltgeschichte des Tanzes. Berlin, 1933

Sachsen, M.: Newe Keyser Chronica. T. IV, p. 187. Magdeburg, 1607

Sahlin, Margit: Etude sur la Carole médiévale. Diss. Upsala, 1940

Sainte-Palave, La Curne de: Dictionnaire historique de l'ancien langage françoise depuis son origine jusqu'au siècle de Louis XIV. Paris, 1879

Samter, E.: Geburt, Hochzeit und Tod. Leipzig, 1911

Sartori, P.: Sitte und Brauch, Handb. z. Volkskunde. I. Leipzig, 1910

Sauer, J.: Votive und Weihegaben. In Buchberger: Lexikon f. Theol. u. Kirche. 10. Freiburg, 1938

Schedel, Hartmann: Liber chronicorum germanica. Buch der Chroniken und Geschichten. Nürnberg, 1493

Scheftelowitz, I.: Das stellvertretende Hahnopfer mit besonderer Berücksichtigung des jüdischen Volksglauben. Relig.-gesch. Vers. u. Vorarb. 14, H. 3. Giessen, 1914

— Das Schlingen- und Netzmotiv im Glauben und Brauch der Völker. Religions-gesch. Vers. u. Vorarb. 12, H. 2. 1912

Schenck à Grafenberg: Observationum medicarum, rarum, novarum, admirabilium et monstrosarum. p. 155. Francofurti, 1609

Scherr, J.: Deutsche Kultur- und Sittengeschichte. Leipzig, 1858

Schiffers, H.: Aachener Heiligthumsfahrt. Reliquien-Geschichte-Brauchtum. Veröffentl. d. Bischöfl. Diözesenarch. Aachen. 5. Aachen, 1937

Schiller, K. u. Lübben, A.: Mittelniederdeutsches Wörterbuch. Bremen, 1880

Schiltern, Joh.: Die älteste Teutsche so wol Allgemeine Als insonderheit Elsassische und Strassburgische Chronicke von *Jacob von Königshoven* /Priestern in Strassburg von Anfang der Welt biss ins Iahr nach Christi Geburth MCCCLXXXVI beschrieben. p. 1085, 1087, 1098. Strassburg, 1698

Schmid, H. A.: Gemälde und Zeichnungen von Matthias Grünewald. Leipzig, 1907

Schneegans, H.: Die italienischen Geisslerlieder. In *Runge*

Schneegans, L.: Das Fest der Chorknaben im Münster zu Strassburg. Zeitschr. deutsche Kulturgesch. 3, 22. 1858

Schnurrer, Fr.: Chronik der Seuchen. Tübingen, 1823

Scholzius, L. à. Rosenaw: Epistolarum Philosophicarum, Medicinalium ac chymicarum. col. 329. Hanoviae, 1610

Schoockius, M.: Fabula Hamelensis sive Disquisitio Historica de infausto Exitu Puerorum Hamelensium. Groningae, 1662

Schreiber, G.: Wallfahrt und Volkstum in Geschichte und Leben. Düsseldorf, 1934

Schreiber, W. L.: Holzschnitte aus d. Kgl. Samml. zu München. I. Strassburg, 1912

Schröder, E.: Die Tänzer von Kölbigk. Zeitschr. f. Kirchengesch. 17, 94. 1897

Schrörs, H.: Religiöse Gebräuche in der alten Erzdiözese Köln. Ann. d. Hist. Ver. f. d. Niederrhein. H. 82, p. 149, 1907

Schubring, P.: Donatello. Stuttgart, 1907

— Luca della Robbia. Bielefeld, 1921

Schultz, A.: Deutsches Leben im XIV und XV Jahrhundert. I–II. p. 237, 242, 419, 425. Wien, 1892

Schwebel: Tod und ewiges Leben in deutschen Volksglauben. p. 197. Minden, 1887

Schück, H.: Ur gamla papper. Andra serien. Ett helgon, p. 1. Stockholm, 1894

Schönbach, A. E.: Ein Zeugnis zur Geschichte der MHD. Lyrik. Zeitschr. f. Deutsche Alterth. u. Litt. 34, 215. 1890

Schöppenchronik von Madgeburg. Die Chroniken d. niedersächs. Städte. Magdeburg. T. I. Leipzig, 1869

Scribonius, G. A.: Thesaurus Pauperum. Frankfurt, 1576

Sébillot, P.: Le Folklore de France. I–IV. Paris, 1904

Segange, L. du Broc de: Les Saints patrons des corporations et protecteurs spécialement invoqués dans les maladies et dans les circonstances critiques de la vie. I–II. Paris, 1887

Seligmann, S.: Der böse Blick und Verwandtes. I–II. Berlin, 1910

— Die magischen Heil- und Schutzmittel aus der unbelebten Natur. Stuttgart, 1927

Sennert, Dan.: Practicae medicinae lib. pr. Wittebergae, 1628

— Opera omnia. I, p. 411. II, p. 166. Parisiis, 1641

Siwertz, S.: En färd till Abessinien. p. 296. Stockholm, 1926

Sjöberg: Rituala Bruk vid våra hälsokällor. Fataburen. p. 46, 1911

Sköldberg, S. E.: Om Choræan inom Jönköpings län. Jönköping, 1843

Slichtenhorst, A. v.: Gelsersee Geschiedenissen, blz.157, fol.1654. In: *Frédéricq:*Corpus

Sondén, C. U.: Anteckningar över den epidemiska religiösa ecstas som herrskade i Sverige åren 1841–1842. En sjukdom under medeltiden känd under namnet Chorea S: t Viti. Stockholm, 1843

Sonny, A.: Rote Farbe im Totenkult. Arch. f. Relig.-Wiss. 9, 525. 1906

Sowa, R. v.: Wörterbuch des Dialekts der deutschen Zigeuner. Abh. f. d. Kunde d. Morgenlandes. II, I. 1898

Spangenberg: M. C.: Adels-Spiegel. Buch 12, cap. 8, p. 403 b. Schmalkalden, 1591

Spanke, H., Tanzmusik in der Kirche des Mittellalters. Neuphilologische Mitteil. 30, 143. 1929

Specklini Collectanea. Mittheil. d. Ges. f. Erh. d. Geschicht. Denkm. im Elsass. II Folge. 13, 1888; 14, 1889

Sprengel, K.: Beiträge zur Geschichte der Medizin. Halle, 1794

— Handbuch der Pathologie. III, 271. Leipzig, 1810

— Institutiones medicae. IV. p. 625. Amstelodami, 1814

Sprengel, K.: Institutions medicae. Pathologiae spec. Vol. II, p. 221. Mediolani, 1817

Stadler, J. E.: Vollständiges Heiligen-Lexikon. Augsburg, 1882

Stammler, W.: Die Totentänze des Mittelalters. München, 1922

Stapelmohr, S. v.: Helgon, sjukdom och läkekonst. Sv. Läkartidn. N:o 29, 1943

Stavelot, Jan van: Chronica. In *Frédéricq:* Corpus

Stegemeier, H.: The Dance of Death in Folksong, with an Introduction on the History of the Dance of Death. Diss. Chicago, 1939

Stenström, M.: Dansen. Stockholm, 1918

Sticker, G.: Paracelsus, Ein Lebensbild. Nova Acta Leopoldina. 10, 66. 1941

Stieren, A.: Ursprung und Entwicklung der Tänzersage. Diss. München, 1905

Stoeber, A.: Sagen aus den Elsass. Zeitschr. f. Deutsche Mythol. u. Sittenk. I, 399. 1853

Stramberg, v.: Jülich. Allg. Encycl. d. Wiss. u. Künste. 27. Leipzig, 1850

Stubenvoll: Heidenthum im Christenthum. Heidelberg, 1891

Szamota, I. u. Zolnai, G.: Magyar Klevel-Sztár. Budapest, 1902

Sächsische Weltchronik. Thüringische Fortsetzung. Mon. Germ. Hist. Deutsche Chroniken. T.2, p. 301. Hannover, 1877

Taczak, Th.: Dämonische Besessenheit. Diss. Münster, 1903

Taube, J.: Die Geschichte der Kriebel-Krankheit, besonders derjenigen welche in den Jahren 1770 und 1771 in dem Zellischen Gegenden gewütet hat. Göttingen, 1782

Tegengren, J.: Dödstro, dödskult och dödsmagi i svenska Sydösterbotten. Skrifter utg. av Svenska Litt. sällsk. i Finland. 112. Förh. o. upps. 26, 289. 1913

Theodoretos: Church history. Lib. III. c. 22. *Migne:* P. Gr. 82, col. 1119. Paris, 1859

— The heretic sects. IV: 7. *Migne:* P. Gr. 83, col. 425. Paris, 1859

Thoemmes, Elisabeth: Die Wallfahrten der Ungarn an den Rhein. Veröffentl. d. Bischöfl. Diözesenarch. Aachen. 4. Aachen, 1937

Thompson, W.: The People of Mexico. p. 178. New York, 1921

Thüringisch-Erfurtische Chronik von *Konrad Stolle.* Herausgegeb. v. L. Fr. Hesse in Bibliothek d. Litt.-Ver. in Stuttgart. 32. 1854

Tihon, F.: Encore les Croix de Verviers. Bull. Pér. de la Soc. Verviét. d'archéol. et d'hist. 3, 228. 1902

Tilliot, du: Mémoires pour servir à l'histoire de la fête des fous. Lausanne, 1751

Trausch. Cf. Chronique strasbourgeoise

Tresch, M.: Evolution de la Chanson Française savante et populaire. Bruxelles et Paris, s.a.

Trithemius, J.: Chronica Sponheimensis. Chronica insignia duo. Chronicon huius Monasterii Sponheimensis. p. 332. Francofurti, 1601

Tulpius, N.: Observationes Medicae. Ed. quinta. Lugduni Batav. p. 34. 1716

Tylor, E. B.: Die Anfänge der Cultur. I–III. T. II, p. 29. Leipzig, 1873

Unser lieben Frauen Wunder. Insel-Büchlerei, N:o 145. Leipzig, s.a.

Ursprung, O.: Die katholische Kirchenmusik. p. 150. Potsdam, 1931–33

Veit, L. A.: Volksfrommes Brauchtum und Kirche im deutschen Mittelalter. Freiburg, 1936

Verwijs, E. en Verdam, J.: Middelnederlandsch Woordenboek. 's-Gravenhage, 1929

Villanueva, J.: Viage literario a las iglesias de España. 7, 151, Valencia, 1821. 17, 236, Madrid, 1851. 20, 67. Madrid, 1851

Villetard, H.: La Danse ecclésiastique à la Métrópole de Sens. Bull. de la Soc. Archéol. de Sens. 26, 105. 1911

Virchow, R.: Eiserne Kröten. Verh. d. Berlin. Ges. f. Anthropol., Ethnol. u. Urg. p. 314. 1882

Virgin, E.: Abessinska minnen. Stockholm, 1936

Vistrand, P. G.: Signelser från Småland, antecknade under några på Nord. museets bekostnad företagna resor 1879 och 1880. Medd. fr. Nord Museet. p. 15. 1897

Vloberg, M.: Les fêtes de France. Grenoble, 1936

Voss, R.: Der Tanz und seine Geschichte. Berlin, 1869

Vuicelius, G.: Psaltes ecclesiasticus. p. 163. Meutz, 1550

Vuillier, G.: La Danse. Paris, 1898

Vögelin, S.: Geschichte der Wasserkirche. Neujahrsblatt v. d. Stadtbibl. in Zürich auf das Jahr 1842–1848

Wackenroder, E.: Die Kunstdenkmaler des Kreises Bitburg. In *P. Clemen:* Die Kunstdenkmäler der Rheinprovinz. Düsseldorf, 1927

Wackernagel, Ph.: Das deutsche Kirchenlied von den ältesten Zeit bis zu Anfang des XVII Jahrhundert. Bd. II, N:o 605. Leipzig, 1867

Wackernagel, W.: Abhandlungen zur Deutsch. Alterthumsk. u. Kunstgesch. p. 302; Der Totentanz. Leipzig, 1872

Wagner, P.: Ursprung und Entwicklung der liturgischen Gesangformen bis zum Ausgange des Mittelalters. Leipzig, 1911

Waldau, A.: Geschichte des böhmischen Nationaltanzes. Prag, 1861

Wallensteen, J. P.: Vidskepelser, Vantro och Huskurer i Danderyd och Lidingö i slutet av 1700-talet. Stockholm, 1899

Walter, A.: Das Eselsfest. Caecilien Kalender. p. 75. Regensburg, 1885

Wauters, A.: Histoire des environs de Bruxelles. I: 323. Bruxelles, 1855

Weber, Fr.: Eiserne Votivfiguren aus Oberbayern. Zeitschr. d. Ver. f. Folksk. 14, 215. 1904

Weber, N. H.: Sect and Sects. The Catholic Encyclop. 13, 674. London, 1912

Weege, Fr.: Der Tanz in der Antike. Halle, 1926

Weinhold, K.: Zur Geschichte des heidnischen Ritus. Abh. d. K. Pr. Akad. d. Wiss. 1896

Weinsberg, Das Buch. Kölner Denkwürdigkeiten aus dem 16. Jahrh. Herausgegeb. v. K. Höhlbaum. II: 38, 132, 232. III: 67, 379. Leipzig, 1886

Wencker. Cf. Chroniques Strasbourg

Westerdahl, Fr.: Beskrifning om Svenska Allmogens Sinnelag, Seder . . . Stockholm, 1774

Wetter, G.: Altchristliche Liturgien: Das christliche Mysterium. Göttingen, 1921

— La Danse rituelle dans l'Eglise ancienne. Revue d'histoire et de Litt. relig. 8, 254. 1922

Wierus, J.: De praestigiis Daemonum et incantationibus ac ueneficijs Libri sex. Lib. I, c. XV, p. 85. Basileae, 1568

Wichmann, J. E.: Beytrag zur Geschichte der Kriebelkrankheit im Jahre 1770. Leipzig u. Zelle, 1771

Wicke, E. C.: Versuch einer Monographie des grossen Veitstanzes und der unwillkürlichen Muskelbewegungen, nebst Bemerkungen über den Taranteltanz und die Beriberi. Leipzig, 1844

Wilhelm, J. Fr.: De Chorea Sti Viti. Diss. Path.-Ther. Lipsiae, 1825

Willis, Th.: Pathologiae Cerebri et Nervosi generis Specimen. Amstelodami, 1670

Wingenroth, M.: Angelico da Fiesole. Bielefeld, 1906

Winkler, Fr.: Altdeutsche Tafelmalerei. München, 1941

Witkowski, L.: Einige Bemerkungen über den Veitstanz des Mittelalters und über psychische Infection. Allg. Zeitschr. f. Psychiatrie. 35, 591. 1879

Wittius. Cf. *Historia Westphalica*

Wunderlich, E.: Die Bedeutung der roten Farbe im Kultus der Griechen und Römer. Religionsgesch. Vers. u. Vorarb. Giessen, 1925

Wuttke, A.: Sächsische Volkskunde. p. 338. 1900

Wyss, A.: Die Limburger Chronik des Tilemann Elhen von Wolfhagen. Mon. Germ. Hist. 4, I. Hannover, 1883

Young, G. F.: The Medici. I, 217. London, 1911

Zantfliet. See Chronicon C. Zantfliet

Zoepfl, Fr.: Nacktwallfahrten. In *G. Schreiber:* Wallfahrt und Volkstum. Düsseldorf, 1934

Zwingerus, Th.: Theatrum Praxeos Medicae. p. 237. Basiliae, 1710

INDEX

Aachen, Hungarian pilgrimages to, 216-19, 225; relics at, 220-21

Abyssinia, and Coptic Church dance, 93-95

Acrodynia, 312

Adamites, 293

Adrenalin, and Ergot, 304-5, 319

Aegidius, St, 108, 112

Aegilis, St, 86

Aix, Corpus Christi procession of, 111

Aksum, church festival at, 93, 94

Alaro, dance at, 100-1

Albigenses, 292-93

Alcwyn, Abbot, 58, 59

Alicante, 103

All Hallows, and Bernhardine Order, 44

Almedha, St, 177, 268

Alphabet, and magic, 267

Alsace, 6

Altar, the, dance round, 3-4, 19, 282-83

Amalricians, 293

Ambrose, 2, 21, 25-30, 328

America, South, 130-31

Amru Ben el-Haris Ben Modh-adh, 147

Andacollo, 130-31

Andoenus of Rouen, 171

Andrew, St, 17, 260, 261

Angels, dance of, 19, 21, 22, 24, 25, 34, 48, 328, 329; and Alaro festival, 101; and Death, 152, 154; magic power of, 327; in 'Paradise', 160, 234, 270; and Seville choristers, 79; and St Ursula, 45-46

Annales Fossenenses, 209

Anteranna, 3

Anthony, St, the Hermit, 104, 110, 116, 263, 298, 321-26, 333-34; Hospitals, 279, 321; hymns to, 298-99; relics of, 297; symbols of, 299-301

Anthony's, St, Fire, 279, 295-306, 333-34; curse of, 234; and Ergot poisoning, 303-6, 320-25; and puppets, 288; in Sweden, 310

Antidotum Tarantulae, 8

Apostles, Acts of, 14, 15-16, 17

Aquinas, St Thomas, 301

Arabic Mohammedanism, and Plotinus, 17

Arnstadt, and children's dance, 178

Asceticism, 161, 162

Aschaffenburg, Faust von, 204-5

Asia Minor, 5

Ass, its role in Church festivals, 59, 64; songs of, 54, 55

Asses Festival, *see* Fools, Festival of

Assurbanipal, 2

Astrology, and St Vitus dance, 238

Augustine, St, 15, 33-34, 43, 154, 329

Aurelius, 132

Auxerres Cathedral, and Pelota, 66-68, 73

Babylonians, and Nakedness, 285; and Temple Dance, 2-3

Bailleul funeral dance, 138-39

Balde, Jakob, 141

Bâle, and Choreomania, 243; and Dance of Death, 149-50

Ball games, and the Church, 66-68

Balsamon, 58-59

Banquets, symbolism of, 74

Baptism, and dance, 26, 27, 328; by fire, 39-40, 302-3; improper, 191, 193, 195, and Choreomaniacs, 214; and running water, 283; threefold, 75

Barbarossa, Emperor, 262

Barbastro, 98

Barcelona, 98

Barde, of Hamelin, 184, 187

Barger, 311, 324

Barjol, 109-10

Baronius, Caesar, 22

Bartholomew, St, 260, 261

Basileios, 24-25; and Coptic Church, 93; and the martyrs, 42-43; and music for the dead, 41, 271

Becherer, 186

Beckmann, 178

Beghards, 291-92, 294-95

Beguines, 291-92

Beham, Hans Sebald, 273

Beka, Joannes de, 198

Beleth, John, 50-51

Belgium, 111-116

Bells, and exorcism, 135-36, 301

Bergerette, The, 73-76, 330

Bernhard, The Little Fool, 90-91

Bernhardine Order, and All Hallows, 44

Bertelius, 213

Berthold, Abbot, 140

Besançon, and The Bergerette, 73-74

Besseler, 55
Billengren, 310–11
Binding, of Choreomaniacs, 318-19
Bircherod, Bishop, 135
Birth, dance at, 5-6
Bjuráker, death dance of, 133-34
Black Death, 161, 169, 190
Bloch, 6
Blood baptism, 39-40
Blood pressure, and Ergot, 318-19
Bodinus, 85, 143, 186, 313
Boemus, Johannes, 128
Boersch, 316
Bohemia, and immorality, 290; as starting-point of Choreomania, 190, 198
Böhme, 7, 169
Bollandists, 263
Bonnet, 3
Bordeaux, Palm Sunday in, 110
Boy Bishops, 64-66
Brandt, Heinrich of Prüm, 117, 126
Brant, Sebastian, 236
Brazil, death dance in, 130, 137
Breisgau, dance at, 252, 269
Bridges, and running water in magic, 283-84
Brittany, 110
Broberg, 280
Brömel, 22
Brothers and Sisters of the Free Spirit, 292
Browerus, 213
Brueghel, Pieter, the Elder, 144-46, 244-51, 332
Bulgaria, sick healing in, 5
Bulls, as symbols of devils, 101-2
Bünting, 183
Burchard from Worms, and Festival of Fools, 58; and Flagellation, 162; and death watch, 137, 156
Burdach, 21
Burgos, 98
Burial rites, Jewish, 11. See also Dead, Death
Byzantine Mass, 21
Bzovius, 179, 209, 210, 315

Caesarius, 35; and the Asses Festival, 57
Calmet, 211
Camerarius, Philippus, 214, 243-44, 253
Candle Dance, in Catalonia, 103-4
Cantón, Sánchez, 96-97
Capmány, 95, 96
Casel, 3

Castellón de le Plana, 97
Castil-Blaze, 107
Catalonia, 102, 103-4
Cathars, 292
Cahusac, 4-5
Cedrenus, 59
Cervulus, 57
Châlons-sur-Marne, 109, 155
Charcot, 244
Charlemagne, 231
Chassidim, 12
Child-bishop, song to, 64
Children('s), choruses, 19; Dance of, 237, 177-79; death of, 136-37; Festival, 51, 64-66; learning to walk, 110
Chile, 130-31
Chorea, 13. See also Ring dance
Choreae Mortuales, 141
Choreomania(cs), and St Anthony's Fire, 321-25; and Astrology, 238; binding of, 318-19; and bystanders, 201, 233-34; and Consecrated Oil and Water, 281-82; contemporary medical evidence on, 214-15, 252-54; descriptions of, 191, 194-95, 198, 200, 203-4, 205-7, 209, 211, 212, 243, 244-51; Dutch chronicles on, 191-202; end of, 306-7; as epilepsy, 202; exorcism of, 191, 195-98, 199, 200; French chronicles on, 211-13; German chronicles on, 202-10; and heresy, 191, 193, 290-95; and Hungarian pilgrimages, 226; and immorality, 289-90; and naked-ness, 285-86; opinions on, 315-16; as a pilgrimage, 210; and red, 199, 201; and red shoes, 236; route followed by, 225, 228-29; and running water, 283-84; and Saints, 260-69; song of, 226; starting-point of, 190; of Strassburg, care of, 237; survey of symptoms of, 269, 317-21; and St Vitus' Dance, 265, 315-16. See also Dance Epidemics
Choristers, Festival of, see Children's Festival
Chorus, 13
Christ, birth of, 61, 63; and Dance of Death, 151; His Martyrdom, dance and hymn before, 14-15, 16; as sun of righteousness, 71-73
Christianity, and dancing, 1, 328; and Paganism, 9
Christians' Spring, 106-7
Christina of Stumbelen, 224-25, 261-62
Christmas dances, 127-28; and the dead, 133
Chronicon Belgicum Magnum, 202

Gordon, Bernard de, his *Lilium Medicinae*, 262

Gottestracht, 89-91

Gougaud, 36-37, 74

Gout, formula against, 143

Grafenberg, Schenk à, 214, 252-53, 320

Greece, 4, 5; and labyrinths, 69; and mysteries, 18; Orthodox Church of, 21, 129

Gregory IV, Pope, and Children's Festival, 66

Gregory the Great, 35

Gregory of Nazianzus, 30-32, 329; and Coptic Church, 93; and Demons, 143; and the martyrs, 41, 42, 43; and the ox and ass, 63

Gregory of Nyssa, 22, 62-63; and the Martyrs, 40, 41, 42; and Plotinus, 17

Gregory the Wonder-Worker, 22, 72

Grundtvig, 135

Gurdon, 258

Guy, St, *see* Vitus, St

Haase, 315-16

Hades, 283

Haeser, 316

Hagberg, Louise, 133

Hahn, 114-15, 290-91, 292

Hamburg chronicle, 205-8, 215

Hamelin, 181-90

Hand-clapping, as a protection against demons, 142

Harvest, dance at, 6

Healers, groups of, 125-26

Healing, and dance, 176; and processions, 86; and Religion, 335

Heathens, and dragons, 259, 260

Heavenly bodies, and dancing, 2, 3, 15, 16

Hebraeus, Bar, 157

Hecker, 191, 311, 316

Hedion, Caspar, 210

Hedqvist, 310

Heiligtag, 310

Helena, Empress, 262, 263

Héliot, Father, 11

Hell, 283-84

Helmet House, of Water Church, 233-34

Hemricourt, Jacques de, 114

Henne-am-Rhyn, 146

Henry of Albano, 192

Henry II, King, 174

Herbs, in magic, 273, 274

Herenthal, Petrus de, 191, 192, 197, 291

Heresy, and Choreomania, 290-95, 333

Heretical sects, 291-94

Heribert, Bishop, 89

Hermas, his 'Shepherd', 18, 20

Herr, J. D. G., 183

Hilderheim, and Easter ceremonies, 88

Hind, Festival of the Little, 57, 58, 59, 60

Hof, 127-28

Hohlenstein, St Vitus' Grotto of, 235, 236, 240, 241, 242-43

Holy Trinity, as occasion for healing, 6

Hondius, Hendrik, 248

Hondorff, 179, 185, 186-87, 243

Honorius, 36-37

Hopping-dance, 13; Jewish, 10-11; in magic, 275-76

Hopping Saints, dance of the, 116-26

Horstius, 253

Hoven, 315

Hungarian pilgrimages, 331-32; and Choreomaniacs, 225-26

Hungary, colonists in, 216-17; and Dance of Death, 152; death customs, 140

Hus, John, 278

Huy's College, 111

Huyskens, Professor, 225

Hydrophobia, 262

Hyltén-Cavallius, 6-7, 129-30, 133

Hymns, and dancing, 13, 44-50, 334-35

Ignatius, his letter to the Ephesians, 10

Ignis sacer, 295-97, 301, 311. *See also* Anthony's, St, Fire

Ilmoni, 309-10

Images, magical use of, 313-14

Imlin's chronicle, 236-37

Immorality, magical significance of, 289-90; of priests, etc., 191, 192

Incantationes, 142-43

In hac die Dei, 76

Indecency in dance, 25, 26, 32, 33, 290

Innocent III, Pope, and Festival of Fools, 51, 53, 157

Intestines, Dance of the Small, 109-10

Iron, as symbol of Underworld, 289

Isaiah, and death, 141

Isidor, Bishop of Seville, 35, 57

Italy, Church dances in, 107-8; and dances for the dead, 4; and labyrinths, 69; and Tarantism, 7

James, St, 268; and St Vitus Dance, 255-58

Jannensus, Hermann, 179

Janus, and Festival of Fools, 53, 56, 58

359

Schookius, 183, 186
Schöppenchronik of Magdeburg, 190
Schröder, 172, 173, 175
Scribonius, his *The Treasury of the Poor*, 146
Sebastian, St, 119
Sedemünde, battle of, 185, 187, 188
Sennert, 307, 312-13
Sens, Easter dance of, 75
Servatius, St, 116, 260; relics of, 180, 222
Seville, and *Christians' Spring*, 106-7; Choristers of, 76-85, 330, 335
Shoes, pointed, *see* Poulaines
Shrove Tuesday, dance on, 108
Simon of Thessalonica, 129
Sköldberg, 310
Slavs, 8-9; influence of, 2; and nakedness, 286
Slichtenhorst, 209-10, 291
Sondén, 310
Songs, and dances, 335
Spain, and *Ignis sacer*, 297; and Dance of Death, 153; and death dance, 136-37, 138; popular Church dances in, 95-107; and Prohibition of dancing, 155
Spangenberg, 214
Spechtshart, Hugo, 166
Specklin, Daniel, 235
Spring(s), of St Gertrude, 267; at Moelenbeek, 112-13, 245-46; and superstitious cults, 6-7; at Zürich, 232. *See also* Water
Stapelmohr, von, 6
Stavelot, Jan van, 201
Stenström, 249
Stephen, St, 263; relics of, 43, 221, 224
Stieren, 180-81
Strassburg, and Children's Festival, 65-66; and Choreomania, 235-38, 269; start of 314-15
Sub-deacons Festival, 51
Sudor Anglicus, 310, 318
Suicide, and ghosts, 146
Sun, as symbol for Christ, 71-73
Sunrise, greeting of, 25
Suso, Henrik, 151
Svantevit, sun-god, 8-9
Svennung, Professor Joseph, 202
Sweden, dances in, 129-30; death customs, 134-35, 138; healing springs in, 6; labyrinths in, 71; and ergotism, 309-11; and St Anthony's Fire, 310; and Verviers dance, 115

Symbolism, in dance, 2, 4; and Honorius' 36-37
Syrian, Ephraim, 303

Talavera, Hernando de, 98
Talmud Jews, 11
Tarantism, Tarantella, 7, 8
Tarragona, Archbishop's procession of, 99-100
Taube, 308
Tax-paying, and Verviers dance, 114-15
T cross, 300-1
Temkat festival, of Coptic Church, 93
Tertullian, and music for the dead, 41, 271
Theodor, Bishop of Cologne, 89
Theodor, St, 40, 41
Theodoretos, 34-35
Theofrid, Abbot, 117
Theophylactes, 59
Therapeutae, Jewish sect, 11-12; and Coptic Church Dance, 95
Thoemmes, Elizabeth, 217
Thomas of Celano, 303
Thomas, St, 264; Acts of, 16
Thullier, the Elder, 303
Toads, iron, offerings of, 242-43, 288-89
Toledo, and prohibition of Dancing, 155; sacral dance of, 84
Tournay, procession at, 113
Trier, Cathedral and relics of, 221-22; and Choreomaniacs, 207, 213
Tripettos, danso dei, 109-10
Tripudium, 13, 117, 123, 130
Thrithemius, 210
Trojan contest, games, 5, 69
Trudo, St, invocation of, 260; relics of, 180
Tulpius, 313
Two-and-one dance, 275

Urine, and medicine, 145
Ursula, St, 263; hymn to, 45

Valencia, festivals at, 101, 102, 105
Valentine, St, 116, of Terni, and of Rhaetia, 264
Valpurgis Nacht, 272
Västergötland, 134-35
Verdi, his *requiem*, 141-42
Verviers, 113-16
Victimae Paschali Laudes, 67, 68, 73
Vigils, 11, 39; in Spain, 95, 96; and women, prohibition of, 155
Villanueva, 99

363